Dictionary OF PHYSICS

Covering Terms, Definitions
Laws & Theories

Dictionary

OF

PHYSICS

Covering Terms, Definitions
Laws & Theories

Covering all Terms of NCERTs

arihant

Arihant Prakashan (Series), Meerut

arihant

Arihant Prakashan (Series), Meerut

Administrative & Production Offices

Regd. Office

'Ramchhaya' 4577/15, Agarwal Road, Darya Ganj, New Delhi -110002
Tele: 011- 47630600, 43518550

Head Office

Kalindi, TP Nagar, Meerut (UP) - 250002 Tel: 0121-7156203, 7156204

Sales & Support Offices

Agra, Ahmedabad, Bengaluru, Bareilly, Chennai, Delhi, Guwahati, Hyderabad, Jaipur, Jhansi, Kolkata, Lucknow, Nagpur & Pune.

ISBN : 978-93-88128-92-6

PRICE: ₹ 200.00

PO No. : TXT-59-T052193-3-23

Published by Arihant Publications (India) Ltd.

For further information about the books published by Arihant, log on to www.arihantbooks.com or e-mail at info@arihantbooks.com

Follow us on

Preface

Arihant Dictionary of Physics aims to provide concise explanation of terms of physics. It tries to cover all branches of Physics that are useful for students of schools & colleges along with all those who are preparing for competitive examinations.

There are many popular dictionaries in the market but they are for the reference purpose and common school & college students do not find these dictionaries easy to handle/comprehend because they are not meant for the specific purpose. Keeping all these things in mind I have tried to fill the space by preparing this dictionary. Information provided in this dictionary is apt and to the point without going into lengthy details that are not useful for the students. You are going to find each and every such word which you are looking for. Most of the entries are more than just a definition. Explanations are clear, straight forward and up-to-date. There is a network of cross references, some entries are simply referred to another entry, it may indicate that terms are synonyms.

At last, not the least, it is only your success that is our sole aim and for which we have consummated this ambitious project. The success of this dictionary rests with / lies in your success.

With Best Wishes

Contents

A

A

1. A symbol for Ampere (unit of current).
2. Represents Å (Angstrom).
   1 Å = 10^{-8} cm.
3. A symbol for area.

abbe refractometer An instrument used to measure the refractive index of liquids.

aberration A defect in the image formed by a lens or curved mirror due to which image of a white object is obtained coloured or blurred. The image of a white object formed by a lens is usually coloured and blurred. This defect of the image is called chromatic aberration. Paraxial and marginal rays after refraction through a lens focus at a point near and far away from lens respectively due to which image is obtained blurred. This defect is called spherical aberration.

ablation A process used to remove material from surface by decomposition or by vaporisation.

abnormal reflection The reflection of radio waves from the ionosphere at frequencies higher than the critical frequency of the layer.

absolute altimeter An electronic device which indicates altitude above the surface of the Earth.

absolute error The magnitude of the difference between the true value and individual measured value of any physical quantity. This is denoted by $|\Delta a|$.

absolute expansion The true expansion of a liquid.

absolute humidity The amount of water vapour per unit volume of air.

absolute permeability Absolute permeability of a substance is the ratio of the magnetic flux density (B) in a substance to the applied external magnetic field strength (H), i.e.

$$\mu = \frac{B}{H}$$

Its unit is 'henry per metre' (H-m^{-1}).

absolute permittivity Permittivity of free space is called absolute permittivity.

absolute refractive index Absolute refractive index of a medium is equal to the ratio of speed of light in vacuum (c) to the speed of light in that medium (v). It is denoted by 'μ'.

$$\mu = \frac{c}{v}$$

absolute rest A state in which any object is at rest with respect to all objects in the universe. This is an imaginary state because practically absolute rest is not possible.

absolute scale of temperature A scale of temperature which measures the temperature in kelvin.

absolute temperature A temperature expressed on the thermodynamic scale measured from absolute zero is called absolute temperature.

absolute unit Unit defined in terms of fundamental quantities, e.g. length, mass, time, electric current, luminous intensity, etc.

a

absolute value (modulus) Positive value of a quantity is called absolute value.

absolute zero Theoretically, the lowest possible temperature at which a substance has no heat energy. The pressure and volume of any gas becomes zero at this temperature. Its value is – 273.15°C or 0 K or – 459.67°F.

absorptance Ability of a medium to absorb radiation. It is the ratio of radiant energy absorbed by the medium in a given time to the total radiant energy incident on the medium in the same interval of time. It is also called absorptivity.

absorption The process of taking up of light, heat or other radiant energy by molecules when radiations are incident on them. e.g. When a metallic chair is placed in sunlight, it becomes hot by absorbing heat radiations from sunlight.

absorption band *See* band spectrum.

absorption coefficient When electromagnetic radiation passes through any medium, it is partially absorbed by the molecules of that medium. The rate of decrease in intensity of electromagnetic radiation when it is passed through a medium is called absorption coefficient.

absorption edge The X-ray wavelength at which a discontinuity is seen in the intensity of an X-ray absorption spectrum.

absorption hygrometer A device used for measuring the humidity of air.

absorption of radiation The loss of energy while transmitting through a medium. There is no medium which transmits energy with some energy loss, this energy loss is called absorption of radiation.

absorption spectrum When radiations of all frequencies are passed through a medium, then in the spectrum of transmitted light dark lines are obtained. This spectrum is called absorption spectrum. Dark lines in spectrum correspond to those wavelengths which are absorbed by the molecules of the medium.

absorptivity A measure of the ability of a substance to absorb radiation.

abundance The number of nuclides of a given isotope in a mixture relative to the other nuclides of isotopes present in an element. For example, in chlorine the abundance of ^{35}Cl is 75.5% and that of ^{37}Cl is 24.5%.

acceleration (Symbol *a*) The time rate of change of velocity is called acceleration. It is a vector quantity. Its SI unit is ms^{-2}.

acceleration due to gravity (Symbol *g*) The time rate of change of velocity of a freely falling under gravity. Its SI unit is ms^{-2}. Its international standard value is 9.80665 ms^{-2}.

accelerator A machine used to increase the kinetic energy of charged particles or ions such as protons, deuterons, etc. An electric field is used to accelerate the charged particle and a magnetic field is used to move the charged particle in a circular path in a desired region. Cyclotron, synchrotron, synchrocyclotron etc., are popular accelerators used in nuclear physics.

acceptor Atoms of a trivalent substance added as an impurity in a semiconductor to increase its conductivity are called acceptors. These atoms have a tendency to accept one electron from valence bond. Adopted semiconductor having acceptor atoms (trivalent atoms) is called *p*-type semiconductor.

acceptor circuit A circuit having inductance (L) and capacitance (C) connected in series and a high alternating current flows through it at resonating frequency.

acceptor level An energy level containing acceptor atom in an extrinsic semiconductor.
Acceptor level is very close to the top of the valence band.

access time A mean time interval between demanding any particular information from a computer storage device and obtaining it.

accommodation The ability of the eye to change its focal length to obtain a clear image of near by and far away objects at retina. This process is accomplished by ciliary muscles.

accumulator A source of electric current which can be recharged after use. In such a device, chemical energy changes into electrical energy and *vice-versa* by reversible process. Lead-acid accumulators and alkali accumulators are commonly used accumulators.

accuracy Closeness of a measurement to the standard value of that quantity.

AC generator A machine which converts mechanical energy into electrical energy in the form of alternating current. It is also called an AC generator or alternator.
An AC generator consists of following four parts :

(i) **armature** It is a coil of large number of turns of insulated copper wire wound over a cylindrical soft iron core. It rotates normally to a magnetic field through a rotor shaft, which is along the axis of the core.

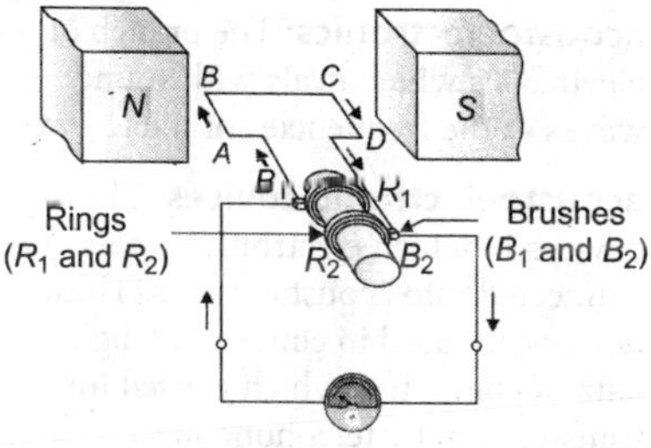

AC generator

(ii) **field magnet** These are rectangular or concave shaped magnetic pole pieces. Armature rotates about an axis in the magnetic field between field magnets.

(iii) **slip rings** Slip rings are of two metallic circular rings fixed on shaft. The two ends of the armature are connected to slip rings. Slip rings are responsible for the generation of alternating current in armature.

(iv) **brushes** Brushes are two metal or carbon rods which are fixed and are in contact with revolving slip rings. Through brushes the alternating current is supplied to the outer circuit.

achromatic colours Colours having no hue or saturation but only lightness. e.g. White, grey and black.

achromatic lens A combination of two or more lenses of different kinds of glass which is free from the defect chromatic aberration.

aclinic line Aclinic line or magnetic equator is a line that join points of zero inclination. This is an imaginary line on the earth's surface.

acoustics The study of production and properties of sound waves.

a

acoustoelectronics The branch of electronics which deals with sound waves at the frequencies of microwaves.

acoustoelectronic devices The devices in which electronic signals are connected into acoustic waves. These devices are used in converting digital data of computers which is used for transmission by telephone lines.

acre Unit of area used in the imperials and US customary system.
1 Acre = 4046.8 square metre.

actinic radiation The electromagnetic radiation such as ultra-violet radiation that can cause a chemical reaction.

actinometer An instrument used to measure the intensity of radiation.

action Alternative name of force.

action-reaction force Pair of forces involved in an interaction which are equal in magnitude and opposite in direction.

adapter A device which is used for connecting parts of different size and shape.

additive process The process of colour mixing in addition.

adhesion The force of attraction acting between atoms or molecules of different substances. e.g. the adhesion between the molecules of water and glass.

adiabatic process A thermodynamic process in which no exchange of heat takes place between the thermodynamic system and its surroundings.
For an adiabatic process,

$$pV^{\gamma} = TV^{\gamma-1} = T^{\gamma}p^{1-\gamma} = \text{constant}$$

where, p = pressure
V = volume
T = absolute temperature
and $\gamma = \dfrac{C_p}{C_V}$, ratio of specific heat at constant pressure and specific heat at constant volume. Adiabatic process is very fast process.
e.g. puncturing of a cycle tube, sudden expansion or compression of gas, etc.

admittance The reciprocal of impedance. Its unit is siemens (S). It is the measure of the response of an electric signal to an alternating signal.

adsorbate A substance that is absorbed on a surface.

adsorbent The substance over the surface of which adsorption takes place.

adsorption The process of accumulation of molecules or atoms of one substance (usually a gas) on the surface of another substance (a solid or a liquid).

advection The transfer of matter through the atmosphere such as water vapour or heat as a result of horizontal movement of air.

aerial (antenna) A straight or curved wire, rod or other device used to transmit or receive radio waves.

aerodynamics The branch of physics which deals with the study of motion of solid objects in air or in moving gas.

aerofoil It is a shape of a using a blade which move through a fluid smoothly.

aerogel A colloidal solution of a gaseous phase in a solid phase, obtained usually by replacement of liquids in the passed phase in air.

aerogenerator An electrical generator which is driven by wind energy.

aeronautics The branch of aerodynamics which deals with the design, construction, operation of aircrafts and rockets.

aerospace The earth's atmosphere and the space beyond it.

agonic line A line drawn on a map which connects the places of zero magnetic declination.

air A mixture of gases in earth's atmosphere. The average composition of dry air in percentage by volume is

nitrogen	78.1%
oxygen	20.9%
argon	0.9%
other gases	0.1%

air foil American english of aerofoil a lifting wing on an aircraft or bird.

air pollutant The substances which contaminate the air. The main sources of air pollutants are factories, automobiles exhausts and burning of fire wood.

air pressure The pressure exerted by atmosphere at any point on earth.

air resistance Force of air on object moving through it.

albedo The ratio of amount of light reflected from a body to the amount of light incident on it. The albedo of earth is 34%.

alcohol thermometer Thermometer that uses ethanol as its working substance. The ethanol used here contains a red or blue dye to make the liquid more visible.

alloy A mixture of two or more metals or a metal with small amount of non-metal. e.g. bronze, brass, manganin, constantan, etc.

alnico An alloy containing iron, aluminium, nickel, cobalt and copper. It is used to make permanent magnets.

alpha decay A radioactive decay in which radioactive nucleus emits an alpha particle (a helium nucleus, ${}^4_2He$). After an alpha decay, the resulting nuclide has mass number decreased by 4 and atomic number decreased by 2. e.g. ${}^{238}U_{92}$ transforms to ${}^{234}Th_{90}$ after an alpha decay.

$${}^{238}U_{92} \longrightarrow {}^{234}Th_{90} + {}^4He_2$$

alpha particle A positively charged particle emitted by radioactive materials. It consists of two protons and two neutrons.

alternating current An electric current whose magnitude changes continuously and changes its directions periodically.

The instantaneous value of alternating current is given by

$I = I_0 \sin \omega t$

I_0 = peak value of alternating current where, $\omega = 2\pi f$, is the angular frequency and f is the frequency of alternating current.

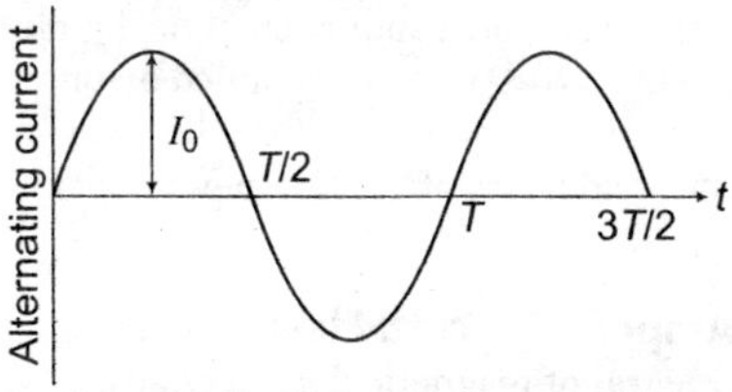

Magnitude of current at any instant of time t

alternator A generator that produces alternating current.

altimeter An instrument for measuring altitude (height above a certain reference level usually mean sea-level).

The atmospheric pressure changes with altitudes and therefore by measuring atmospheric pressure, we can measure altitude. An aneroid barometer can be used as an altimeter.

a

altitude

1. The height of any object above a certain reference level usually mean sea-level.
2. One coordinate out of two required to specify the position of any star.

AM Abbreviation of amplitude modulation.

amalgam An alloy of mercury with one or more than one metals. It may be liquid or solid.

ammeter An instrument used to measure electric current. Ammeter is always connected in series because it has very low resistance. Generally, a shunt moving coil galvanometer is used as an ammeter.

amorphous Solids that has no crystalline structure, i.e. they have no long-range order of atoms. Glass is an example of amorphous.

Ampere The SI unit of electric current. One ampere is that steady current which when flows through two infinite parallel conductors of negligible circular cross-section separated by one metre would produce a force between the conductors of 2×10^{-7} newton per metre.

Ampere's circuital law The line integral of magnetic field over any closed path is μ_0 times the total threading current through the closed path. $\oint \mathbf{B} \cdot d\mathbf{l} = \mu_0 I$

where, μ_0 is the magnetic permeability of free space and I is the total threading current theory the closed path.

Amperes' rule The rule which states that the direction of the magnetic field surrounding a conductor will be clockwise when viewed from the conductor if the direction of current flow is away from the observer.

Ampere turn The SI unit of magnetomotive force (mmf). One ampere turn is the magnetomotive force produced by a current of one ampere which flows through one turn of a coil.

amplification factor The ratio of change in plate voltage that cause a certain change in plate current to change in grid voltage which can effect the same change in plate current.

amplifier A device used to increase the strength of an electrical signal which is applied to it as an input.

amplitude

1. The maximum value (peak value) of any quantity varying periodically.
2. The maximum displacement of oscillations from the mean position on its either side.

It is represented by *a*.

amplitude modulation In this type of modulation, the amplitude of carrier wave is varied in accordance to the instantaneous value of modulating signal. Now, carrier wave is imposed over audio signal and we get amplitude modulated wave.

amplitude of accommodation The human eye's range of accommodation in terms of power (in D).

analog computer A computer that represents numerical values by continuously variable quantities such as voltage, current, etc.

analog/digital converter A device that converts the output of an analog computer into a digital signal for a digital computer.

analog signal A signal that varies continuously in amplitude with time.

analyser A device which is used to observe and detect plane polarised light. It may be a polaroid or a Nicol prism. If intensity of emerging light from an analyser varies from zero to maximum when it is rotated, then incoming light rays are plane polarised.

anastigmatic lens A lens which is specially designed for minimizing astigmatic aberration. It has different curvatures in different directions.

anemometer An instrument used for measuring wind speed.

angle of contact The angle subtended between the tangent to the liquid surface at the point of contact and the tangent to the solid surface inside the liquid. It is denoted by θ. If angle of contact is acute angle, then liquid will wet the solid surface and if obtuse angle then liquid will not wet the solid surface.

angle of deviation When light is incident on a prism then the angle subtended between the direction of incident and emergent light rays is called angle of deviation. It is denoted by δ.

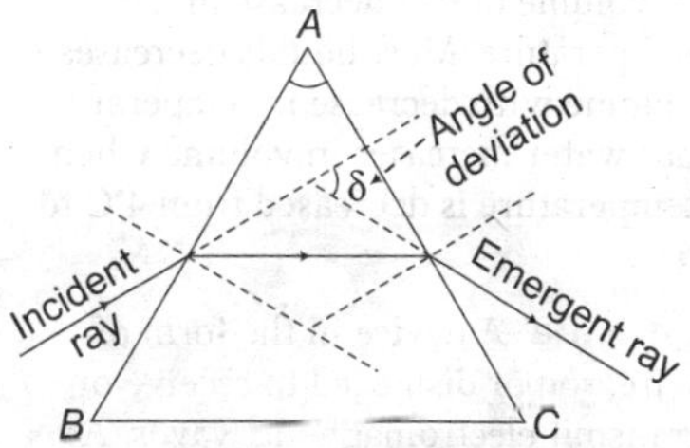

Deviation by prism

angle of dip or inclination The angle that the total strength of earth's magnetic field makes with the horizontal. Its value is 90° at magnetic poles and 0° at magnetic equator.

angle of friction In the state of limiting friction, the angle subtended between the normal reaction and resultant of normal reaction and limiting friction is called angle of friction. It is denoted by θ.
The tangent of angle of friction is equal to the coefficient of friction.

$$\mu = \tan\theta$$

angle of incidence The angle between the incident ray and the normal at the point of incidence. It is denoted by *i*.

angle of reflection The angle between the reflected ray and the normal at the point of incidence. It is denoted by *r*.

angle of refraction The angle between the refracted ray and the normal at the point of incidence. It is denoted by *r*.

angle of repose The angle of inclination of a plane from the horizontal when a body placed on it just begins to slide. It is denoted by α.
Coefficient of friction,

$$\mu = \tan\alpha = \tan\theta$$

where, θ is the angle of friction.

angstrom A small unit of length equals to 10^{-10} m. It is denoted by Å.

$$1\ \text{Å} = 10^{-10}\ \text{m} = 0.1\ \text{nm}$$

It is used to measure the intermolecular distances and to express wavelength of electromagnetic radiations.

angular acceleration The time rate of change of angular velocity of a rotating body is called angular acceleration.
It is denoted by α.

$$\alpha = \frac{d\omega}{dt} = \frac{d^2\theta}{dt^2}$$

where, ω is angular velocity and θ is angular displacement.
Its unit is rad/s^2.

a

angular displacement The rotational displacement of an object about an axis. It is denoted by θ. If radius vector *r* of the object subtends an angle Δθ at axis while object travels a distance Δ*s*, then

$$\Delta\theta = \frac{\Delta s}{r}$$

Its unit is radian.

angular frequency Number of rotations or vibrations per unit time multiplied by 2π is called angular frequency. It is denoted by ω. If *T* is the time period and *n* is the frequency, then

$$\omega = 2\pi\nu = \frac{2\pi}{T}$$

Its unit is hertz.

angular magnification The ratio of visual angles subtended at eye by an image formed by an optical instrument to that subtended at eye by the object. It is denoted by *M*.

$$M = \frac{\beta}{\alpha}$$

where, β and α are visual angles subtended by the image and by the object at eye.

angular momentum The moment of linear momentum of a body in rotational motion. It is equal to the product of the moment of inertia (I) of the body and its angular velocity (ω). It is denoted by L.

$$L = \mathbf{r} \times \mathbf{p} = I\omega$$

Its unit is joule-second.

angular velocity The time rate of change of angular displacement. It is denoted by ω.

$$\omega = \frac{d\theta}{dt}$$

Its unit is rad/s.

anharmonic oscillator The system whose vibrations are periodic but cannot be described in terms of simple harmonic motion.

anisotropic A substance showing different physical properties in different directions.

annealing The process of heating a solid substance to a temperature below its melting point and the cooling it slowly. Crystal imperfections and strains can be removed by annealing.

annihilation A process in which a particle and its antiparticle is destroyed and energy released is equal to the sum of their rest energies and their kinetic energies. e.g. in the annihilation of an electron and a positron, two photons each of energy 0.51 MeV is produced.

annual variation The direction and strength of the Earth's magnetic field at any point that changes with time.

annular space The space between two inner and outer rings.

anode Positive terminal of an electrolytic cell. In any electronic system such as a discharge tube or a solid state electronic device, the anode is the terminal at which electrons flow out of the system.

anomalous expansion An increase in volume due to decrease in temperature. Most liquids decreases in volume with decrease in temperature but water increases in volume when temperature is decreased from 4°C to 0°C.

antenna A device in the form of a wire, rod or dish used to receive or transmit electromagnetic waves. At transmitting end, it converts electrical signal into electromagnetic waves and at receiving end it converts electromagnetic waves into electric signal.

anti-clockwise A rotational or circular motion taking place opposite to the direction of motion of a clock.

antiferromagnetism A kind of magnetism found in solids at low temperature. At lowest temperature, the molecular magnets are arranged in equal number in opposite direction, giving zero resultant magnetization.

antimatter Matter which consists of antiparticles. Nuclei of antimatter would consists of antiprotons and antineutrons and would be orbiting by positrons.

antinode When a stationary or standing wave propagates in a medium, then the points where amplitude is maximum but strain is zero, are called antinodes. Two successive antinodes are separated by a distance of $\lambda/2$, where λ is the wavelength of the wave.

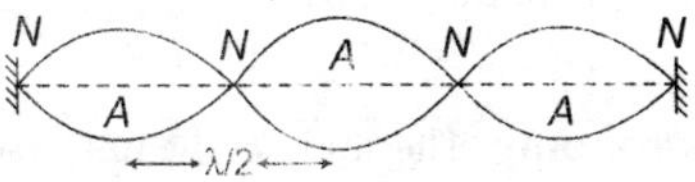

Mode of vibration of string

antiparallel Having parallel and opposite lines of action.

antiparticle A particle of equal mass and same spin but of opposite charge to its corresponding particle.
e.g. antiparticle of electron is positron.

aperture The effective diameter of a lens or a mirror through which light is allowed to incident on it.

aphelion The point or time in the orbit of a planet or a satellite in solar orbit at which it is farthest from the sun. It is opposite to perihelion.

aplantic lens Lens designed so as to minimize both its astigmatic and coma aberration.

apochromatic lens A lens designed to correct chromatic aberration at three different wavelengths.

apogee The largest distance of a satellite from the earth during its orbital motion around the earth.

apparent depth

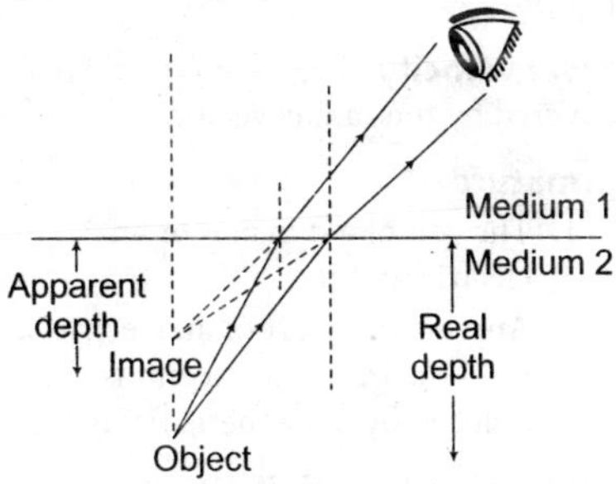

Change in path of light on change in the medium

The depth observed through any transparent medium and is different from the real depth is called apparent depth.

$$\text{Apparent depth} = \frac{\text{real depth}}{\text{refractive index of the medium 2}}$$

apparent expansion The observed expansion of a liquid without taking into account the expansion of the vessel in which liquid is filled.

appleton layer The upper layer of the ionosphere at about 200 km altitude by day and at 300 km by night. It reflects radio waves in the medium wave band back to the earth.

aqueous humour The watery substance present between cornea and the lens in the eye.

Archimedes' principle When a body is partially or fully immersed in a fluid, it experiences an upward thrust which is equal to the weight of the liquid displaced by the submerged part of the body.

a

arc lamp A light source in which light is produced by an electric arc between two electrodes. Arc lamps are used in light houses and in search lights.

areal velocity The time rate of area covered by the radius vector.

armature

1. The coil of a dynamo or an electric motor.
2. Any moving part of an electrical machine in which an emf is induced by a magnetic field.

artificial radioactivity Radioactivity produced in any substance by nuclear reactions, generally by the bombardment of neutrons or by other ionising radiations.

e.g. $^{59}Co_{27} + {}^{1}n_{0} \longrightarrow {}^{60}Co_{27} + \gamma$ - rays

$^{59}Co_{27}$ is a beta active radioactive material.

aspect ratio It is the ratio of longer length to the shorter length of a physical body.

aspirator A device used to produce a partial vacuum for high vacuum pumps. It is based on Bernoulli's principle.

asteroids A large number of small bodies revolving around the sun between the orbits of the Mars and Jupiter. Each asteroid has its own orbit. The size of an asteroid vary from one kilometre to few hundred kilometres.

astigmatism

1. An eye defect in which observer cannot focus clearly on objects at any distance. The cause of astigmatism is the non-spherical cornea. This defect can be corrected by using cylindrical lens of suitable curvature.
2. The defect of an optical system such as a lens or a mirror in which the horizontal and vertical objects at the same distance from the lens are not focused simultaneously.

astronomical telescope A telescope designed to observe astronomical objects. It consists of two convex lens one of large aperture and large focal length and towards the object, called objective and the other is of small aperture and small focal length and towards the eye, called eye-piece.

astronomical unit The mean distance of earth from the Sun. It is taken as a unit to express distance in solar system.

1 astronomical unit (AU)

$$= 1.496 \times 10^{11} \text{ m}$$

astronomy The study of the universe beyond the earth's atmosphere.

astrophysics A branch of astronomy in which we deal with the physical and chemical process involving astronomical phenomena.

athermanous bodies The bodies that absorb the heat radiation falling on them.

atmosphere The envelope of air or gases surrounding the earth or any heavenly body. The earth's atmosphere extends outward up to several hundred kilometres.

atmospheric pressure The weight of the air column of unit area of cross-section on the surface of the earth. At sea level its value is 1.013×10^{5} Pa.

atomic bomb A great explosive bomb whose working is based on nuclear fission. It is also called nuclear bomb.

atomic clock A time measuring device whose working is controlled by an atomic or molecular process. It is accurate to within one second per 30000 years.

atomic energy The energy released by nuclear fission or nuclear fusion.

atomic physics Branch of physics in which different properties of atom or nucleus are studied.

atomic pile A type of nuclear reactor constructed by piling up graphite blocks and uranium rods.

atomic radius An imprecise measurement usually expressed as half of the distance between neighbouring atoms of the same kind in a crystal or molecule. It depends on the type of chemical bonding between the atoms.

atomic spectra A spectrum emitted by the substance when it is present in atomic state.

atomic weight Relative mass of an atom given in terms of atomic mass unit.

atomiser A device used for reducing liquids to a fine spray.

attenuation The loss of strength of a signal while propagating through a medium is known as attenuation.

atto A prefix denoting 10^{-18}.

audio frequency The frequency of sound waves with in the audible frequency range, i.e. from 20 hertz to 20 kilohertz.

audiometer An instrument used for measuring the frequency range of the human ear and the minimum intensity of sound that can be detected at different frequencies.

Auger effect Radiationless ejection of an electron from an ion. It results from the de-excitation of an excited electron within the atom. It is named after the French physicist Picrrc Auger. This effect is also called autoionization.

aurora boriolis During a solar flare, a large number of electrons and protons are ejected from the sun. Some of them get trapped in the earth's magnetic field and move in helical paths along the field lines. The field lines come closer to each other near the magnetic poles. Hence, the density of charge increases near the poles. These particle collide with atoms and molecules of the atmosphere. Excited oxygen atoms emits pink light. This is called Aurora Boriolis.

autoionization Spontaneous ionization of excited atoms, molecules or fragments of an ion. Alternatively, it is called preionization.

autoradiography Technique of photographing a specimen by injecting it with radioactive material so that it produces its own image on a photographic film or plate.

autotransformer A transformer having a single winding trapped at intervals, instead of two or more independent windings. The voltage drop across each trapped section is related to the total applied voltage in the same proportion.

avalanche A stream of particles formed by collision of a high energy ionising particle with matter. The electrons and ions formed in the first collision ionize atoms and the process continues.

a

avalanche breakdown This occurs at junction which light by doped have wide deflection layer and electric field is not so strong enough to produce zener effect. When in reverse bias condition.

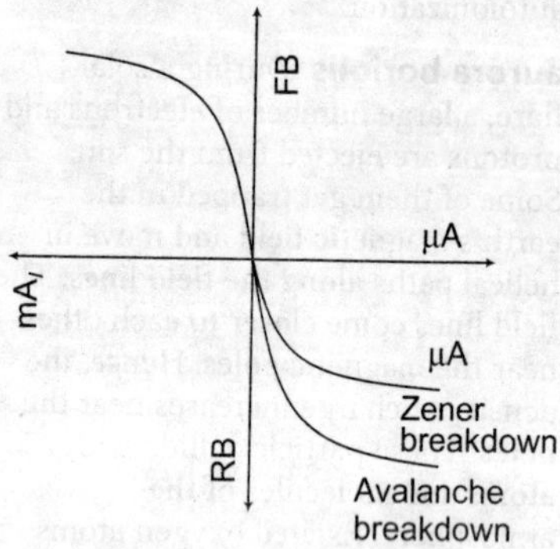

Representation of avalanche breakdown

avalanche diode A specially designed lighted doped diode, designed to go through avalanche breakdown at a specified reverse bias voltage. This diode prevent current concentration at hot spot, so that the diode is undamaged by the breakdown.

average acceleration Average acceleration is the change in the velocity divided by the time interval during which the change occurs

$$\mathbf{a} = \frac{v_2 - v_1}{t_2 - t_1} = \frac{\Delta v}{\Delta t}$$

average life The sum of the life times of all atoms divided by the total number of atoms.

average speed Average speed is the ratio of total path length traversed and the corresponding time interval.

$$\text{Average speed} = \frac{\text{total path length}}{\text{total time interval}}$$

Its unit is ms^{-1}. It is a scalar quantity. It is always positive and cannot be zero or negative.

average velocity Average velocity is the ratio of change in the position or displacement (Δx) to the time interval (Δt) in which the displacement occurs.

$$\mathbf{v}_{av} = \frac{\text{total displacement}}{\text{total time taken}} = \frac{x_2 - x_1}{t_2 - t_1} = \frac{\Delta x}{\Delta t}$$

Its SI unit is ms^{-1}.

axial chromatic aberration Formation of images of different colours in different positions.

axial vector A vector that does not reverse its sign when coordinate system is changed to a new system by a reflection in the origin.

axis For spherical lenses, it refers to a straight line perpendicular to each face joining the centres of two surfaces. For cylindrical and sphero-cylindrical lenses, it refers to a line parallel to the geometrical axis of the cylindrical surface.

axis of rotation The line along which the body is kept to be fixed.

azimuth Position as measured by an angle around some fixed point or pole.

B

babbit metal The group of related alloys used for making bearing surface in a plain bearing (antimony in 10% and copper 1-2%).

Babinet's principle A diffraction pattern for an aperture as same as the pattern for an opaque object of the same shape, illuminated in the same manner. It is used for making measurement of very small objects, for which an aperture is as same as the pattern. It states that the diffraction pattern from an opaque body is identical to that from a hole of the same size and shape except for the overall forward beam integrity.

back electromotive force An emf force appearing in an inductive circuit in such a direction, so that it opposes any change of current in the circuit.

back focal length The distance between the last surface of an optical system and the second principal focus.

back focal plane The plane perpendicular to the optic axis, which pass through the front and rear focal points.

background noise The unwanted sound present whether or not the sound source being studied, is in operation.

background radiation The low intensity radiations which are produced by the bombardment of the earth by cosmic rays and from the naturally occurring radionuclides; such as C^{14}, K^{40}, etc., in rocks, soil, air, etc. Therefore, when radiations are measured, a correction must be made for the background radiation.

backing store Large-capacity computer storage device, in which programes and data are kept when not required for processing by a computer.

backlash A sudden or forceful recoil or reaction. It is the difference between the thickness of a gear tooth and the width of the space between teeth in gear. It is designed to allow room for lubricants expansion, etc.

backward When any physical quantity lags behind in phase with another quantity, then first quantity is called backward with respect to second physical quantity.

balance An instrument used for comparing two masses or measuring weight. Common balance is used as a beam balance, a spring balance, a torsion balance, etc.

balanced forces If any object is pulled with several forces in different directions and there is no change in its state of rest or state of motion, then the applied forces are called balanced forces. e.g. tug of war, ice-skating ring.

ball-bearing

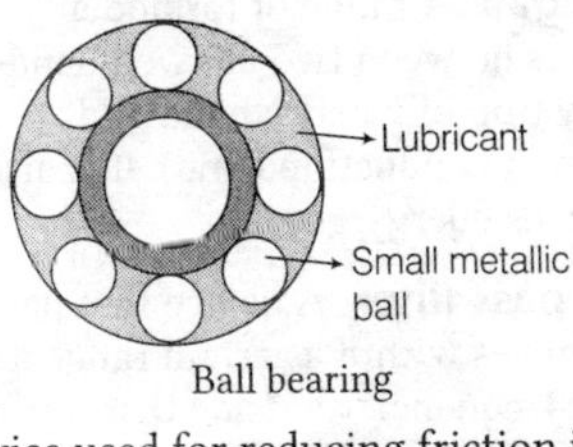

Ball bearing

A device used for reducing friction in rotational motion and support radial and axial loads. It consists of two concentric circular rings and small spherical metallic balls are fitted between them. The remaining part between the spherical balls is filled by a lubricant.

ballistic galvanometer An instrument that measures the total electric charge passing through it in a sudden pulse of current. The maximum deflection of its pointer is directly proportional to the total charge passing through it.

ballistic missile A ground-to-ground missile that moves under gravity after the influence of initial power.

ballistic pendulum An instrument used to measure the velocity of a projectile, such as a bullet. A heavy bob of ballistic pendulum is allowed to strike with the projectile. The displacement of bob is studied and velocity of projectile is found using law of conservation of energy.

ballistics The science of mechanics that deals with the launching flight, behaviour and effects of projectiles, especially bullets, gravity bombs, rockets, etc.

band

1. A specific range of very closely spaced electron energy levels in solids. The distribution and nature of it determines the electrical properties of a material.
2. A range of frequencies within specified limits used for a definite purpose in communications.

band gap A range of forbidden energies between two allowed bands of energy (top of valence band and bottom of conduction band). It is also known as energy gap.

band pass filter A device that passes frequencies within a certain range and rejects frequencies outside that range.

band spectrum A spectrum consisting of a number of bands, each having a sharp boundary and composed of large number of closely spaced lines. Band spectrum is a characteristic of the molecular state.

band theory A theory that explain the crystalline state of matter using quantum theory. It also accounts the electrical and thermal properties of solids and forms the basis of technology of solid state electronics.

bandwidth The frequency range over which an electronic device can work efficiently. This shows the difference between the upper and lower frequency limits.

bar A unit of pressure in CGS system and equal to 10^5 pascal. 1 bar is the pressure exerted by 76 cm of mercury column.

$$1 \text{ bar} = 10 \text{ dyne/cm}$$

bar magnet A small rectangular shaped permanent magnet having two poles as North and South. They are usually made of ferromagnetic materials.

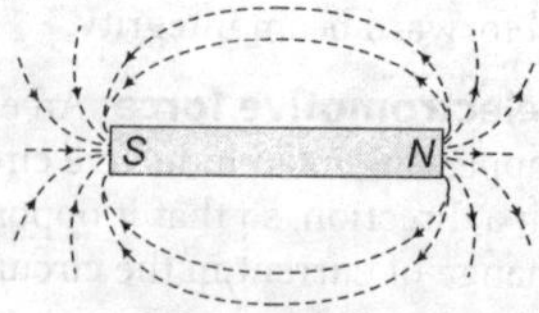

Bar magnet

Bardeen-Cooper-Schrieffer (BCS) **theory of superconductivity** First discovered in 1911. The quantum theory of superconductivity in which interaction between pairs of electrons gives, for the electron system, a ground state which is separated from the excited states by an energy gap. This energy gap accounts for the superconducting phase transition and the critical magnetic field which leads to the destruction of superconductivity.

Barkhausen effect First discovered by Heinrich Barkhausen in 1919 which was caused by rapid changes of size of magnetic domain. During the magnetisation of a ferromagnetic substance, when magnetising field is increased or decreased steadily, then magnetisation of the substance does not increase or decrease steadily but proceeds in a series of minute jumps. This effect is called Barkhausen effect. This effect supports the domain theory of magnetism.

Barlow lens Named after Peter Barlow. A plano concave lens placed between the objective and eyepiece in a telescope. It is used for magnification.

barn A unit of area equal to 10^{-28} square metre. It is denoted by b. It is used in nuclear physics for expressing the cross-sectional area of nuclei and nuclear reactions.

barograph A meteorological instrument that records on paper variations in atmospheric pressure over a period.

barometer An instrument used for measuring atmospheric pressure. e.g. liquid barometer, mercury barometer and aneroid barometer.

barometric height The height of liquid column in a barometer. The standard barometric height of atmospheric pressure is 760 mm of mercury.

barostat A device used to maintain constant pressure in a closed chamber.

barrier potential The potential difference across the depletion region and acts as a barrier to the majority charge carriers that are electrons in *n*-type and holes in *p*-type semiconductors. It stops the flow of diffusion current.

bary centre The point between two objects where they balance each other. The centre of mass of a system, where two or more celestial bodies orbit each other.

barye A CGS unit of pressure equals to 1 dyne per square centimetre. It is denoted by Ba.

$$1 \text{ Ba} = 0.1 \text{ Pa}$$

base The middle region in a Bipolar Junction Transistor (BJT) that separates the emitter and the collector. It is a very thin layer of lightly doped *n*-type or *p*-type semiconductor sandwiched between two thick layers of comparatively highly doped other type of semiconductor.

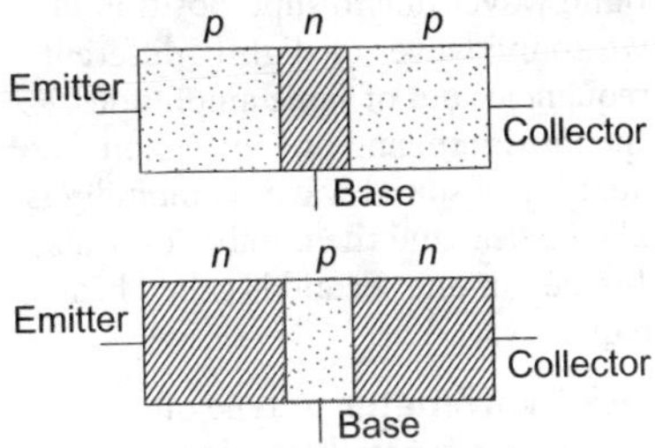

Junction transistor

base quantity One of the seven physical quantities corresponding to the seven base units in SI. They are length, mass, time, electric current, temperature difference, amount of substance and luminous intensity.

base unit A unit that is defined arbitrarily rather than other units. e.g. kilogram, metre, second, ampere are base units of SI system.

battery The combination of a number of cells connected in series or parallel and used as a single unit.

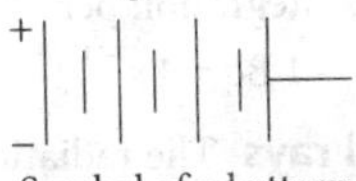

Symbol of a battery

baud A unit for measuring signal speed in a computer or communication system.

beam A bundle or group of light rays or other type of radiation, moving in a single direction. A beam is a group of light rays coming from a point or diverging towards a point.

beam balance An instrument to determine the mass of an object. It consists of two pans suspended from a horizontal beam pivoted at centre.

The object (whose mass is to be found) is placed in one pan and known mass is placed in other pan. When the beam is horizontal, the masses in both pans will be equal.

beats The phenomena of a regular increase or decrease in intensity of sound waves due to superposition of two sound waves of slightly different frequencies but of same amplitudes. One maximum and one minimum intensity of sound waves combindly is called a beat and the number of beats obtained in one second is called beat frequency.

Beck hydrometer A type of hydrometer generally used to measure the relative density of liquids which are less dense than water. Such a hydrometer is graduated in degrees Beck, where Beck = 200 (1-relative density).

Beckmann thermometer A device used for measuring small changes in temperature but not absolute temperature values. It was invented by Ernst Otto Beckmann.

becquerel The SI unit of radioactivity. It is denoted by 'Bq'.

1 becquerel

= 1 disintegration per second

i.e. $1\ \text{Bq} = 1\ \text{s}^{-1}$.

Becquerel rays The radiation discovered by H Becquerel (1896) emitted by uranium. They refer to beta rays which Becquerel detected with the help of a photographic plate.

bel A dimensionless unit expressing the ratio of powers or intensities, i.e. 1 bel = 10 decibels.

bell metal A type of bronze used for making bells. It consists of 60-85% copper alloyed with tin, often with some zinc and lead.

Bernoulli's equation When a non-viscous and incompressible fluid is in streamline flow, then total energy per unit volume of the fluid, i.e. sum of pressure energy, kinetic energy and potential energy per unit volume remains constant.

$$p + \frac{1}{2}\rho v^2 + \rho g h = \text{constant}$$

For horizontal flow of fluid,

$$p + \frac{1}{2}\rho v^2 = \text{constant}$$

Bernoulli's principle First derived by Daniel Bernoulli in 1738. It states that for a non-viscous flow (liquid having resistance to move) of a non-conducting fluid, an increase in the speed of the fluid occurs simultaneously, with a decrease in pressure or a decrease in the fluid's potential energy.

Bessemer process Process for converting pig iron from a blast furnace into steel.

beta current gain factor Its symbol is β. The short circuit current amplification factor of a transistor with common-emitter connection given by

$$\beta = \left(\frac{\partial i_C}{\partial i_B}\right) V_{CE} = \text{constant}$$

where, i_C is the collector current and i_B is the base current. β is always greater than unity and can take values upto 500.

beta decay A type of radioactive decay, in which a nucleus decays spontaneously by emitting an electron. With the emission of a β-particle, an antineutrino particle is emitted along with energy.

$$^{13}N_7 \longrightarrow {}^{12}C_6 + \bar{\nu}$$

By the emission of one beta particle β^-, the atomic number increases by one and mass number remains unchanged.

Total energy in β-decay remains constant but not uniformly distributed along β-particle, antineutrino and daughter nucleus. In another type of beta decay, positron β^+ is emitted along with a neutrino particle.

$$^{13}N_7 \longrightarrow {}^{13}C_6 + e^+ + \nu$$

beta particle A high speed, high energy electron or positron emitted by a radioactive nucleus in beta decay. These are emitted in the form of ionising radiation known as beta rays.

B-field A three-dimensional space in which the magnitude of the result out magnetic field strength B at any point, is mostly non-zero.

beta radiation Consists primarily of electrons emitted from radioactive nuclei, but the term also covers streams of positrons (positively charged anti-electrons).

beta transformation

1. Transformation of nucleus due to beta decays.
2. The decay of a neutron to a proton, an electron and an antineutrino.

$$n \longrightarrow p + e^- + \nu$$

betatron A device used for accelerating electrons upto very high energies (of range 300 MeV). If an electron is revolving in a circular orbit in a magnetic field between the poles of an electromagnet, then an increase in magnetic field through alternating current, accelerates the electrons. Electrons completed several hundred thousand revolutions before the current reaches its peak value.

bevatron A device which can accelerate protons to very high energies (of about 10^{-9} joule).

bias A voltage applied to an electronic device to produce the desired characteristics.

biaxial crystal A birefringent type of crystal having two axis along which ordinary and extraordinary rays which are component of polarised light, travel with same speed.

biconcave lens A lens whose both opposing surfaces are concave. It is also called concavo-concave lens.

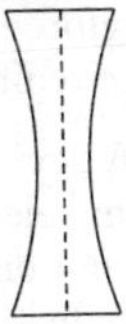

Biconcave lens

biconvex lens A lens whose both opposing surfaces are convex. It is also called as convexo-convex lens.

Biconvex lens

bifurcation A phenomenon that can occur in a dynamical system in which some solutions of a certain type for the system, such as laminar flow in a fluid, suddenly change to another type, such as turbulent flow, when one of the parameters that characterised the system reaches a critical value.

big-bang theory A theory related to the origin of universe. According to this theory, all the matter and energy in the universe originated from a state of enormous density and temperature and it is continuously expanding in size. This theory is also called superdense theory.

big dipper A group of many stars of which seven are comparatively brighter and are easily visible. It is named as Ursa Major or Vrihat Saptarishi or big dipper. It appears like a big ladle or a question mark. The two stars at the top of the ladle are called pointers.

bilateral slit A slit used in spectrometer which consists of two metal strips whose separation can be accurately adjusted.

bimetallic strip A strip consisting of two metals of different coefficient of linear expansion welded at side-by-side. This strip bends on heating and therefore used in thermostats and circuit breakers.

bimorph cell A device which is used for converting electrical signals into mechanical motion making use of the piezoelectric effect.

binary notation A number expressed in the binary numeral system or base-2 numeral system which represents numeric values using two different symbols 0 and 1. The equivalents are given below:

Decimal	Binary	Decimal	Binary
0	0	5	101
1	1	6	110
2	10	7	111
3	1	8	1000
4	100	9	1001

As only two symbols are used, they can be represented by either of two alternatives. Binary notation is used in computing.

binary prefixes A set of prefixes for binary powers designed to be used in data processing and data transmission contexts.

binary star A binary star is a system of two stars attracting each other by gravitational force due to which they revolve around their common centre of gravity.

binary system A number system based on two digits 0 and 1 having base 2.

binding energy The energy released when a nucleus is formed because nucleons enter a more stable lower energy state. It is equal to the energy equivalent to the mass defect (the difference between the mass of the nucleus and the sum of the masses of its constituent nucleons). The required expression is as

$$BE = [Z_{mH} + (A - Z)_{mn} - m({}_Z m^A)]c^2$$

For most nuclei, binding energy lies between about 7 and about 9 MeV per nucleon, reaching a maximum of about 9 MeV for nuclei of mass number about 60.

binoculars An optical instrument giving distance perception as well as magnification and used simultaneous for both eyes. Binocular microscopes are used in Biology and surgery to enable the observer to obtain a stereoscopic view of small objects or parts.

bio-gas plant A plant used for the production of electricity from the slurry of cowdung and water. It has a dome like structure built with bricks. The slurry is fed into a digester, where is no oxygen. Anaerobic micro-organisms decompose the complex compounds of slurry in the absence of oxygen and produces gases like methane, carbon dioxide, hydrogen and hydrogen sulphide. This mixture of gases, called bio-gas is stored in a gas tank. This gas is supplied through pipes for use.

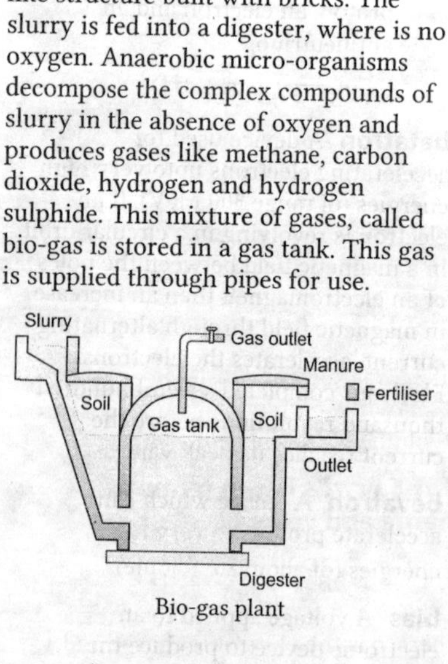

Bio-gas plant

bio-mass The fuel made by dead plants and animals. These fuels, however, do not produce much heat on burning and a lot of smoke is given out when they are burnt. Therefore, technological inputs to improve the efficiency of these fuels are necessary.

biophysics The use of Physics in the study of biological phenomena and living organisms.

biotechnology The development of techniques for the applications of biological processes to the production of materials used in medicines and industry.

Biot-Savart law This law deals with the magnetic field induction at a point due to a small current element.

Biot-Savart's law in terms of current carrying element The magnetic field dB due to a current carrying element $I\,dl$ at distance r is given by

$$dB = \frac{\mu_0}{4\pi}\frac{I\,dl\sin\theta}{r^2}$$

where, θ is the angle between dl and r.

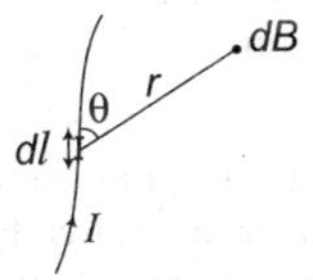

Biot-Savart's law in terms of current density *J*

$$dB = \frac{\mu_0}{4\pi}\cdot\frac{J\times r}{r^3}\,dV$$

where, J is current density at any point on the current element and dV is volume of the element.

Biot-Savart's law in terms of charge and velocity

$$dB = \frac{\mu_0}{4\pi}\frac{q(v\times r)}{r^3}$$

where, q is the electronic charge and v is its velocity.

bipolar transistor A semiconductor device commonly used for amplification. This device can amplify analog or digital signals. It uses two types of charge carriers, electrons and holes, for its operation.

biprism A glass prism with an obtuse angle, used to produce two coherent (virtual) sources of light. A Fresnel's biprism is formed by placing two prisms base-to-base, so that forming a single biprism with an obtuse angle of 179°. It is used to produce two coherent (virtual) sources for light interference experiments. The fringes obtained with this arrangement are brighter than those in Young's experiment.

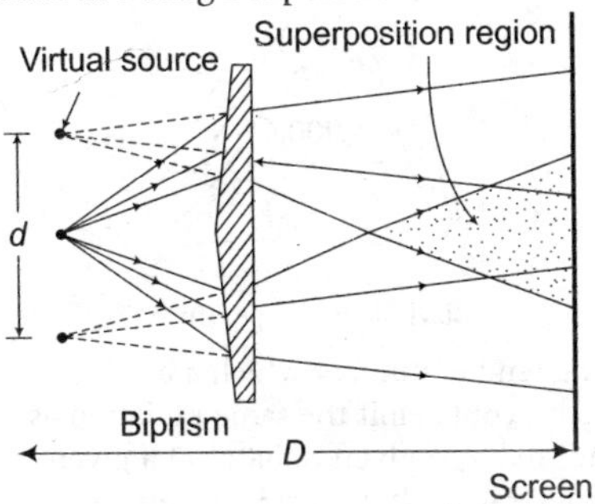

Biprism or Fresnel's biprism

birefringent crystal A crystal that splits the incident light and transmitted through it into two beams, each polarised perpendicular to each other. These rays of light are called ordinary ray (O-ray) and extraordinary ray (E-ray). Ordinary rays follow laws of refraction and extraordinary rays do not follow laws of refraction. This phenomenon of splitting of light rays into two beams is called birefringence or double refraction.

biscope An early form of motion picture projector.

bit A basic unit of information in computing and digital communications used to express the choice between two possibilities. Either of the digit 0 or 1 is called bit in binary notation.

black body An idealised physical body which absorbs all the radiations completely falling on it. Its absorptance and emissivity, both are 1.

black body radiation The electromagnetic radiation emitted by a black body. It extends over the whole range of wavelength and the distribution of energy over this range has a characteristic form with a maximum at a certain wavelength.

black body temperature

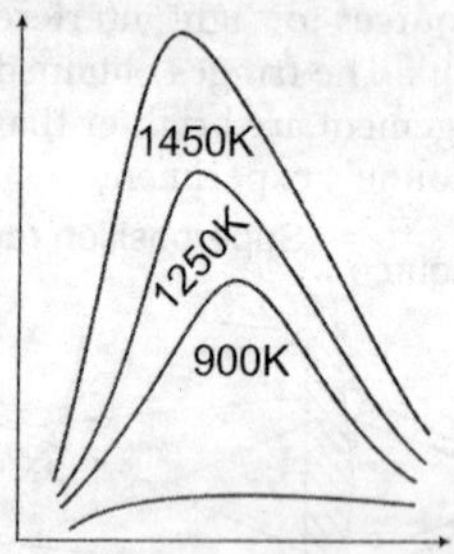

Black body temperature

The temperature, at which a black body would emit the same radiation as emitted by a given radiator at a given temperature. It generally covers the entire wavelength range.

black hole A region of space and time in which the gravitational force is so great that no object or electromagnetic radiation can escape from it. A neutron star of mass more than three times that of the sun, is compressed to a single point due to gravitational pull and converts into a black hole.

blind spot A small area on the retina where the optic nerve leaves the eye which is insensitive to light due to absence of rod and cone cells.

bloch wall A ferromagnetic material in zero magnetic field which will be in equilibrium, if it has minimum potential energy.

blondel A metric unit of luminance. One blondel is the luminance of a uniform diffuser emitting 1 lumen per square metre.

$$1 \text{ blondel} = \frac{1}{\pi} \text{ candela metre}^{-1}$$

blooming Method to coat the lenses to reduce back-reflection from their surfaces. It is done by applying magnesium fluoride on a lens.

blue shift An apparent decrease in wavelength, when waves are received from a source moving towards the observer.

Board of Trade Unit (BTU) The unit of energy equal to the kilowatt-hour (3.6×10^6 joule).

bob A small metallic sphere connected to a thread forming a simple pendulum.

Bohr magneton The unit of atomic magnetic moment. It is the magnetic moment of a single electron spin. It is equal to the

$$\frac{eh}{4\pi\, mc} = 9.273 \times 10^{-24} \text{ A-m}^2$$

where, h = Planck's constant, m = rest mass of electron and c = speed of light in vacuum.

Bohr's radius The mean radius of the orbit of an electron revolving around the nucleus of a hydrogen atom at its ground state.
Its value is approximately equal to

$$a_0 = \frac{4\pi\varepsilon_0\, h^2}{m_e \cdot e^2}$$

$$= 0.5292 \times 10^{-10} \text{ m}$$

boiling point The temperature at which a liquid freely converts into vapour. At this temperature, the saturated vapour pressure of the liquid equals the external pressure and the liquid and vapour states of the substance can coexist simultaneously.

bolometer A sensitive instrument used to measure heat radiations or microwaves. It contains platinum strips and heat is measured by observing the change in resistance of these strips.

Boltzmann constant The ratio of universal gas constant R to the Avogadro constant N.
It is denoted by k or k_B.

$$k = \frac{R}{N} = 1.38 \times 10^{-23} \text{ J/K}$$

Boltzmann equation An equation used in the study of a collection of particles in non-equilibrium statistical mechanics, particularly their transport properties.

bomb calorimeter A thick-walled steel container, used for measuring energy released during combustion of substances.

Bose-Einstein statistics Statistical mechanics of systems of identical particles. It is assumed that all identical particles are absolutely indistinguishable and can have the same set of quantum numbers in a given system.

boson A particle that obeys Bose-Einstein statistics but does not obey Pauli exclusion principle and has zero or integral spin, called boson. Bosons are not conserved in number and can be generated or destroyed singly. e.g. alpha particle, photon, etc.

boundary layer The layer of incompressible fluid of thickness in the range of 50 μm to 100 μm. The behaviour of this layer is important for the study of lift and drag.

Brackett series A series of energy emission levels for infrared region of atomic spectrum of hydrogen.
When an electron jumps from any excited energy state ($n = 5, 6, 7, \ldots$) to fourth energy state ($n = 4$), the emitted spectral line is a member of Brackett series.
Its wavelength is given by

$$\frac{1}{\lambda} = R\left[\frac{1}{(4)^2} - \frac{1}{n^2}\right]$$

where, $n = 5, 6, 7, \ldots$ and R is Rydberg's constant.

Bragg's law When a beam of X-rays is incident at a crystal, then X-rays are reflected from each of its parallel planes and interference takes place between them. Constructive interference occurs at angles θ, where,

$$n\lambda = 2d \sin\theta$$

Here, d = separation distance between its planes,
λ = wavelength of light and
θ = angle between the crystal plane and the incident beam

This law is called Bragg's law.

breakdown The sudden passage of large current through an insulator.

breakdown voltage The reverse voltage at which the covalent bonds near the junction in a p-n junction breaks suddenly and results in a sudden rise in reverse current.

breeder reactor A nuclear reactor that produces more fissile nuclei at a rate greater than that, at which it consumes fuel. Enriched uranium is used as fuel containing ^{235}U and ^{238}U. The surplus neutrons obtained from the fission of ^{235}U converts ^{238}U into ^{239}Pa, which is more fissile.

Bremsstrahlung The X-rays emitted when a charged particle, especially a fast electron, is rapidly slowed down, as when it passes through the electric field around an atomic nucleus.

Brewster angle

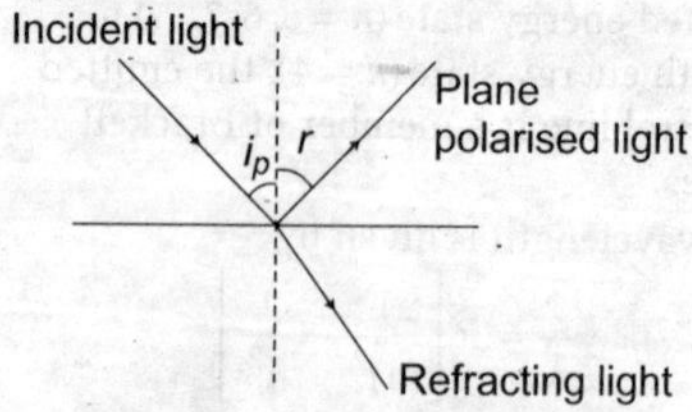

Representation of Brewster angle

The angle of incidence on a partially reflecting surface, for which the reflecting light is fully polarised, is called Brewster angle or angle of polarisation. It is denoted by i_p.

Brewster's law The tangent of the angle of polarisation of light for a substance is equal to the refractive index of the substance.

$$\mu = \tan i_p$$

where, μ = refractive index of the substance.

bridge circuit Arrangement of four electrical components in a square form with an input across two opposite corners and an output across the other opposite corners.

Bridgman effect The absorption or liberation of heat when an electric current passes through an anisotropic crystal. It arises from non-uniformity in the current distribution and is additional to the Peltier and Thomson effects.

brightness An attribute of visual perception, in which a source appears to be radiating or reflecting light.

brinell machine An instrument used for determining the hardness of metals in which hard ball is forced into the material being tested.

British Thermal Unit (BTU) Amount of heat required to raise the temperature of 1 pound of water through 1°F.

$$1 \text{ BTU} = 251.98 \text{ cal} = 1.055 \times 10^3 \text{ J}$$

Brownian movement The erratic random motion of small particles in a fluid. e.g. random motion of smoke particles in air.

brush discharge A luminous discharge from a conductor which occurs when the electric field near the surface exceeds a certain minimum value but is not sufficient to cause a true spark.

buckling It occurs when a rod under compressive stress moves sideways at its centre.

buffer An isolated circuit used to minimise reaction between two circuits. It has a high input impedance and low output impedance.

bulk lifetime The average time lapse between the generation and recombination of minority carriers in the bulk material of a semiconductor.

bulk modulus The ratio of normal stress to the volume strain of any body.

$$\text{Bulk modulus } (B) = \frac{\text{normal stress}}{\text{volume strain}} = \frac{\Delta p}{\Delta V / V}$$

Bunsen cell The first battery to use a carbon electrode. A type of primary cell in which positive electrode of carbon is dipped in nitric acid solution and negative electrode of zinc is dipped in sulphuric acid solution.

Bunsen ice calorimeter Calorimeter is used to measure the specific heat capacity of a solid or liquid only when a small quantity is available.

buoyancy The tendency of an object to float in a liquid.

buoyant force The upward force acting on an object when it is immersed in a fluid. This is equal to the weight of the fluid displaced by the submerged part of the object in fluid.

bypass capacitor A capacitor providely a low impedance path in an electronic circuit over a predetermined frequency range.

C

cadmium A transition metal and is used in polishing the metal objects to protect them from corrosion, in nuclear reactor as a neutron absorber, in alkali batteries and in certain pigments. It is highly toxic and obtained as a by-product during the extraction of zinc.

caesium clock An atomic clock that depends on the energy difference between two states, of the caesium-133 nucleus when it is in magnetic field.

calcite A natural transparent form of calcium carbonate which manifests double refraction.

calibration The determination of the absolute values of the arbitrary indications of an instrument.

caloric theory A former theory concerning the nature of heat, which was regarded as a weightless fluid (called caloric).

calorie The quantity of heat required to increase the temperature of 1g of water through 1°C.

1 calorie = 4.2 joule

calorific value A measurement of the energy content of fuels. It is the amount of heat released when unit weight or volume of a fuel burns completely.

calorimeter

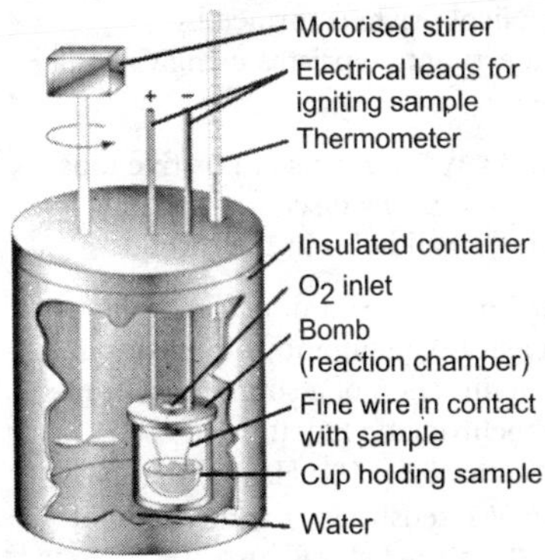

Calorimeter

A device used for the heat measurement. It consists of a metallic vessel and stirrer of the same material like copper or aluminium. Kept inside a wooden jacket which contains heat insulating materials like glass, wool, etc. The outer jacket acts as a heat shield and reduces the heat loss from the inner vessel. There is an opening in the outer jacket, through which a mercury thermometer can be inserted into the calorimeter.

calorimetry Measurement of heat. When a body at higher temperature, is brought in contact with another body at lower temperature, the heat lost by the hot body is equal to the heat gained by the colder body, provided no heat is allowed to escape to the surroundings. Thus, heat lost = heat gained.

camera An optical instrument able to record an image formed by visible light. A lens or system of lenses is used to focus the radiation onto the sensitive surface.

Canada balsam A transparent material with a refractive index of 1.53. Canada balsam has various uses in optical instrumentation.
e.g. Nicol prism is formed by connecting two prisms using Canada balsam.

canal rays Streams of positive ions obtained from a discharge tube by boring small holes in the cathode.

candela The SI unit of luminous intensity. The luminous intensity in a given direction of a source that emits monochromatic radiation of frequency 5.4×10^{15} Hz and that has radiant intensity in that direction of $1/683$ watt per steradian.

candle Former unit of luminous intensity.

cantilever A uniform beam clamped at one end and loaded at the other end.

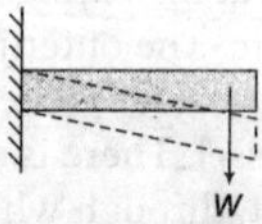

Cantilever

capacitance The ability of a system of conductors and insulators to store electric charge.

Capacitance of a system, $C = \dfrac{q}{V}$

where, q = charge given to the system and V = increase in potential.
Its unit is farad F.
Capacitance of a parallel plate capacitor with a conducting slab of thickness t is given by

$$C = \frac{\varepsilon_0 A}{d - t}$$

Capacitance of a parallel plate capacitor with a dielectric slab of thickness t is given by

$$C = \frac{\varepsilon_0 A}{d - t\left(1 - \frac{1}{k}\right)}$$

where, A = area of plate and
k = dielectric constant.

capacitor A device used for storing electric charge. It usually consists of two parallel conductors separated by some insulating material.

capacitors in parallel In parallel combination of capacitors, the equivalent capacitance of any number of capacitors is equal to the sum of the individual capacitances,

i.e. $C = C_1 + C_2 + C_3 + \ldots + C_n$

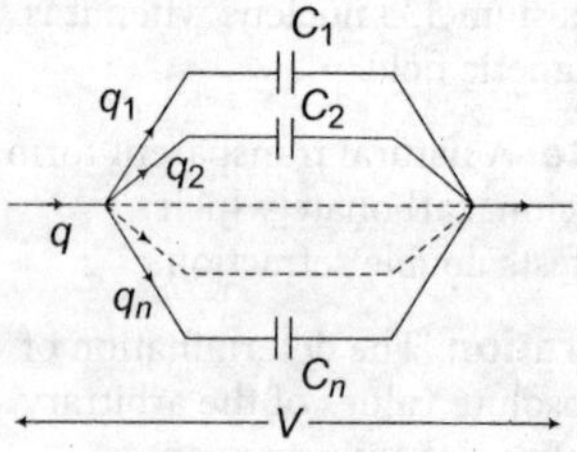

In parallel combination, the potential difference across the plates of each capacitor is same and charge is distributed in proportion to their capacitors. Parallel combination of capacitors is used for charge accumulations.

capacitors in series In series combination of capacitors, the reciprocal of equivalent capacitance of any number of capacitors is equal to the sum of reciprocals of the individual capacitors.

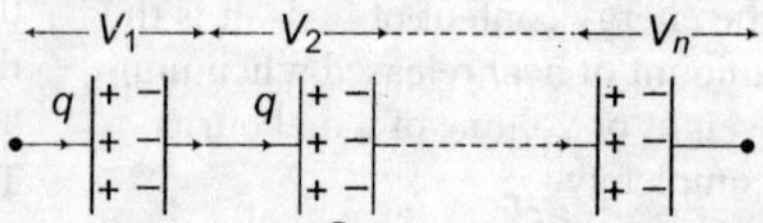

$$\frac{1}{C} = \frac{1}{C_1} + \frac{1}{C_2} + \ldots + \frac{1}{C_n}$$

In series combination, the charges on plates of each capacitor are same but the potential difference between their plates are inversely proportional to their capacitance. Series combination of capacitors is used when high voltage is to be divided on several capacitors.

capacitive reactance The opposition offered by a capacitor to the flow of alternating current. It is given by X_C.

$$X_C = \frac{1}{\omega C} = \frac{1}{2\pi f C}$$

where, f = frequency of alternating current and C = capacitance.

capillarity The rise or fall of liquid in a capillary tube (a tube of very fine bore). It is due to the surface tension of liquid. The height h through which a liquid will rise in a capillary tube of radius r which wets the sides of the tube, is given by

$$h = \frac{2S\cos\theta}{r\rho g}$$

where, S = surface tension of the liquid, θ = angle of contact, ρ = density of liquid and g = acceleration due to gravity.

capillary action The flow of liquid through a fine tube, against the force of gravitation.

capillary tube A tube with a narrow bore. Glass capillary tubes are used in mercury thermometers.

capture The absorption of one particle by a system. e.g. a positive ion may capture an electron to form a neutral atom. In nuclear reactions, an atomic nucleus may capture a neutron with emission of one or more gamma-ray photons.

carbon black A form of amorphous carbon produced by incomplete combustion of gas. It is used in experiments as a coating for surfaces that need to be good absorbers of radiation.

carbon cycle A series of nuclear reactions postulated to account for energy production in stars. In this series, $^{12}_{6}C$ is an intermediatry in the process by which hydrogen nuclei fuse to form helium with release of energy. In this series of nuclear reactions, four hydrogen nuclei combine to form a helium nucleus.

$$^{12}_{6}C + ^{1}_{1}H \longrightarrow ^{13}_{7}N + \gamma$$
$$^{13}_{7}N \longrightarrow ^{13}_{6}C + ^{0}_{1}e$$
$$^{13}_{6}C + ^{1}_{1}H \longrightarrow ^{14}_{7}N + \gamma$$
$$^{14}_{7}N + ^{1}_{1}H \longrightarrow ^{15}_{8}O + \gamma$$
$$^{15}_{8}O \longrightarrow ^{15}_{7}N + ^{0}_{1}e$$
$$^{15}_{7}N + ^{1}_{1}H \longrightarrow ^{12}_{6}C + ^{4}_{2}He$$

carbon dating (Radio carbon dating) A method to find out the age of material that contains living origin. In this method, ratio of carbon-12 to carbon-14 is determined. ^{14}C is a beta emitter of half-life approximately 5730 yr, is being formed continuously in the atmosphere as a result of cosmic-rays action. The ^{14}C becomes incorporated into living organisms. After death of organism, the amount of radioactive carbon decreases exponentially by radioactive decay. The ratio of ^{12}C to ^{14}C is a measure of the time elapsed since, the death of the organic material.

Carey Foster bridge A modified form of a slide wire bridge. It has four gaps instead of two. It is very accurate for determination of low resistances.

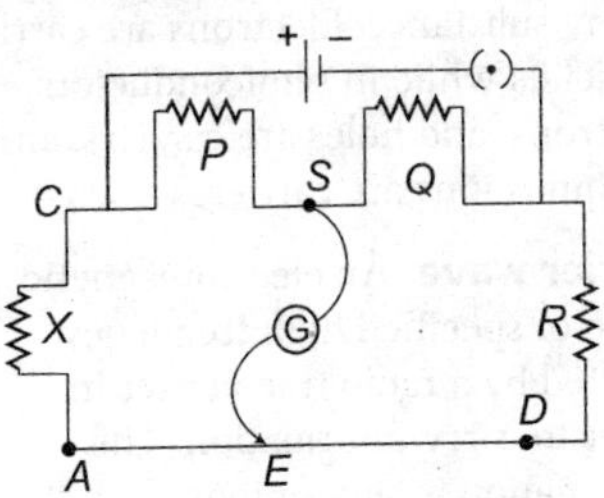

Carey foster bridge

Carnot cycle A reversible cycle in which four processes are involved. The four processes are:

(i) isothermal expansion (AB)
(ii) adiabatic expansion (BC)
(iii) isothermal compression (CD)
(iv) adiabatic compression (DA).

This process occurs in a perfect heat engine.

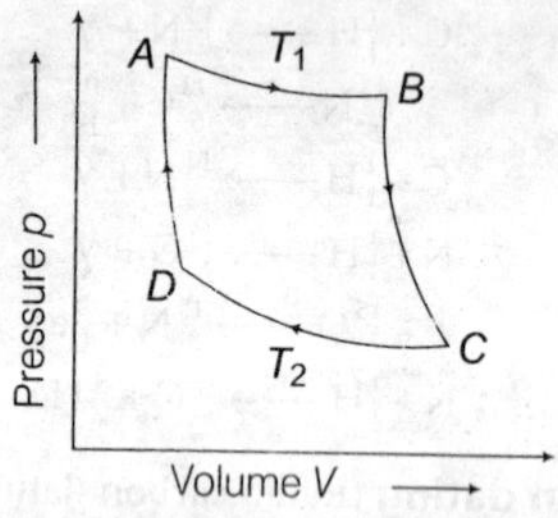

Carnot cycle

Carnot engine A reversible ideal heat engine operating between two temperatures. The body at fixed higher temperature is called source and body at fixed lower temperature is called sink.

Carnot theorem The efficiency of an ideal heat engine working between two specified temperatures is not less than the efficiency of any heat engine working between the same two temperatures. The efficiency of the Carnot engine is independent of the nature of the working substance.

carrier Charge particles, such as electrons or holes whose movements are responsible for the flow of current in any substance. Electrons are carrier in metals while in semiconductors, electrons and holes are carriers, and in liquids ions are carriers.

carrier wave An electromagnetic wave of specified high frequency emitted by a radio transmitter in order to carry information. The information is superimposed on the carrier wave by modulation.

cartesian sign convention While dealing with reflection or refraction of light, we use a certain set of sign convention which is known as cartesian sign convention. The below tables show cartesian sign convention for mirror and lens.

For mirrors

Measurement	Type of mirror	
	Convex	Concave
Focal length	+ ve	– ve
Radius of curvature	+ ve	– ve
Object distance	– ve	– ve
Image distance (real)	NA	– ve
Image distance (virtual)	+ ve	+ ve
Height of image (real)	NA	– ve
Height of image (virtual)	+ ve	+ ve

For lenses

Measurements	For convex lens	For concave lens
Distance of the object	Negative	Negative
Distance of the real image	Positive	
Distance of the virtual image	Negative	Negative
Focal length	Positive	Negative
Height of the object	Positive	Positive
Height of the inverted real image	Negative	
Height of the virtual erect image	Positive	Positive

cascade connection A method of electrical connection in which the output terminals of the first device or network are connected to the input terminals of the second, those of the second to the third, and so on.

cascade process The process taking place in different or number of stages.

Casimir effect The existence force between two macroscopic conducting surfaces in a volume that only contains an electromagnetic field.

cassegrain telescope A reflecting type telescope in which a small hyperbolic mirror is used to converge the incident beam of light.

cataract A defect of eye in which the crystalline lens of people at old age becomes milky and cloudy. This causes partial or complete loss of vision. It is possible to restore vision through a cataract surgery.

cathetometer A telescope or microscope fitted with cross wires in the eye piece and mounted, so that it can slide along a graduated scale. It is used for accurate measurement of lengths without mechanical contacts.

cathode In electrolysis, the electrode that is at a negative potential with respect to the anode, in any electrical system, such as a discharge tube or a solid-state electronic device. The cathode is the terminal at which electrons enter the system.

cathode ray The electron beam emitted in a discharge tube when the pressure falls to about 10^{-4} mm of mercury.

Cathode Ray Oscilloscope (CRO) An instrument for investigating electrical signals. An electron beam is deflected in the horizontal and vertical directions by an electrostatic field from two sets of plates. The horizontal deflection is often a constant repeating sweep of the spot produced by an internal time base. The signal to be investigated, is amplified and applied to the vertical deflecting plates. So, in this way, a graph of the signal is drawn on the screen.

Cathode Ray Tube (CRT) An electron tube which converts the electrical signals into a pattern on a screen. It provides the viewing screen in the television tube, the radar viewer and the cathode ray oscilloscope.
It consists of an evacuated tube containing a heated cathode and two or more ring shaped anodes, through which the cathode rays pass, so that they hit the luminous screen. Any point on the screen that is hit by the cathode ray becomes luminous.

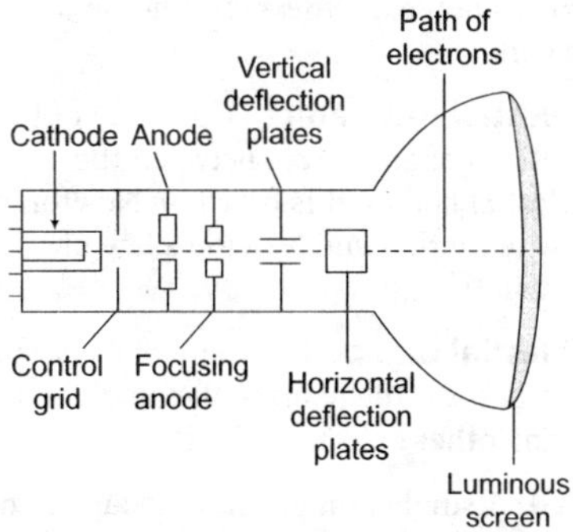

Cathode Ray Tube (CRT)

A control grid is used to control the brightness of illumination on the screen. The assembly of cathode, control grid and anode is called electron gun. The beam from electron gun is focussed and deflected by means of plates providing electric field or coils providing magnetic field.

cation A positively charged ion, formed by removal of electrons from atoms or molecules. In electrolysis, cations are attracted towards the negatively charged electrode.

causality The principle used to analyse the result of scattering experiment and in optics.

caustic The curve or surface formed by the reflection of parallel ray of light in a large-aperture concave mirror.

Cavendish's experiment The first experiment in which gravitational constant G is measured in laboratory performed by Cavendish in 1798.

cavitation The formation of gas or vapour filled cavities in liquids in motion when the pressure is reduced to a critical value while the ambient temperature remains constant. If the velocity of the flowing liquid exceeds a certain value, the pressure can be reduced to such an extent that the Bernoulli's theorem breaks down. At this point the cavitation occurs.

celestial mechanics The study of the motions of and forces between the celestial bodies. It is based on Newton's law of motion and Newton's law of gravitation.

celestial object Heavenly objects; such as the stars, the planets, the moon and many other objects in the sky.

cell A single unit generating current on account of chemical reactions going on inside it. It converts chemical energy into electrical energy.

celsius scale A temperature scale in which lower fix point is melting point of ice (0°C) and upper fix point is boiling point of water (100°C). There are 100 equal divisions between these two fixed points and each division represent 1°C.

central force A force directed towards or away from a fixed point, i.e. along the position vector of the point of application of the force with respect to the fixed point. In the motion under a central force, the angular momentum is always conserved.

centre of buoyancy The centre of mass of the displaced fluid volume. For a floating object to be stable, the centre of mass of the object must lie below the centre of buoyancy, when the object is in equilibrium, the two lie on the same vertical line.

centre of curvature The centre of the sphere of which the mirror or lens is a part.

centre of gravity A point where the total weight of the body may be considered to act and about which the gravitational torque on the body is zero.

centre of mass A point in a body at which the whole mass of the body may be considered to act. It is expressed as

$$r = \frac{m_1 r_1 + m_2 r_2}{m_1 + m_2}$$

where, r_1 and r_2 are position vectors of the two particles of masses m_1 and m_2 constituting the system.

centre of moment The point about which lever in equilibrium is free to move. The reference axis is used in calculating the moments of forces.

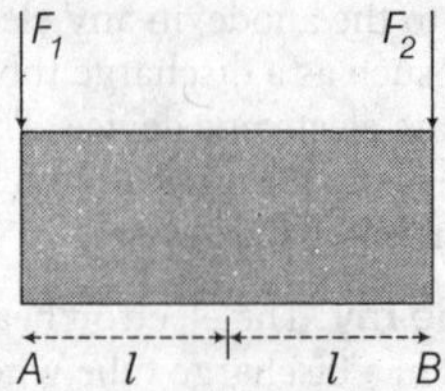

Centre of moment

centre of oscillation The point on a stationary compound pendulum located vertically below the pivot at a distance that equals the length of the equivalent simple pendulum.

centre of pressure The centre of pressure of a submerged surface is the point through which the resultant of the pressure forces acts.

centre of symmetry The point inside a crystal located in such a way that all lines passing through it contact opposite faces of the crystal in corresponding points at equal distances.

centre-tap-transformer A transformer whose secondary coil has three points of connectivity, two at the ends of the length of the wire and one at the middle of the wire.

centi Symbol is *c*, a prefix denoted by 10^{-2}.

centigrade scale *See* celsius scale.

centimetric waves Electromagnetic waves with wavelengths in the range 1-10 cm.

centrifugal force Force acting radially outward when an object is moving in a circular path.
It is an imaginary force and its magnitude is

$$\frac{mv^2}{r}$$

where, r = radius of circle,
m and v = the mass and speed of object, respectively.

centrifuge A device for separating the components of a suspension by spinning. The liquid containing suspended particles is placed in a tube, which is whirled round in a horizontal circle. Light particles move towards the axis of rotation and heavy particles accumulate at the outer surface.

centripetal acceleration The acceleration acting on the object undergoing uniform circular motion. It always acts on the object along the radius towards the centre of the circular path. Its magnitude is given by

$$a_c = \frac{v^2}{r} = r\omega^2 = r\,(2\pi f)^2$$

$$= 4\pi^2 rf^2 = \frac{4\pi^2 r}{T^2}$$

where, v = speed of the body,
r = radius of the circle,
ω = angular speed,
f = frequency and
T = the time period.

centripetal force Force acting radially inward when an object is moving in a circular path.
The magnitude of this force is $\frac{mv^2}{r}$

where, r = radius of circle,
m = mass and
v = speed of object, respectively.

centroid The mean position of all the points in all the coordinate directions.

cesium clock An apparatus used to produce the steady frequency, used in defining the second. In a cesium clock, the number of atoms in the higher state is detected and the signal is used to stabilise the oscillator producing the radiation.

CGS system System of measurement in which unit of length is centimetre, unit of mass is gram and unit of time is second.

chain reaction If in a nuclear reaction, the produced particle, such as neutron further take part in fission then a chain of reaction is started, called chain reaction. In a chain reaction, the number of fissions produced by daughter neutrons in any generation is equal to or more than the number of fissions produced by parent neutrons in the previous generation.

Chandrasekhar limit The maximum possible mass of a star that is prevented from collapsing under its own gravity.

change of state Matter normally exists in three states, such as solid, liquid and gas. A transition from one of these states to another is called a change of state. Two common changes of states are, solid to liquid called melting, and liquid to gas called vaporisation. These changes occurs at constant temperatures.

channel A path for the transmission of electrical signals, generally specified by frequency band.

characteristic In an electronic device, such as diode, triode or a transistor, a graph that shows how voltage or current between two of the terminals varies with respect to voltage or current at other terminals of the device.

charcoal An amorphous form of carbon obtained by heating wood or other organic material in the absence of air. It is used for absorbing gases and for removing impurities from liquids.

charge A property of elementary particles that gives rise to an interaction between them. There are two types of charge described as positive and negative.

charge carrier Any particle that transport electric charge in an electric current. The type of carrier depends upon the nature of conductor. In metals, negatively charged electrons are charge carriers, while in semiconductors, electrons and holes are charge carriers.

charge conjugation A property of elementary particles that determines the difference between a particle and its anti-particle.

Charge-Coupled Device (CCD) A rectangular array of light sensitive pixels which forms the image detection sensor in camcorders and some telescopes.

centre of mass

1. The electric charge per unit volume of a body or medium is called volume charge density. It is denoted by ρ.
2. The electric charge per unit surface area of a body is called surface charge density. It is denoted by σ.
3. The electric charge per unit length of a linear object is called linear charge density. It is denoted by λ.

charge to mass ratio of electron A quantity that was first measured by Thomson using the apparatus in which a beam of electrons was subjected to magnetic and electric fields in a way that they deflected the beam in opposite directions.
The strengths of the deflecting fields were adjusted to give zero deflection of the spot, where the beam struck the fluorescent screen.

Charles' law At constant pressure, the volume of a given mass of gas is proportional to its absolute temperature T, i.e.

$$V \propto T$$

chemical energy The energy stored in the chemical bonds of a substance. It is converted into another form when a chemical reaction takes place.

chip A single crystal of a semiconducting material of very small dimension (millimetre) fabricated in such a way that it can perform a large number of electronic functions.

choke A coil of high inductance and low resistance which is used to reduce or block the high frequency component of any electrical signal.

choroid The pigmented vascular layer of the eyeball between the retina and the sclera.

chromatic aberration The image of white object formed by a lens is obtained coloured and blurred.

chromaticity An objective description of the colour quality of a visual stimulus that does not depend on its luminance.

chromosphere The Sun consists of two layers photosphere and chromosphere. Photosphere is the inner part and chromosphere is the outer layer. It extends to about 13000 km to 16000 km above the photosphere.

Its lower layers from the reversing layer, in which temperature decreases outwards upto about 4300 K. In the main chromosphere, temperature gradually rises to about 10000 K. In a thin layer at its outer boundary, temperature abruptly rises to a few million kelvin.

ciliary muscles They hold the lens in position and help in modifying the curvature of the lens.

circuit The component path of an electric current including the source of the current, resistors, inductors, etc.

circuit breaker A safety device in an electric circuit that interrupts the flow of current in the event of a short circuit or other fault.

circuit element A resistor, capacitor, inductor, transistor or other device used in making up electric circuits.

circular birefringence A phenomenon, in which there is a difference between the refractive indices of the molecules of a substance for right and left circularly polarised light. It depends on the way, in which the electromagnetic field interacts with the molecules.

circular dichroism The production of an elliptically polarised wave, when a linearly polarised light wave passes through a substance that has difference in the extinction coefficients for left and right-handed polarised light.

circular measure Measurement of angles in radians.

circular motion A form of periodic motion of an object which moves around a point keeping a constant distance from that point. For this to be possible, a positive central force must act.

circular polarisation In this type of polarisation of wave, the plane of polarisation rotates uniformly around an axis as the light progresses.
Circularly polarised light is equivalent to the combination of two plane polarised waves having phase difference of 90° and moving together.

cladding A thin covering of a metal around a fuel element in a nuclear reactor to prevent corrosion of the fuel element by the coolant.

clark cell A type of voltaic cell consisting of an anode made of zinc amalgam and a cathode of mercury both immersed in a saturated solution of zinc sulphate. The clark cell has been superseded as a standard by the weston cadmium cell.

classical physics The part of Physics which does not include quantum theory or the theory of relativity.

Clausius statement It is impossible to design a self-acting machine unaided by any external agency, which would transfer heat from a body at a lower temperature to another body at a higher temperature. It is also known as second law of thermodynamics.

clinical thermometer A mercury thermometer used for measuring the temperature of human body. It has a range of 95°F to 110°F. The mercury reaches a maximum value but does not then return to the bulb until shaken down post the kind.

clock face rule Used to find the direction of current face of circular wire. If we look at one face of a circular wire (or coil) through which a current is passing:

1. If the current around the face of circular wire flows in clockwise direction, then the face of the circular wire will be South pole.
2. If the current around the face of circular wire flows in anticlockwise direction, then the face of the circular wire will be North pole.

closed circuit A circuit in which electric current can flow without any interruption.

closed system A physical system which is not subjected to any force whose source is external to the system.

cloud chamber A chamber, containing a liquid and its saturated vapour. It is used to show the tracks of ionising radiation, especially alpha and beta particles.

coaxial Denoting bodies or shapes that have a common axis of rotation or radial symmetry.

coaxial cable An electrical coaxial cable consisting of a central metallic wire in an insulating sheath. It is surrounded by a woven mesh of conductor. It is insulated by an outer plastic jacket. A coaxial cable is not affected by external electric and magnetic fields.

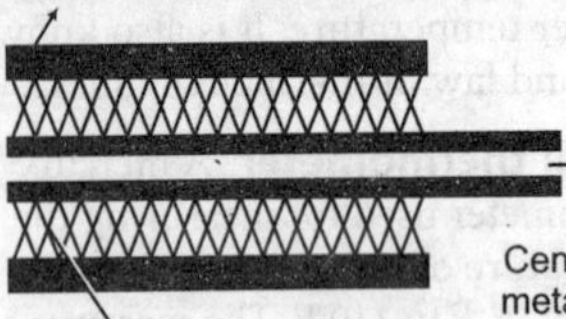

cobalt A lustrous silvery-blue hard ferromagnetic transition metal. It is used in alloys for magnets, cutting tools, electrical heating elements, catalysts and some paints.

coefficient A number that is constant for a given substance, body or process under certain specific condition.

coefficient of area expansion The small charge in surface area ΔS per unit original area S per °C change in temperature ΔT. It is denoted by β and expressed as

$$\beta = \frac{\Delta S}{S\,\Delta T}$$

coefficient of coupling The portion of the flux that links one coil to the other coil. The coefficient of coupling can range from 0 to 1. When all the flux is coupled, the coefficient of coupling is 1. Sometimes, it is expressed as a percentage. Thus, 100 percent coupling means coefficient of coupling of 1.

coefficient of friction The ratio of frictional force F and the normal force R between two forces. It is denoted by μ and expressed as

$$\mu = \frac{F}{R}$$

coefficient of linear expansion If the substance is in the form of a long rod, then for small change in temperature ΔT, the fractional change in length $\Delta l / l$, is directly proportional to ΔT.

$$\alpha_i = \frac{\Delta l}{l\Delta T}$$

where, α_i is known as the coefficient of linear expansion and is characteristic of the material of the rod.

coefficient of performance The ratio of the heat absorbed per cycle from the sink Q_2 to the electric energy supplied W to remove this heat. It is denoted by β and expressed as

$$\beta = \frac{Q_2}{W}$$

coefficient of self-induction The magnetic flux linked with the coil when the unit current flows through it. It is numerically equal to the emf induced in the circuit when the rate of change of current is unity. It is numerically equal to twice the work done against the induced emf in establishing unit current in the coil.

coefficient of thermal conductivity The rate of flow of heat per unit area per unit temperature gradient across the solid. It is denoted by k and expressed as

$$k = \frac{\Delta Q / \Delta t}{A\,\Delta T / \Delta x}$$

Its SI unit is W/mK.

coefficient of viscosity The coefficient of viscosity of fluid is defined as the tangential force required to maintain velocity gradient between two layers of fluid each having its area. It is denoted by η and expressed as

$$\eta = \frac{Fl}{vA} = \frac{F}{A\left(\frac{dv}{dx}\right)}$$

where, F = tangential force,

l = thickness of fluid.

$\frac{dv}{dx}$ = velocity gradient,

A = area of the liquid in contact with glass and

v = velocity.

Its SI unit is N-s/m^2 or Pa-s.

coefficient of volume expansion The fractional change in volume, $\Delta V/V$ of a substance for temperature change ΔT. It is denoted by α_V and expressed as

$$\alpha_V = \left(\frac{\Delta V}{V}\right)\frac{1}{\Delta T}$$

Here, α_V is also a characteristic of the substance but is not strictly a constant. It depends in general on temperature. It is seen that α_V becomes constant only at a high temperature.

coelostat A device that enables light from the same area of the sky to be continuously reflected into the field of view of an astronomical telescope.

coercive force The magnetising field intensity required to reduce the flux density in a material to zero. If the material is magnetically saturated the coercive force is a maximum; it is then referred to as the coercivity.

coherent Two sources of waves are said to be coherent, if there is a constant relationship between the phases of the waves emitted by them.

coherent scattering The scattering for which there is a well-defined relationship between the phase of the incoming wave and the phase of the outgoing wave. Scattering for which there is no well-defined such relationship is called incoherent scattering.

coherent sources Those sources which emit continuous light waves of same amplitude, same wavelength/ frequency in same phase or having a constant phase difference. They are an essential requirement for interference of light. They should be strong with least background lying close to each other.

coherent units A system or subset of units in which the derived units are obtained by multiplying or dividing together base units with no numerical factor involved.

coherent wave Waves are said to be coherent, if there is a regular phase relationship between different parts of a wavefront.

cohesive force The force of attraction between two similar molecules, i.e. of the same substance.

cold emission Emission of electrons from a solid by a process other than thermionic emission.

collector *See* transistor.

collimator The arrangement for producing a parallel beam of radiation to be used in spectrometer or any other optical instrument.

collinear vectors The vectors which are acting along parallel straight lines.

collision A collision refers to the mutual interaction of molecules, atoms, etc. When they encounter one another, although they do not necessarily come into actual contact. These are of two types as perfectly elastic collision and perfectly inelastic collision.

colloid A substance containing very small particles e.g. sols, gels and emulsions.

colorimeter The instrument which able to give readings for any colour in terms of the intensity of each of the three primary colours.

colour blindness The inability to distinguish different colours.

colour code In electronics, it is used to indicate the values or ratings of electronic components usually for resistors but also for capacitors, inductors and others.

colour temperature The temperature of a black body with the same relative spectral distribution as that of the radiation under investigation.

colour vision The ability of eye to distinguish different colours of objects based on the wavelengths or frequencies of the light they reflect, emit or transmit.

coma An aberration of lens or mirror occurs in case of oblique incident. When an unsymmetrical beam of light is incident on it, then image of a point object is comet shaped.

combustion A reaction in which a substance reacts rapidly with oxygen and the results in production of heat and light.

comet Comets are also members of our solar system. They revolve around the Sun in highly elliptical orbits. However, their period of revolution round the Sun is usually very long. A comet appears generally as a bright head with a long tail. The length of the tail grows in size as it approaches the Sun. The tail of a comet is always directed away from the Sun. Many comets are known to appear periodically. One such comet is Halley's comet, which appears after nearly every 76 years.

commercial unit The unit of electrical energy and measured in kilowatt-hour. It is denoted by kWh.

common emitter transistor characteristic When a transistor is used in common emitter configuration, the input is applied between the base and the emitter, the output is obtained between the collector and emitter. The variation of the base current I_B with the base-emitter voltage V_{BE} is called the input characteristic. Similarly, the variation of the collector current I_C with the collector-emitter voltage V_{CE} is called the output characteristic.

commutator The part of a direct-current electric motor or generator that connects the coil to the outside circuit changing the connections round as the coil rotates.

companding A way of reducing the distortion of an analog signal during transmission.

comparator An apparatus used in measurements of the expansivity of solids. A standard bar at constant temperature is used for comparison.

compass needle A compass needle is a small magnet. Its one end, which point towards North, is called a North pole, and the other end, which points towards South, is called a South pole.

complementary colours Two coloured lights that mix to produce the sensation of white. There is an infinite number of pairs of complementary colours. The members of each pair of complementary colours lie at opposite sides of white on this curve.

component vectors Two or more vectors into which a given vector can be resolved. The effect (or resultant) of these vectors is equal to that of the given vector.

compound lens A unit of two or more lenses used together.

compound microscope In a compound microscope, the images are highly magnified. The objective lens forms a real, inverted and magnified image of the object. This acts as an object for eye lens, which forms a virtual, erected magnified image seen by the eye held close to the eye lens. Its magnifying power is given by

$$m = \frac{v_o}{-u_o}\left(1 + \frac{d}{f_e}\right)$$

where, u_o and v_o are distances of object and image from optical centre of objective lens, f_e is the focal length of eye lens.

compound pendulum In such a pendulum, the moment of the restoring force is $\tau = -mgd \sin\theta$, if θ is sufficiently small, then $\tau = -mgd\,\theta$. Time period of such a pendulum is

$$T = 2\pi\sqrt{\frac{I}{mgd}}$$

compressibility The reciprocal of bulk modulus.

compression When a vibrating object moves forward, it pushes and compresses the air infront of it creating a region of high pressure. This region is called a compression *C*. This compression starts to move away from the vibrating object. Compressions are the regions, where particles are crowded together and represented by the upper portion of the curve. The peak represents the region of maximum compression. Thus, compressions are regions, where density as well as pressure is high.

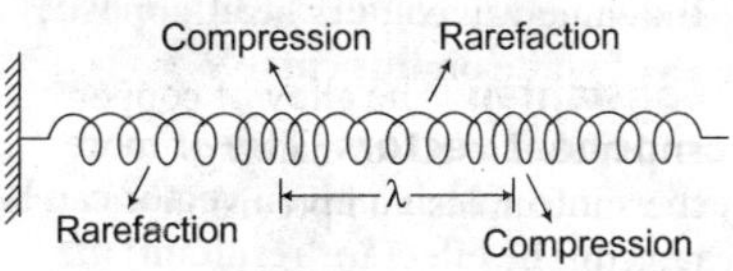

compton effect An increase in the wavelength of X-rays or gamma rays when scattered by loosely bound electrons in substances, the electrons being ejected. This type of inelastic scattering is known as compton scattering.

concave mirror Spherical mirror in which the reflection of light takes place at the concave surface or bent in surface.

concavo-convex Describes a lens with one concave surface and other convex surface.

concord A combination of two or more notes sounded together that produce a pleasing effect on the ear is known as a concord.

condenser The former name of capacitor. It is a device used to cool a vapour to cause it to condense to a liquid. In steam engine, it acts as a reservoir.

condition for constructive interference The path difference between two waves should be zero or an integral multiple of full wavelength.

condition for destructive interference The path difference between two waves should be an odd integral multiple of half wavelength.

conductance Reciprocal of resistance in DC circuits. In AC circuit, conductance is the resistance divided by the square of its impendence. Unit of conductance is mho or Siemen S or reciprocal ohm.

conduction A process of heat transfer through a substance without movement of the substance itself. This transfer depends on temperature difference and nature of the material.

conduction band An energy band occupied by conduction electrons, which can move freely in solid. It is generally empty or partially filled.

It may also be defined as the lowest unfilled energy band. On acquiring sufficient energy, valence electrons may leave the valence band and come to the conduction band. They are then almost free or are only weakly held to the nucleus and are called the conduction electrons.

conduction current A current in the electric circuit which arises due to the flow of electrons in the connecting wires of the circuit in a definite closed path. It exists even, if the flow of electrons is at uniform rate.

conductivity

1. The ability of a material to conduct electricity.
2. The ability of a material to conduct heat (energy).

conductor

1. The materials having high electrical conductivity are called electric conductors, e.g. all metals.
2. The materials having high thermal conductivity are called thermal conductors.

cones The cells present in the retina of an eye which are sensitive to bright light. The cone cells of our retina respond to colours. They do not function in dim light.

configuration The arrangement of electrons in shells around the nucleus of an atom. The electron configuration largely determines the chemical behaviour of an element as well as some physical properties, such as electrical conductivity.

conjugate points Any pair of points relative to a lens, reflector, or other optical system as that either is imaged at the other.

conjunction When a planet approaches closest to Sun as seen from Earth during its orbital motion, the planet is said to be in conjunction with the Sun. At that time, it may actually be a little to North or to South of the Sun, but due to glare of the Sun, it cannot be seen.

conservation law A physical law, that some property of an isolated system remains constant throughout a series of changes.

conservation of angular momentum If no external torque acts on a system, then the total angular momentum of the system remains conserved.

conservation of linear momentum The vector sum of linear momenta of all the bodies in an isolated system is conserved and is not affected due to their mutual action and reaction.

conservative field The vector field, for which the line integral depends on the end points of the path only and is independent of the path.

conservative force When an external force does work in taking a body from a point to another against a force like spring force or gravitational force, that work gets stored as potential energy of the body. When the external force is removed, the body moves, gaining kinetic energy and losing an equal amount of potential energy. The sum of kinetic and potential energies, is thus conserved. Forces of this kind are called conservative forces. e.g. spring forces and gravitational forces.

constant A quantity that remains at the same value.

constantan The alloy of copper and nickel used for making thermocouples and precision resistors.

C

constructive interference Interference in which the resultant intensity of two interferring waves is maximum.

contact angle An angle formed between solid and liquid surfaces.

continuous spectrum The spectrum having continuous range of wavelengths or frequencies.

continuous wave The electromagnetic wave which is transmitted continuously over a period of time.

contour map A map showing irregularities of land surface.

control grid These are used in nuclear reactor to control the number of thermal neutrons produced during nuclear fission reaction.

control rods Neutrons absorbing rods that can be moved into or out of the core of a nuclear reactor to control the chain reaction.

convection The transfer of energy by flow of a liquid or gas, convection can be natural or forced. In natural convection, gravity plays an important part. When a fluid is heated from below, the hot part expands and therefore, becomes less dense. e.g. in an electric kettle the heating element raises the temperature of the water next to it, which expands and rises. Colder water then flows in beneath it, setting up a convection current.
In forced convection, material is forced to move by a pump or by some other physical means. e.g. in the human body, the heart acts as a pump, that circulates blood, through different parts of the body, transferring heat by forced convection.

conventional current The electric current which flows from points at positive potential to the points at negative potential.

conventional sources of energy The traditional sources of energy which are familiar to the most people. It is also known as non-renewable sources of energy.

convergent A convergent beam becomes narrow as it travels. After passing through the focus, the beam will be divergent.

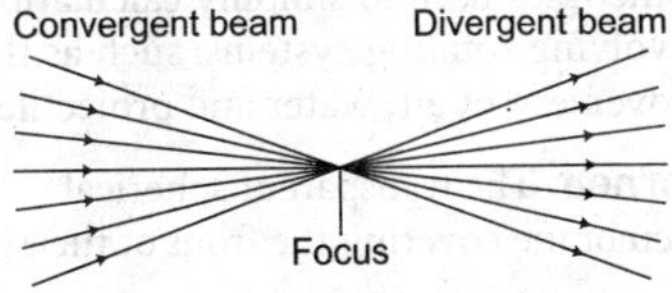

Convergent and Divergent beams

convergent beam The beam of light meeting at a point.

converging lens The lens which converges all the parallel rays of light incident on it (after refraction) at particular point.

converging mirror The mirror which converges all the parallel rays incident on it (after reflection) on at particular point.

converter A device used for converting alternating current to direct current.

convex mirror A convex mirror is one with a convex reflecting surface or bulging-out surface. It is a spherical mirror which is commonly used as rear-view (wing) mirrors in vehicles. It has a wider field of view as it is curved outwards.

coolant Any substance that is generally a liquid or a gas and is used to reduce the temperature of a system below a specific level.

cooling correction A method of correcting for errors due to energy loss in experiments that involve temperature changes.

coplanar forces All the forces acting in the same plane.

core

1. A piece of iron or other any other magnetic material used to concentrate the magnetic lines of force in a transformer.
2. Central part of a nuclear reactor, where the chain reaction occurs.

coriolis force A fictitious force sometimes used to simplify calculations involving rotating systems; such as the movement of air, water and projectiles.

cornea The transparent spherical membrane covering the front of the eye.

corona or crown

1. The outer most layer of the Sun's atmosphere. Its temperature is a few million kelvin. The corona may extend as far as our Earth and some astronomers are of the opinion that it may reach even farther.
2. A glowing region of the air surrounding a conductor when the potential gradient near its surface exceeds a critical value. It is due to ionisation of the air and may be associated by hissing sounds.

corpuscular theory According to this theory, light travels as a particle or corpuscle. This theory successfully explained the phenomenon of reflection, refraction, dispersion, etc. but cannot explain the results of interference, diffraction, etc.

cosmic radiation High-energy particles that fall on the Earth from space.

cosmology The study of the nature, origin and evolution of the universe.

Coulomb Its symbol is *C*. The SI unit of electric charge, equal to the charge transmitted by an electric current of 1 ampere flowing in one second.

Coulomb barrier The atomic nucleus surrounded by a strong electrostatic potential barrier. The Coulomb barrier is about 3 MeV in height for carbon nuclei and 20 MeV for lead nuclei.

Coulomb's law The mutual electrostatic force between two point charges q_1 and q_2 is proportional to the product $q_1 \times q_2$ and inversely proportional to the square of the distance r_{21} separation them. Mathematically,

$$\mathbf{F}_{21} = \text{force on } q_2 \text{ due to } q_1$$
$$= k\,\frac{q_1 \cdot q_2}{r_{21}^2}\,\hat{\mathbf{r}}_{21}$$

where, $\hat{\mathbf{r}}_{21}$ = unit vector in the direction from q_1 to q_2 and $k = \dfrac{1}{4\pi\varepsilon_0}$ is the constant of proportionality. In SI units, the unit of charge is coulomb. The experimental value of the constant ε_0 is

$$\varepsilon_0 = 8.854 \times 10^{-12}\ \mathrm{C^2N^{-1}m^{-2}}$$

The approximate value of k is

$$k = 9 \times 10^9\ \mathrm{Nm^2\,C^{-2}}$$

couple A pair of equal and parallel forces in opposite directions, whose of line of action is not same.

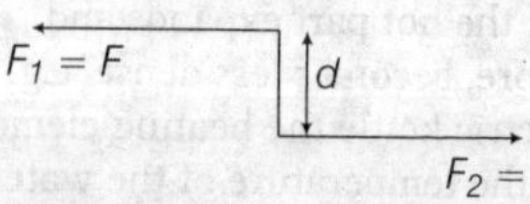

coupled oscillations When two or more oscillating bodies connected to each other oscillate together and affect each others oscillations are called coupled oscillations.

crank A type of lever that impart rotary or oscillatory motion to rotating shaft.

creep Slow deformation of a solid due to continuous applied stress.

crest A point of maximum positive displacement in a wave.

critical angle The value of angle of incidence in denser medium corresponds to which angle of refraction in rarer medium is 90°. It is denoted by *C*. If μ is refractive index of denser medium w.r.t. rarer medium, then

$$\mu = \frac{1}{\sin C}$$

critical exponents Numbers that quantify how thermodynamic quantities, such as the specific heat capacity, diverge at the critical temperature of a second-order phase transition.

critical field The critical value of the magnetic flux density of a magnetic field, above which the superconductivity of a super conductor is destroyed.

critical frequency The highest frequency of radio wave which sent straight towards the layer of ionosphere gets reflected from ionosphere and returns to the Earth. It is found as

$$\nu_c = 9\,(N_{max})^{1/2}$$

critical mass The minimum mass of a fissile material required to produce a self-sustained chain reaction without any supply of neutrons from outside.

critical pressure The pressure of a fluid in its critical state, i.e. when it is at its critical temperature and critical volume.

critical speed The speed at which the behaviour of the fluid switches from that of laminar flow to that of turbulent flow.

critical state The state of a fluid in which the liquid and gas phases both have the same density.

critical temperature The temperature above which a gas cannot be liquefied by an increase of pressure.

critical velocity The velocity of liquid flow upto which its flow is streamlined and above which its flow becomes turbulent.
It is denoted by v_c and expressed as

$$v_c = K\eta^a\rho^b r^c = \frac{K\eta}{\rho r}$$

where, η = coefficient of viscosity of liquid,
ρ = density of liquid,
r = radius of the tube,
K = dimensionless constant and
a, b and c = dimensions of v_c.

critical volume The volume of a fixed mass of a fluid in its critical state i.e. when it is at its critical temperature and critical pressure.

cryogenics The physics of very low temperatures, including techniques for producing low temperatures and the study of behaviours of materials when cooled.

cryoscopy The determination of freezing points.

cryotron A switch that relies on superconductivity and take very little current.

crystal oscillator A fixed frequency oscillator in which the output is derived from a crystal of Rochelle salt or quartz specially cut, so that its natural frequency of mechanical vibration is the desired value.

crystal spectrometer A type of spectrometer for use with X-rays which are dispersed by diffraction from the face of a single crystal.

CT scanner An X-ray machine used to produce images of slices through a patient or other subject. CT stands for 'Computed Tomography'.

Curie's law The magnetisation I of a paramagnetic substance is directly proportional to the applied field B and inversely proportional to the absolute temperature T.

$$I = C \cdot \frac{B}{T}$$

where, C = Curie's constant.

Curie temperature The particular temperature at which a ferromagnetic substance losses it ferromagnetism.

current Its symbol is I the flow of electric charge from one place to other. Its SI unit is ampere.

current balance A device for measuring electric current to a high degree of accuracy, by measuring the electromagnetic force produced between two conductors carrying the current.

current carriers The charged particles whose flow in a definite direction constitutes the electric current. e.g. electron in conductors, ions in electrolyte, electrons and holes in semiconductos.

current density The amount of current flowing per unit area of the conductor around that point provided the area is held in a direction normal to the current. It is denoted by J and expressed as $J = \frac{I}{A}$. The SI unit of the current density is A/m^2.

current sensitivity of a galvanometer The deflection produced in the galvanometer when unit current flows through it. It is denoted by I_s and expressed as

$$I_s = \frac{Q}{I} = \frac{nBA}{K}$$

Its SI unit is rad/A or div/A.

Current-voltage characteristics The graphs which show how the circuit component varies with the voltage across it.

cut-off potential The minimum negative potential given to anode in a photocell for which the photoelectric current becomes zero. It is also called as stopping potential.

cybernetics The science that deals with communication and control, particularly with regard to machines. It includes details about the input and output of information, feedback and so on.

cyclic process Consists of a series of changes which return the system back to its initial state.

cyclotron It was invented by E.O. Lawrence and M.S. Livingston in 1934 to investigate nuclear structure. A machine used to accelerate charged particles or ions to high energies. The cyclotron uses both electric and magnetic fields in combination to increase the energy of charged particles. As the fields are perpendicular to each other, they are called crossed fields. Cyclotron uses the fact that the frequency of revolution to the charged particle in a magnetic field is independent of its energy.

cyclotron frequency In a uniform magnetic field B, a charge q executes a circular orbit in a plane normal to its frequency of uniform circular motion is called the cyclotron frequency and is given by

$$\nu_c = \frac{qB}{2\pi m}$$

This frequency is independent of the particle's speed and radius. This fact is exploited in a machine, the cyclotron, which is used to accelerate charged particles.

D

D'Alembert's principle A formulation of Newtonian mechanics that reduces dynamics to an equilibrium condition like statics by extending Newton's third law to the case of forces acting on bodies.

damp Retarding the action of a vibration string to cause a decrease in its amplitude.

damped Progressive energy loss and decrease in amplitude of oscillations due to friction, viscosity or other means.

damped harmonic motion The harmonic motion in which amplitude decreases due to the dragging force. The resting force,

$$F = -kx$$

The differential equation of motion,

$$\frac{d^2x}{dt^2} + 2\beta\frac{dx}{dt} + \omega_0^2 x = 0$$

$$\omega_0^2 = k/m$$

damped oscillation When a simple harmonic system oscillates with a decreasing amplitude with time. The energy of the system executing damped oscillations will go on decreasing with time.

damped vibration Vibration with decreasing amplitude. The cause of decreasing amplitude is loss of energy as heat in overcoming frictional and viscous force.

damping A decrease in the amplitude of an oscillation as a result of energy loss from the oscillating system to overcome frictional or other resistive force.

Daniell cell A kind of primary cell in which copper is used as positive electrode dipped in $CuSO_4$ solution. The amalgamated zinc rod is used as negative electrode dipped in dilute H_2SO_4. The emf of Daniell cell is about 1.08 V with sulphuric acid and 1.10 V with zinc sulphate.

dark energy Energy in the universe associated with the fact that the expansion of the universe is accelerating and the cosmological constant could have a non-zero value.

dark galaxy A galaxy that is composed largely of dark matter. There is some evidence for the existance of such galaxies.

dating Methods of determining the age of archaeological or geological specimens, the Earth, meteorites etc. It is assumed that some radioactive nuclide is disappearing by decay and a product is formed. Measurements of the amount of parent nuclide or product nuclide, or the ratio of parent to product can give an estimate of the age in certain circumstances as carbon dating, fission-track dating, potassium-argon dating, rubidium-strontium dating, thermo-luminescent dating, uranium-lead dating, etc.

dating techniques Methods applied for estimating the age of rocks, palaeontological sites, etc.

daughter neutron When one neutron, called the parent neutron is captured by U^{235}, the nucleus splits up into two parts with the release of more than two neutrons called the daughter neutrons.

daughter nucleus A nuclide produced by radioactive decay of another nuclide.

day The time taken for the earth to make one complete rotation on its own axis. The solar day is the time between two successive transist of the Sun across the meridian.

DC current gain in CB transistor The ratio of collector current I_c to the emitter current I_e. It is denoted by α and expressed as

$$\alpha = \frac{I_c}{I_e}$$

DC current gain in CE transistor The ratio of the collector current I_c to the base current I_b. It is denoted by β and expressed as

$$\beta = \frac{I_c}{I_b}$$

DC generator (or dynamo) Produces direct current energy from mechanical energy of rotation of a coil. Its principle and working are same as those of AC generator.

DC motor Converts direct current from a battery into mechanical energy of rotation of a coil. It is based on the fact that when a coil carrying current is held in a magnetic field. It experiences a torque which rotates the coil.

deadbeat Refers to damping. This term is used in electricity for describing an instrument that is damped, so that its oscillations die away very quickly.

deadbeat galvanometer A galvanometer which is damped, so that its oscillations die away very quickly.

de-Broglie's hypothesis A wave is associated with every moving particle, whatever be its nature.
Its wavelength is called de-Broglie wavelength and is given by

$$\lambda = h/mv$$

where, h is Planck's constant.
de-Broglie's wavelength is associated with an electron and accelerated under a potential difference V is given by

$$\lambda = \frac{h}{\sqrt{2eVme}} = \frac{12.27}{\sqrt{V}} \text{ Å}$$

debye A unit of electric dipole moment used for the dipole moments of molecules.

$$1 \text{ debye} = 1 \times 10^{-10} \text{ esu}$$
$$= 3.33 \times 10^{-28} \text{ coulomb-cm}$$

deca A prefix used in metric system to denote multiple of 10. Its symbol is da.

1 decametre = 10 m.

decay The spontaneous disintegration of unstable (radioactive) nuclei to give other nuclei by the emission of particles. Decay follows an exponential law. At any time t, the number N of original nuclei present is given by

$$N = N_0 \, e^{-\gamma t}$$

where, N_0 is the original number and γ is a constant (the decay constant or disintegration constant).

decay constant The reciprocal of the time during which the number of atoms in a radioactive substance reduces to 36.8% of their initial number.

decay sequence A plot of neutron number N against proton number Z for nuclides which belong to radioactive series. Each point represents the member of the series.

deceleration Accelera ion of an object is the rate of change of velocity. If the rate of change of velocity is negative, then the acceleration is said to be deceleration.

deci A prefix used in metric system to denote multiple of 10^{-1}. Its symbol is d.

$$1 \text{ decimetre} = 10^{-1} \text{ m}$$

decibel A unit of sound level. The threshold of hearing is taken as 0 db in sound measurement. The fundamental unit is the bel, but the decibel is almost exclusively used (10 db = 0.1 bel).

declination The angle between the geographic and magnetic meridians at a given point on the Earth's surface.

decoherence A process in which a quantum mechanical state of a system is altered by the interaction between the system and its environment.

defect The irregularity in the ordered arrangement of particles in a crystal lattice.

defects of vision Any fault in the eye which causes the formation of an imperfect image.

deflection The deviation of the indicator of an instrument from the position taken as zero.

deflection magnetometer The form of compass used for comparing magnetic field strengths. It consists of very small bar magnet, pivoted so that it is due to more in a horizontal plane.

deforming force The force which when applied to a body, changes the configuration of the body.

degaussing The process of neutralisation of an object's magnetic field by the use of an equal and opposite field. It is used in colour television sets to neutralise the Earth's magnetic field.

degeneracy The state of matter when it is at such a high temperature that all the electrons have been stripped from the atoms.

degenerate Different quantum states that have the same energy.

degradation The irreversible loss of energy available to do work, with a consequent increase in entropy.

degree An interval on a scale of measurement, such as a temperature scale.
A unit of angle is 1/360 of a complete turn.

degrees of freedom The number of independent parameters required to specify the configuration of a system. It is denoted by f and expressed as

$$f = 3N - K$$

where, N = number of particles and
K = number of coordinates of the particles.

demagnetisation The process due to which a magnetic material losses its magnetic properties. This can be done by hammering or heating of the material.

demodulation The process of retrieval of information from the carrier wave at the receiver is termed demodulation. This is the reverse process of modulation.

densitometer An instrument used for measuring the density of exposure of a photographic emulsion.

density The mass per unit volume of a substance. It is expressed as

$$\rho = \frac{M}{V}$$

Its SI unit is kg/m^3.

d

depletion layer The region at the *p-n* junction containing no mobile charge carriers, but only immobile charges of opposite kind on its two sides. The width of the depletion layer depends on the doping level.

For heavy doping, depletion layer is thin because the *p-n* junction contains a large number of free electrons and holes and a diffusing charge carrier has not to travel far across the junction for recombination. Opposite is the case for light doping. But, generally, the width of the depletion layer is of the order of a few μm.

depolariser The prevention of polarisation in a primary cell. A substance used in a voltaic cell to prevent polarisation.

derived quantity Any physical quantity which is not a base quantity in SI.

derived unit Units of physical quantities which are derived from fundamental units.

desorption Reverse process of adsorption. The removal of adsorbed atoms, molecules or ions from a surface.

destructive interference The interference in which the resultant intensity or amplitude of interfering waves is minimum. The resultant amplitude = $a - b$, where a and b are amplitude of two waves.

detector

1. An electronic circuit used to separate original signal from modulated signal.
2. A device which responds to a physical effect and used to detect the presence of the effect.

deuterium A naturally occurring stable isotope of hydrogen (^2_1H) in which the nucleus contains one proton and one neutron. Deuterium is known as heavy hydrogen. The natural abundance of deuterium is somewhat below 0.015% but this varies slightly with source.

deuteron A nucleus of a deuterium atom which consists of one proton and a neutron bounded together.

deviation The turning of a ray during reflection or refraction.

dew Water droplet developed due to condensation of water vapour in air when the temperature of air falls and air becomes saturate.

dew point The temperature at which dew starts forming. At this temperature, water vapour present in the atmosphere begins to condense.

dewar flask A double walled container of thin glass with the space between the walls evacuated and sealed to stop conduction and convection of energy through it.

dextrorotatory Denotes a substance which rotates the plane of polarisation of polarised light in a clockwise direction, as viewed by an observer looking in the direction opposite to that of incidence of the light.

diamagnetism The magnetic behaviour of substances with a negative susceptibility. Diamagnetic substances are those which are feebly magnetised opposite to the direction of field when placed in strong magnetic field and have tendency to move from stronger to the weaker part of the external magnetic field.

For diamagnetic substances, the susceptibility is small and relative permeability is slightly less than one. e.g. gold, silver, copper, lead, silicon, nitrogen (at STP), water, sodium chloride, etc.

diaphragm A device used in optical instruments to reduce or control the aperture of the system. An iris diaphragm is variable aperture in human eye. Diaphragms are used to control the light admitted. A thin sheet of metal or plastic that vibrates to produce, or is vibrated by sound waves, as in a loudspeaker or some types of microphone.

dichroism Property of a few substances that makes them transmit some colours and reflect others, or which display certain colours when viewed from one angle and different colours when viewed from another.

dielectric Non-conductor of electricity in which an electric field persists in the presence of an inducing field. The external electric field induces dipole moment by stretching or re-orienting molecules of the dielectric. The collective effect of all the molecular dipole moments is net charges on the surface of the dielectric which produce a field that opposes the external field.

dielectric constant The dielectric constant (or relative permittivity) of a medium is the ratio of the magnitude of force between the two charges placed at a given distance apart in vacuum, to the force between the same two charges, when they are similarly placed, the same distance apart, in the given medium. It is denoted by ε_r.

Thus,

$$\varepsilon_r = F_{(\text{vacuum})}/F_{(\text{medium})} = \frac{\varepsilon}{\varepsilon_0}$$

ε_r is a dimensionless constant and it has no unit.

dielectric heating The production of heat due to rapid alternation of the electric field across an insulator. This effect is used as a heating technique for certain materials.

dielectric loss The dissipation of power in a dielectric under alternating electric stress.

dielectric polarisation The phenomenon that is explained by the formation of doublets (dipoles) of elements of dielectric under stress.

dielectric strength The maximum electric field that a dielectric medium can withstand without break-down (of its insulating property). For air, it is about 3×10^6 Vm^{-1}. For a separation between conductors of the order of 1 cm or so, this field corresponds to a potential difference of 3×10^4 V between the conductors.

diesel engine An internal combustion engine in which heavy oil is used as fuel.

differential amplifier An amplifier with two inputs in which the output is a function of the difference between the inputs.

diffraction Bending of waves at the corners of the object in their path whose size is one of the order of wavelength of wave.

diffraction grating Optical device that is used for producing spectra.

diffraction of light The phenomenon of bending of light around corners of an obstacle or aperture in the path of light. On account of this bending, light penetrates into the geometrical shadow of an obstacle. The diffraction pattern due to a single slit consists of a central bright band having alternate dark and weak bright bands of decreasing intensity on both sides.

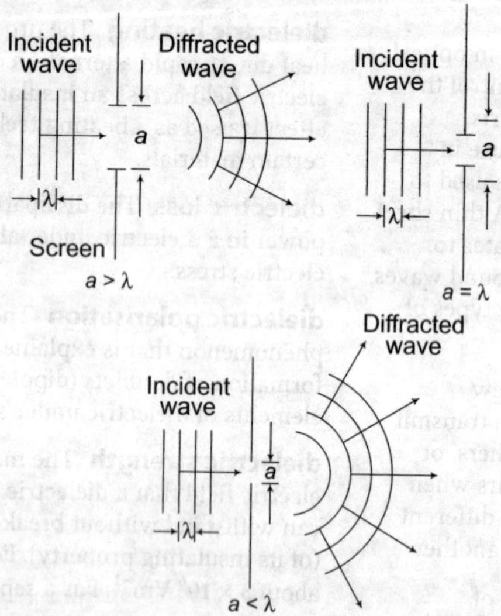

Diffraction of waves for slits of different width

diffuse reflection The reflection of light from the surface, such that an incident ray is reflected at many angles rather than at just one angle.

diffuse refraction The process similar to diffuse reflection except that the rays rather than bouncing back from the surface, pass through a block of translucent material.

diffusion

1. The process by which fluids and solids mix with one another due to the kinetic motions of the particles. Mixing occurs completely unless one set of particles is much heavier than the other, in which case dynamic equilibrium between diffusion and sedimentation under gravity occurs.
2. The scattering of a beam of light on reflection or transmission. A light beam that is reflected from a rough surface does not obey the laws of reflection but is scattered in many directions. Similarly, light that is transmitted by certain materials does not obey the laws of refraction and is scattered in the medium.
3. The movement of charge carrier from a region of higher concentration to a region of lower concentration across the junction.

digital The use of numerical digits for representing discretely all variables occurring in a problem.

digital circuit Any circuit that responds to discrete value of input voltage and produce discrete output voltage level. Usually two levels are used.

digital computer Computer that operates on data supplied and stored in digital or number form.

digital recording A method of recording or transmitting sound in which the sound itself is not transmitted or recorded.

digital signal A signal that is made up of bits. Each bit has two possible values labelled 1 or 0.

digital to analog conversion The reverse of analog to digital conversion. It is sometimes referred to as decoding.

digital transmission systems The systems which transmit a voltage signal in the form of a succession of square pulses.

digital voltmeter A voltmeter that displays the measured values as numbers composed of digits.

dimension The dimensions of a physical quantity are the powers (or exponents) to which the base quantities are raised to represent the unit of that quantity.

dimensional analysis A method of checking an equation or a solution to a problem by analysing the dimensions in which it is expressed.

dimensional equation The equations which represent the dimensions of a physical quantity in terms of the base quantities.

dimensional formula The expression which shows how and which of the base quantities represent the dimensions of a physical quantity.

diode Any electronic device with only two electrodes. Diodes are usually use as rectifiers. Semiconductor diodes consist of a single *p-n* junction. Current flows when forward voltage is applied to the diode and increases exponentially with voltage. If voltage is applied in the reverse direction, only a very small leakage current flows until the break down voltage is reached.

dioptre The unit of power of a lens and is equal to the reciprocal of the focal distance in metre. Power measures the ability of a reflector, refracting surface or lens to converge a parallel beam.

dip The angle between the Earth's total magnetic field and the freely suspended magnetic needle when suspended in magnetic meridian is called angle of dip at the place or inclination. Its value is 0° at the magnetic equator and 90° at magnetic poles. It is denoted by δ.

dip circle An instrument used for determining the angle of dip. It consists of a thin magnet supported, so as to be free to rotate about a horizontal axis through its centre of gravity, its inclination to the horizontal being read on a vertical circle, divided into degrees.

dipole A system of two equal and opposite charges placed at a very short distance apart.

dipole moment The product of either charge **q** of an electric dipole and length 2a of electric dipole. It is denoted as **p** and expressed as

$$\mathbf{p} = \mathbf{q} \times (2a)$$

Its unit is coulomb-metre.

direct current An electric current flowing in one direction only.

discharge

1. In case of cell, conversion of chemical energy into electrical energy.
2. The release of charge from capacitor to external circuit.
3. The passage of charge carrier through a gas at low pressure in a discharge tube.

disintegration Break-up of an atomic nucleus either through bombardment by subatomic particles or through radioactive decay.

disintegration constant The reciprocal of the time after which number of particles remains in the sample is $1/e$ times, the value of its initial number of particles.

dispersion Splitting of an electromagnetic radiation into its component wavelengths when it passes through a medium because different wavelengths undergo different degrees of diffraction or refraction.

dispersion of light The phenomenon of splitting of white light into its constituent colours on passing through a prism and the band of seven colours is obtained. The cause of dispersion is that different colours having different wavelengths deviate through different angles on passing through the prism.

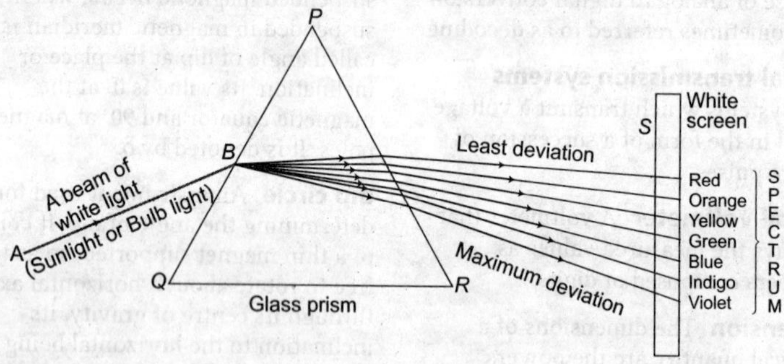

Dispersion of light

dispersion of sound Means the change in the speed of sound with frequency.

dispersive power A measure of the variation for a medium of refractive constant n with wavelength λ. It is given by the ratio

$$\omega = (n_b - n_r)/(n_y - 1)$$

where n_b, n_r and n_y are absolute refractive constant for blue, red and yellow light.

displacement The change in position of the object along a particular direction during that time and is given by the vector drawn from the initial position to final position. It is expressed as

$$\Delta x = x_2 - x_1$$

where, x_1 and x_2 are initial and final positions of the object. It can be positive, zero or negative.

displacement current Maxwell found an inconsistency in the Ampere's law and suggested the existence of an additional current, called displacement current. This displacement current is that current which comes into play in the region, whenever the electric field and hence, the electric flux is changing with time.

It is expressed as

$$i_d = \varepsilon_0 \frac{d\phi_E}{dt}$$

where, ε_0 is absolute permittivity of space, $\frac{d\phi_E}{dt}$ is rate of change of electric flux.

displacement in SHM The displacement of a particle executing SHM at an instant is defined as the distance of the particle from the mean position at that instant.
It is expressed as

$$y = a \sin \omega t \text{ or } y = a \cos \omega t$$

The first relation is valid when the time is measured from the mean position and the second relation is valid when the time is measured from the extreme position of the particle executing SHM along a straight path.

dissipation The removal of energy from a system to encounter some form of resistive force.

distance The total length of the path covered by a moving object from initial point to the final point. It is a scalar quantity.

distance of closest approach The distance r_0 from the nucleus, when whole of the kinetic energy of α-particle converts into electrostatic potential energy. It is expressed as

$$r_0 = \frac{1}{4\pi\varepsilon_0}\frac{2\,Ze^2}{K}$$

where, m = mass of α-particle,
Z = atomic number and
Ze = charge on α-particle.

distance-time graph A graph which shows how distance travelled along a line varies with time.

distortion Change from the ideal shape of an object or image, or in the form of a wave pattern.

divergent The property that makes the rays move in different directions.

divergent beam A beam of light rays that move away from a point. The separation between the rays increases as it moves in space.

diverging lens (or mirror)A lens/mirror that convert a parallel beam of light falling on it into divergent beam.

domain The ferromagnetic substance small regions in which all magnetic dipoles are fully aligned in a direction.

d

donor A pentavalent impurity added to semiconductor to increase its conductivity, results in n-type semiconductor.

dopant Small quantities of material added to semiconductor to increase electrical conduction.

doping The deliberate introduction of impurities into an extremely pure crystal. Doping with an element of valency 5, e.g. antimony, arsenic, phosphorus donates electrons to form an n-type semiconductor doping with a element of valency 3, e.g. aluminium, boron, gallium donates holes to form a p-type semiconductor.

Doppler's effect in light The phenomena that whenever there is a relative motion between a source of light and observer, the apparent frequency of light received by observer is different from the true frequency of light emitted actually from the source of light.

The apparent frequency ν' is given by

$$\nu' = \nu\left(1 \pm \frac{v}{c}\right)$$

where, v = velocity of star and velocity of light in vacuum and
ν' = frequency of light emitted from the source.

The positive sign indicates that the source is moving towards the observer and *vice-versa*. Its effect in light is symmetrical.

Doppler's effect in sound The phenomena of apparent change in frequency of the source observed by the observer due to the relative motion between the source and observer. For sound, the observed frequency ν is given in terms of the source frequency ν_0 by

$$\nu = \nu_0 \left(\frac{v + v_o}{v - v_s} \right)$$

where, v = speed of sound through the medium,

v_o = velocity of observer relative to the medium and

v_s = source velocity relative to the medium.

Its effect in sound is asymmetrical.

dot product A product of two vectors which results a scalar quantity. This is also known as scalar product. The dot product of two vectors, A and B is given by $A \cdot B = AB \cos\theta$, where A and B are magnitudes of A and B and θ is the angle between them.

double refraction Phenomenon shown by certain crystals, e.g. calcite that splits an incident ray of light into two refracted rays termed ordinary and extraordinary rays, polarised at right-angles to each other in an isotropic medium.

doublet A compound lens consists of two lenses in contact. It is used to reduce aberrations.

drag The frictional force exerted by fluids.

drift mobility In a semiconductor, the average velocity of excess minority carriers per unit electric field.

drift velocity An average velocity with which free electrons get drifted towards the positive end of the conductor under the influence of an external electric field. It is denoted by v_d and expressed as

$$v_d = \frac{eE}{m} \tau$$

where, e is the charge on electron, m is the mass, E is the electric field applied and τ is the average time of relaxation.

dry cell A leclanche cell in which the electrolyte is in the form of a paste of ammonium chloride.

dual nature of matter Radiation has dual nature, so it possesses both the properties of wave and particles and Universe is composed of radiation and matter. Thus, de-Broglie concluded that the matter must also possess dual nature.

ductility Property of a metal that allows it to be drawn out into a wire. e.g. copper and silver are very ductile metals.

Dulong and Petit's law For a solid element, the product of the relative atomic mass and the specific heat capacity is a constant and is equal to 25 J mol^{-1} K^{-1}.

dynamic resistance of a diode The ratio of a small change in voltage ΔV applied across the p-n junction to a small change in current ΔI. Thus,

$$r_d = \frac{\Delta V}{\Delta I}.$$

dynamics Branch of mechanics which deals with the study of the behaviour of bodies under the action of forces which change their motion.

dynamometer An instrument used to measure a force offer a spring balance.

dyne In CGS system, dyne is the unit of force.

$$1 \text{ dyne} = 1 \text{ g cm s}^{-2}$$

$$1 \text{ N} = 10^5 \text{ dyne}$$

E

e The charge of an electron, the natural unit of electric charge. It is equal to

$$1.60210 \times 10^{-19} \text{ C}$$

or $$4.803 \times 10^{-10} \text{ esu}$$

or $$1.602 \times 10^{-20} \text{ emu}$$

ear The sense organ which helps us in hearing sound. It helps us to convert pressure variations in air with audible frequencies into electrical signals which travel to the brain *via* auditory canal.

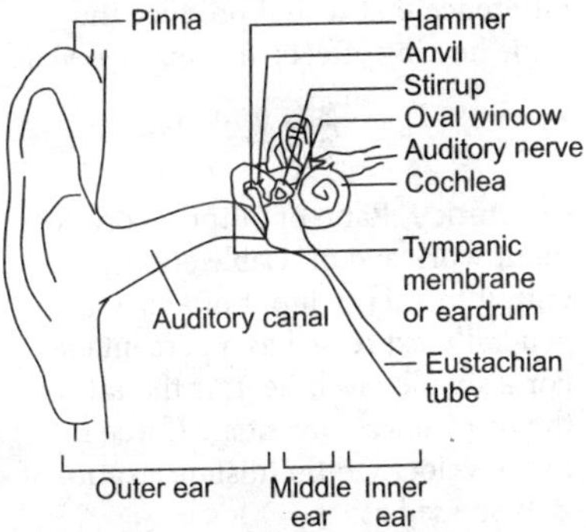

Human ear

Earth Third planet in terms of distance from the Sun. It has one natural satellite, the Moon. The Earth rotates about an imaginary axis that passes through its North and South poles and slightly tilted with respect to the plane of its orbit.

The day and the night on the Earth occur due to this rotation. It also revolves around the Sun in its orbit. The Earth completes its journey around the Sun in 365.25 days, which we call a year.

Earth inductor An instrument used for measuring large uniform fields.

earth wire The wire which have green plastic covering.

earthing The process of transferring charge from a charged object to the earth.

earthquake A sudden movement or fracturing within the Earth's lithosphere, causing a series of shocks.

Earth's atmosphere The gaseous cover that surrounds the Earth. The composition of dry air at sea level is: nitrogen 78.08%, oxygen 20.95%, argon 0.93%, carbon dioxide 0.03%, neon 0.0018%, helium 0.005%, krypton 0.0001% and xenon 0.0001%.

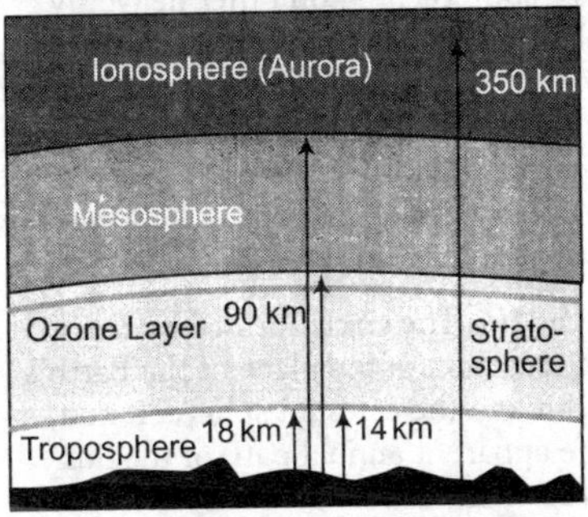

Earth's atmosphere

Earth's magnetic field Earth has its own magnetic field and it resembles that of a magnetic dipole located at the centre of the Earth. A freely suspended magnet always points in the North-South direction even in the absence of any other magnet. The shape of the Earth's magnetic field resembles that a bar magnet of length one-fifth of the Earth's diameter buried at its centre.

echelon A form of inferometer consisting a stock of glass plates arranged stepwise with a constant offset. It is used to study hyperfine line structure in spectroscopy.

echo The result of reflection of sound waves (or other waves) usually by a hard surface. The sensation of sound persists in our brain for about 0.1 s. To hear a distinct echo, the time interval between the original sound and the reflected one must be atleast 0.1 s.

echo location The method used by animals to detect objects in the dark. The animal emits a series of high-pitched sounds that echo back from the object and are detected by the ear or some other sensory receptor.

echo sounder An apparatus used for determining depths by echo sound method.

eclipse The hiding of one heavenly body behind on other due to the prevention of light from a source such as a star reaching on other heavenly object. In solar eclipse, shadow of the Moon falls on Earth when the Moon is in between the Sun and Earth. In lunar eclipse, shadow of the Earth falls on the moon when the Earth is in between the Sun and the Moon.

ecliptic The circle formed by the intersection of the place of the Earth's orbit and the celestial sphere. It marks the apparent annual path of the Sun around the Earth.

eddy current The current induced in the body of a conductor when the amount of magnetic flux linked with the conductor charges. This current is also called Foucault current. The magnitude of eddy current is given by

$$i = \frac{-e}{R} = \frac{d\phi/dt}{R}$$

where, R is the resistance of the conductor.

The direction of eddy current is given by Lenz's law or Fleming's right hand rule.

Eddy currents are used to advantages in certain applications like

(i) Magnetic braking in trains,
(ii) Electromagnetic damping,
(iii) Induction furnace and
(iv) Electric power meters.

effective current DC current that would produce the same heating effects as by AC. It is expressed as

$$I_e = \frac{I_0}{\sqrt{2}} = 0.707\ I_0$$

effective resistance The resistance of a conductor or other element of an electric circuit when used with alternating current.

effective voltage DC potential difference that would produce the same heating effects. It is expressed as

$$E_e = \frac{E_0}{\sqrt{2}} = 0.707\ E_0$$

efficiency Ratio of output work to input work and of usable energy output to energy input of a machine, generally expressed as a percentage. For a simple machine, it is the ratio of the mechanical advantage (force ratio) to the velocity ratio (distance ratio). It is expressed as

$$\eta = \frac{\text{MA}}{\text{VR}} \times 100$$

effort In a simple machine, the force that is applied to move a load. The ratio of the load L to the effort E is the mechanical advantage (force ratio). It is expressed as

$$\text{MA} = \frac{L}{E}$$

eigen function An allowed wave function of a system in quantum mechanics. The associated energies are eigen values.

Einstein coefficients Coefficients used in the quantum theory of radiation, related to the probability of a transition occurring between the ground state and an excited state in the process of induced emission and spontaneous emission.

Einstein's equation for photoelectric effect In the emission of electrons from metals by the incidence or radiation, if ϕ_0 is the work required to pass the electron through the surface, the maximum energy of the emitted electron is given by

$$KE_{max} = h\nu - \phi_0$$

where, ν is the frequency of the radiation used and h is Planck's constant. ϕ_0 is known as the work function of the metal. It is also expressed as

$$V_e = h(\nu - \nu_0)$$

where, V_e is the magnitude of the retarding potential required to decrease the velocity of the electron to zero, and $\nu_0 = \phi_0 / h$ is the minimum frequency which causes photoelectric emission from the given surface and is known as the photoelectric threshold.

Einstein mass-energy equation A fundamental equation connecting the mass m of the particle with its energy, $E = mc^2$.

Einstein theory of specific heat A theory of specific heat of solids proposed by Albert Einstein in 1906. In this theory, Einstein attributed the specific heat of solids to the vibrations of the solid and made the simplifying assumption that all the vibrations have the same frequency.

elastance The reciprocal of capacitance. Its unit is farad^{-1} (F^{-1}). Sometimes called a daraf.

elastic after effect The delay of regaining of original shape after being deformed within elastic limit when external forces are removed. It is also known as elastic lag. It is least for quartz or phosphor bronze.

elastic collision A collision in which the kinetic energy as well as momentum remains constant before and after collision.

elastic fatigue It is the property of the elastic body by virtue of which its behaviour becomes less elastic under the action of repeated deforming force.

elastic hysteresis The work done by the material in returning to its original shape is less than the work done by the deforming force when it was deformed. Thus, the material absorbs a certain amount of energy in cycle that appears as heat. This phenomenon is called elastic hysteresis. It has an important application in shock absorbers.

elastic limit The maximum value of strain for which a body shows elastic property. Body beyond the elastic limit behaves like a plastic body.

elastic modulus The ratio of the stress on a body to the produced strain, within the limit of elasticity. It is expressed as,

$$\text{Modulus of elasticity} = \frac{\text{Stress}}{\text{Strain}}.$$

Its unit is N/m^2 or Pa.

There are three types of modulus of elasticity :

(i) Young's modulus
(ii) Bulk modulus
(iii) Shear modulus

elastic potential energy in wire The work done against the internal restoring forces acting between particles of the wire.

It is denoted by U and expressed as,

$$U = \frac{1}{2} \times \text{stress} \times \text{strain}$$

$$= \frac{1}{2} \times \text{Young's modulus} \times (\text{strain})^2$$

elastic strain energy The energy stored in a material under stress.

elasticity The property of a body by virtue of which it tends to regain its original configuration (size and shape), when the applied force is removed, is known as elasticity and the deformation caused is known as elastic deformation.

elastomer The substances in which stress and strain are not proportional to each other. Substances like tissue of aorta, rubber, etc. which can be stretched to cause large strains are called elastomers.

electret A permanently electrified substance or body that has opposite charges at its extremities. An electret can be made by cooling certain waxes in a strong electric field.

electric arc A luminous electrical discharge between two electrodes in a gas having high current density and low potential difference.

electric arc furnace A furnace used in melting metals to make alloys, especially in steel manufacture, in which the heat source is an electric arc.

electric bell An instrument in which an electromagnetically control hammer strikes a bell. On pressing the button, circuit is closed, causing current to flow through electromagnet. The electromagnet attracts a piece of soft iron attached to the hammer, which strikes the bell and at the same time, breaks the circuit.

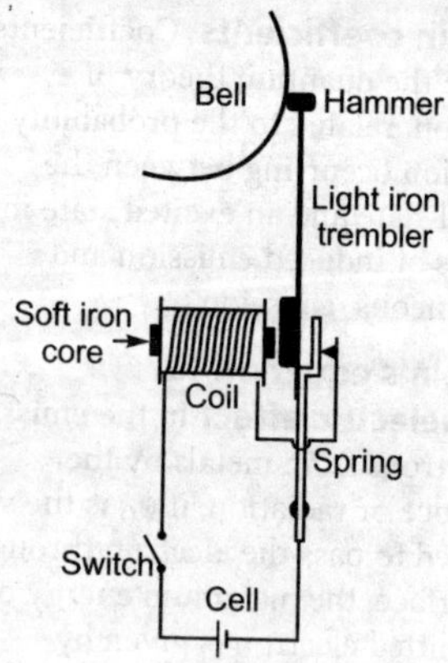

Electric bell

electric capacitance The ability of the conductor to store charge on it. If the charge on a conductor is gradually increased, its potential also increases.

$$q \propto V$$

or $$q = CV$$

or $$C = \frac{q}{V}$$

where, C is constant of proportionality and is called capacity or capacitance of the conductor. The SI unit of C is farad.

electric charge *See* charge.

electric circuit A continuous and closed path of an electric current. Conventionally, in an electric circuit, the direction of electric current is taken as opposite to the direction of the flow of electrons, which are negative charges. There are two types of circuit such as open circuit and closed circuit.

electric constant *See* permittivity.

electric current Drift of electrons through a conductor in the same direction, usually because there is a potential difference across it. It is denoted by I and expressed as,

$$I = \frac{\text{charge flowing}}{\text{time taken}} = \frac{q}{t}$$

SI unit of current is ampere (A).

electric dipole Consists of a pair of equal and opposite point charges separated by some small distance.

electric displacement The electric flux density in a dielectric material

$$D = \varepsilon_r \varepsilon_0 E$$

where, E is the electric field strength in free space and $\varepsilon_r\ \varepsilon_0$ is the permittivity of the material.

electric energy Energy associated with charged particle in an electric field. It is defined as the total work done in maintaining the current in an electric circuit for a given time. It is expressed as

$$E = VIt = Pt = I^2Rt = V^2t/R$$

Its SI unit is joule.

electric field A region in which a force would be exerted on an electric charge. Like magnetic fields, electric fields can be represented by lines of force. Electric fields can be produced by electric charges or by changing magnetic fields. Like coulomb force, electric field also satisfies superposition principle.

electric field intensity The electric field intensity at any point in electric field is defined as the force experienced per unit positive test charge placed at that point without disturbing the source charge. It is expressed as

$$E = \frac{F}{q_0}$$

Its unit is N/C.
Here, E is electric field intensity (strength) and F is the force acting on the test charge q_0 at that point. It is a vector quantity and its direction is same as the direction of F on positive charge.

electric flux Total number of lines of force passing through an area placed normally in an electric field E is known as flux. It is usually denoted by ϕ_E or ψ.
The electric flux through a surface is defined as the product of the area S and the component of the electric field normal to the surface E_n.

$$\phi_E = E_n \times S$$

Its SI unit is N-m^{2}C^{-1}. Electric flux through a closed surface will be positive or negative depending on whether the field lines emerge from the surface or enter into the surface.

electric flux density *See* electric displacement.

electric fuse Used to protect the individual domestic electrical appliances from damage which is caused due to excessive current flowing through them.

electric image A fictitious charge used in finding the electric field setup by fixed electric charges in the neighbourhood of a conductor.

electric lighting Illumination provided by electric currents. The devices used are the arc lamp, the light bulb and the fluorescent tube.

electric lines of force In an electric field, it is an imaginary smooth curve, such that tangent at any point of which gives the direction of the electric field at that point. No two electric lines of force can intersect each other.

electric meter Instrument for measuring the consumption of electricity.

electric motor An electric motor is a rotating device that converts electrical energy into mechanical energy. A simple electric motor consists of a current-carrying coil that rotates in the magnetic field between the poles of a permanent magnet.
Electric motors can be designed to work with direct-current supply or, more commonly with alternating current.
Electric motor is used as an important component in electric fans, refrigerators, mixers, washing machines, computers, mp3 players, etc.

electric polarisation Difference between the displacement of charge and the electric field strength in a dielectric.

electric potential The electric potential at a point in an electric field is the work required to bring unit positive electric charge from infinity to that point. It is measured in volt V.

electric potential difference The difference in the values of the electric potentials at the two points. In other words, it is the work done in moving a unit positive charge from one point to another, within the electric field of any arbitrary charge configuration.

electric power Energy liberated per second in an electric device. The power P is given by

$$P = VI = I^2 R = \frac{V^2}{R}.$$

The SI unit of electric power is watt W. It is the power consumed by a device that carries 1 A of current when operated at a potential difference of 1 V. Thus,

$$1 \text{ W} = 1 \text{ volt} \times 1 \text{ ampere} = 1 \text{ V-A}$$

The unit watt is very small. Therefore, in actual practice, we use a much larger unit called kilowatt. It is equal to 1000 watt. The other unit of electric energy is, therefore, watt hour Wh. One watt hour is the energy consumed when 1 watt of power is used for 1 hour. The commercial unit of electric energy is kilowatt hour kWh, commonly known as unit.

$$1 \text{ kWh} = 1000 \text{ watt} \times 3600 \text{ s}$$
$$= 3.6 \times 10 \text{ watt second}$$
$$= 3.6 \times 10^6 \text{ joule (J)}$$

electric spark A discharge of electricity in a gas accompanied by light and sound. The discharge occurs between two points of opposite high electric potentials. The spark can only occur when the potential difference exceeds a certain value, called the sparkling potential.

electric susceptibility The ratio of P and E is called electric susceptibility, where P is the polarisation density which is produced in the dielectric when it is subjected to an external electric field E. It is denoted by χ and expressed as,

$$\chi = \frac{P}{\varepsilon E} = k - 1$$

where, k is dielectric constant.

electrical charge The property of protons and electrons which give rise to electric force between them. It is a scalar quantity. The value of

$$e = 1.6 \times 10^{-19} \text{C}.$$

electrical conductivity *See* conductivity.

electrical energy A form of energy related to the position of an electric charge in an electric field. For a body with charge Q and an electric potential V, its electrical energy is QV.

electricity The nature and effects of moving or stationary electric charges, and the branch of physics that studies them.

electrified If an object possesses an electric charge, it is said to be electrified or charged. When it has no charge, it is said to be neutral.

electrocardiogram (ECG) A sensitive instrument that records that voltage and current waveforms associated with the action of the heart.

electrochemical cell *See* cell.

electrochemical equivalent Defined as the mass of the element deposited when one coulomb of charge flows through an electrolyte containing the element. Its symbol is Z.

electrochemical series *See* electromotive series.

electrochemistry The study of the formation and behaviour of ions in solutions. It includes electrolysis and the generation of electricity by chemical reactions in cells.

electrochromatography *See* electrophoresis.

electrode Any part of an electrical device or system that emits or collects electrons or other charge carriers. An electrode may also be used to deflect charged particles by the action of the electrostatic field that it produces.

electrode efficiency The ratio of the actual yield of metal deposited in an electrolytic cell to the theoretical yield.

electrode potential A measure of the tendency of a metal to lose electrons to a surrounding solution. It is the potential difference, at equilibrium, between the metal and a solution of its ions. It can't be measured directly and is usually compared against that of a hydrogen electrode.

electrodeless deposition A method of coating objects with a thin layer of metal without using any electric current and any kind of additives.

electrodeposition The process of depositing one metal on another by electrolysis.

electrodialysis A method of removing salts (crystalloids) from a colloidal solution using two semipermeable membranes.

electrodisintegration The disintegration of a nucleus that occurs when it is bombarded by electrons.

electrodynamics The branch of science that studies the mechanical forces generated between neighbouring circuits when carrying electric currents.

electroencephalogram (EEG) A tracing or graph of the electrical activity of the brain. The pattern of an EEG reflects an individual's level of consciousness and can be used to detect such disorders as epilepsy, tumours or brain damage.

electroforming A method of forming intricate metal articles or parts by electrodeposition of the metal on a removable conductive mould.

electroluminescence *See* luminescence.

electrolysis The process of conduction of electricity through solutions and through molten salts. Flow of current causes a chemical reaction. Chemical reactions at the anode are different from those at cathode.

electrolyte Aqueous solution of inorganic salts, acids and bases conducts electricity and these are called electrolytes. Conduction in electrolytes is due to ions that are produced by the separation of electrolyte in the solvent. Here, matter is actually transported through the solution.

electrolytic capacitor A capacitor in which one plate is a thin metal plate coated with a thin oxide layer dipped in a suitable electrolyte H_2SO_4. Such capacitor provides high capacitance.

electrolytic cell A cell in which current is passed through the electrolyte from an external source.

electrolytic rectifier A rectifier consisting of two dissimilar electrodes immersed in an electrolyte, e.g. lead-aluminium cell with ammonium phosphate as an electrolyte.

electrolytic separation The separation of isotopes by electrolysis.

electromagnet A strong magnetic field produced inside a solenoid can be used to magnetise a piece of magnetic material, like soft iron, when placed inside the coil. The magnet so formed is called an electromagnet.

electromagnetic damping The retarding force due to the eddy currents inhibits the motion of the magnet. Such phenomena are referred to as electromagnetic damping.

electromagnetic deflection Method of deflecting an electron beam using an electromagnet. The most common application is in the cathode ray tube of a television or radar receiver.

electromagnetic force The force between charged particles. In the simpler case, when charges are at rest, the force is given by Coulomb's law, i.e. attractive for unlike charges and repulsive for like charges. Charges in motion produce magnetic effects and a magnetic field gives rise to a force on a moving charge. Electric and magnetic effects are, in general, inseparable, hence the name electromagnetic force. Like the gravitational force, electromagnetic force acts over large distances and does not need any intervening medium. It is enormously strong compared to gravity.

electromagnetic induction The phenomenon of inducing an emf or an electric current by changing the magnetic field. The magnetic field may change due to a relative motion between the coil and a magnet placed near to the coil. The emf so developed is called induced emf. If the conductor is in the form of a closed circuit, a current flows in the circuit called induced current. It is based on the working of power generators, dynamos, transformers, etc. The direction of the induced current is given by the Fleming's right hand rule.

electromagnetic interaction (fundamental interaction) The interaction between two charged particles or systems that is intermediate in between the strong and weak strengths.

electromagnetic moment *See* magnetic moment.

electromagnetic pump A pump with no moving parts, used for circulating electrically conducting fluids.

electromagnetic radiation The propagation of vibrating electric and magnetic fields in the form of waves.

electromagnetic spectrum The classification of EM waves according to their wavelength or frequency. Electromagnetic waves include visible light waves, X-rays, gamma rays, radio waves, microwaves, ultraviolet and infrared waves. There is no sharp division between one kind of wave and the next. The classification is based roughly on how the waves are produced and/or detected.

electromagnetic units (emu) A system of electrical units formerly used in the CGS system. The emu of electric current is the abampere (all emu have the prefix *ab*-attached to the names of practical units). The abampere is current that, flowing in an arc of a circle (1 centimetre in diameter), exerts a force of 1 dyne on unit magnetic pole at the centre of the circle. In emu the magnetic constant is of unit magnitude. The system has now been replaced by SI units for most purposes. Compare electrostatic units, gaussian units, heaviside-Lorentz units.

electromagnetic wave The wave which consist of oscillating electric and magnetic fields at right angle to each other and to the direction of propagation of the wave.

electrometer An instrument that is used for determining the potential difference between two charged bodies by measuring the electrostatic force between them.

electromotive force (emf) The work done by a source of electric potential in driving a unit charge round the circuit is called the electromotive force. Its symbol is *E*.

electromotive series (electrochemical series) Series of elements arranged in the order of their standard electrode potentials.

electron A fundamental negatively charged sub-atomic particle (radius = 2.81777×10^{-15} m; rest mass = 9.109558×10^{-31} kg; charge = 1.602192×10^{-19} C).

electron affinity The energy released when an electron is attached to an atom or molecule. It is frequently positive, i.e. the negative ion is often more stable than the neutral species. Its symbol is *A*.

electron beam Consists of electrons released from a hot cathode, all moving through vacuum with the same acceleration from cathode to anode.

electron biprism An arrangement of fields that splits a beam of electrons or other charged particles in an analogous way to an optical biprism.

electron capture

1. Formation of negative ion by an atom or molecule, by acquiring an extra free electron.
2. A radioactive transformation in which a nucleus captures an electron from an inner orbit, this capture transforms a proton into a neutron. This capture is also followed by emission of an X-ray photon and the nucleus, thus transformed has same mass number but atomic number one less than that of the original.

electron charge The charge carried by an electron. It is a fundamental constant, equals to 1.6×10^{-19} C.

electron counting rules Rules for counting the number of electrons that give rise to stable structures in atoms, molecules and solids.

Electron Cyclotron Maser (ECM) A type of maser in which the operation is based on the stimulated emission of radiation caused by the motion of high energy electrons moving as in a cyclotron.

electron density The number of electrons per unit mass of a given material. Most of the light elements (except hydrogen) have an electron density of about 3×10^{26} electrons per kilogram.

electron diffraction The diffraction of electrons by atoms or molecules.

electron emission The phenomenon of emission of electrons from the surface of a metal. The electron emission can be obtained by the following processes:

1. Thermionic emission
2. Photoelectric emission
3. Field emission
4. Secondary emission

electron gas The free electrons in the solid or liquid state behaves as a gas.

electron gun Electrode assembly for producing a narrow beam of electrons.

electron lens An instrument used for focussing beam of electrons. Electron lenses use electric or magnetic fields.

electron microscope An instrument that uses a beam of electrons from an electron gun to produce magnified images of extremely small objects, beyond the range of an optical microscope.

electron-nuclear double resonance *See* endor.

electron optics Study of the control of free electrons by curved electric and magnetic fields.

Electron Probe Microanalysis (EPM) A technique used for analysing amount of a substance as small as 10^{-13} g. A very fine beam of electrons of diameter about 10^{-6} m is focused on the sample and the resulting characteristic X-radiation emitted by the sample is examined. From the intensity of this radiation, the quantity of substance present can be deduced.

electron spectroscopy One of the techniques in which information is obtained by analysing the energy spectrum of electrons, e.g. photoelectron spectroscopy.

Electron-Spin Resonance (ESR) A spectroscopic method of locating electrons within the molecules of a paramagnetic substance in order to provide information regarding its bonds and structure.

electron temperature The temperature at which gas molecules would have the same average kinetic energy as the electrons of the plasma.

electron volt 1 eV is the energy acquired by an electron when it is accelerated through a potential difference of 1 volt and its value is 1.602×10^{-19} joule.

electronegative Describing elements that tend to gain electrons and form negative ions.

electronics The branch of physics in which we study semiconductor devices, thermionic tubes and other vacuum devices.

electrophoresis (cataphoresis) Movement of charged colloid particles in a solution placed in an electric field. It is also called electrochromatography.

electrophorus Device for producing electric charges by electrostatic induction.

electroplating The process of depositing a thin layer of a metal on a solid surface by means of electrolysis.

electropositive elements Elements which tend to lose electrons and so form positive ions.

electroscope Instrument used for detecting and measuring electric charges or gaseous ions.

electrostatic field The electric field that surrounds a stationary electric charge.

electrostatic generator A device which produces continuous supply of electric charge by electrostatic force.

electrostatic induction The production of electric charge by separation of positive and negative charges in an electric field.

electrostatic potential The electrostatic potential V at any point in a region with electrostatic field is the work done in bringing a unit positive charge (without acceleration) from infinity to that point. It is expressed as

$$\Delta V = \frac{W_{AB}}{q_0} = -\int_A^B E.dl$$

If A is at ∞, $V_A = 0$

$$\therefore \quad V_B = \frac{W_{\infty B}}{q_0} = -\int_\infty^B E.dl$$

Its unit is volt (V).

electrostatic potential energy The total amount of work done in bringing the various charges to their respective positions from infinitely large mutual separation. It is denoted by U and expressed as

$$U = \frac{q_1 q_2}{4\pi\varepsilon_0 r_1 r_2}$$

electrostatic shielding The process of protecting certain region from external electric field. Whatever be the charge and field configuration outside, any cavity in a conductor remains shielded from outside electric influence; the field inside the cavity is always zero. The effect can be made use of a protecting sensitive instrument from outside electrical influence.

electrostatic units (esu) A system of electrical units in the CGS system. The esu of electric charge is the statcoulomb.

electrostatics Branch of electricity concerned with the study of electrical charges at rest. The charges are produced which is due to actual transfer of electrons.

electrostriction Change in the dimensions of a dielectric that is caused by the reorientation of molecules, when an electric field is applied.

electroweak theory A gauge theory (or quantum flavour dynamics, QFD) that gives a unified description of the electromagnetic and weak interactions.

element Substances that cannot be decomposed into simpler substances. In an element, all the atoms have same number of electrons or protons, but number of neutrons may vary.

elementary particles Fundamental constituents of all the matter in the universe. Initially, atoms were believed to the elementary particles but later, it was realised that they were divisible. These particles are characterised by their mass, charge, spin and certain other properties.

elliptical galaxy *See* galaxy.

elliptical polarisation Electromagnetic radiation in the visible region that can be resolved into two polarised planes. Vibrations of same frequency but having unequal amplitudes, which are out of phase of 90°.

emission line spectrum When an atomic gas or vapour is excited at low pressure, usually by passing an electric current through it, the emitted radiation has a spectrum which contains certain specific wavelengths only. A spectrum of this kind is termed as emission line spectrum and it consists of bright lines on a dark background.

emissive power The total energy of thermal radiation emitted from unit surface area of body per second at any given temperature.

emissivity The ratio of emissive power of a body to the emissive power of a perfectly black body at the temperature and wavelength.

emitter *See* transistor.

Emitter-Coupled Logic (ECL) A set of integrated logic circuits. The input part of an ECL consists of an emitter-coupled transistor pair which is a very good differential amplifier. The output is through an emitter follower.

emitter follower An amplifying circuit using a bipolar junction transistor with a common collector connection. The output is taken from the emitter.

empirical Something which is only based upon the result of experiment and observation is called empirical.

end correction (resonance tube) In a resonance tube, the reflection of sound waves takes place slightly above the open end and not at the open end itself. The length measured from the open end, therefore, requires a correction which is known as the end correction. It is equal to $0.3D$, where, D is the diameter of the resonance tube.

endor Electron-nuclear double resonance. A magnetic resonance technique involving excitation of both electron spins and nuclear spins.

endothermic Describing a process in which heat is taken in, e.g. in many chemical reactions.

endothermic process The process in which heat is absorbed.

endothermic reaction Reaction that take place only when energy is supplied from outside.

energy The energy possessed by an object is thus measured in terms of its capacity of doing work. The unit of energy is the same as that of work done, i.e. joule J. 1 J is the energy required to do 1 joule of work. Sometimes, a larger unit of energy called kilojoule kJ is used. 1 kJ equals to 1000 J. Energy is in many different forms. The various forms include potential energy, kinetic energy, heat energy, chemical energy, electrical energy and light energy.

energy bands of solids *See* band theory.

energy levels According to quantum theory, atoms and molecules can exist only in certain allowed energy states. These energy states are known as energy levels.

energy-separation curve A graph which shows how the energy stored in the bond between two atoms vary with their separation.

energy sources These are of two types:

(i) **Primary** These are those which occur in their natural state. e.g. fossil fuels.

(ii) **Secondary** These are sources produced from primary fuels. e.g. petrol.

energy stored in capacitor The total work done in charging the capacitor to a given potential. It is denoted by U and expressed as

$$U = \frac{Q^2}{2C} = \frac{1}{2}CV^2$$

engine A device that can convert one form of energy into mechanical energy.

enrich Increase in the percentage of a particular isotope in a mixture of isotopes.

enrichment The process of increasing the concentration of one particular isotope in a mixture of isotopes.

ensemble A set of systems of particles used in statistical mechanics to describe a single system.

enthalpy The sum of the internal energy U and product of pressure p and volume V of a system. It is denoted by H, i.e.

$$H = U + pV$$

entropy In thermodynamics, quantity that is a measure of a system's disorder, or the unavailability of its energy to do work. It is denoted by the letter S. It is a measure of randomness.

It is expressed as, $\Delta S = \dfrac{\Delta Q}{T}$

where, ΔS is change in entropy, ΔQ is change in heat and T is absolute temperature.

ephemeris A tabulation showing the calculated future positions of the Sun, Moon and planets together with other useful information for astronomers.

ephemeris time A time system that has a constant uniform rate as opposed to other systems that depend on the Earth's rate of rotation, which has inherent irregularities.

epidiascope An optical instrument used by lecturers, etc. for projecting an enlarged image of either a translucent object or an opaque object onto a screen.

epitaxy The process of growing a thin layer of material upon a single crystal substrate, so that the lattice structure is identical to that of the substrate.

equal vector The two vectors are said to be equal, if they have equal magnitude and same direction.

equation of continuity According to this equation, product of area of cross-section of tube and speed of liquid flowing through that tube remains constant. Since,

$av = \text{constant}$

$\Rightarrow v \propto \frac{1}{a}$, i.e. deep water runs slow.

equation of state An equation which describes the relation of pressure, volume and temperature of a substance. Equation of state for an ideal gas, $pV = nRT$ where, R is the molar gas constant and n is the number of moles.

equations of motion (kinematic equations) Equations that apply to bodies moving linearly with uniform acceleration (a). The equations, which relate distance covered s to the time taken t, are

$$v = u + at$$
$$s = (u + v)t/2$$
$$s = ut + at^2/2$$
$$v^2 = u^2 + 2as$$

where, u is the initial velocity of the body and v is its final velocity.

equator The imaginary circular line drawn on the surface of the Earth. The equatorial plane divides the Earth into two hemispheres:

(i) The Northern hemisphere and
(ii) The Southern hemisphere.

equilibrium The state of a system in which forces influences reactions, etc. balance each other in, such that there is no net change.
A body is said to be in **static equilibrium**, if the resultant of all the forces and all the couples acting on it, both are zero. The body in static equilibrium returns to its original position after a slight displacement.
A body is said to be in **thermal equilibrium** If there is no heat exchange within it or between it and its surroundings.
A system is in **chemical equilibrium** if a reaction and its reverse are proceeding at equal rates, both these equilibrium are dynamic equilibrium.

equipartition of energy The total energy of a molecule which is equally distributed among the available degrees of freedom. The energy associated with each degree of freedom is $\frac{1}{2}kT$, where k is Boltzmann constant and T is absolute temperature.

equipotential surface An imaginary surface drawn in electric field at which all points are at same potential. Electric lines of force are always normal to equipotential surfaces.

equivalent circuit An arrangement of simple circuit elements which has the same electrical characteristic as a more complicated circuit or device under specified conditions.

equivalent sine wave A sine wave with the same root mean square values as the given wave and also the same fundamental frequency.

erect Describing an image formed by a mirror or lens which is the same way up as the object.

erecting lens The lens used in an optical instrument to produce an erect image from an inverted image.

erecting prism A glass prism used in optical instruments to convert an inverted image into an erect image.

erg Unit of energy in the CGS system, transferred when a force of 1 dyne moves through 1 cm equivalent to 10^{-7} joule.

ergodic hypothesis A hypothesis in statistical mechanics concerning phase space. The ergodic hypothesis states that the orbit of the representative point in phase space eventually goes through all points on the surface.

error The difference between the measured value of a quantity and the exact value of that quantity. The errors are communicated in different mathematical operations.

Esaki diode *See* Tunnel diode.

escapement A device in a clock or watch that controls the transmission of power from the spring or falling weight to the hands. It is usually based on a balance wheel of pendulum.

escape velocity The minimum velocity with which an object is projected vertically upwards from the surface of Earth, it crosses the gravitational field of Earth and never returns on its own. It is expressed as,

$$v_e = \sqrt{\frac{2Gm}{R}}$$

where, G is gravitational force of attraction, m is mass of object and R is radius of object.
Its value on Earth is 11.2 km s^{-1}.

ESR *See* electron-spin resonance.

etalon It is an interferometer. It is used to study fine spectrum lines.

evaporation The process in which a liquid changes to its vapour. It can occur (slowly) at a temperature below the boiling point, but is faster if the liquid is heated and fastest when the liquid is boiling.

even-even nucleus A nucleus containing an even number of protons and an even number of neutrons.

even-odd nucleus A nucleus that contains an even number of protons but an odd number of neutrons.

excess electron Electron that is added to a semiconductor from a donor impurity.

exchange force A force between two particles because of exchange of another particle between them.

excitation The process whereby a particle acquires excitation energy, that increases its energy to a value greater than that in its ground state. The particle is then said to be in an excited state.

excitation energy The energy required to change an atom from one quantum state to a higher energy state.

excited state Energy level of an atom higher than the ground state.

exclusion principle Alternative name for the Pauli exclusion principle. Two electrons of an atom cannot have same set of four quantum numbers.

exoergic process A nuclear reaction in which energy is ejected.

exothermic reaction A chemical reaction in which energy is given out by heat or light.

expansion (thermal) The change in size of an object on heating or cooling. This effect is due to increased or decreased energy of the atoms or molecules. It is of three types for solids:

(i) **Linear expansion** The expansion of solids only in one dimension on heating it.

(ii) **Areal expansion** The expansion of solids in two dimensions on heating it.

(iii) **Volume expansion** The expansion of solids in three dimensions on heating it.

expansion of the universe The hypothesis, which is based on the evidence of the red shift, that the distance between the galaxies is continuously increasing.

expansitivity (thermal expansion) The measure of tendency of substances to undergo thermal expansion. Coefficient of expansivity is of three types:

1. Coefficient of linear expansivity α, defined as the change in length of a rod on increasing its temperature by 1°C.
2. Coefficient of areal expansivity β, defined as the increase in area of a solid on increasing its temperature by 1°C.
3. Coefficient of volume expansivity γ, defined as the increase in volume of a solid on increasing its temperature by 1°C.

   Relation between α, β and γ is

   $$\alpha : \beta : \gamma = 1 : 2 : 3$$

explosion A situation in which bodies that are initially close together, move apart when energy is supplied to the system.

exposure meter A photocell connected to a suitable display to indicate illumination for photography.

expressions for time period The various expressions for time period in different cases are :

1. Simple pendulum, $T = 2\pi\sqrt{\frac{l}{g}}$
2. Oscillations of a liquid in U-tube.

   $$T = 2\pi\sqrt{\frac{h}{g}}$$

   where, h is the height of undisturbed liquid in each limb of U-tube.
3. Oscillations of a floating cylinder,

   $$T = 2\pi\sqrt{\frac{L\rho}{\sigma g}} = 2\pi\sqrt{\frac{l}{g}}$$

   where, L is vertical length of cylinder of density ρ, σ is the density of liquid floating in cylinder and l is the length of the cylinder dipping in liquid.
4. Oscillations of a loaded spring

   $$T = 2\pi\sqrt{\frac{m}{k}}$$

   where, m is the mass of body attached and k is the spring constant.

extensive variable A quantity in a macroscopic system that is proportional to the size of the system. e.g. volume, mass and total energy.

extensometer Any device for measuring the extension of a specimen of a material under longitudinal stress.

extinction coefficient A measure of the extent, by which the intensity of a beam of light is reduced by passing through a distance d of a solution having a molar concentration C of the dissolved substance. If the intensity of the light is reduced from I_1 to I_2, the extinction coefficient is $[\log (I_1 / I_2)]/Cd$.

extra-nuclear electrons Electrons with orbits that take up a large fraction of the atom's volume and whose number equals the number of protons in the nucleus.

extraordinary ray *See* double refraction.

extrasolar planet (exoplanet) A planet that orbits a star other than the Sun. Such planets are mostly detected by the change in the radiation associated with the 'wobble' they cause in the star they orbit.

extremely high frequency The radio frequency lying in the range 30 GHz - 300 GHz.

extrinsic semiconductors Semiconductors in which some impurity atoms are embedded. These are basically of two types:

(i) ***n*-type semiconductors** The semiconductors in which majority charge carriers are electrons and minority charge carrier are holes.

(ii) ***p*-type semiconductors** The semiconductors in which majority charge carriers are holes i.e. positively charged and minority charge carriers are electrons.

eye

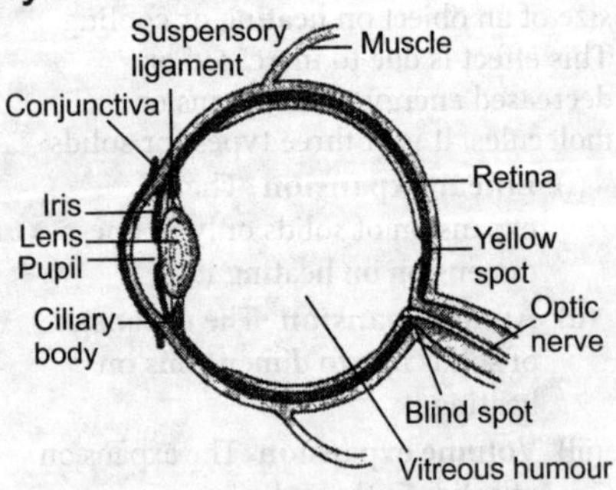

Human eye

A sense organ able to produce optical images and to send corresponding nerve signals to the brain. These normally occur in pairs, are nearly spherical and filled with fluid. Light is refracted by the cornea through the pupil into iris and onto the lens, which focuses the images onto the retina.

eye lens The lens which is nearest to the eye in any optical instrument.

eye piece A magnifier, usually a combination of lenses to give a magnified, aberration free image in a telescope or a microscope.

eye ring The position of the eye, when using an optical instrument, for which most light enters the eye. It coincides when the image of the object is formed by the eyepiece.

Fabry-Perot interferometer A type of interferometer in which a monochromatic light is passed through half-silvered glass plates which produces circular interference fringes.

fading The variation in the strength of a signal at a receiver due to interference of waves. It is more at high frequencies.

Fahrenheit scale A temperature scale in which lower fix point (melting point of ice) is taken as 32°F and upper fix point (boiling point of water) is taken as 212°F. There are 180 equal divisions between these two fix points and each division represent 1°F. If we convert Fahrenheit into Celsius scale, the expression is as

$$C = \frac{5(F - 32)}{9}$$

fall-out (radioactive fall-out) Radioactive substances that fall to Earth from the atmosphere after a nuclear explosion. The most worrying fission fragments are

(i) ^{131}I having half-life 8 days. If it is ingested, then it is concentrated in the thyroid glad.

(ii) ^{90}Sr having half-life 28 years. It is accumulated in bones. Both of them may reach to us in milk from cows grazing on land contaminated by fall-out.

false vacuum In quantum field theory, a state in which a local minimum (but not the minimum energy state) of the system occurs overall. The minimum energy state of the system is called true vacuum. e.g. tunnelling occurs from false vacuum to true vacuum and is calculated by using instant on techniques.

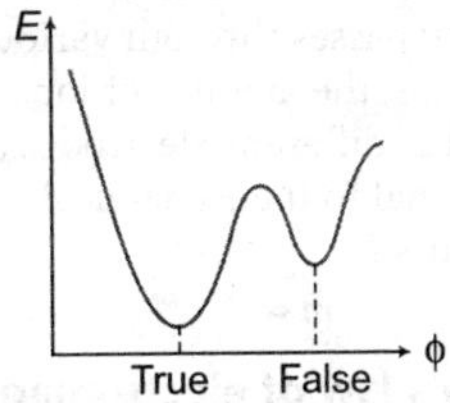

farad The SI unit of capacitance,

1 farad = 1 coulomb volt^{-1}

farad meter A device used to measure the capacitance directly.

Faraday balance Balance to measure the susceptibilities of diamagnetic and paramagnetic materials.

Faraday cage A hollow inclosed conductor used to protect delicate instruments from external electric field.

Faraday constant The quantity of electricity equivalent to one mole of electrons, i.e. the product of the Avogadro constant and the change on an electron in coulomb. Its value is 9.648×10^4 C mol^{-1} and symbol is F.

Faraday effect In this, rotation of the plane of polarisation of radiation in a dielectric medium is exposed to a magnetic field. The angle of rotation is proportional to Bl, where l is the length of the path of radiation in the medium and B is the magnetic flux density.

Faraday tube A tube through which charged particles can pass without coulomb force.

Faraday's laws of electrolysis There are two Faraday's laws of electrolysis, such as

First law The mass liberated on an electrode during electrolysis is directly proportional to the amount of charge q passing through the electrolyte,

i.e. $m \propto q$ or $m = Zq = ZIt$

where, Z is the electrochemical equivalent of the substance liberated on the electrode.

Second law If the same quantity of electricity passes through various electrolytes, the amount of ions liberated at different electrodes are proportional to their chemical equivalents E.

i.e. $m \propto E$

Faraday's law of electromagnetic induction There are two Faraday's laws of electromagnetic induction such as

First law Whenever the magnetic flux linked with any circuit changes an emf is induced in it, which lasts so long as the change in magnetic flux is continuing.

Second law The magnitude of induced emf is proportional to the rate of change of magnetic flux linked with the circuit. It is expressed as

$$e = \frac{-d\phi}{dt}$$

Negative sign indicates that induced emf always opposes any change in magnetic flux associated with the circuit.

far infrared The part of longer wavelength of infrared region of the electromagnetic spectrum. This part is farthest in wavelength from the visible region and nearest to the radio wave region.

far point The farthest point from the eye at which an object can be seen clearly. For a normal adult person, the far point is at infinity.

far sight General name for hypermetropia (vision defect).

fast breeder reactor A fast nuclear reactor that breeds (generates) more fissile material than it consumes. These reactors are able to utilise 75% of the uranium ore as it comes from the Earth compared to thermal reactor which utilise less than 1% of the uranium ore.

fast-ion conductor They are solid conductor of electricity, in which the moving particles are ions and transport electric charge by moving rapidly between vacancies in the lattice of a crystal. Such substances are also called as solid electrolytes.

fast neutrons Neutrons produced in the nuclear fission having energies above 0.1 MeV.

fatigue The progressive decrease of a property due to repeated stress. e.g. elastic fatigue of a metal under continuous vibrations.

fault A defect in any apparatus or machine due to which its normal working is interrupted.

feedback The process of returning of the output signal to the input. It is generally used in amplifiers.

There are two types of feedback, such as positive feedback and negative feedback. The feedback is positive, if the output voltage is in phase with the input voltage and negative, if it is out of phase with the input voltage.

femto *Symbol* f, prefix denoting 10^{-15}.

Fermat's principle States that the path taken by a ray of light between any two joints in a system, is always the path that takes the least time. It leads to law of rectilinear propagation of light and the laws of reflection and refraction.

fermi A unit of length equal to 10^{-15} m. It is denoted by f_m.

fermi constant The coupling constant associated with the weak interaction which gives rise to beta decay. It is denoted by G_w and its value is $1.435 \times 10^{-36}\ \mathrm{J/m^3}$.

fermi energy The maximum kinetic energy of a free electron at absolute zero temperature.

fermi level The highest occupied energy level at absolute zero. It lies in conduction band in conductor, in valence band, in insulator and in forbidden energy gap, in semiconductor.

fermion An elementary particle with half-integral spin.

Ferranti effect The increase of voltage along a powerline when the load falls quickly, as a result of electromagnetic induction.

ferrimagnetism A type of magnetic behaviour shown by certain solids. In these solids, the magnetic moment of neighbouring ions align in anti-parallel directions, producing a net magnetisation.

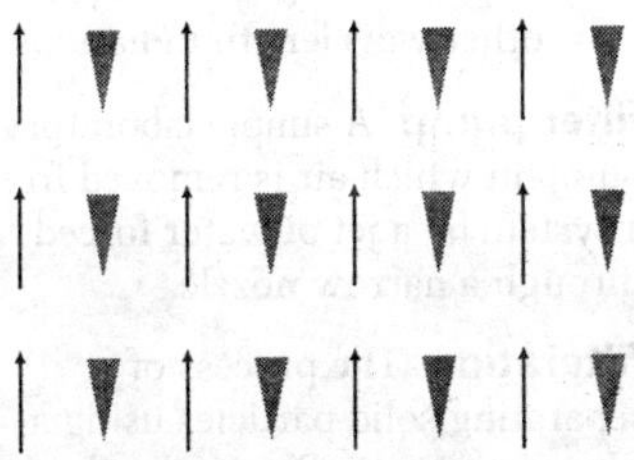

ferrite A group of non-conducting ceramic materials that exhibits ferrimagnetism. These materials have weak but permanent magnetism and used to make powerful magnets for radars and other high-frequency electronic apparatus.

ferro alloys Alloys of iron with other elements made by smelting mixtures of iron ore and the metal ore.

ferroelectric materials It belongs to ceramic dielectrics that have a domain structure making them analogous to ferro-magnetic materials.

ferromagnetism Those substances which gets strongly magnetised when placed in an external magnetic field, are called ferromagnetic substance. e.g. iron, nickel, cobalt, etc. They have a tendency to move from a region of weak magnetic field towards a strong magnetic field in a non-uniform magnetic field. The individual atoms or ions or molecules in a ferromagnetic material possess a permanent dipole moment.
They interact with one another in such a way that they spontaneously align themselves in a common direction over a macroscopic volume called domain. Each domain has a net magnetisation. Typical domain size is 1 mm and the domain contains about 10^{11} atoms. The magnetisation varies randomly from domain-to-domain. When it is placed in external magnetic field either domain whose magnetic moment is in the direction of external magnetic field, extends their boundaries or all domain rotate and align themself in the direction of external magnetic field, due to which substance is strongly magnetised.

fertile material Materials that can be converted into fissile materials by irradiation with neutrons. ^{238}U and ^{232}Th are fertile materials which are converted into ^{239}Pu and ^{233}U respcctively. This process is carried out in breeder reactors.

fibre optics The branch of optics which deals with the transmission of light along optical fibres. In optical fibres the light propagates due to multiple total internal reflections.

field A region in which a body experiences a force as the result of the presence of some other body or bodies.

field coil It is the coil in an electrical machine that produces the magnetic field.

Field Effect Transistor (FET) A solid state device like transistor, used in amplifiers. This device controls the current between two terminals, the source and the drain, by the voltage at a third, called the gate.

field emission The release of electron from a surface as a result of a strong external electric field.

Field-Emission Microscope (FEM) A type of electron microscope, in which a high negative voltage is applied to a metal tip placed in an evacuated vessel at some distance from a glass screen coated with fluorescent material. The tip produces electrons due to field emission, which form an enlarged pattern on the fluorescent screen.

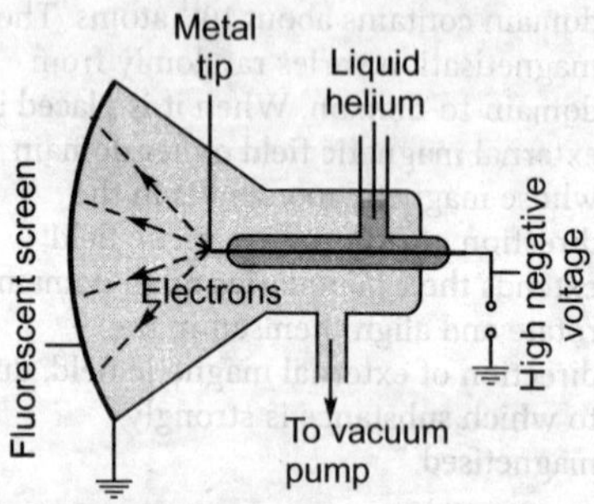

Field-emission microscope

field-ionisation microscope A type of electron microscope that have a high positive voltage. It is applied to the metal tip which is surrounded by low-pressure gas rather than a vacuum. It is abbreviated as FIM.

field lens The lens in the compound eye-piece of an optical instrument which is away from the eye is called field lens. It increases the field view.

field magnet A permanent magnet or an electromagnet used to provide magnetic field in an electric machine.

field of view The area which can be seen through an optical instrument is called its field of view.

field strength The direction and size of any force at a given point.

figure of merit (factor of merit) Measure of the sensitivity of a mirror meter. In other words, it is the corrected value of the deflection in millimetres for a current of 10^{-6} A and at a distance of 1m.

filament A thin wire of tungsten or any other metal having high melting point, used in incandescent electric bulbs or thermionic values.

film resistor Resistor that contains a conduction layer on the surface of an insulating core.

filter

1. An electronic circuit that allows only certain frequencies to pass through and stop all other frequencies.
2. An optical fibre passes only certain wavelength radiations to pass through and stop all other wavelength radiations.

filter pump A simple laboratory pump in which air is removed from a system by a jet of water forced through a narrow nozzle.

filteration The process of separating solid particles using a filter. In vacuum filteration, the liquid is drawn through the filter by vacuum pump. Ultrafiltration is filtration under pressure.

finder A small low powered astronomical telescope with a wide field of view. It is fixed to a large astronomical telescope, so that the large telescope can be pointed in the actual direction to see a particular celestial body.

fine structure Closely spaced lines seen at high resolution in a spectral line or band. It is caused due to vibration motion of the molecules or by electron spin.

fine structure constant The dimensionless constant having its value of about $\frac{1}{137}$, that characterises quantum electrodynamics. It is expressed as

$$\alpha = e^2/\hbar c$$

where, e is the charge, $\hbar$ is Dirac constant $\left(\hbar = \frac{h}{2\pi}\right)$ and c is the speed of light in free space.

first harmonic The fundamental frequency of any musical instrument is called its first harmonic. It is also known as fundamental mode.

first law of thermodynamics It states that "The heat energy ΔQ supplied to a system is partly utilised in doing work ΔW and the remaining part increases the internal energy of the system ΔU,

i.e. $$\Delta Q = \Delta W + \Delta U$$

or $$\Delta U = \Delta Q - \Delta W$$

This law is general law of conservation of energy.

fissile material A material that undergoes nuclear fission by thermal neutrons is called fissile material. e.g. ^{232}Th, ^{233}U, ^{239}Pu, etc. These materials are used in nuclear reactors and nuclear weapons.

fission The splitting of a heavy nucleus into two or more small fragments of comparable size when a neutron strike on it, is called nuclear fission. In this process, new neutrons and a large amount of energy is produced.

fission products The stable and the unstable isotopes produced as a result of nuclear fission.

fission reactor The nuclear reactor in which energy is produced by nuclear fission reaction.

fission tracking dating A method of calculating the age of glass and other mineral objects by observing the tracks made in then by the fission fragments of uranium nuclei that they have.

fixed point The temperature that can be accurately reproduced to enable it to be used as the basis of a temperature scale.

Fizeau's method A method to measure the speed the light, invented be Armand Fizeau in 1849. It has a rotating log wheel that transmits flashes to a distant mirror. Speed of light is calculated from the reflected light (flashes) and rotation of wheel to produce an eclipse of returning light.

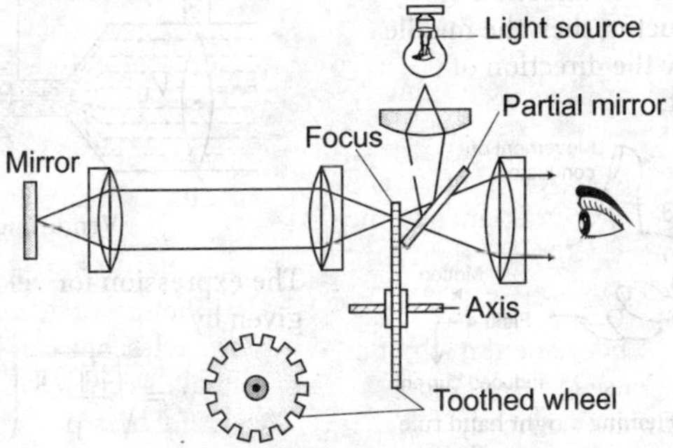

Apparatus for Fizeau's method

flame A hot luminous mixture of gases undergoing combustion. The chemical reactions occurring in a flame are mainly free radical chain reactions.

flash photolysis A technique use for studying free-radical reactions in gases.

flash point The lowest temperature, at which a volatile substance produces enough flammable vapour to produce a flash when a small flame is applied.

Fleming's left-hand rule It states that, "If we stretch the thumb, forefinger and middle finger of our left hand, such that they are mutually perpendicular, then if the forefinger points in the direction of magnetic field and the middle finger in the direction of current, then the thumb will point in the direction of motion or the force acting on the conductor.

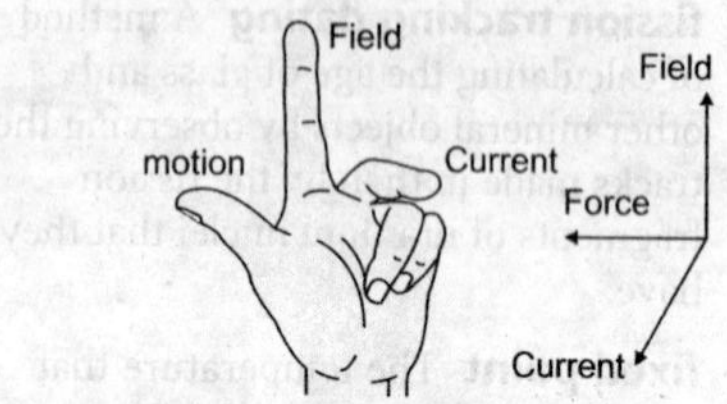

Illustration of Fleming's left hand rule

Fleming's right-hand rule If we stretch the thumb, forefinger and middle finger of our right hand, such that they are perpendicular to each other, then if the forefinger indicates the direction of the magnetic field and the thumb shows the direction of motion of conductor, then the middle finger will show the direction of induced current.

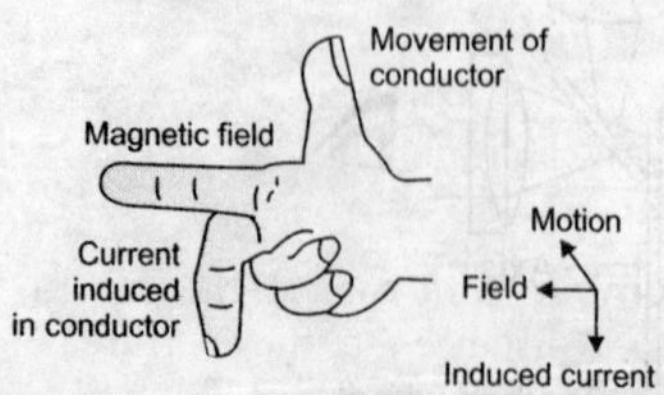

Illustration of Fleming's right hand rule

flint glass A type of glass containing lead silicate. It is used in optical instruments.

flip-flop An electronic circuit that has two stable states. It is switched from one stable state to the other by means of triggering phase. It is a bistable multivibrator.

floatation law A body will float in a liquid, if the weight of the liquid displaced by the submerged part of the body is equal to the weight of the body. The two forces acting on it, are weight of the body w acting downwards and upthrust w' equal to the weight of the liquid ϕ displaced acting upwards. The following cases arises

(i) $w < w'$, the body in sinks.

(ii) $w = w'$, the body floats completely immersed in liquid.

(iii) $w < w'$, the body floats with a part of it outside the liquid.

flow meter (*venturimeter*) A device used to measure the rate of flow of liquid through a pipe. The device is connected to the flow pipe. It essentially consists of manometer, with its two limbs connected to a tube having two different cross-sectional areas at its ends, respectively.

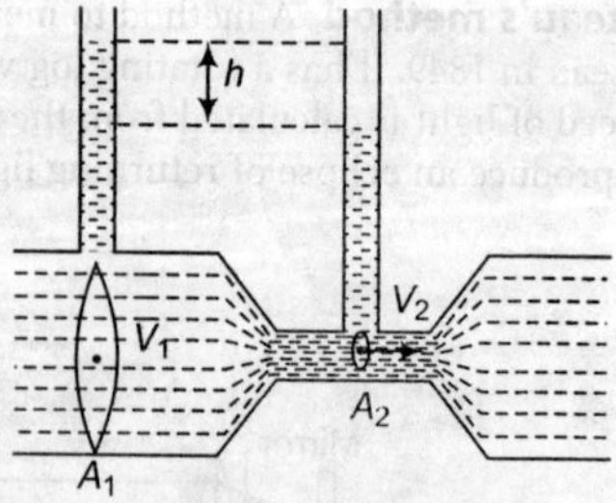

Venturimeter

The expression for velocity of flow is given by

$$v_1 = \sqrt{\frac{2h\rho_m g}{\rho}}\left(\frac{A_1^2}{A_2^2} - 1\right)^{-1/2}$$

and volume of liquid is

$$V = A_1 A_2 \sqrt{\frac{2(p_1 - p_2)}{\rho(A_1^2 - A_2^2)}}$$

where, p_1 and p_2 are liquid pressure, A_1 and A_2 are cross-sectional area of tube, ρ_m is liquid density and h is the difference in height.

fluctuations Random changes in the value of a quantity above some average value.

fluence Measure of the intensity of radiation in a space.

fluid A substance which can flow, i.e. a liquid or a gas.

fluid coefficient (fluid constant) Reciprocal of the value of fluid friction.

fluid friction Friction within a fluid with some other substance.

fluid mechanics The study of fluids both in rest or motion.

fluid pressure The pressure exerted by a fluid at any point inside it.

fluid resistance The restriction offered by a fluid in the motion of any body moving through it.

fluidics The use of jets of fluid in pipes to perform the control functions performed by the electronic devices.

fluidity The property of a fluid that enables it to flow easily, is called fluidity. It is opposite to viscosity.

fluidisation The method of passing a gas through a finely powdered solid, so that it acquires the characteristics of a fluid.

fluorescence The absorption of energy by atoms, molecules, etc., followed by immediate emission of electromagnetic radiations, when atoms or molecules return to their lower energy state. In fluorescence, the emission of light stops as the incident radiation is cut-off.

fluorescent lamp A lamp consisting of an electric glow discharge tube. Its inner surface is coated with a fluorescent material, such as phospher. The tube is filled with a gas generally mercury vapour. The gas produces visible light and ultraviolet radiations. The ultraviolet radiations produces visible light in the phosphor by fluorescence.

fluoroscope Instrument which makes invisible radiation (like X-rays) visible by means of a fluorescent screen.

flux The rate of flow of mass or energy per unit area perpendicular to the direction of flow.

flux density *See* magnetic flux density.

flux leakage The magnetic flux that does not pass through an air gap or other part of a magnetic circuit which is required.

flux meter An instrument used to measure magnetic flux.

flux quantum A quantum of magnetic flux that occurs in a superconducting ring, such as hollow cylinder. The magnetic flux is quantised in multiples of $\frac{h}{2e}$ where, h is Planck's constant and e is the charge of an electron.

flywheel A large heavy wheel having a large moment of inertia. It rotates at a constant speed even though a fluctuating torque is acting on it due to its large moment of inertia. Therefore it prevents jerky motion and ensure a smooth ride.

FM An aberration of frequency modulation.

F-number For a camera, the ratio of the focal distance f to the aperture diameter d. It is express as F-number

$$= \frac{f}{d}$$

focal length (focal distance) The distance between the pole and the principal focus of a spherical mirror is called its focal length. It is represented by the letter f.

focal plane A plane perpendicular to the principal axis of a lens or mirror and centred at its focus.

focal point A point on the principal axis through which incident light rays close and parallel to the principal axis possess or appear to pass through it after refraction through a lens or reflection through a spherical mirror, is called principal focus (or second focus).

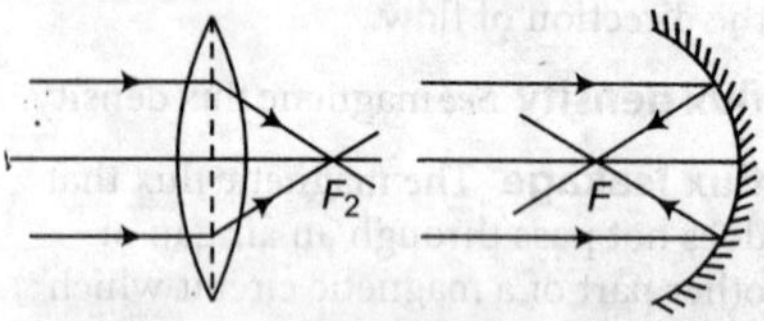

Focal points

A point on principal axis the light rays coming or appear to come from it becomes parallel to the principal axis after refraction through a lens or reflection through a spherical mirror is called its first focus.

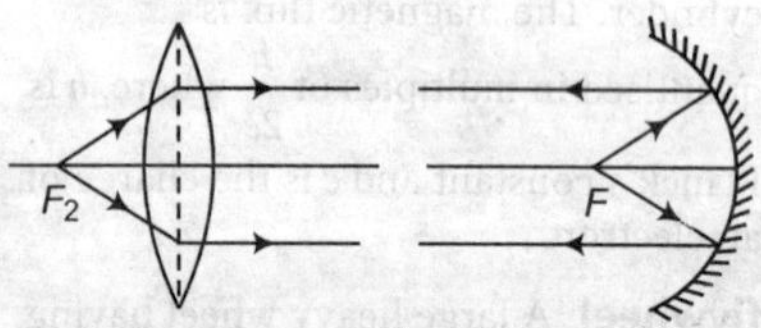

Focal points

focal power The ability of a lens to converge or diverge the light rays. Its unit is dioptre D.

Power of lens $P = \frac{1}{f}$ (in metre)

where, f= focal length of lens.

focal ratio *See* aperture

focus *See* focal point.

foot The unit of length in the FPS system. It is equal to 0.3048 m or one-third of a yard.

foot print Area of the Earth's surface to which Earth satellite send signals or receive them.

forbidden band The range of energies in an atom or molecule, in which there are few or no quantum states.

forbidden transitions Transitions between the energy levels in quantum mechanics that does not occur because of selection rules.

force An external cause (push or pull) which can change or tries to change the state of rest or state of motion of any body. It is equal to the product of the mass of the body m and its acceleration a. It is expressed $F = ma$. Its SI unit is newton (N).

force constant The magnitude of restoring force required to produce a unit displacement in a system. Its SI unit is Nm^{-1}.

force of buoyancy A force exerted by a liquid in upward direction when a body is submerged partly or fully in it.

force meter The device for measuring the force (in newtons).

force ratio (mechanical advantage) The ratio of the output force (load) and the input force (effort). It is expressed as

$$MA = \frac{L}{E}.$$

forced convection When energy is carried away from the source by flow produced by an external machine.

forced oscillation Oscillation induced in a body by the applications of an external periodic force. The external force is of sinusoidal nature of the form,

$$F = F_m \sin \omega t$$

where, ω is the angular frequency.

formula A rule or law expressed in algebraic symbols.

fortin barometer *See* barometer.

forward biasing

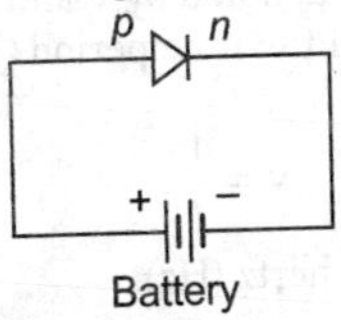

When an external voltage V is applied across a semiconductor diode, such that p-side is connected to the positive terminal of the battery and n-side to the negative terminal.

Foucault pendulum Pendulum having a bob attached to a long wire and can swing in any direction.

Fourier principle Any periodic function that can be expressed as a superposition of sine and cosine function of different time periods with suitable coefficients.
$A \sin\omega t + B \cos \omega t$ is a periodic function.

four-wave mixing The production of a photon in a medium as a result of the interaction of three photons. The photon produced has a wavelength, different from the wavelength of the three original photons.

fovea Most sensitive central region of the retina that subtends about 2°.

FPS system of unit The system of units in which the unit of length is foot, the unit of mass is pound and the unit of time is second.

frame of reference A reference point, a set of three axes alongwith a clock, is called a frame of reference. Commonly, three mutually perpendicular axes, labelled X, Y and Z-axes are taken as axes and their common intersection point is called origin and taken as a reference point. The coordinates (X, Y, Z) describe the position of the object.

Fraunhofer diffraction A form of diffraction in which the light source and the receiving screen are at infinite distances from the diffracting object, so that the wavefronts can be treated as planar rather than spherical. In practice, it involves parallel beams of light.

It occurs when $\frac{\omega^2}{L\lambda} << 1$

where, ω is aperture of lens, λ is wavelength and L is distance from aperture.

free body diagram A graphic dematerialised, symbolic representation of the body, in which all connecting pieces have been removed. It is a concerned method to model the structure, structural element or segment that is under scrutiny.

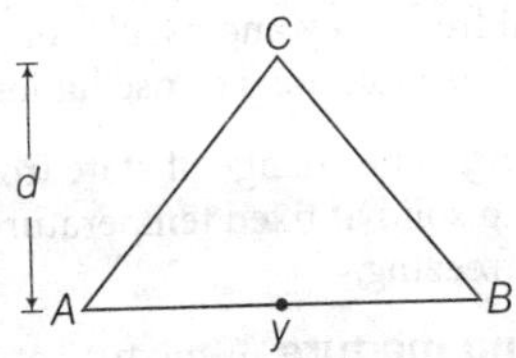

Fraunhofer lines Dark lines obtained in Sun spectrum due to the absorption of few wavelength in the chromosphere, the outer region of the Sun.

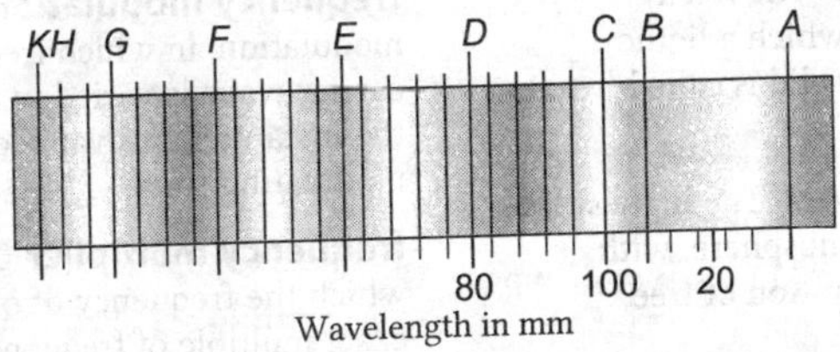

free electron An electron which is free to move in the lattice of the substance.

free electron laser A type of laser that works by the stimulated emission of electromagnetic radiation produced by the motion of electrons moving rapidly in external magnetic fields.

free electron theory The theory which treats electrons as moving freely within the body of a metal crystal or fluid.

free energy Measurement of the ability of a system to do the work.

free fall The movement of an object under the gravitational force only.

free oscillations When a system oscillates with its own natural frequency without the help of an external periodic force.

free space A region, in which there is no matter and no electromagnetic or gravitational fields.

free vibration When an oscillatory system is displaced from its mean position and then released, it oscillates to and fro about its mean position with a definite frequency called its natural frequency and oscillations are called free vibrations or oscillations.

freezing The change of state from liquid to solid at fixed temperature is called freezing.

freezing mixture A mixture of components which produces low temperature.

freezing point The fixed temperature at which a liquid converts into a solid is called freezing point.

F-region (*F*-layer) The highest layer of the Earth's ionosphere, with highest concentration of free electrons.

frequency The number of oscillations completed by the oscillating body in one second. It is denoted by ν and is the reciprocal of the time period (T) of the oscillation,

i.e., $$\nu = \frac{1}{T}.$$

Its SI unit is hertz (Hz).

frequency band A range of frequencies within prescribed limits.

frequency changer An electrical machine or circuit which converts alternating current of one frequency into alternating current of another frequency.

frequency converter A device which converts frequency of the received signal to giga hertz. It is also called a transponder.

frequency discriminator Circuit whose output frequency is equal to the difference between input frequency and reference frequency.

frequency distribution Set of all related frequencies of all events that are concerned.

frequency divider An electrical apparatus or circuit of the output frequency which is an exact integral sub-multiple of the frequency of the input.

So, $$f_{\text{out}} = \frac{f_{\text{in}}}{n}$$

where, n is an integer.

frequency meter An instrument used for measuring the frequency of an alternating current.

frequency modulation A type of modulation, in which frequency of carrier wave is varied in accordance to the instantaneous value of amplitude of modulating wave.

frequency multiplier A device in which the frequency of output is an exact multiple of frequency of input.

frequency of a vibrating string The fundamental frequency f of a stretched string of length l under tension T, is given by

$$f = \frac{1}{2l} \cdot \sqrt{\frac{T}{m}}$$

where, m=mass per unit length of the wire.

fresnel A unit of frequency which is equal to 10^{12} Hz.

Fresnel diffraction When either source or screen are placed closed to the diffractor, the diffraction observed is called Fresnel diffraction. In Fresnel diffraction, the wavefronts are not flame and analysis is difficult. The approach is useful in explaining diffraction around a circular obstacle.

Fresnel distance The minimum distance that a beam of light has to travel before its deviation from straight line path. It is expressed as

$$x \geq \frac{a^2}{\lambda}$$

$\frac{a^2}{\lambda}$ is the Fresnel distance.

where, a is width of slit, x is travelling distance and λ is the wavelength.

Fresnel lens A lens consisting of a large number of strips. Each strip have a convex surface of the same curvature. It is used as a field lens in spotlights, camera, etc., for producing a large increase in image brightness.

Fresnel's biprism A glass prism with a large angle (= 178°) which produces two coherent virtual sources which can produce interference patterns when monochromatic light is passed through it.

friction A force between two surfaces in contact which opposes the relative motion between them.

The two causes of friction are

(i) Roughness of surfaces in contact.

(ii) Force of adhesion between the molecules of the surfaces in contact.

Frictions can be reduced by

(i) Polishing

(ii) Lubricating

(iii) Using ball bearing

Friction as evil

1. Some force is wasted in overcoming friction and so the efficiency of a machine decreases due to friction.
2. The heat produced due to friction has adverse effect.
3. It wears out the rubbing surfaces.

frictional electricity When two appropriate bodies are rubbed with each other, then each of them get electrified. The electricity produced on bodies due to friction is called frictional electricity.

fringes The bright and dark bands obtained in interference and diffraction of light.

frost A deposit of ice crystals on the ground or other exposed surfaces by direct condensation of water vapour when temperature is below the freezing point.

frost point (frost temperature) The temperature lower 0°C is called frost point or frost temperature in which moisture present in the air becomes condense as frost rather than dew or mist.

fuel A substance that is oxided or changed in a furnace or heat engine to release useful heat or energy.

fuel cell A type of cell, in which fuel is directly converted into electricity.

fuel element Smallest package of fuel in a nuclear reactor.

fugacity A thermodynamic function used in place of partial pressure in reactions involving real gases and mixtures.

It is denoted by f and expressed as

$$d(\ln f) = \frac{dH}{RT}$$

where, H is the chemical potential.

fulcrum A point, where the lever or a rod is pivoted or supported along which it can turn.

full moon day The day on which the whole disc of the Moon is visible, is known as a full Moon day.

full wave rectifier A rectifier which converts both the half cycles of alternating current into direct current.

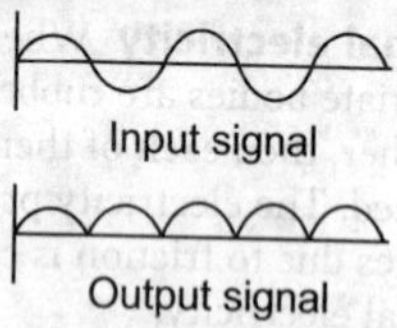

fundamental constant The quantities that do not change under any physically known conditions, e.g. speed of light in vacuum, change of an electron.

fundamental frequency The frequency of that component of sound which has the lowest frequency.

fundamental interactions Interactions that can occur between bodies. They can be

(a) Gravitational interaction
(b) Weak interaction
(c) Electromagnetic interaction
(d) Strong interaction.

fundamental mode The mode of vibration of object at the fundamental frequency.

fundamental note The musical note of the largest wavelength or lowest frequency possible within the given parameters.

fundamental particles Those particles of which all materials are composed, are called fundamental particles. e.g. quarks, leptons, etc.

fundamental quantities Those physical quantities which are made up of themselves only, like mass, length and time.

fundamental tone The sound of lower frequency produced by any musical instrument is called its fundamental tone.

fundamental units These units are independent and cannot be obtained from one another. There are seven fundamental units; such as metre, kilogram, second, ampere, kelvin, candela and mole.

fuse A safety device in the form of a metal wire of low melting point. It is made of tin and lead alloy. It is always connected in series.

fusion

1. The change of state from solid to liquid.
2. The process of interacting of light nuclei to form a heavy nucleus.

fusion reactor The nuclear reactors which produce energy by nuclear fusion. However, there are immense practical problems in sustaining a controlled fusion reaction, these reactors are still in development stage.

G

gain The ratio measuring the efficiency of an amplifier or an antenna. It is the ratio of the output signal to input signal. It has no unit.

galaxy A huge group of stars, gases and dust, held together by gravitational attraction. Our planet, Earth lies in milky way galaxy.

galaxy cluster A group of galaxies containing hundreds of members extending over a radius of upto a few megaparsecs.

Galilean telescope A type of refracting telescope having a converging lens as its objective and a diverging lens as its eyepiece. It produces an upright final image. This arrangement is used in cheap binoculars (opera glasses).

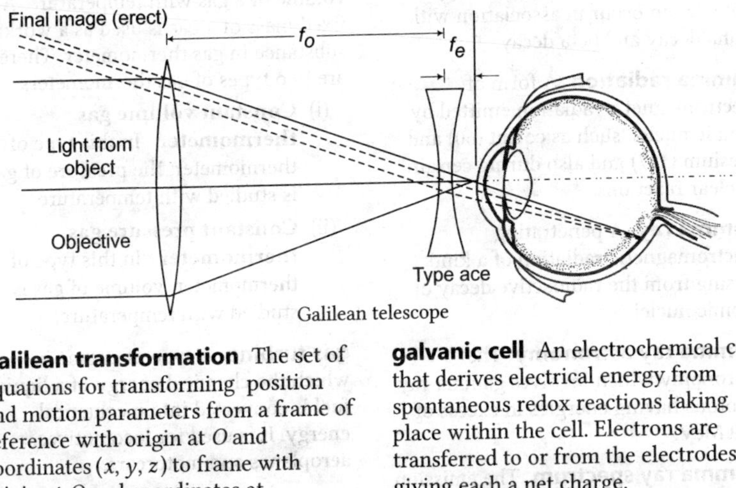

Galilean telescope

Galilean transformation The set of equations for transforming position and motion parameters from a frame of reference with origin at O and coordinates (x, y, z) to frame with origin at O and coordinates at (x', y', z').

Thus,

$$x' = x - vt$$
$$y' = y$$
$$z' = z$$
$$t' = t$$

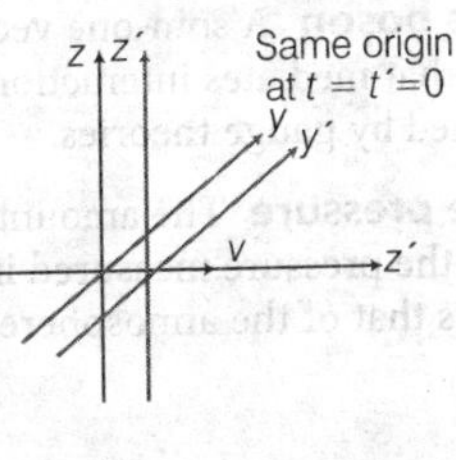

galvanic cell An electrochemical cell that derives electrical energy from spontaneous redox reactions taking place within the cell. Electrons are transferred to or from the electrodes giving each a net charge.

galvanised iron The material, such as iron or steel which is coated with a layer of zinc to protect from corrosion.

galvanising Process of coating iron with zinc to prevent corrosion (rusting).

galvanometer A galvanometer is an instrument used to detect the presence of current in a circuit. Its working is based on the fact that a torque acts on a current carrying coil when placed in a uniform magnetic field. This torque tries to rotate the coil.

galvanometer sensitivity The current in microampere required to consume 1 mm deflection on a scale 1 m away from the mirror.

gamma The measure of the convexity of a derivatives value γ. It is denoted by γ.

gamma camera A device that detects and records the spatial distribution of radioactive compounds in the human body.

g

gamma decay A type of radioactive decay, in which gamma rays are emitted by a nucleus. Gamma decay occurs due to transition of a nuclide from excited state to lower energy state. It can occur in association with alpha decay and beta decay.

gamma radiation A form of electromagnetic radiation emitted by atomic nuclei, such as cobalt (60) and caesium (137) and also during certain nuclear reactions.

gamma ray A penetrating electromagnetic radiation of a kind arising from the radioactive decay of atomic nuclei.

gamma ray astronomy The astronomy which involves gamma-ray photons having energies in excess of 100 MeV.

gamma ray spectrum The emission spectrum of sharp lines, corresponding to well defined quantum energies, which results from nuclear transitions between different energy levels.

gamma ray transformation A radioactive disintegration accompanied by the emission of gamma rays.

gas cooled reactors The nuclear reactors, in which cooling of the core is achieved by circulation of a gas. It uses graphite as a neutron moderator and carbon dioxide as coolant.

gas discharge tube An electron tube whose behaviour is markedly influenced by the presence of a gas.

gas giants A large, massive, low-density planet composed primarily of hydrogen, helium, methane and ammonia in either gaseous or liquid state. Jupiter, Saturn, Uranus and Neptune are known as the gas giants because of their gaseous composition and relatively large size. These planets are also called Jovian planets because Jupiter was the first planet whose gaseous nature was recognised.

gas thermometer A thermometer based on the variation in pressure or volume of a gas with temperature. A fixed mass of a gas is used as a working substance in gas thermometer. There are two types of gas thermometers:

(i) **Constant volume gas thermometer** In this type of thermometer, the pressure of gas is studied with temperature.

(ii) **Constant pressure gas thermometer** In this type of thermometer, volume of gas is studied with temperature.

gas turbine A type of engine in which the chemical energy of a liquid fuel is converted into mechanical energy. It is used for locomotives, aeroplanes and motorcars.

gate An electronic circuit which produces a single output signal from two or more input signals.

gauge A device used for measuring and indicating a quantity such as thickness of wire.

gauge boson A spin-one vector boson that mediates interactions governed by gauge theories.

gauge pressure The amount by which the pressure measured in a fluid exceeds that of the atmosphere.

gauge theory It involves various number of quantum field theories put forward to elaborate fundamental interactions. It involves a symmetry group for the fields and potentials.

Gauss The unit of magnetic flux density in the CGS system. It is equal to 10^{-4} tesla.

Gauss meter An instrument that indicates the strength of a magnetic field at any point directly in gauss.

Gauss's law in electrostatics The total normal electrical flux linked with a closed surface is equal to $\frac{1}{\varepsilon_0}$ times, the net charge enclosed by that surface (where, ε_0 is the permittivity of the free space).

Mathematically, it is expressed as,

$$\phi_E = \oint \mathbf{E} \cdot d\mathbf{s} = \frac{q}{\varepsilon_0}$$

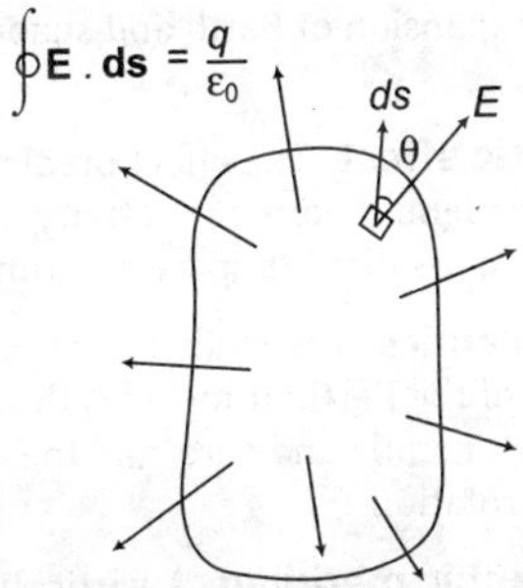

Gauss's law in magnetostatics A magnetic *N*-pole always occurs together with a magnetic *S*-pole. Therefore, this law states that "the total normal magnetic flux linked with any closed surface is always zero." As many lines come out of any surface enclosing any magnet, will enter into it. Mathematically, it is expressed as,

$$\phi = \oint \mathbf{B} \cdot d\mathbf{s} = 0$$

This means that isolated monopoles do not exist. Therefore, it is also known as law of absence of isolated magnetic poles.

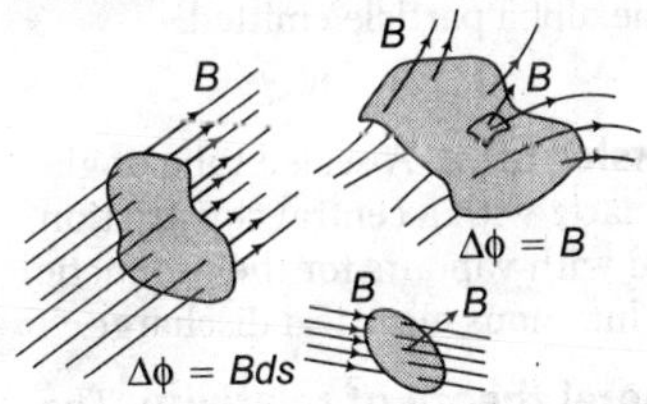

Gaussian distribution *See* frequency distribution.

Gaussian surface A closed surface in three-dimensional space, through which the flux of a vector field is calculated usually the gravitational field, electric field or magnetic field.

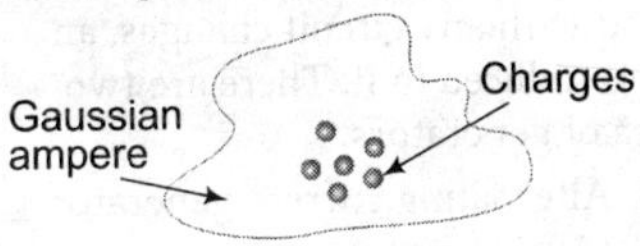

Gaussian surface

Gaussian units A type of CGS units which employ both electrostatic and electromagnetic units.

Gay Lussac's law It states that "at constant pressure, the density of an ideal gas is inversely proportional to its absolute temperature.".

gear A toothed wheel that meshes with another toothed wheel to transfer rotation from one shaft to another. The ratio of the numbers of teeth on two meshing gear wheels is called the gear ratio. If two meshing gears have different numbers of teeth, then the second (driven) shaft rotates at a different speed from the first (drive) shaft.

gegenschein A patch of any faint nebulous light, sometimes seen in the night sky opposite to the position of the Sun. It is though to be the image of the Sun reflected from gas and dust outside the atmosphere.

Geiger-Nuttall law The relation between the decay constant γ of an alpha emitter and the kinetic energy, E of the alpha particle emitted.

$$E \propto \log \gamma$$

Geissler tube A sealed tube of glass or quartz with a central constriction, filled with vapours for the production of a luminous electrical discharge.

general theory of relativity The theory given by Einstein to explain the gravity and accelerated motion.

generator A device which converts mechanical energy into electrical energy. Its working is based on the electromagnetic induction according to which whenever the magnetic flux linked with any circuit changes, an emf is induced in it. There are two types of generators:

(i) Alternating current generator (AC generator)

(ii) Direct current generator (DC generator)

A generator has four main parts:

(i) **Armature** A coil of large number of turns.

(ii) **Field magnets** Coil is placed between two magnetic poles.

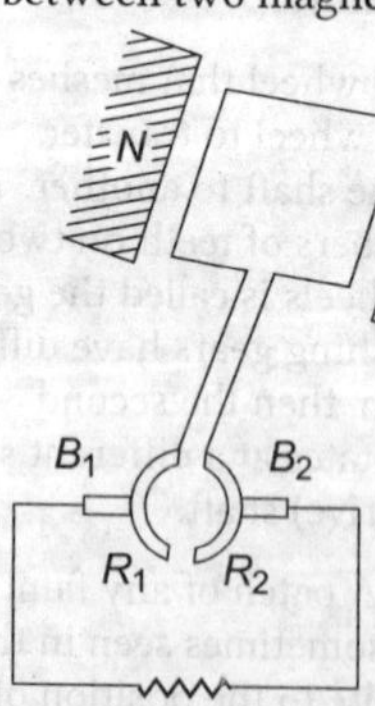

Generator

(iii) **Commulator rings or slip rings** Two ends of the coil are connected to two full or half rings.

(iv) **Brushes** Two carbon metal pieces slightly in contact with rings.

geocentric In which Earth is at the centre.

geocentric theory This theory was given by Ptolemy. It is an astronomical theory that describes the universe as a geocentric system ,such that the Earth is the centre of the universe and all other planets and Sun revolve around it.

geodesic The shortest distance between two points on a curved surface.

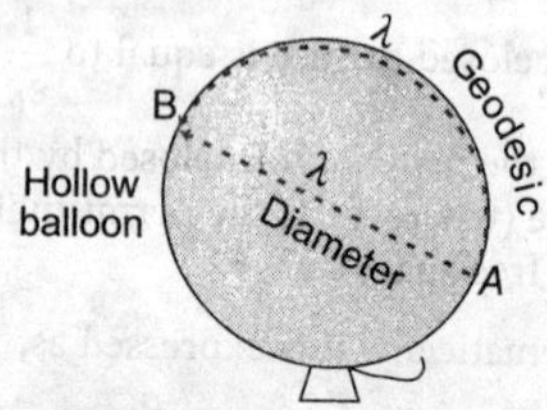

Representation of geodesic

geodesy The branch of Science in which expansion of Earth and shape is studied.

geodetic effect The effect predicted by the general theory of relativity, in which a mass distorts space and time.

geodynamics The study of the motion of the Earth. It includes those of the crust, mantle and core, and the Earth's rotation.

geographic meridian A vertical plane passing through the geographic axis of the Earth is called geographic meridian.

geoid A surface in the Earth's gravitational field, at which all points are at same gravity. These are approximately, an oblate spheroid in shape.

geometrical optics The branch of Physics in, which we study the reflection and refraction of light neglecting the finiteness of the wavelength.

geo-neutrinos Neutrinos that are emitted as a result of radioactivity inside the Earth.

geophysics The branch of Physics concerned with the study of the Earth and its interior.

geostationary orbit Orbit of the Earth artificial satellite at a height 35900 km in which the satellite takes 24 hours to make one complete orbit which is exactly same in which the earth completes one rotation about its own axis. Therefore, the satellite appears stationary with respect to any place on the Earth.

geostationary satellite A satellite revolving around the Earth in geostationary orbits. Its time period is 24 h exactly the same as, in which the Earth completes one rotation about its own axis. These satellites appear stationary with respect to any place on the Earth, therefore these satellites are used for communication purposes. The height of geostationary satellite is 36000 km and its orbital velocity is 3.1 km/s.

geosynchronous orbit An orbit of the Earth made by an artificial satellite in 24 h, i.e. Earth's period of rotation on its axis.

geothermal energy The energy within the Earth's interior. Volcanoes, geysers, heat springs are the sources of geothermal energy. The temperature of Earth increases with depth at a rate of 24°C km^{-1}. The temperature of upper mantle is about 1200°C and therefore, rocks are in molten state. Due to geological changes, molten rocks formed in the deeper hot regions of Earth's crust are pushed upwards and trapped in certain regions called 'hot spots'. When underground water comes in contact with the hot spot, steam is generated. Sometimes, hot water from that region finds outlets at the surface. Such outlets are known as hot springs. The steam trapped in rocks is used to run turbines which produces electricity.

GeV Abbreviation of gigaelectron volt, equals 10^9 electron volts.

giant magnetoresistance Change in electrical resistance that occurs in thin films consisting alternating layers of ferromagnetic and non-magnetic metals.

giant star A very large star that is highly luminous. Giant star represents a late stage in stellan evolution.

Gibbs function (Gibbs free energy) Thermodynamic function of a system given by its enthalpy *H* minus the product of its entropy *S* and its thermodynamic temperature *T*,

i.e. $$G = H - TS$$

In a reversible change taking place at constant temperature and pressure, the change in Gibbs function of a system is equal to the work done on it. If change in volume of a system is taking place at constant temperature and pressure then system is in equilibrium, when *G* is minimum.

giga A prefix denoting 10^9.
e.g. 1 gigahertz (GHz) = 10^9 Hz.

gilbert The CGS unit of magnetomotive force equal to $\frac{10}{4\pi}$ ampere-turn. It is denoted by Gb.

gimbal A device for keeping an instrument, such as a compass or chronometer horizontal in a moving vessel or aircraft.

glancing angle The angle between an incident beam and the surface upon which it is incident. The complement of the angle of incidence *i*, i.e. the angle $90° - i$.

glass A non-crystalline solid in which there is a non-regular arrangement of atoms. The atoms of glass are randomly arranged and are soft over a range of temperature. It has no definite melting point.

glass electrode A type of ion-selective electrode made of a doped glass membrane that is sensitive to a specific ion. It is used in pH measurement.

glass fibre Melted glass which is drawn into thin fibres having 0.005 mm to 0.01 mm in diameter. The fibres may be spun into threads and woven into fabrics.

glass transition The transition that occurs when a liquid is cooled very rapidly to become a glass.

Glauber model In this model, it describes the critical dynamics in which the dynamics is dissipative and the order of parameter is not conserved.

glide The movement of one atomic plane over another in a crystal.

global positioning system A space-based satellite navigation system that provides location and time information in all weather conditions, anywhere on or near the Earth, where there is an unobstructed line of sight to four or more GPS satellites.

gloss The ratio of light reflected by a mirror to the total light reflected.

glovebox A metal box that has gloves fitted to ports in its walls. It is used to manipulate mildly radioactive materials and in laboratory techniques.

glow discharge The silent discharge of electricity through a gas at low pressure. It is usually luminous, consisting of a dark and light bands between the electrodes.

golay cell A transparent cell containing gas, used to detect infrared radiations.

gold-leaf electroscope An apparatus used to detect charge on a body. It consists of a vertical metal rod housed in a box, with two thin gold leaves attached to its bottom end. When a charged object touches the metal knob at the top of the rod, charge flows onto the leaves and they diverge. The degree of divergence is an indicator of the amount of charge.

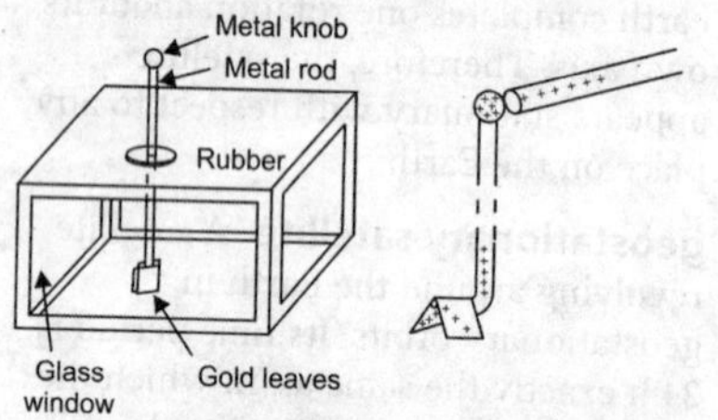

Gold-leaf electroscope

Goldstone's theorem Examines a generic continuous symmetry which is spontaneously broken, such that its currents are conserved, but the ground state is not invariant under the action of the corresponding charges.

Gouy balance A method used in measuring magnetic susceptibility.

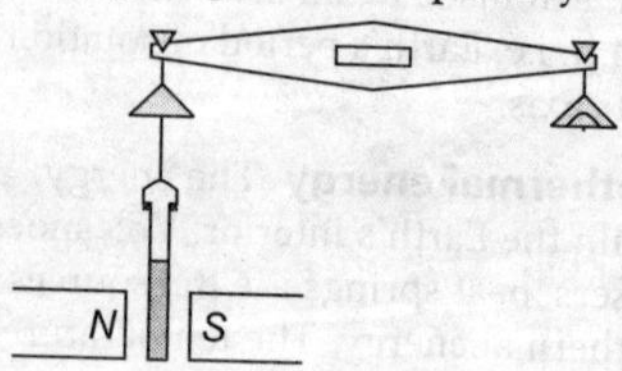

grad The unit of angle equal to $\frac{1}{100}$ of a right angle.

$$1^g = 0.9°$$

gradient Rate of change of a variable quantity with distance, such as temperature gradient ,means rate of change of temperature with distance. Similarly, pressure gradient, velocity gradient, potential gradient can be defined.

Graham's law States that "the rate of diffusion of a gas through a porous partition is inversely proportional to the square root of its density".
According to the kinetic theory of gases, the rate of diffusion of a gas through a fine hole is directly proportional to the root mean square velocity $\bar{c}$ of the gas.

grand unified theory A theory attempting to give a single explanation of the strong, weak and electromagnetic interactions between subatomic particles.

graphite-moderated reactor A nuclear reactor that uses as a neutron moderator and carbon dioxide as coolant.

graticule A series of fine lines or fibres in the eyepiece of an optical device, such as microscope or on the screen of an oscilloscopes ,used as a measuring scale or aid ,in locating objects.

grating A device for producing spectra by diffraction and interference. It usually consists of a glass or metal sheet with a very large number of fine parallel grooves rules on the surface by a diamond point.

gravimeter An instrument used to measure variations in the Earth's gravitational field by detecting changes in the force acting on a suspended weight. It is used to find the deposits of minerals including petroleum inside the Earth.

gravitation The force of attraction acting between two bodies due to their mass. It is the weakest force in nature but becomes sufficient when large massive bodies are involved.

gravitation law The alternative name of Newton's law of gravitation. According to which the gravitational force acting between two point masses is directly proportional to the product of their masses and inversely proportional to the square of the distance between them, i.e.

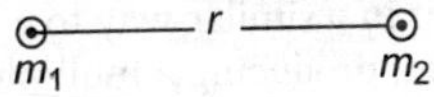

$$F \propto \frac{m_1 m_2}{r^2} \quad \text{or} \quad F = G\frac{m_1 m_2}{r^2}$$

where, G is gravitational constant.

gravitational acceleration *See* acceleration due to gravity.

gravitational collapse The tendency of matter to move towards a common centre of gravity.

gravitational constant A constant of proportionality in the Newton's law of gravitation. It is denoted by G and its value is $6.67 \times 10^{-11}\ \text{Nm}^2\text{kg}^{-2}$.
Its value is independent of size and shape of bodies, intervening medium, temperature, weather, etc., and remains same at all places. Therefore, it is also called universal gravitational constant. The dimensional formula is $[\text{M}^{-1}\text{L}^3\text{T}^{-2}]$.

gravitational field The space in the surrounding of a body in which its gravitational force can be experienced by other bodies is called gravitational field. The strength of gravitational field at a point is the measure of gravitational intensity at that point. The intensity of gravitational field at a point distance r from the centre of the body of mass m is given by

$$I_G = \frac{Gm}{r^2}$$

gravitational force The force between two masses as a result of gravity.

It is given by $F = \dfrac{Gm_1 m_2}{r^2}$

where, m_1 and m_2 are the masses and G is the gravitational constant.

gravitational lens A region of space containing a massive object whose gravitational field distorts electromagnetic radiation passing through it in a similar way to a lens, sometimes, producing a multiple image of a remote object.

gravitational mass The ratio of gravitational force to the object's acceleration.

gravitational potential The amount of work done in bringing a body of unit mass from infinity to that point in gravitational field, is called gravitational potential at that point. Its SI unit is J/kg.

It is expressed as,

$$V = -\frac{GM}{r}$$

gravitational potential energy The amount of work done in bringing any body from infinity to that point in gravitational field, is called gravitational potential energy of that body, at that point.

It is expressed as

$$U = \text{gravitational potential} \times \text{mass of the body}$$

$$= \frac{-GM}{r} \times m$$

gravitational shift The process by which electromagnetic radiation originating from a source that is in a gravitational field is reduced in frequency or red shift, when observed in a region of a weaker gravitational field.

gravitational waves They are ripples in the curvature of space time that propagate as a wave ,travelling outwards from the source.

graviton A hypothetical particle which is assumed as a quantum of gravitational energy. Graviton has not yet been observed. Rest mass of this particle is supposed to be zero.

gravity Force of gravitation applied by the Earth towards its centre on any other object lying on or near the surface.

gravity cell A primary electric cell in which two electrolytes (zinc electrode in zinc sulphate solution at top and copper electrode in copper sulphate solution at bottom) are kept apart by their different densities.

gravity wave The wave produced by the restoring force due to the pull of gravity. These waves tend to keep the water surface at its lowest level. The wavelength of these waves ranges from few metres to several hundred metres.

gray The derived SI unit of absorbed dose of ionising radiations. Its symbol is Gy.

gray body A body that emits radiant energy and has the same relative spectral energy distribution as a black body at the same temperature but in smaller amount.

greenhouse effect The surface of the Earth absorbs most of the solar radiation incident on it and re-emitting it as infrared radiation. These radiations are absorbed by carbon dioxide, water and ozone in the atmosphere as well as by clouds and re-radiated back to Earth. At night, this absorption prevents the temperature from falling rapidly after a hot day, especially in regions with a high atmosphere water content. This effect is called greenhouse effect.

grid In electricity, network of wires and cables that distribute electricity from power station to that places where it is used. In electronics, grid is an electrode other than anode and cathode, is thermionic valves, such as triode valve, tetrode, etc., which can control the flow of current through valves.

grid bias The potential difference applied between the cathode and control grid of a thermionic ,valve so that operation on any chosen part of the characteristic curve may be obtained.

grid circuit The part of a circuit that consists of the grid and cathode of a vacuum tube.

grid current The current that moves within a vacuum tube from grid to the cathode.

grounding or earthing The process of sharing charge of any conducting body with the Earth when it is connected to Earth or placed in contact with Earth, is called grounding or earthing. It is used as a safety measure for electrical circuits and appliances. For earthing, a thick metal plate is buried deep into the Earth. A thick copper wire is connected to this plate and wire is taken upto the electric mains. Householding electric wiring have three wires such as live, neutral and earth. The Earth wire is connected to the buried metal plate.

ground state The lowest energy level of an electron in an atom.

ground wave The radio waves that travel directly from a transmitting antenna to a receiving antenna following the Earth's surface are called ground waves. These waves cannot bend round the curvature of the Earth. Ground wave transmission becomes weaker for higher frequencies and therefore, it is useful for wavelength zoom or above. The maximum range of ground wave depends on the frequency of the radio waves and power of the transmitter.

group velocity If the wave motion has a phase velocity that depends on wavelength or frequency, then disturbance of a progressive wave travels with a different velocity from the phase velocity, it is called group velocity.

gun metal An alloy of copper of 88-90%, tin of 8-10% and zinc of 2-4% which is used for chains, belt buckles, etc.

gyration The motion of a body around a fixed centre or axis.

gyrator A device which reverse the phases of signals transmitted in one direction, but has no effect on the phase of signals transmitted in the opposite directions.

gyrocompass A gyroscope free to swing in any plane, rotated by an electric motor about a North-South axis.

gyrodynamics The study of rotating bodies having gyroscopic features.

gyromagnetic ratio The ratio of magnetic moment and angular momentum of an atom or nucleus. It is denoted by γ and is expressed as

$$\gamma = \frac{\mu_L}{|L|2}$$

Its unit is radian per second per tesla ($rads^{-1}T^{-1}$).

gyroscope A rotating heavy wheel that tends to resist any change in its axis of rotation.

GZK limit The Greisen-Zatsephin -Kuzmin limit is a theoretical upper limit on the energy of cosmic rays coming from distant source. The limit is 6×10^{19} eV or above 8 J.

g

H

Halation A blurred effect around the edges of high light areas in a photographic image caused by reflection and scattering of light through the emulsion from the back surface of the film support or plate. (in astronomy: The formation of a halo around bright star images by light reflected from the emulsion).

half-cell An electrode in contact with solution of the metal ions, forming part of a cell. The simplest half-cell consists of metal electrode immersed in a solution of metal ions. Half-cells are commonly referred as electrodes.

half-life Time taken for half of a sample of radioactive material to decay. The half-life of unstable substances may be from few seconds to thousands of years.

$\ln t = T, N = \frac{N_0}{2}, T = \frac{0.6931}{\lambda},$

where, λ is the wavelength.
e.g. Lawrencium has a half-life of 8 seconds and the isotope plutonium-239 has a half-life of 24400 years.

half-thickness The thickness of a specified material which reduces the intensity of a beam of radiation to half of its original value.

Half-wave dipole A straight wire used as aerial for passing radio wave twice of its length. The wave sets up resonance in the wire with a current antinode at the centre and voltage antinodes at the ends.

half-wave rectifier

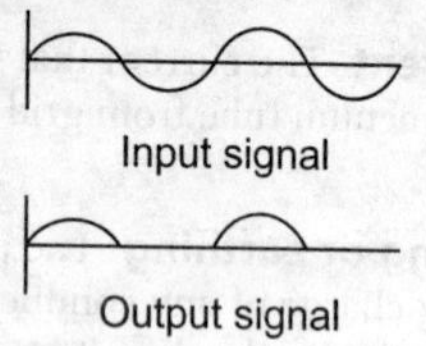

A rectifier which rectifies only one half cycles of input alternating current and suppresses the other.

half-width The width of a spectrum line measured at half of its height.

Hall coefficient The ratio of the induced electric field to the product of the current density and the applied magnetic field. It is denoted by R_H and expressed as

$$R_H = \frac{E_y}{j_x B}$$

where, E_y is the induced electric field j_x is the current density and B is the magnetic field.

Hall effect The phenomenon of the development of a potential difference between two opposite surface of a conductor or semiconductor when an electric current is passed through it.

Hall mobility The ratio of hall angle to the magnetic field strength involved.

Halley's comet A bright comet with a period of 76 years, its last visit was in 1986. It moves around the Sun in the opposite direction to the planets.
Its orbit was first calculated by Edmund Halley in 1705, after when it is named.

halo A type of luminous ring that sometimes can be observed around the Sun or the Moon.

Hamiltonian A function that is used to describe a dynamic system in terms of momentum, coordinates of space and time. It is equal to the total energy of the system when time is not explicitly part of the function.

hardness The resistance offered by a solid substance to scratching or local deformation by indentation.

hard radiation The ionising radiation of high penetrating power, usually gamma rays or short wavelength of X-rays.

Hard vacuum Refers to extremely low pressure.

harmonic An oscillation of a periodic quantity whose frequency is an integral multiple of the fundamental frequency.
The fundamental frequency of a sinusoidal oscillation is usually called the **first harmonic**. The **second harmonic** has a frequency twice that of fundamental and so on.
A stretched string or column of air will sound upper harmonics at the same time as the fundamental sounds.

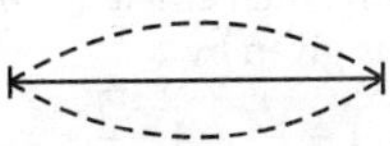

1st harmonic
(fundamental)

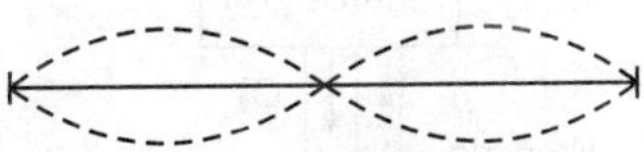

2nd harmonic
(1st overtone)

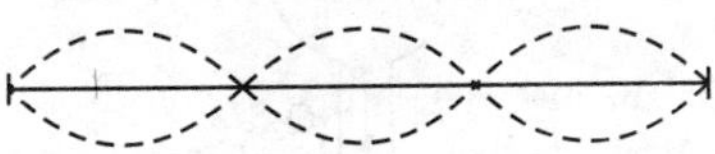

3rd harmonic
(1st overtone)

harmonic analyser Devised by Olaus Henrici in 1894 for determining the fundamental and harmonic components of complex sound waves. It consists of multiple pulleys and glass spheres, called rolling-sphere integrators, connecting to measuring dials. The image of a curve is placed under the device. The user moves a mechanical stylus along the curve's path tracing out the waveform.

harmonic motion A regularly repeated motion that can be expressed as the sum of a set of sine waves is called harmonic motion. This motion takes place to and fro or back and forth about the mean position.

harmonic oscillator A system that, when displaced from its equilibrium position, experiences a restoring force *F*, is directly proportional to the displacement *x* such as

$$F = -kx$$

where, *k* is a positive constant.

harmonic series A sequence in which each term is a harmonic of first term, such as in sound. Each sound produced by a musical instrument, is a harmonic of the fundamental note.

harmonic wave The wave whose frequencies are the integral multiple of the fundamental frequency. If f is the fundamental frequency, then frequency of 2nd, 3rd, 4th, ..., *n*th harmonic are $2f$, $3f$, $4f$, ..., nf.

hassium Made by Peter Armbruster and his team, in 1984. It is a radioactive transactinide element having atomic number 108. Its symbol is Hs.

Hawking process A form of radiation which emanate from black holes, arising from the creation of pairs of subatomic particles in the space adjacent to the black hole and with one particle falling into the black hole and the other radiating away.

head of liquid Difference in liquid levels between its free surface and in delivery pipe through which the liquid is supplied. It is measured in metre.

head on collision If the initial and final velocities of colliding masses lie along the same line, it is called head on collision. From law of conservation of linear momentum,

$$m_1u_1 + m_2u_2 = m_1v_1 + m_2v_2$$

From principle of conservation of kinetic energy, $\frac{1}{2}m_1u_1^2 + \frac{1}{2}m_2u_2^2$

$$= \frac{1}{2}m_1v_1^2 + \frac{1}{2}m_2v_2^2$$

We have, $v_1 = \frac{m_1 - m_2}{m_1 + m_2}u_1 + \frac{2m_2u_2}{m_1 + m_2}$,

$$v_2 = \frac{2m_1v_1}{m_1 + m_2} + \frac{m_2 - m_1}{m_1 + m_2}u_2$$

hearing aid People with hearing loss may need a hearing aid. A hearing aid is an electronic battery operated device. The hearing aid receives sound through a microphone.

The microphone converts the sound waves to electrical signals. These electrical signals are amplified by an amplifier. The amplified electrical signals are given to a speaker of the hearing aid. The speaker converts the amplified electrical signal to sound and sends to the ear for clear hearing.

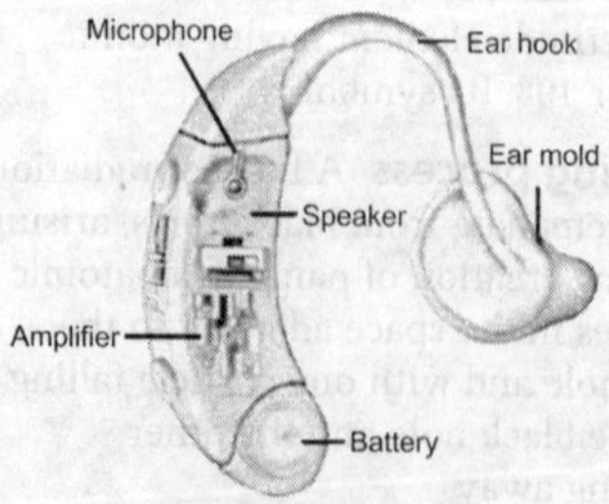

Hearing aid

heat A form of energy that transfers between two bodies due to temperature difference between them. Its SI unit is joule but its another popular unit is calorie and

$$1 \text{ calorie} = 4.186 \text{ joule}$$

heat balance The distribution of the heat energy supplied to a thermomechanical system among the various drains upon it including both useful output and losses.

heat capacity The heat capacity of a body is equal to the amount of heat required to raise its temperature through one degree. It is also called as thermal capacity of the body.

i.e. heat capacity of the body is given by

$$\Delta Q = mC$$

where, m = mass of the body and

C = specific heat of the body.

The unit of heat capacity in SI system is J/K.

heat engine A device which converts heat energy into mechanical energy. It takes in heat from a hot body called source ,then do some work and remaining heat is rejected to a colder body called sink. If Q_1 heat energy is taken from source at temperature T_1 and Q_2 heat energy is rejected to the sink at temperature T_2, then efficiency of the heat engine is given by

$$\eta = 1 - \frac{Q_2}{Q_1} = 1 - \frac{T_2}{T_1}$$

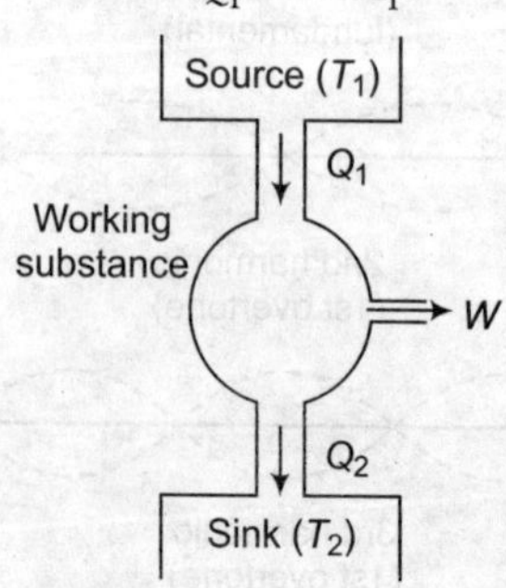

Symbolic diagram of heat engine

heater A resistor used to provide a source of heat when carrying an electric current.

heat exchanger A device used for transferring heat from one fluid to another without the fluids coming in contact. Simply, it is a two coaxial pipes and fluids flow through the pipe in opposite directions.

heat insulator A substance through which heat cannot flow.

heat of atomisation The energy required to dissociate one mole of a given substance into atoms.

heat of combustion The energy liberated when one mole of a given substance is completely oxidised.

heat of formation The energy liberated or absorbed when one mole of a compound is formed from its constituents in its standard state.

heat of fusion The amount of heat energy required to change a unit mass of a substance from solid to liquid state at the melting point.

heat of neutralisation The energy liberated in neutralising one mole of an acid or base.

heat of reaction The energy liberated or absorbed as a result of the complete reaction of molar amounts of the reactants.

heat of vaporisation The amount of heat energy required to change a unit mass of a substance from liquid state to gaseous state at the boiling point.

heat pipe A device which combines the principle of both thermal conductivity and phase transition. It efficiently manage the transfer of heat between two solid interfaces.

heat pump A device which continuously takes heat energy from a low temperature body and rejects it to a higher temperature body. It is similar to a refrigerator or a heat engine driven in reverse.

heat radiation The energy in the form of electromagnetic waves emitted by a solid, liquid or gas due to its temperature.

heat shield A device or coating for protection from the excessive heat.

heat sink A device used in association with transistors and other electronic components to dissipate undesirable heat and prevent a damaging due to rise in temperature.

heat transfer The transfer of energy from one body or system to another as a result of a difference in temperature. The heat is transferred by conduction, convection and radiation.

heaviside layer It is also called E-layer or Kennelly-Heaviside layer. A layer in the ionosphere at an altitude of 90 to 150 km that reflects medium frequency radio waves.

heavy fermion system A solid material in which the electrons have a very high effective mass.

heavy water Deuterium oxide (D_2O) is called heavy water. Water in which hydrogen atoms are replaced by the heavier isotope deuterium.

hecto Symbol h, a prefix denoting 10^2.

helicon A low frequency electromagnetic wave that can exist in plasmas in the presence of a magnetic field. The first helicons observed were atmospheric whistlers. Helicals have special ability to propagate through pure metals hence utilised in research metal properties.

heliocentric model According to this model, the Sun is the centre of our solar system and all other planets revolve around it in different orbits.

helioseismology Deals with the study of waves in the Sun.

helix A type of smooth space curve i.e. a curve in three dimensional space. It has the property that the tangent line at any point makes a constant angle with a fixed line called the axis. e.g. Spiral staircase, spring etc.

Helmholtz coils A pair of identical coaxial cylindrical coils separated by a distance equal to the radius of the coils. A uniform magnetic field is produced in the region between them, when a current is passed through the coils, connected in series.

Helmholtz free energy A thermodynamic potential that measures the useful work obtainable from a closed thermodynamic system at a constant temperature.

Helmholtz function It is also called Helmholtz free energy function. It is a thermodynamic function and is equal to the difference of internal energy U and the product of absolute temperature T and entropy S,

i.e. $$F = U - TS$$

Helmholtz galvanometer An improved form of tangent galvanometer. Helmholtz galvanometer has uniform magnetic field using two coils at centre, thus its sensitivity is increased.

henry The SI unit of self induction and mutual induction.

1 henry = 1 weber/ampere

Henry's law At constant temperature, the mass of gas dissolved in a liquid at equilibrium is proportional to the partial pressure of the gas. It is expressed as,

$$p = K_H C$$

where, p = partial pressure of the gas, C = concentration of the dissolved gas and K_H = constant.

hertz The SI unit of frequency defined as one cycle per second.

Hertzspring-Russell diagram Abbreviated as H-R diagram. It is a scatter graph of stars showing the relationship between the stars' absolute magnitudes or luminosities *versus* their spectral classifications on effective temperature.

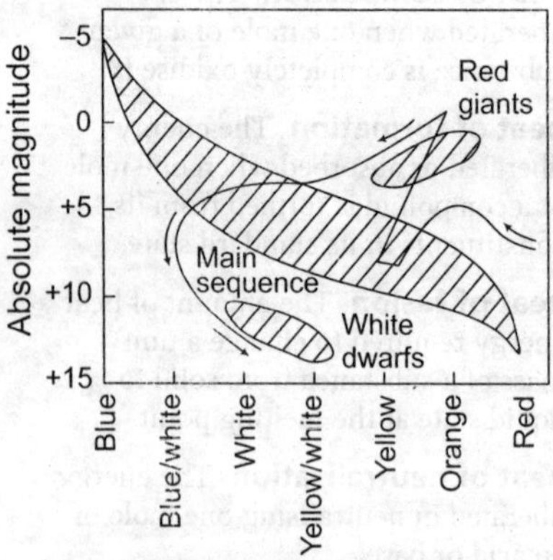

heterodyne A method of radio reception in which beats are produced by superimposing a locally generated radio wave on an incoming wave.

heterogenous multiplexing Multiplexing in which two or more information bearer channels operate at different data signaling rates (DSRs) i.e. multiplexing such that the information bearing channels resulting from multiplexing do not all operate at the same DSR.

heterogenous radiation Radiation consisting of different frequencies, various energies or a variety of particles.

Heusler alloys A ferromagnetic alloys containing no ferromagnetic elements.

high energy collision A collision of high energetic particles.

high frequency A radio frequency in the range between 3 MHz and 30 MHz.

high-speed steel A steel that will remain hard at dull red heat and can therefore be used in cutting tools for high speed lathes. It usually contains 12-22% of tungsten upto 5% chromium and 0.4 to 0.7% carbon.

high tension Refers to high voltage and sometimes written as HT.

Hilbert space A linear vector space that can have an infinite number of dimensions

histogram A graphical representation of a frequency distribution. In it, rectangular areas standing on each interval into which the observations are taken, represent the frequency of the observations in that interval.

hole

1. A deficiency of electron in a semiconductor is called a hole. It also works as a charge carrier.
2. A vacancy in the valence band that acts as a positively charged carrier.
3. Hole has a positive charge equal to that of electron and mobility of hole is smaller than that of electron.

hologram The intermediate photographic record which contain the information for reproducing a three dimensional image.

holographic optical element An optical device consisting of a hologram used to focus or deflect electromagnetic radiation.

holography A method of recording a three-dimensional image of an object. The object is illuminated with laser light and the reflected light from the object is combined with direct light from the source, to produce an interference pattern on a photographic plate. When original light is incident on the interference pattern, a three-dimensional image of the object is reconstructed.

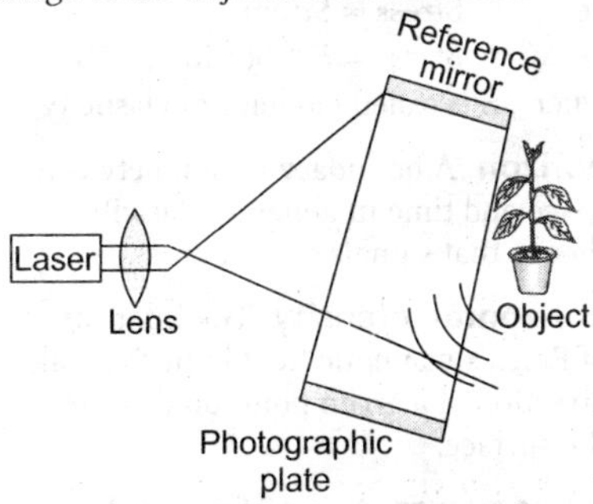

Representaion of holography

homo Prefix used for same or similar.

homocentric Converging to or diverging from a common point.

homogeneous Describing a system of uniform composition.

homogeneous body A body which has same lattice structure and has same properties everywhere.

homogeneous multiplexing Multiplexing in which all the information bearer channels operate at the same data signaling rate (DSR).

homogenous radiation Radiation consists of a narrow band of frequencies of the same energy or of a single type of particle.

homogenous substance A substance that contains only one kind of compound or element.

homopolar generator A simple electric generator consisting of a metal disc rotating between two poles of a magnet.

At constant rotational speed, the device produces a steady direct current and generators of this type are used in certain specialised applications.

Hooke's law It states that "within the limit of elasticity, the strain produced in a body is directly proportional to the applied stress,

i.e. Stress $\propto$ Strain

or Stress $= E \times$ Strain

where, E is called modulus of elasticity.

horizon A boundary region between space and time in general relativity theory that signals cannot cross.

horizontal intensity The intensity of Earth's magnetic field in horizontal direction at a given point on or near the surface.

horse power A unit of power. It is equal to the power needed to lift 33,000 pounds through one foot in one minute.

1 horse power = 745.7 watt

$\approx$ 746 watt

hot cathode A cathode which is operated at a high temperature and acts as a source of electrons by thermionic emission.

hot-wire instrument An electrical instrument in which the current to be measured is pressed through a thin wire and causes its temperature to rise.

howl A high-pitched audio frequency tone caused by feedback.

Hubble space telescope A telescope used to take pictures from space, avoiding the difficulties arising from the Earth's atmosphere.

Hubble's constant The constant which determines the relationship between the distance to a galaxy and its velocity of recession due to the expansion of the universe.

Hubble's law An empirical law in astronomy stating that the velocity v at which a distant galaxy is receding from the Earth is proportional to its distance d from the earth. It is expressed as

$$v = Hd$$

where, H is Hubble's constant.

human ear *See* ear

humidity The amount of water vapour in air. Relative humidity is the amount of vapour divided by the maximum amount of vapour the gas can hold.

Huygens' principle A geometrical construction of a wavefront at any instant. It states that:

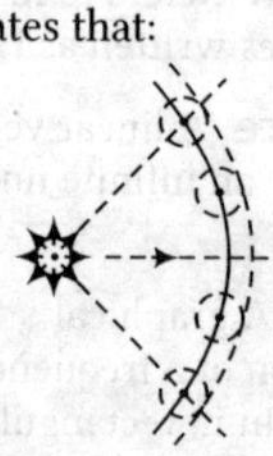

1. Each point on a wavefront is a new source of disturbance and emits secondary waves.
2. The new wavefront is the forward envelope of the secondary waves.
3. The secondary wavelets travel in all the directions with the speed of light in the medium.

hydraulic pressure A device which is used as a force multiplier. Its working is based on Pascal's law, according to which pressure is transmitted equally throughout the liquid. Force F_1 is applied on small area of cross-section A_1 and force F_2 is obtained at large area of cross-section A_2.

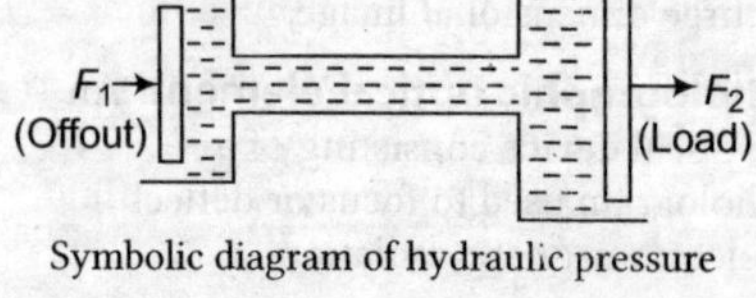

Symbolic diagram of hydraulic pressure

Here, $\dfrac{F_1}{A_1} = \dfrac{F_2}{A_2}$ or $F_2 = \dfrac{A_2}{A_1} F_1$

Therefore, a magnified force is obtained.

hydraulic stress When a solid spherical body placed in the fluid under high pressure, then it is compressed uniformly on all sides and the body is said to be under hydraulic compression. This leads to decrease in its volume without any change of its geometrical shape. The body develops internal restoring forces that are equal and opposite to the forces applied by the fluid. The internal restoring force per unit area in this case is known as hydraulic stress and in magnitude is equal to the hydraulics pressure (applied force per unit area).

hydraulic system Machine that uses fluid to transmit energy.

hydraulics The branch of engineering which deals with the flow by liquids in pipes and channels, the pumping of liquids and their use for the transmission and generation of power.

hydrodynamics The branch of science which deals with the mathematical study of the force, energy and pressure of liquid in motion.

hydroelectric power The electric power generated by flow of water.

hydrogen electrode An electrode system, in which hydrogen is in contact with a solution of hydrogen ions.

hydrogen spectrum The atomic spectrum of hydrogen which is characterised by lines corresponding to radiation quanta of sharply defined energy.

hydrometer An instrument used to measure the relative density of a fluid.

hydrostatic pressure The pressure exerted by the stationary liquid at any point inside the liquid.

It is given by, $p = \dfrac{F}{A} = h\rho g$

hydrostatics The branch of mechanics concerned with the hydrostatic properties of liquid.

hygrometer An instrument used for measuring humidity of air.

hypermetropia Alternative name for long-sightedness or far-sightedness. A person suffering with hypermetropia can see distant objects clearly but cannot see nearby objects distinctly. The near point for the person is farther away from the normal near point (25 cm). This is because the light rays from a close by object are focussed at a point behind the retina.

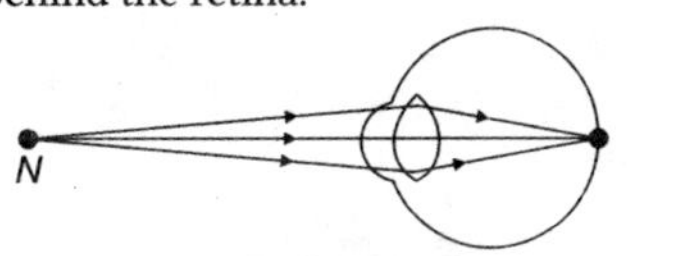

Near point of a hypermetropic eye

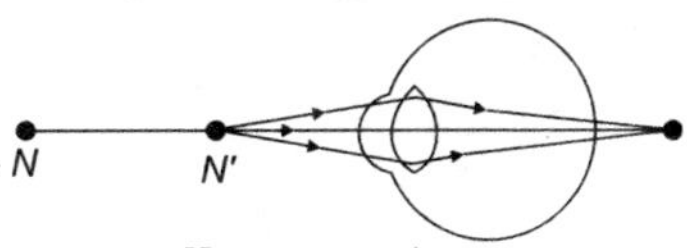

Hypermetropic eye

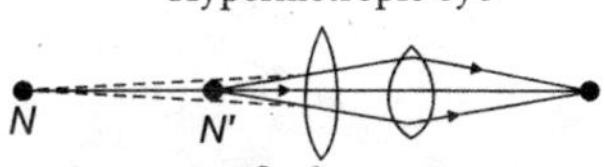

Correction for hypermetropic eye

This defect arises either because

(i) The focal length of the eye-lens is too long or

(ii) The eyeball has become too small. This defect can be corrected by using a convex lens of appropriate power.

hypernova An explosive event in which a large star collapses with the formation of a black hole.

hyperon A short-lived elementary particle whose mass is greater than the neutron.

hypersonic The speed which is greater than (more than 5 times) the speed of sound in the same medium.

Hypsometer A device for calibrating thermometers at the boiling point of water at a known height above sea level or for estimating height above sea level by finding the temperature at which water boils.

hysteresis When a ferromagnetic substance is taken across a complete cycle of magnetisation and demagnetisation, i.e. first magnetised by external applied field H and then demagnetised, then the flux density lags behind the field H. This is called hysteresis.

I

ice The solid form of water. Its density at 0°C is 916.0 kg m^{-3} as compared to water at 0°C with density of 999. 8 kg m^{-3}.

ice line A curve expressing the relation between the melting point of ice and the applied pressure. It is also called solidification curve.

ice point Freezing point of water. Its value is 0°C and used as a lower fixed point for celsius scale of temperature. It is the temperature at which there is an equilibrium between ice and water at standard atmospheric pressure.

iconoscope A form of television camera tube in which the beam of light from the scene is focused onto a thin mica plate.

ideal crystal Crystal structure considered as perfect, containing no defect.

idle current The average power associated over a complete cycle with a pure inductor or pure capacitor is zero. Hence, the current through L and through C is said to be idle current or wattless current.

ignition temperature

1. The lowest temperature at which a combustible substance when heated takes fire in air and continues to burn.
2. The lowest temperature at which the fusion energy generated in a plasma.

illuminance Intensity of illumination, i.e. luminous flux incident on a given surface per unit area. Illuminance is given by

$$E = \frac{\Delta F}{\Delta A}$$

where, ΔF is the luminous flux incident on surface area ΔA. Its unit is lumen-metre^{-2} or lux.

illuminated object An object over which light is incident.

illusion A false appearance or deceptive impression of reality (like in a mirror, illusion of real depth can happen).

image If light rays coming from a point actually meet at another point after reflection and/or refraction, that point is called the image of the first point. The image is real if the light rays actually converge to the point and it is virtual if the light rays do not actually meet but appear to diverge from the point when produced backwards. A real image can be obtained on a screen but a virtual image cannot. A real as well as virtual image can be photographed.

image converter An evacuated electron tube which converts infrared or other invisible images into visible images.

image intensifier A device used to produce a brighter image than an initial image.

image plane The plane perpendicular to the axis centered on the image.

immersion objective An optical microscope objective in which the front surface of the lens is immersed in a liquid on the cover glass of the microscope specimen slide.

impact

1. The striking of one body against another.
2. The force transmitted by a collision.

impact parameter The perpendicular distance of the velocity vector of an alpha particle from the central line of the nucleus, when particle is far away from the atom. It is denoted by b and expressed as

$$b = \frac{1}{4\pi\varepsilon_0}\frac{Ze^2 \cot(\theta/2)}{\left(\frac{1}{2}mv^2\right)}$$

impedance The resistance offered by an AC circuit containing two or three components out of inductance L, capacitance C and resistance R. It is denoted by Z and is given by

$$Z = \sqrt{R^2 + (X_L - X_C)^2}$$

Its unit is ohm.

impedance triangle A right angled triangle whose base represents ohmic resistance R, perpendicular represents reactance $(X_L - X_C)$ and hypotenuse represents impedance Z of the R-L-C circuit. From this triangle, we can calculate Z and ϕ such that

$$Z = \sqrt{R^2 + (X_L - X_C)^2}$$

and $\quad \phi = \tan^{-1}\left(\frac{X_L - X_C}{R}\right)$

implosion An inward collapse of a vessel and results of evacuation.

impulse When a strong variable force acts on a body for a short interval of time and produces a large change in momentum, then the product of the average force and time interval is called impulse and it is equal to the change in momentum, i.e.

Impulse = force × time interval
= change in momentum

Its SI unit is kg-ms^{-1}.

impulsive force A strong force acting for a short interval of time and produces a large change in momentum.

impulsive generator An electrical apparatus which produces very short high-voltage or high-current surges. Such devices can be classified into two types; impulse voltage generators and impulse current generators. Impulse generators are used in various technical applications such as lasers, plasma devices and nuclear fusion.

in phase Having waveforms that are of the same frequency and that pass through corresponding values at the same instant.

in series A number of objects or events arranged or coming one after the other in succession.

incandescence The emission of light from a high temperature surface such as the filament in an electric lamp.

incandescent body A body that emits light due to its high temperature such as the filament in an electric lamp is incandescent.

incandescent lamp See incandescent body.

incident ray The light ray which strikes any surface. The angle between this ray and perpendicular or normal to the surface is the angle of incidence. The reflected ray corresponding to incident ray, is the ray that represents the light reflected by the surface.

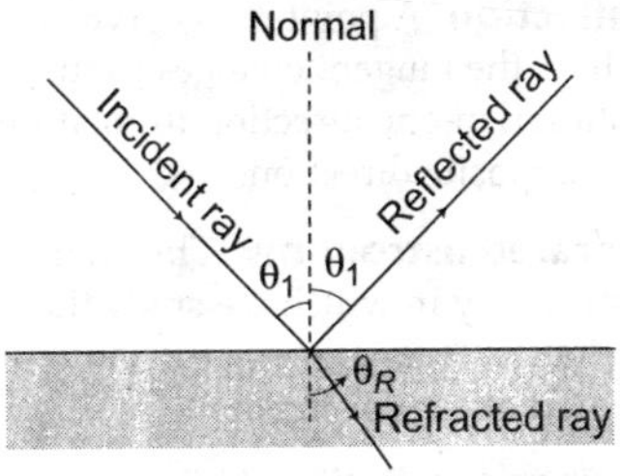

inclination An alternative name of angle of dip. The angle subtended between the magnetic axis of Earth and horizontal at any point is called inclination or angle of dip at that place. Its value is 0° at magnetic equator and 90° at magnetic poles.

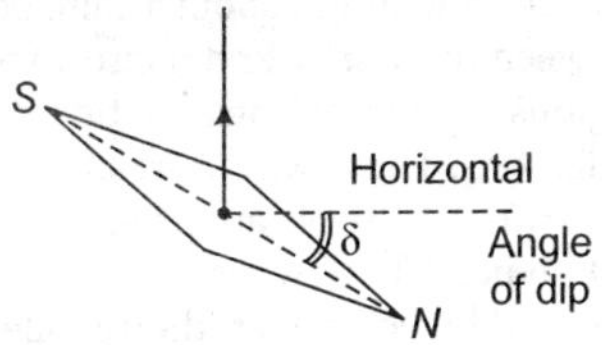

inclined plane A plane making an angle with the horizontal. It is a simplest machine.

incoherent scattering *See* coherent scattering.

incoherent source The sources in which phase difference is not constant.

index error A scale error on a measuring instrument. So that the instrument shows some reading when it should show zero reading.

indicator tube An electron-beam tube in which useful information is conveyed by the variation in cross-section of the beam at luminescent target.

induced current The current produced in any circuit due to change in magnetic flux linked with it.

induced emission (stimulated emission) Emission of a photon by an atom in the presence of electromagnetic radiation. On absorption of a photon, the atom becomes excited and emits a photon.

induced magnetism Creation of a magnet by aligning the magnetic domains in a ferromagnetic substance by placing it in a magnetic field.

inductance Property of a current carrying electric circuit that causes it to form a magnetic field and store magnetic energy. It is equal to the ratio of the flux-linkage to current.

induction Electrification or magnetisation produced in an object such as electrostatic induction is the production of an electric charge on a body when another charged body is placed near to it, electromagnetic induction is the production of an electric current in a conductor by means of a varying magnetic field near it.

induction coil An instrument that can produce high voltage impulses from a source of low emf. It is made up of a soft iron core over which two coils (primary and secondary) are wound. The number of turns in secondary coil are much larger than those in primary.

induction furnace A furnace in which very high temperature is produced by converting electrical energy into heat energy by electromagnetic induction.

induction heating The heating of an electrically conducting material by eddy currents induced by varying electromagnetic field.

induction motor An electric motor consisting two coils, one stationary primary coil called the stator and one moving secondary coil called the rotor. When AC is passed through primary winding, it induces a current in secondary coil of the rotor. The magnetic interaction between the two coils produces a motion in the rotor.

inductive reactance The resistance offered by an inductor. It is denoted by X_L and expressed as

$$X_L = \omega L = 2\pi fL$$

where, ω = angular frequency,
L = inductor and
f = frequency.

Through a pure inductor, alternating current lags behind the alternating emf by phase angle of 90°.

inductor A component of an electrical circuit that possesses significant inductance, generally a coil.

inelastic collision A collision in which kinetic energy does not remain conserved, but linear momentum remains conserved.

inertia The property of an object by virtue of which it cannot change its state of rest, state of motion or direction of motion its own.

inertial frame of reference The frame of reference in which bodies move with uniform velocity with respect to each other. In an inertial frame of reference, the Newton's laws of motion hold good.

inertial mass The ratio of the net force acting on an object to its acceleration. It is identical to the gravitational mass of that body.

inertial system The frame of reference in which an observer sees an object which is free of all external forces to be moving at constant velocity.

inextensible Which cannot be extend further.

inferior planet Mercury and Venus are known as inferior planets because their orbits lie inside the orbit of the earth.

inflection A point on a curve at which the tangent changes from rotation in-one direction to rotation in the opposite direction.

infrared astronomy The branch of astronomy in which we study the radiation from space in the infrared region of the spectrum.

infrared radiation Electromagnetic radiation having wavelength longer than that of red light but shorter than radio waves. Its wavelength lie in the range 0.7 μm - 1 mm.

infrared wave Electromagnetic radiation whose wavelength lies between 730 nm to about 1 mm, i.e. between the visible and microwave regions of the electromagnetic radiations. These waves are also called heat waves as these are produced by hot bodies. These waves can be detected by bolometer, thermopile and photoconductive cell.

infrasonic Sound waves with frequencies below the audible range, i.e. less than 20 Hz are termed as infrasonic.

infrasound Vibrations having frequencies below the audible limit (20 Hz).

inject

1. To force or drive into something.
2. To place into an orbit or trajectory (*inject* a satellite into a geosynchronous orbit).

inner planet The first four planets starting from Sun. The rest five are called outer planets.

input device A part of computer which feeds in data and program instructions. Different types of input devices are keyboard, mouse, punched card reader, etc.

input resistance The ratio of change in base-emitter voltage (ΔV_{BE}) to the resulting change in base-current (ΔI_B) at constant collector-emitter voltage (V_{CE}) is called input resistance of a transistor. This is dynamic and its value varies with the operating current in the transistor.

$$r_i = \left(\frac{\Delta V_{BE}}{\Delta I_B}\right)_{V_{CE} = \text{constant}}$$

Its value can be from a few hundreds to a few thousand ohms.

insolation The solar radiation which is received at the Earth's surface per unit area.

instantaneous Means momentarily or at that particular moment.

instantaneous acceleration Acceleration at a particular moment or acceleration at that instant. It is defined as the limit of the average acceleration as time interval tends to zero, i.e.

$$a = \lim_{\Delta t \to 0} \frac{\Delta v}{\Delta t} = \frac{dv}{dt} = \frac{d^2x}{dt^2}$$

instantaneous position Position of any object at that instant.

instantaneous speed The speed of an object at a given instant of time. It can be also defined as the first derivative of distance w.r.t. time at the given instant of time.

instantaneous value Value of a varying quantity at a particular instant of time.

instantaneous velocity Velocity of an object at that instant of time. It is defined as the limit of the average velocity as time interval tends to zero, i.e.

$$v = \lim_{\Delta t \to 0} \frac{\Delta x}{\Delta t} = \frac{dx}{dt}$$

insulator A substance which does not allow the passage of current through. It has no free electrons. e.g. mica, quartz, glass, ebonite, etc. In insulators, the valence electrons are tightly bound to their parent atom. The valence band is completely filled, the conduction band is totally empty and there is a large forbidden energy gap of several eV between them.

integrated circuit (IC) Many logic gates, resistances, condensers and other components integrated in on single chip.

intensity The intensity of a wave is the average amount of energy transported by the wave per unit area of cross-section of the medium per second.

interaction An effect involving a number of particles, bodies or systems as a result of which some physical or chemical changes take place to one or more of them.

interelectrode capacitance The capacitance between the electrodes tube. A capacitor is simply two conductors separated by an insulator or dielectric. The electrodes in an electron tube are the conductors and the vacuum is the dielectric. High frequency signals can feed back from one electrode to another through the interelectrode capacitance inside a tube.

interface The common surface of two adjacent bodies, either or both of which may be solid, liquid or gaseous.

interference The phenomenon of redistribution of energy when two or more waves of same frequency having a constant phase difference travel simultaneously in the same direction in a medium.

interference of light The phenomenon of redistribution of light energy on account of superimposition of light waves from two coherent sources. At the points, where resultant intensity is maximum, interference is said to be constructive. At the points, where the resultant intensity is minimum, interference is said to be destructive.

interferometer The instrument made to produce optical interference fringes for measuring wavelengths, testing flat surfaces, measuring small distance, etc.

intermediate neutron A neutron having energy in a range from 100 eV to 100 keV. ($1eV = 1.6 \times 10^{-19}$ J)

intermodulation The amplitude modulation of signals containing two or more different frequencies, caused by non-linearities in a system. It is caused by non-linear behaviour of the signal processing being used.

intermolecular force Force of attraction acting between the molecules and neutral atoms.

internal absorptance The value of absorptance, corrected to eliminate the effects of scattering and of reflection from the surfaces of the substance. The ratio of the radiant power absorbed between the entry and exit surfaces of the substance to the radiant power leaving the entry surface.

internal combustion engine A heat engine in which the fuel is burnt inside the cylinder of the engine and the gases so produced constitute the working substance.

internal conversion A transition from a higher to a lower electronic state in a molecule or atom. Sometimes, it is also called as radiationless de-excitation because no photons are emitted.

internal energy The sum of the kinetic energy and intermolecular potential energies of the molecules of a body. It is denoted by the letter *U*. Internal energy of a system depends on temperature and state of the system. The internal energy of an ideal gas is wholly kinetic.

internal force Forces acting between the bodies within a system.

internal friction *See* viscosity.

internal kinetic energy The total kinetic energy of all the molecules or particles of a system.

internal potential energy The energy possessed by a system due to the intermolecular attraction.

internal resistance The restriction offered by an electrolyte of a cell in the path of flow of current. It is denoted by *r*.

international system of units (SI) General conference on weights and measures in 1971 accepted an international system of units called Systeme Internationale d units (in French). This system contains seven fundamental units as metre, kilogram, second, ampere, kelvin, candela, mole and two supplementary fundamental units as radian and steradian.

international temperature scale A practical temperature scale, based on the meaning of thermodynamic temperature and employing experimentally determined values of particular temperature and specified experimental methods for measuring other temperatures.

interplanetary space The space between the Sun and the planets in the solar system. This space is occupied by interplanetary matter which originates from Sun.

interstellar space The space between the stars. This space is occupied by the interstellar matter, from which new stars are formed.

interval

1. An interval is the difference between two pitches (in music).
2. A gap between two points, limits, time, etc.

intrinsic semiconductor A semiconductor in its pure form. e.g. pure germanium and pure silicon. In an intrinsic semiconductor, the number of conduction electrons is exactly equal to the number of holes in the valence band, i.e. $n_e = n_h$.

invar An alloy of iron containing 36% of nickel. Its coefficient of thermal expansion is very small. It is used in making clocks and accurate standards of lengths.

Inverse Compton Effect The gain in energy of low-energy photons when they are scattered by free electrons of much higher energy.

inverse square law (light) The illuminance of a surface is inversely proportional to the square of its distance from the (point) source. The law holds for isotropic sources and at distance larger compared to the size of the source.

inversion temperature At a given pressure, the temperature of the gas at which the rise in temperature from the Boyle's law deviation, is balanced by the fall from the Joule's law deviation. Above the inversion temperature, the gas is heated by expansion.

inverter

1. A device that converts DC into AC.
2. An amplifier that inverts the polarity of a signal.
3. A logic circuit which gives low output when input is high and *vice-versa.*

inverting prism A prism such as porro-Abbe prism to correct for the inverted image produced by the eye-pieces.

ionisation The process of forming ions. Ionisation occurs in an electrolyte when it dissolves in a suitable solvent. Ionisation in gases take place by ionising radiation; such as X-rays, α-rays, β-rays, γ-rays, etc.

ionisation energy The energy required to remove an electron from the ground energy state ($n = 1$) to ionisation state ($n = \infty$).

ionisation gauge Composed mainly of three electrodes, all acting as a triode, wherein the cathode is the filament. The three electrodes are a collector or plate, a filament and a grid. Electrons from cathode are attracted to grid, which is positively charged. Some of the electrons collide with gas molecules and ionise them. Due to ionisation these molecules are attracted towards anode (plate). The resulting anode current can be used as a measure of number of gas molecules present. Thus pressure upto 10^{-10} torr can be measured efficiently in this way.

ionisation potential The potential which can provide energy to an electron to jump from ground energy state ($n = 1$) to ionisation state ($n = \infty$).

ionising radiation The radiation of sufficiently high energy to cause ionisation in the medium through which it passes. It may consist of stream of high energy particles or a electromagnetic radiation of short wavelength.

ionosphere A region in the Earth's upper atmosphere containing ions and free electrons. It is formed by ionisation of Earth's upper atmosphere by ultraviolet radiations from the Sun.

It has three main layers of higher ion concentration :

(i) *D*-layer from 50 km to 90 km,
(ii) *E*-layer from 90 km to 150 km and
(iii) *F*-layer from 150 km to 1000 km.
Radio waves are reflected back to the Earth by the ionosphere due to which radio transmission is possible.

ionospheric wave *See* radio transmission.

iridescence The property of certain surfaces that appear to change colour as the angle of view or the angle of ilumination changes (like iridescence in soap bubble).

iris An arrangement which is used to vary the amount of light that enters an optical instrument. In mammalian eye, it is a circular coloured diaphragm that changes the size of the pupil.

iron loss Energy wasted by hysteresis or eddy currents in the core of a transformer.

irradiance The rate of energy incidence per unit area of a surface, i.e. the radiant flux per unit area. Its unit is watt-metre^{-2}.

irradiation The apparent extension of the edges of an illuminated object seen against a dark background.

irregular reflection When a non-parallel reflected beam of light is obtained for incident parallel beam of light, then it is called irregular or diffused reflection.

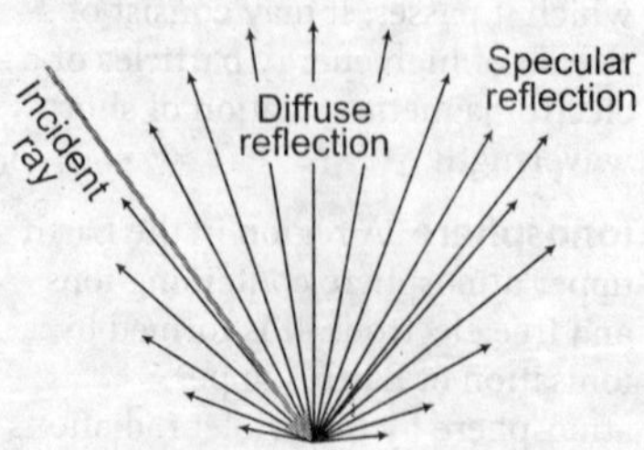

Representation of irregular reflection

irreversible process The process which cannot be retraced along the same equilibrium state from final to the initial state.

irrotational flow A flow in which each element of the moving fluid undergoes no net rotation with respect to a chosen coordinate axes from one instant to other.

isobaric process A thermodynamic process that occurs at constant pressure. Work done in an isobaric process is given by

$$W = p(V_2 - V_1) = \mu R(T_2 - T_1)$$

isochoric process A thermodynamic process that occurs at constant volume. Work done by or on the gas in an isochoric process is zero. The heat given to the gas entirely increases the internal energy of the gas.

isoclinic line Imaginary lines drawn on the surface of the Earth joining the places of equal angle of dip.

isodynamic line An imaginary line drawn on Earth's surface joining points at which the Earth's total magnetic field strength is same.

isoelectronic Describes compound that have same number of valence electrons.

isogonal lines Imaginary lines drawn on the surface of the Earth joining the places of equal magnetic declination.

isolated system If no exchange of heat takes place between a system and its surroundings, then it is called an isolated system.

isolating transformer A transformer used to transfer electrical power from a source of AC power to some device while isolating the powered device from the power source, usually for safety reasons.

Isolating transformers block transmission of the DC components in signals from one circuit to the other, but allow AC components in signals to pass.

isolator A two-port device that transmits microwave or radio-frequency power in one direction only. It is used to shield equipment on its input side, from the effects of conditions on its outer side. e.g. to prevent a microwave source being detonet by a mismatch load.

isotherm A line on a chart or a graph joining points of equal temperature.

isothermal process A thermodynamic process that occurs at constant temperature. This process takes place at a very slow speed and follows Boyle's law. According to which

$$pV = \text{constant}$$

Free exchange of heat between the system and the surroundings is allowed. Work done is given by

$$W = 2.303\ RT\ \log_{10} \frac{V_2}{V_1}$$

J

Jaynes-Cummings model A model used in quantum optics and atomic physics to describe the interactions between an atom with two energy level and a quantised mode of an electromagnetic field.

jet A free stream of liquid, gas or small solid particles shooting forcefully from a nozzle orifice.

jet engine Alternative name for a gas turbine engine used in aircraft.

jet propulsion Propulsion of a body force produced due to the discharging of fluid in form of a jet. This backward moving jet reacts on the body on which it was produced and create a reactive force that drives the body forward (in accordance with Newton's third law of motion).

***j-j* coupling** A type of coupling in various fermion systems such as electrons in atoms and nucleons in nuclei, in which the energies associated with the spin-orbit interactions are higher than the energies associated with electrostatic repulsion.

Joly's steam calorimeter An apparatus use to measure the specific heat capacity of a gas at constant volume.

Josephson effect An electrical effect which is observed when two superconducting materials at low temperature are separated by a thin layer of insulating material.

Joule Its symbol is J. The SI unit of work and energy. One joule is equal to the work done when the point application of a force of one newton moves in the direction of the force of a distance of one metre.

1 Joule = 1 newton-metre

Joule heating Production of heat in a conductor due to flow of electric current through it.

Joule Thomson effect A temperature change that occurs when a thermally insulated gas expands through a small hole or a porous barrier into a region of lower pressure. If the gas is above a certain temperature (inversion temperature of the gas), the temperature rises. This effect is also known as Joule-Kelvin effect.

Joule's equivalent Constant which is also called the mechanical equivalent of heat. It is denoted by J and its value is 4.18 joule calorie^{-1}.

Joule's law of heating The electrical work done per unit time (or the electric power) when a current I flows through a resistor of heating resistance R with a potential difference V is given by

Electric power = $VI = RI^2 = V^2/R$

Its SI unit is Watt or Joule per second, J/s.

junction Point at which two or more conductors are connected to the source.

junction detector A sensitive detector of ionizing radiating in which the output is a current pulse proportional to the energy falling in or near the depletion region of a reverse-biased semiconductor junction.

junction diode Two terminal semiconductor devices consisting of a layer of *p*-type semiconductor and *n*-type semiconductor. It can be used as a rectifier.

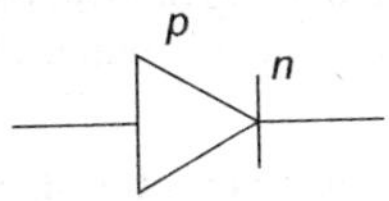

p-n junction

junction rule The algebraic sum of the currents meeting at any given junction in a circuit is zero, i.e. $\Sigma I = 0$. This law supports the concept that moving charges are not accumulated at a junction i.e. the law of conservation of charge.

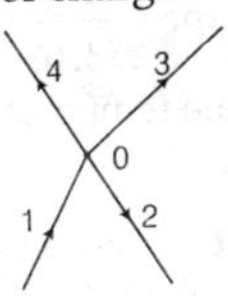

$$I_1 - (I_2 + I_3 + I_4) = 0$$

junction transistor A semiconductor device which is obtained by growing a thin layer of one type semiconductor in between two thick layers of other similar type semiconductor. A junction transistor is having two junctions and three terminals.

If central thin layer is of *p*-type and outer thick layers are of *n*-type semiconductor, then we get *n-p-n* transistor.

If central thin layer is of *n*-type and outer thick layers are of *p*-type semiconductor, then we get *p-n-p* semiconductor.

The thin layer of the junction transistor is said to form the base *B*.

One of the thick layers serves as emitter *E* and the other thick layer serve as collector *C*.

The function of emitter is to emit the majority carriers.

Function of collector is to collect the majority carriers and base provides the proper interaction between the emitter and the collector. The following figures *p-n-p* and *n-p-n* transistors are shown. In these figures, the arrow head indicates the direction of flow of positive charge between emitter and base.

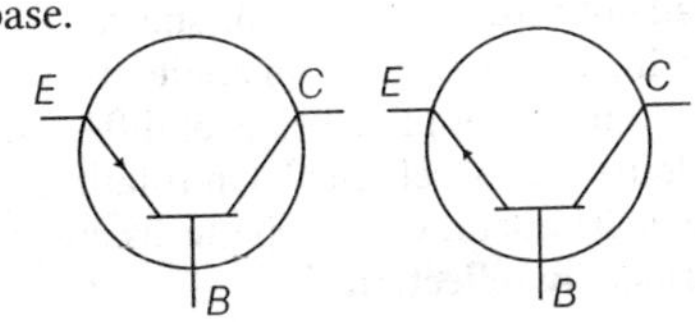

p-n-p transistor *n-p-n* transistor

A junction transistor is a transformer of resistance, which can be achieved by interchanging the biasing across the junction triode, hence the name junction transistor is given. In operation of a transistor, $I_e = I_b + I_c$. where, I_e = emitter current, I_b = base current and I_c = collector current.

junction rectifier Device which allows the current to flow through it in one direction only. A junction rectifier consists of a single *p-n* junction. A *p-n* junction can be used as rectifier in two ways such as half wave rectifier and full wave stiffer.

***J*-particle** Alternative name for psi particle.

Jupiter Largest planet of the solar system. It mainly consists of hydrogen and helium in gaseous form. It has 28 satellites or Moons. Its mass is more than the combined mass of all other planets.

K

k It represents the Boltzmann constant. Its value is 1.38×10^{-23} J/K.

K-capture An absorption of electron from the innermost shell (K-shell) of an atom into its nucleus.

kaleidoscope An optical instrument made of three plane mirror sheets inclined each other at an angle of 60°. Small pieces of glass beads of different colours are loosely held. On rotating the instrument, various patterns are formed by reflections.

Kaluza-Klein theory This is an unified field theory that postulates a generalisation of the relativity theory to higher than four space-time dimensions. In five space-time dimensions, it gives general relativity and electromagnetic interactions.

kange band Form of energy band commonly occurring in semiconductors which have a narrow gap between the valence and conduction bands.

kaom (K-meson) A type of meson. It is denoted by K^+, K^-, K° and 0. There are four types of meson;such as positively charged, negatively charged and two types of neutral particles.

kaon A type of meson. It is denoted by K^+, K^-. Kaon is of two types, having negative or positive charge.

Kater's pendulum A pendulum used to measure the acceleration of free fall.

katharometer An instrument used for comparing the thermal conductivities of two gases by comparing the rate of loss of heat from two heating coils surrounded by the gases.

keeper A piece of soft iron used to bridge the poles of a permanent magnet when it is not in use. It reduces the leakage field and preserves the magnetisation.

kelvin Its symbol is K. SI unit of thermodynamic temperature named after the British physicist Lord Kelvin. One kelvin is the $\frac{1}{273.16}$ of the thermodynamic temperature of triple point of water.

Kelvin effect Alternative name for the Thomson effect. Heat is evolved at a rate approximately proportional to the product of the current and the temperature gradient, when current flows along a conductor whose ends are at different temperatures.

Kelvin-Planck's statement It is impossible to derive a continuous supply of work by cooling a body to a temperature lower than that of the coldest of its surrounding. This statement is also called as second law of thermodynamics.

kelvin temperature The scale of temperature that originates at absolute zero.

Kepler's laws of planetary motion There are three Kepler's laws of planetary motion.

(i) **Law of orbit** All planets revolves around the Sun in elliptical orbits with Sun at its one focus.

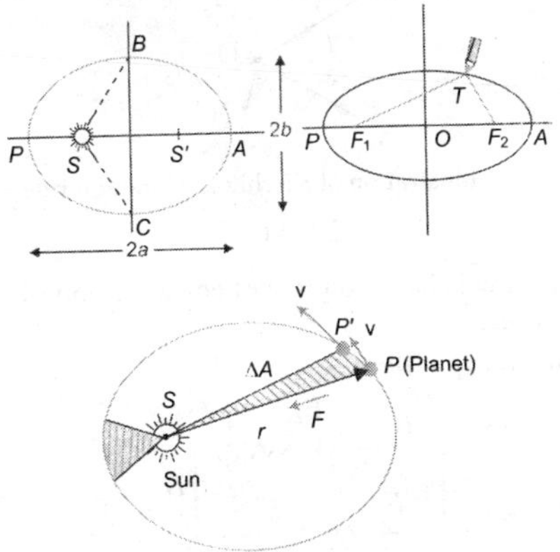

Illustrations of Kepler's laws

(ii) **Law of areas** The line joining any planet to the Sun sweeps equal area in equal intervals of time, i.e. its areal velocity remains constant.

(iii) **Law of periods** The square of the time period of revolution of a planet is directly proportional to the cube of the semi-major axis of the ellipse traced out by the planet,

i.e. $T^2 \propto a^3$

where, a is the semi-major axis of the elliptical orbit.

Kerr effect The ability of substances to refract different light waves whose vibrations are in two directions, substance is placed in an electric field.

keV Abbreviation of kilo-electron volt. It is a unit of energy equivalent to 10^3 eV.

kilocalorie Unit of energy equals to 1000 cal.

kilogram Its symbol is kg. It is equal to the mass of the international prototype of the kilogram which is a piece of platinum-iridium alloy cylinder or kept at International Bureau of Weights and Measures, at Sevres, near Paris, France.

kilohertz Its symbol is kHz. The unit of frequency equal to 1000 Hz.

kilojoule A unit of energy equals to 1000 J.

kilometre A unit of length equal to 1000 m.

kilowatt hour Unit of electrical energy equals to the rate of consumption of 1000 watt per hour.

$$1 \text{ kWh} = 1000 \text{ watt} \times 1 \text{ hour}$$
$$= 3.6 \times 10^6 \text{ joule}$$

kinematics The branch of mechanics which deals with the study of motion without taking into reference to force.

kinematic viscosity The ratio of a fluid's viscosity to its density.

kinetic energy The energy possessed by an object due to its motion is called its kinetic energy. If any object of mass m is moving with velocity v, then its kinetic energy is given by

$$\text{KE of translation} = \frac{1}{2} mv^2$$

If the body is rotating about an axis with angular velocity ω, then kinetic energy is given by

$$\text{KE of rotation} = \frac{1}{2} I\omega^2$$

where, I is moment of inertia of the body.

kinetic equations of rotational motion about a fixed axis
The three equations are

1. $\omega = \omega_0 + \alpha t$
2. $\theta = \omega_0 t + \frac{1}{2} \alpha t^2$
3. $\omega^2 - \omega_0^2 = 2\alpha(\theta - \theta_0)$

where, ω_0 is the initial angular velocity, θ_0 is the initial angular displacement, ω is final angular velocity, θ is final angular displacement and α is the angular displacement.

kinetic friction Friction which acts between two objects, when one body actually moves over the surface of another body.

Kinetic friction $(f_k) = \frac{\mu_k}{R}$

where, μ_k is the coefficient of kinetic friction and R is normal reaction.

kinetic theory A theory which explains the behaviour of gases. According to this theory

(i) An ideal gas is assumed to be made of perfectly elastic molecules.
(ii) These molecules do not exert any appreciable force on each other except during collisions.
(iii) The total volume of all molecules of a gas is negligible as compared to the total volume of the gas.

Kirchhoff's law of emission
The emissive power divided by the absorption coefficient, for any substance, depends only on the frequency and plane of polarisation of the radiation and is independent of the nature of the substance.

Kirchhoff's rule There are two Kirchhoff 's rule for solving simple electrical circuits.

(i) **Junction rule** At any junction in an electric circuit, the algebraic sum of all meeting currents is zero. i.e.

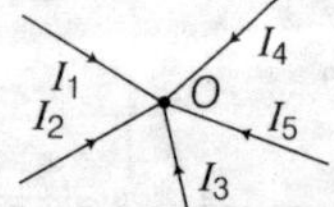

Illustration of Kirchhoff's junction rule

$$\Sigma I = 0$$

This law is based on law of conservation of charge.

(ii) **Loop rule**

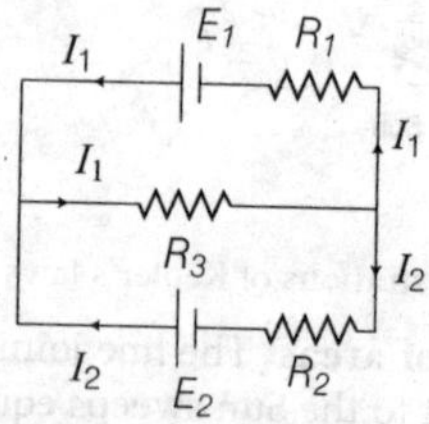

Illustration of Kirchhoff's loop rule

The algebraic sum of all potential differences in any closed loop is zero, i.e.

$$\Sigma V = 0 \text{ or } \Sigma E = \Sigma IR$$

This law is based on law of conservation of energy. While traversing a closed loop in clockwise or anti-clockwise, if negative pole of the cell is encountered first, then its emf is – ve, otherwise +ve .

K-lines The characteristics X-ray frequency from atoms because of excitation of electrons from K-shell ($n = 1$).

knee voltage The forward voltage for a *p-n* junction at which the current through the junction starts to increase rapidly with linear variation. But below the knee voltage, the characteristic curve is non-linear. The knee voltage for Si is 0.7 V and for Ge is 0.3 V.

Kundt's tube A device used for showing stationary waves in a gas or liquid. It consists of a glass tube fitted with a movable piston connected to a rod. This rod is clamped at its mid-point. A fine power is sprinkled along the inside of the tube. The rod is stroked, due to which sound waves are produced by the piston.

These waves are reflected by the other end of the tube and stationary waves are produced.

The power collected is regularly spaced heaps which are pressure antinodes.

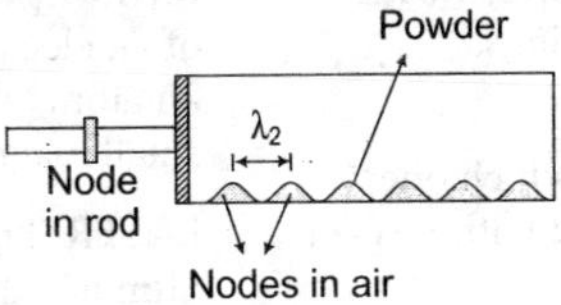

Symbolic diagram of Kundt's tube

L

labile Unstable, usually applied with respect to particular conditions, e.g. heat labile.

lag The time or angle by which one periodic quantity is delayed with respect to another.

lambda particle Type of elementary particle with no electric charge.

lambda point The temperature at which liquid helium I becomes the super fluid helium II.

Lambert Unit of a luminance, equal to 1 lumen of flux emitted per square cm of a surface. The foot-Lambert is a luminance of 1 lumen per sq. ft.

$$1 \text{ lambert} = \frac{1}{\pi} \text{ Cd cm}^{-2} = 3.18 \text{ stilb}$$

Lambert's cosine law The luminous intensity of a diffuse surface varies as,

$$I = I_0 \cos^2\theta$$

where, I_0 is the intensity along the normal, I is the intensity along a line at an angle θ to the normal.

lamina Thin flat sheet of a material of uniform thickness.

laminar flow Steady flow in which the fluid moves past a surface in parallel layers of different velocities.

laminated iron A piece of iron consisting of thin sheets of insulating material. Such a piece of iron is used for core of transformers. Laminated iron cores reduce eddy currents caused by a changing magnetic field.

Langmuir effect The ionisation produced when atoms of low ionisation potential come into contact with hot metal of high work function.

larmor precession Orbital motion of an electron about the nucleus of an atom when it is subjected to a small magnetic field.

LASER (Light Amplification by Stimulated Emission of Radiation) A device able to produce a beam of radiation with unusual properties. It is a source of highly coherent, powerful, monochromatic source of light.

latch Electric circuit designed to stay functioning, even when the original signal that triggered, it is switched OFF.

latent heat Heat energy that is needed to produce a change of state during the melting or vaporisation of a substance, it causes no rise in temperature. This heat energy is released when the substance reverts to its former state.

latent heat of fusion (Enthalpy of fusion) The change in enthalpy resulting from heating a given quantity of substance to change its state from solid to liquid. When the heat of fusion is referenced to a unit mass, it is called specific heat of fusion, while the molar heat of fusion refers to one mole of atom.

lateral aberration It occurs when different wavelengths of colour coming at an angle focus at different positions along the same focal plane.

lateral inversion A phenomenon in which an image formed by a mirror, the left side of the object appears on the right side and *vice-versa*.

lateral pressure Pressure or stress at right angles to the length of a body.

lateral shift When a ray of light is incident obliquely on a parallel sided glass slab, the emergent ray shifts laterally. The perpendicular distance between the direction of the incident ray and emergent ray is called lateral shift.

latitude Circular lines parallel to the equator are called latitudes measured in terms of angle θ with reference to equator at 0°. The latitudes are 0° North or 0° South.

lattice A regular network of geometrical point about which atoms, molecules or ions move in crystal.

lattice energy Strength of an ionic bond, the energy required for the separation of the ions in 1 mole of a crystal to an infinite distance from each other.

lattice parameter or lattice constant The length of the edge of a unit cell in a crystal.

launch window Period of time during which a rocket may be launched on a particular trajectory.

law of conservation of energy Whenever energy gets transformed, the total energy remains unchanged. This is the law of conservation of energy. According to this law, energy can only be converted from one form to another; it can neither be created nor be destroyed. The total energy before and after the transformation remains the same. The law of conservation of energy is valid in all situations and for all kinds of transformations.

law of conservation of momentum The total momentum of a system remains conserved, if no external unbalanced force is acting on it.

law of equipartition of energy Total kinetic energy of a dynamic system is equally divided among all its degrees of freedom and it is equal to $\frac{1}{2}kT$ per degree of freedom, where, k is Boltzmann's constant and T is absolute temperature.

law of floatation An object floating in a fluid displaces its own weight of fluid.

law of gravitation Gravitational force between two objects depends directly on the product of their masses and inversely on the square of their separation.

law of inertia Also known as Galileo law of motion, it states that a body will remain in state of rest or motion unless an external force is not applied on it.

law of magnetic poles The like magnetic poles repel each other while unlike magnetic poles attract each other.

law of radioactive disintegration It states that rate of disintegration is proportional to number of atoms left undecay in the sample at that time.

law of resistances

1. $R \propto l$, l = length of conductor
2. $R \propto \frac{1}{a}$, a = area of cross-section of conductor.

Thus, $R \propto \frac{1}{a} = \rho \cdot \frac{l}{a}$

where, ρ = specific resistance of the material. Specific resistance is also known as resistivity.

laws of dynamic friction

1. Dynamic friction is proportional to the normal reaction. It is less than static friction.
2. It does not depend on the velocity if velocity is neither too large nor too small.

laws of limiting friction

1. The force of limiting friction is directly proportional to normal reaction and it takes place in direction which is opposite to the direction of the force of pull. Limiting friction is maximum static friction,

   i.e. $F \propto R$

   $\Rightarrow F = \mu R$

   where, μ is the coefficient of friction.
2. Limiting friction is independent of the size and shape of the surface in contact as long as the normal reaction remains the same.

laws of reflection

1. Angle of incidence is always equal to the angle of reflection.
2. The incident ray, the normal at the point of the incidence and the reflected ray all lie in the same plane.

laws of refraction

1. The incident ray, refracted ray and the normal at the point of incidence, all lie in the same plane.
2. The ratio of sine of angle of incidence to the sine of angle of refraction is a constant, for the light of a given colour and for the given pair of media. This law is also known as Snell's law of refraction. If i is the angle of incidence and r is the angle of refraction, then

$$\frac{\sin i}{\sin r} = \text{constant}$$

This constant value is called the refractive index of the second medium with respect to the first.

laws of thermodynamics The four law of thermodynamics define fundamental physical quantities (temperature, energy and entropy) that characterised thermodynamic system.

1. **zeroth law** If two systems are in thermal equilibrium respectively with a third system, they must be in thermal equilibrium with each other.
2. **first law** It states that energy is always conserved. It can neither be created nor be destroyed but can be transformed from one form to another.
3. **second law** It states the state of entropy of the entire universe in a closed isolated system, will always increase over time.
4. **third law** The entropy of a system approaches a constant value as the temperature approaches absolute zero.

laws of transverse vibrations of strings These are three fundamental laws :

1. $n \propto \frac{1}{L}$ 2. $n \propto \sqrt{T}$

3. $n \propto \sqrt{m}$

Combining the above laws, we get

$$n = \frac{k}{l}\sqrt{\frac{T}{m}}$$

The value of k (constant) $= \frac{1}{2}$

$$\therefore \quad n = \frac{1}{2l}\sqrt{\frac{T}{m}}$$

If D is the diameter of the wire and d is the density of the material of the wire,

then $m = \pi \cdot \frac{D^2}{4} \times l \times d$

or $n = \frac{1}{2l\sqrt{\frac{4T}{4D^2 \cdot d}}} = \frac{1}{l \cdot d}\sqrt{\frac{T}{\pi d}}$

***L*-capture** Refers to a absorption of an electron from the L-shell into nucleus, giving rise to X-rays of characteristic wavelength depending on atomic number of the element.

***L-C* circuit** (resonant circuit, tank circuit, or tuned circuit) An electrical circuit consisting of inductor and capacitor. The circuit acts as an electrical resonator or also for storing energy of the circuit consisting an electrical resonator or also for storing energy of the circuit oscillating at resonant frequency. *L-C* circuits are generally used either for generating signals at a particular frequency, or picking out a signal at a particular frequency from a more complex signals.

***L-C-R* circuit** A circuit containing an inductance L, a capacitance C and a resistance R in series or in parallel or a combination of these.

LDR Refers to Light Dependent Resistor, the resistor whose resistance decreases on illuminating it.

lead A dense, dull, gray, soft metallic element, the end product of radioactive decay series. It is used in accumulators, alloys, radiation shielding and water and sound proofing.

lead acid accumulator A type of electrical accumulator used in vehicle batteries. It has two sets of plates : spongy lead plates, connected in series to the negative terminal and lead, slightly different for each colour. The reverse breakdown voltage for a LED is very low around 5 V.

lead equivalent Factor that compares any form of shielding against radioactivity to the thickness of lead that would provide the same measure of protection.

leakage The flow of an electric current caused by imperfect insulation in a path other than that intended.

least count The smallest value that can be measured by the measuring instrument is called its least count. All the readings or measured values are good only up to this value. e.g. the least count of vernier callipers is 0.01 cm and of screw gauge is 0.001 cm.

least count error The least count error is the error associated with the resolution of the instrument. Least count error belongs to the category of random errors but within a limited size, it occurs with both systematic and random error.

least energy In equilibrium, it is the state of a system and all other states give it a greater potential energy which relates to Le-Chatelier's principle.

leclanche cell A primary cell, in which positive electrode is carbon rod and negative electrode is zinc rod. The electrolyte is 10-20% ammonium chloride (NH_4Cl) solution. A mixture of MnO_2 used as a dipolariser and carbon powder is placed in a fabric bag or porous pot surrounding carbon rod. The emf of cell is approximately 1.5 volt.

LED An abbreviation of Light Emitting Diode. It is a heavily doped *p-n* junction. In forward biasing, it emits spontaneous radiation and the electrons are sent from *n*-region to *p*-region and holes are sent from *p*-region to *n*-region. On recombination of electrons and holes, energy is released in the form of photons. For a LED threshold voltages are much higher.

left hand rule Alternative name for Fleming's left hand rule. According to which, if the thumb, first and second fingers are held at right angles, then if the fore finger indicates the direction of the magnetic field and the middle finger indicates the direction of current flowing through the conductor, then the thumb will represents the direction of force acting on the conductor.

L-electron An electron having an orbit of such dimensions, that the electron constitute part of the second shell of electron's surrounding the atomic nucleus orbitals in L-shell are characterised by the principle quantum number value of 2.

Length The straight line distance between the two points along an object. Its SI unit is metre, while the CGS system of units takes the centimetre as its base unit.

lens A transparent medium bounded between two spherical surfaces or between one spherical and one plane surface.

A lens which is thicker at middle and thinner at edges is called a convex lens.

A convex lens converges light rays, therefore, it is also called a converging lens.

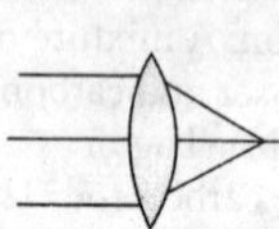

Double convex lens

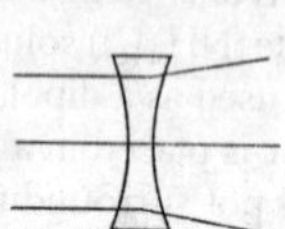

Double concave lens

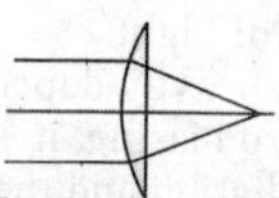

Plano-convex lens

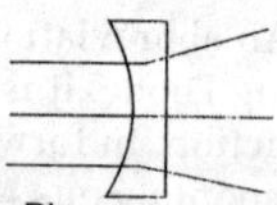

Plano-concave lens

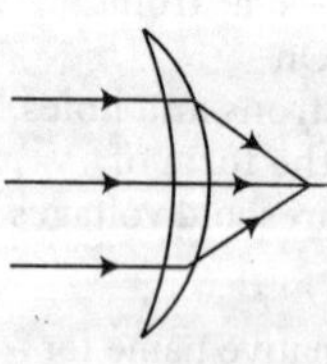

Concave-convex lens

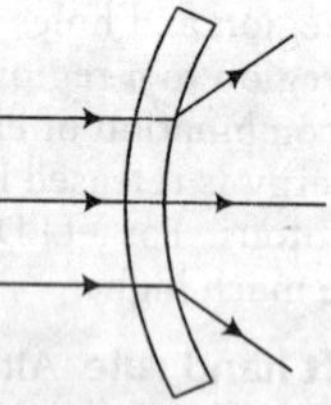

Convex-concave lens

A lens which is thicker at edges and thinner at middle is called a concave lens. A concave lens diverges light rays, therefore, it is also called a diverging lens.

lens maker's formula A relation between the focal length of a lens f, its radii of curvature R_1 and R_2 and refractive index of its material n.

$$\frac{1}{f} = (n-1)\left(\frac{1}{R_1} - \frac{1}{R_2}\right)$$

Lenz's law It states that "the direction of induced emf is always in such a way, that it opposes the causes due to which it is produced." This law follows the law of conservation of energy.

lepton A type of elementary particle including the electron, the muon and the neutrino.

lever A simple machine in the form of a straight or curved rod pivoted at a fixed point, around which it can turn. The weight which has to be lifted is called load L, the applied force is called effort E and the point, around which it can turn is called fulcrum F.

According to the positions of load, effort and fulcrum, there are three types of levers :

(i) **Class I lever** In this class of lever, fulcrum is between the load and the effort. e.g. simple balance, seesaw, scissor, etc.

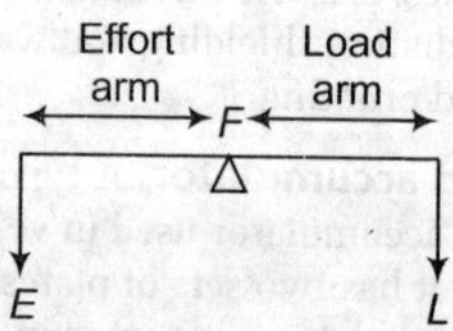

(ii) **Class II lever** In this class of lever, fulcrum is at one end and load is between the fulcrum and effort. e.g. net cracker.

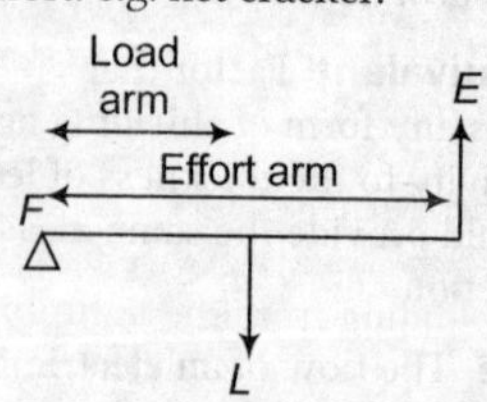

(iii) **Class III lever** In this class of lever, fulcrum is at one end, and effort is between the load and fulcrum. e.g. tongs.

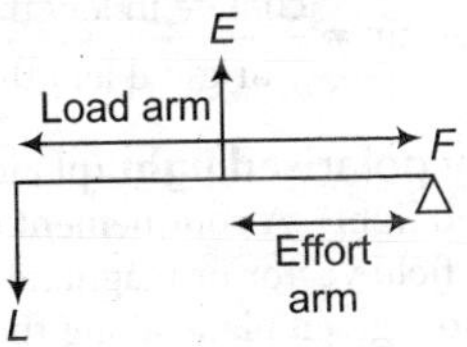

life time The average time spent by an elementary radioactive nucleus in a certain state, before it decay.

lift The force exerted in upward direction by a fluid on an object in its flow. This is the force that enables birds and winged aircraft to fly.

light A form of electromagnetic radiation which produces the sensation of sight on human eye. Its wavelength range is from 400 nm to 700 nm, which corresponds to red and violet colour.

light exposure The amount of light per unit area reaching a photographic film. It is measured in lux seconds and can be compoted from exposure value (EV). It is the product of illuminance and illumination time.

light year One light year is the distance travelled by light in one year in vacuum.

1 light year = speed of light in vacuum × one year

$$= 3 \times 10^8 \times (365 \times 24 \times 3600)$$

$$= 9.46 \times 10^{15} \text{ m}$$

lightning An electric discharge in atmosphere between the clouds or charged clouds and the earth.

lightning conductor Lightning conductor is a safety device used to protect building from the lightning. A metallic rod is installed in the walls of the building during its construction. One end of the rod is kept out in the air and the other buried deep in the ground. The rod provides easy route for the transfer of electric charge to the ground. When a charged cloud passes over the lightning conductor, opposite charge is induced at the sharp edges of the lightning conductor. It neutralise the cloud and transfer the charge to the earth without any loss to the building.

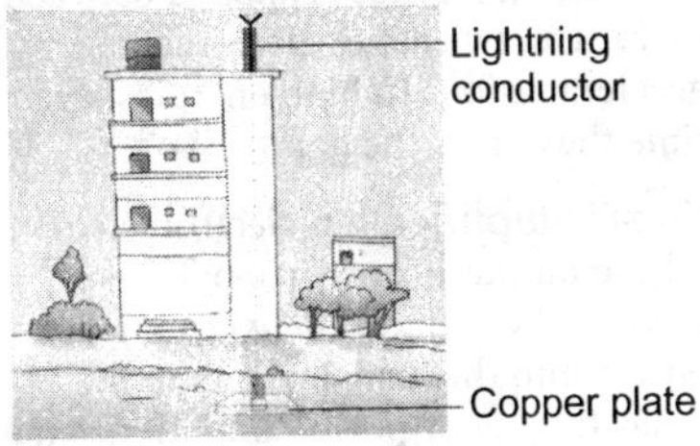

limiting current The limiting value of a faradaic current, which is approached rate of charge transfer to an electrode is increased. It can be approached e.g. by increasing the electric potential or decreasing the rate of mass transfer to the electrode.

limiting friction The maximum value of static friction when the body is at the verge of moving over the surface of another body.

Limiting friction $f_s = \mu_s R$

where, μ_s is the coefficient of limiting friction.

line of sight An imaginary straight line showing the visual range.

lines of force Imaginary lines in the field of force (electrostatic or magnetostatic) that represent the direction and strength of the field. The tangent drawn at any point on the line of force gives the direction of the field at that point.

line spectrum A spectrum composed of a number of discrete lines and each line correspond to a well defined wavelength. Line spectrum is produced by atoms or monoatomic ions of gases.

line width The width of a spectral line in wavelength terms.

linear accelerator A device used to accelerate the charged particles or ions. It consists of a series of cylindrical electrodes in a row having a common axis and separated by small gaps. Alternate electrodes are connected to each other and high frequency potential difference is applied between them. The two set of electrodes accelerates ions to high energies, every time they cross the gap.

linear amplifier An electronic circuit whose output is proportional to its input, but capable of delivering more power into the load. It refers to the radio-frequency power amplifier, some of which have output power measured in kilowatts and are used in a amateur ratio.

linear charge distribution Uniform charge distributed over a wire or rod is called linear charge distribution. Charge per unit length on wire or rod is called linear charge density and denoted by λ.

linear expansion Increase in length on heating is called linear expansion. If l_1 and l_2 are lengths of a rod at temperatures t_1°C and t_2°C, then

$$l_2 = l_1[1 + \alpha\,(t_2 - t_1)]$$

where, α is the linear coefficient of expansion.

linear magnification The ratio of size of image to the size of object.

linear momentum Linear momentum of a particle is equal to the product of its mass and velocity. It is denoted by p. It is expressed as

$$p = mv$$

Its SI unit is kg-ms^{-1}.

linear motor A type of induction motor, in which the rotor is rectangular and travels along rails.

linear strain The fractional change in length, i.e. the ratio of change in length Δl to the original length l is called linear strain.

$$\text{Linear strain} = \frac{\text{change in length } \Delta l}{\text{original length } l}$$

linearly polarised light (plane polarised light) A confinement of electric field vector or magnetic field vector to a given plane along the direction of propagation.

linkage A quantity related with the magnetic flux in a coil or current, which equals the product of the number of lines of magnetic flux times the number of turns in the coil or circuit.

liquefication A change of state from gases to their liquid state.

liquid crystal A substance that flows like a liquid but has some order in its arrangement of molecules. Few liquid crystals change orientation in an electric field and therefore, are used in liquid crystal displays (LCDs).

Liquid Crystal Display (LCD) A type of digital display used in calculators, watches and other electronic equipments. Its working is based on properties of liquid crystals.

liquid drop model Model of the atomic nucleus in which the nucleons are regarded as being analogous to the molecules in a liquid, the interactions between which the droplet shape is maintained by surface tension.

Lissajous figures Patterns obtained by combining two simple harmonic motions in different directions. Different patterns are obtained depending on the frequencies and phase differences. When two periodic motions are of same frequency and right angles to each other, are combined the resultant figure varies from straight line to an ellipse.

lithium battery A type of voltaic cell containing lithium or lithium compounds.

litre A unit of volume equal to 10^{-3} m^3. One litre is the volume of kilogram of pure water at 4°C and standard pressure.

live wire The electric power is supplied by two wires. One of them is at higher potential and called live wire. Generally, it is red in colour. The other wire is at low potential and is called neutral wire. In general, it is of black colour.

Lloyd's mirror An arrangement in which light needs a mirror at grazing incidence and is reflected to interfere with the direct radiation. Interference of the reflected light with the direct light produces fringes.

load (electrical)

1. A device or material, where in signal power is dissipated or received.
2. Refers to the power delivered by a machine, generator or electronic circuit or device.

locomotive A self-propelled vehicle.

lodestone Naturally occurring magnetic rocks. It is oxide of iron called magnetite.

logic gate A digital circuit which follows certain logical relationship between input and output voltages. A logic gate is designed to perform a particular logical function based on the concepts of either-or and neither-nor. The five common logic gates are OR, AND, NOT, NAND and NOR. Each logic gate is indicated by a symbol and its function is defined by a truth table.

(i) OR **gate** A logic gate whose output is zero, if both inputs are zero.

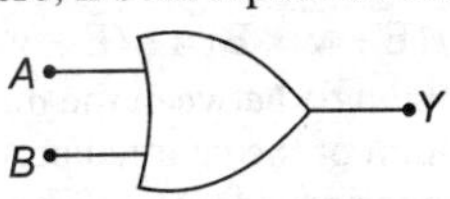

$Y = A + B$

Symbol of OR gate

Truth Table

A	B	Y
0	0	0
0	1	1
1	0	1
1	1	1

(ii) AND **gate** A logic gate having two or more inputs and one output. This is obtained only when both inputs are 1.

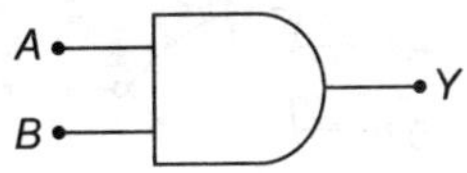

$Y = A \cdot B$

Symbol of AND gate

Truth Table

A	B	Y
0	0	0
0	1	0
1	0	0
1	1	1

(iii) NOT **gate** A logic gate with one input and one output.

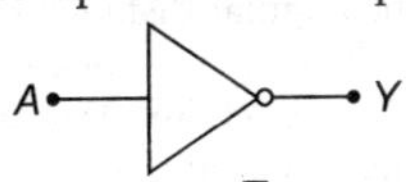

$Y = \overline{A}$

Symbol of NOT gate

Truth Table

A	B
0	1
1	0

(iv) NAND **gate** This is an AND gate followed by a NOT gate. If inputs are 1, then output is not 1.

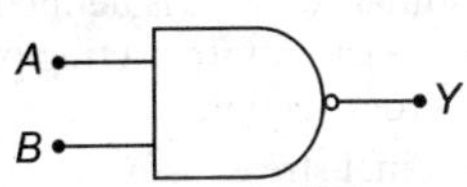

$Y = \overline{A \cdot B}$

Symbol of NAND gate

Truth Table

A	B	Y
0	0	1
0	1	1
1	0	1
1	1	0

(v) NOR **gate** A logic gate having two or more inputs and one output. Its output is 1 only when both inputs are 0.

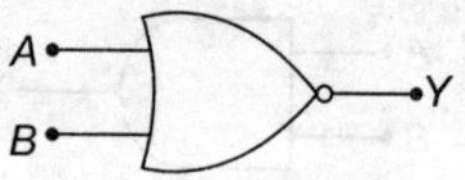

$Y = \overline{A + B}$

Symbol of NOR gate

Truth Table

A	B	Y
0	0	1
0	1	0
1	0	0
1	1	0

longitude Imaginary lines drawn on Earth globe that passes through both poles. The angular distance around the globe is 360°, which is measured as 180° East of Greenwich and 180° West Greenwich. Any place on the Earth can be specified by the combination of longitude and latitude.

longitudinal strain The ratio of change in length Δl to the original length l is called longitudinal strain.

$$\text{Longitudinal strain} = \frac{\Delta l}{l}$$

longitudinal stress If the deforming forces are along the length of the body, then the stress produced is called longitudinal stress. It is defined as internal reaction force acting per unit area of cross-section.

Longitudinal stress

$$= \frac{\text{internal reaction force}}{\text{area of cross-section}}$$

longitudinal wave The wave produced when the vibration of the particles of the medium are parallel to the direction of propagation of wave. Velocity of longitudinal wave is

$$v = \sqrt{E/\rho}$$

where, E = coefficient of elasticity of the medium and ρ = density of the medium.

long sightedness A visual defect in which a person can see far away objects clearly but cannot see near by objects clearly. The cause of this defect is shorting of eye ball or increase in focal length of the eye lens, due to which the eye form an image behind the retina. This defect can be removed by using convex lens of suitable is spectacles.

loop The closed path of an electric circuit.

Lorentz-Fitzgerald contraction Contraction in length of a moving object by a factor of $\sqrt{1 - \frac{v^2}{c^2}}$ in the direction of motion, where, v speed of the object and c speed of light in vacuum. The failure of the Michelson-Morley experiment to show the motion of the Earth with respect to other was explained by Lorentz and Fitzgerald by the above hypothesis. According to the theory of relativity, the length of a body as measured by an observer in uniform relative motion is less than that measured by an observer at rest.

Lorentz force The force F acting on any moving charge q in a uniform magnetic field **B** and electric field **E** is given by

$$\mathbf{F} = q\,(\mathbf{E} + \mathbf{v} \times \mathbf{B}) = q\,(\mathbf{E} + v\,B\sin\theta\,\hat{\mathbf{n}})$$

where, θ angle between the direction of the motion of the charged particle and the magnetic field. Sometimes, the magnetic term in the force is referred as Lorentz force.

lossy Involves huge amount of loss in the case of a circuit or power line.

loudness The magnitude of the sensation produced when a sound reaches the ear. The sensation produced by any sound is related to sound intensity. It is determined by the amplitude of the sound waves and it is expressed in decibels.

loudspeaker An apparatus that converts electrical impulses into sound.

low frequency A radio frequency in the range between 3 kHz and 300 kHz.

low pass filter A filter that passes signals with a frequency lower than a certain cut-off frequency and attenuates signals with frequencies higher than the cut-off frequency.

***L-R* circuit** An AC circuit containing a resistance R and inductance L in series is called an L-R circuit.

lumen The SI unit of luminous flux. One lumen is defined as the luminous flux, emitted by a uniform point source of intensity one candela in a cone of solid angle one steradian.

luminance A measure of surface brightness expressed as the luminous flux, per unit solid angle per unit projected area. Its unit is candela per square metre.

luminance intensity The luminous flux emitted per unit solid angle by a point source in a given direction. Its unit is candela.

luminescence The emission of light by a substance not resulting from heat; it is thus a form of cold body radiation. It can be caused by chemical reactions, electrical energy, subatomic motions or stress on a crystal.

luminosity The observed brightness or luminous intensity of a source of visible radiation.

luminous flux The rate of flow of energy of visible radiation.

luminous object An object which emits its own light is called a luminous object. e.g. Sun and other stars.

lunar eclipse When the Sun, the Earth and the Moon are in a straight line and the Earth lies between the Sun and the Moon and therefore, Moon is not visible at Earth. This is called lunar eclipse.

lunar time Time based on the lunar month (the time between successive New Moons).

lux The SI unit of illumination equal to the illumination produced by a luminous flux of one lumen, falling on a surface of one square metre.

Lyman series A series of lines in the ultraviolet spectrum emitted by excited hydrogen atoms. When an electron jumps from energy levels $n = 2, 3, 4, \ldots$ to energy level $n = 1$, then the obtained spectral line is a member of Lyman series. Its wavelength is given by

$$\frac{1}{\lambda} = R\left[\frac{1}{1^2} - \frac{1}{n^2}\right]$$

where, $n = 2, 3, 4, \ldots$ and R is Rydberg's constant.

M

mach angle If a body moves with a supersonic velocity *v*, through a fluid from a point *X* to a point *Y* in time *t*, then when the body is at *Y*, the spherical pressure wave originating from *X* will have a radius *ct*, where, *c* = local speed of sound in the fluid.

mach number The ratio of speed of body to the local speed of sound. The speed of body is therefore called supersonic, if its mach number is greater than unity.
Similarly, the pressure waves from the other points between *X* and *Y* will have corresponding radii, such that all the spherical pressure waves combine to form a right conical wavefront with its vertex at *Y*. The semiangle of the cone β is called the mach angle.

machine A device for transmitting power from one place to another or a device for doing work, in which small force overcomes a longer force.

macro Prefix meaning large or long in size, or duration.

macroscopic Visible to naked eye without use of any instrument.

macroscopic state The state of matter characterised by the statistical properties of its components. Kinetic theory is an analysis of the macroscopic state.

magic number Several numbers of neutrons or protons characterise stable atomic nuclei. They are 2, 8, 20, 28, 50 and 82.

magnet Substance which has a tendency to attract iron towards itself. Some of the commonly known properties of a magnet are

(i) When a bar magnet is freely suspended, it points in the North-South direction. The tip which points to the geographic North, is called the North pole and the tip which points to the geographic South is called the South pole of the magnet.
(ii) Like magnetic poles repel and unlike magnetic poles attract each other.
(iii) We cannot isolate the North, or South pole of a magnet. If a bar magnet is broken into two halves, we get two similar bar magnets with somewhat weaker properties. Therefore, isolated magnetic North and South poles known as magnetic monopoles do not exist.

magnetic amplifier transducer A device, so arranged that a small controlling direct current input can produce large changes in coupled alternating current circuits.

magnetic axis The line joining the two poles of a magnet inside its body.

magnetic bottle Magnetic bottle refers to the magnetic field applied to contain a plasma in controlled fusion experiments.

magnetic circuit A closed path formed by lines of magnetic flux of a magnetic field.

magnetic compass A magnetic needle which always direct in North-South direction.

magnetic constant *See* permeability.

magnetic cooling A method of attaining very low temperatures. In this method, a salt is magnetised isothermally and demagnetised adiabatically.

magnetic core Computer storage device consisting of a ferromagnetic ring wound with wires, a current flowing in the wires polarises the core, which can therefore adopt one of two states (making it a bistable device).

magnetic declination The angle subtended between the geographic meridian and magnetic meridian. It is the angle by which North as shown by a magnetic compass deviates from true North.

The position of magnetic North is subject to significant variation with time, and for this reason magnetic declination is not a constant factor.

magnetic deviation The error induced in a compass by local magnetic fields which must be allowed for, along with magnetic declination, if accurate bearings are to be calculated. Magnetic deviation is used by some to mean the same as magnetic declination.

magnetic dip The angle subtended between the magnetic axis of Earth and horizontal. Its value is 0° at magnetic meridian and 90° at magnetic poles of the Earth.

magnetic dipole A system of two equal and opposite magnetic poles separated by a very small distance.

e.g. a small bar magnet, magnetic needle, an electron revolving in an orbit, etc.

magnetic dipole moment If m is the magnetic pole strength and 2l is the magnetic length for a magnetic dipole moment **p**, then dipole moment is expressed as

$$\mathbf{p} = m \times 2\mathbf{l}.$$

It is a measure of the strength of the magnet. Its direction is from S-pole to N-pole. Its unit is ampere-metre.

magnetic domain Group of atoms which are aligned in such a way, that their magnetic moments are in same direction. It occurs in a ferromagnetic material. There are many randomly oriented domains in a permanent magnet.

magnetic drum Computer storage device consisting of a rotatable drum coated with magnetic material, such as iron oxide. Data is stored or retrieved through one or more read-write heads.

magnetic effect An optical effect observed in a magnetic field.

magnetic elements of Earth There are three elements of the magnetic field of Earth. These are the magnetic declination, magnetic dip and horizontal component of Earth's magnetic field. These elements can define the Earth's magnetic field at any point on the Earth's surface.

magnetic energy (potential energy) Defined as the work of magnetic force on re-alignment of the vector of the magnetic dipole moment.

Energy stored in a magnetic field is

$$u = \frac{1}{2}\frac{B^2}{\mu}$$

where, μ = permeability

magnetic equator of Earth An imaginary circle on the surface of Earth equidistant from magnetic poles. At the magnetic equator, magnetic field is horizontal and of intensity 0.35 gauss or 0.35×10^{-4} tesla.

magnetic field The region surrounding a magnet, in which the force of the magnet can be detected. Magnetic field is a quantity that has both direction and magnitude.

m

The direction of the magnetic field is taken to be the direction, in which a North pole of the compass needle moves inside it. Therefore, the field lines emerge from North pole and merge at the South pole. Inside the magnet, the direction of field lines is from its South pole to its North pole. Thus, the magnetic field lines are closed curves.

The relative strength of the magnetic field is shown by the degree of closeness of the field lines.

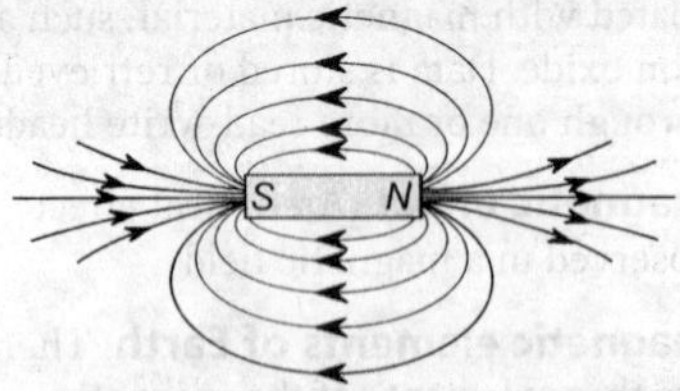

Magnetic field of bar magnet

magnetic field line An imaginary line drawn in magnetic field, of which a free magnetic North pole will move. The direction of magnetic field **B** at any point, is the tangent to the field line at the point. The number of field lines that pass through unit area of a surface held perpendicular to the lines is proportional to the strength of magnetic field in that region. The field lines are closed curves. They start from the North pole and end at North pole itself *via* South pole.

magnetic field strength Its symbol is *H*. Force exerted on a unit *N*-pole at a given point in a magnetic field. Its unit is ampere per metre.

magnetic flux The magnetic flux for a surface, is the surface integral of the magnetic field over that surface.

Thus $\phi_n = \mathbf{B} \cdot \mathbf{dS}$.

The SI unit of magnetic flux is weber Wb, with

$$1 \text{ Wb} = 1 \text{ T-m}^2.$$

magnetic flux density Product of magnetic intensity and permeability. It is also called magnetic induction. It is a vector which specifies the magnitude and direction of magnetic field at a point. It is equal to the magnetic flux passing through a unit area of a magnetic field in a direction perpendicular to the direction of the magnetic force.

magnetic focusing Focusing of charged particle (beam) making use of magnetic field.

magnetic hysteresis The relationship between field strength *H* and magnetisation *m*. For ferromagnetic material, it is not linear. This curve increases rapidly at first and then, approaches an asymptote called magnetic saturation. On reducing, the magnetic field, *M* follows a different curve and results in hysteresis loop which is also called main loop.

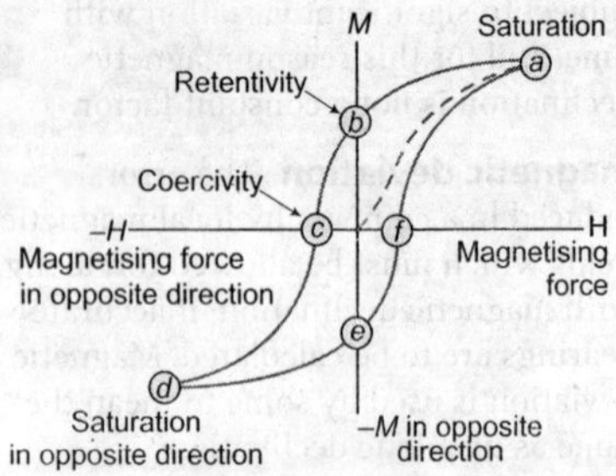

Hysteresis loop

magnetic induction In a magnetic material, magnetisation include in it, by placing it in the electromagnetic field of a current carrying coil or by stroking it with a permanent magnet.

magnetic intensity The force experienced by a unit *N*-pole placed in a magnetic field. Its unit is Am^{-1} and also called magnetic field strength.

magnetic leakage A magnetic method of non-destructive testing which is used to defect corrosion and pitting in steel structures, most commonly pipelines and storage tanks. The basic principle is that a powerful magnet is used to magnetise the steel.

magnetic length The distance between the magnetic poles, when the poles of magnet are not located at the ends but are slightly inside the body.

magnetic lens Arrangement of electromagnets used to focus a beam of charged particles.

magnetic levitation A method by which an object is suspended with no support other than the magnetic fields. Magnetic force is used to counteract the effects of gravitational acceleration and any other accelerations.

magnetic meridian A vertical plane,passing through the axis of a freely suspended magnet.

magnetic moment A measure of the strength of a magnet. It is possessed by an individual atom or molecule, a moving charge, a permanent magnet or a current carrying coil. It is defined as the torque τ observed in a unit field at 90° to the magnetic axis,

$$m = \frac{\tau}{B}$$

Its unit is ampere-metre^2.

magnetic monopole A hypothetical single magnetic pole as existence of single magnetic pole is not possible.

magnetic north Point on the Earth's surface towards which a magnetic compass points. The exact location of magnetic North varies seasonally and from year-to-year.

magnetic permeability The measure of the ability of a material to support the formation of a magnetic field within itself. It is the degree of magnetisation that a material obtains in response to applied magnetic field.

magnetic polarisation The vector field that expresses the density of permanent or induced magnetic dipole moments in a magnetic material.

magnetic poles One of the two points, called North and South poles to and from which magnetic field appear to radiate. Magnetic lines of force move from magnetic North pole towards magnetic South pole outside the magnet and from South pole towards North pole inside the magnet.

magnetic poles of Earth Points where the magnetic axis of Earth meets the surface of Earth. Magnetic poles of Earth do not coincide with Earth's geographic poles. The positions of magnetic poles of Earth is not permanent but changes over a long period of time.

magnetic potential Magnetic potential at a point in a magnetic field is numerically equal to work done in bringing a unit North pole from infinity to that point against the direction of field.

magnetic resistance The ratio of magnetomotive force to total magnetic flux in a magnetic circuit. Its SI unit is henry metre^{-1}.

magnetic shielding The process of protecting certain rêgion from external magnetic field. A screen made of high permeability material, is used to isolate any device from unwanted magnetic fields.

magnetic shunt A piece magnetic material in parallel with a portion of a magnetic circuit so arranged so as to vary the amount of magnetic flux in that portion of the circuit.

magnetic storm Local disturbances in the Earth's magnetic field, which can disrupt telecommunications and which are probably caused by gusts of charged particles emanating from the Sun.

magnetic strip Commonly used in magnetic strip cards which are capable of storing data.

magnetic substance Substances which on being placed in a magnetic field get attracted by magnet are known as magnetic substance. They are classified as

(i) Diamagnetic substances
(ii) Paramagnetic substances
(iii) Ferromagnetic substances

Diamagnetism which is common to all substances, is due to orbital motion of electrons. Paramagnetism is due to electron spin, it is a property of materials containing unpaired electrons. Ferromagnetism, the strongest effect, also involves electron spin and the alignment of magnetic moments in domains.

magnetic susceptibility The magnetisation per unit field strength. It is denoted by χ. It is a dimensionless quantity, hence it has no units. For a large number of magnetic materials, the magnetisation I is directly proportional to the magnetic field strength H.

$$I \propto H$$

or $$I = \chi H$$

$$\therefore \quad \chi = I/H$$

magnetic tape Plastic tape coated with a ferromagnetic powder used in tape recorders. The tape is passed over the gap in a magnetic circuit which is modulated in accordance which can be played back through a suitable circuit. Magnetic tape is also used in the backing storage of computers.

magnetic variation The changes in different magnetic elements with time at a point on the Earth's surface.

magnetisation Difference between the ratio of the magnetic induction to the permeability and the magnetic intensity, its SI unit is Am^{-1}. It represents departure from randomness of magnetic domains. It is a vector quantity. Its magnitude is defined as the magnetic moment per unit volume

$$I = \frac{\text{magnetic moment}}{\text{volume of the substance}}$$

magnetism The phenomena associated with magnetic fields. It also refers to the presence of magnetic properties in materials. Different types of magnetic behaviour result from the type of atom.

magnetite An ore of iron, Fe_3O_4.

magneto An electric generator that uses permanent magnets to produce pulses of alternating current.

magnetocaloric effect The change in temperature of a sample on changing the external magnetic field.

magneto elastic effect A name given to the change of the magnetic susceptibility of a material when subjected to a mechanical stress. It is also known as the inverse magnetostrictive effect.

magnetohydrodynamics (MHD) Branch of Physics that deals with the behaviour of a conducting fluid under the influence of a magnetic flux.

magnetometer The form of compass used to compare magnetic field strengths. *See* deflection magnetometer.

magneton A term used for atomic, molecular or nuclear magnets to represent their respective magnetic moments.

magnetoresistive effect The property of a material to change the value of its electrical resistance when an external magnetic field is applied to it.

magnetostatics Study of the effect of stationary magnetic poles. Although, free magnetic poles do not exist.

magnetostriction The change in length and section area of a ferromagnetic rod with change in external field.

magnetron Electronic device that is used to provide pulsed emissions in microwave telecommunications, radar, transmitters and microwave cookers.

magnification The ratio of height of the image I to the height of the object O. It is represented by m.

Magnification, m

$$= \frac{\text{height of the image, } I}{\text{height of the object, } O}$$

For a spherical mirror,

$$m = \frac{I}{O} = -\frac{v}{u}$$

For a lens, $m = \frac{I}{O} = \frac{v}{u}$

where, u = distance of the object and v = distance of the image from the mirror lens.

magnifying glass A convex lens of small focal length. The lens is usually fixed to a frame with a handle to make it easy to use.

It is used to get magnified and erect image of small objects. A watchmaker's glass is also a magnifying lens.

magnifying power The ratio of angles subtended by image and object at eyelens, when both are assumed to be placed atleast distance of distinct vision.

magnitude It refers to the quantitative aspect of any attribute. So, a substance has a mass of certain magnitude. Speed is an indication of the magnitude the more a particular substance is.

magnox A type of alloy containing magnesium 88%, aluminium 11% and traces of other elements. It is used for canning the uranium rods in some types of nuclear reactors.

magnus effect A ball which is spinning, drags air along with it. If the surface is rough, more air will be dragged.

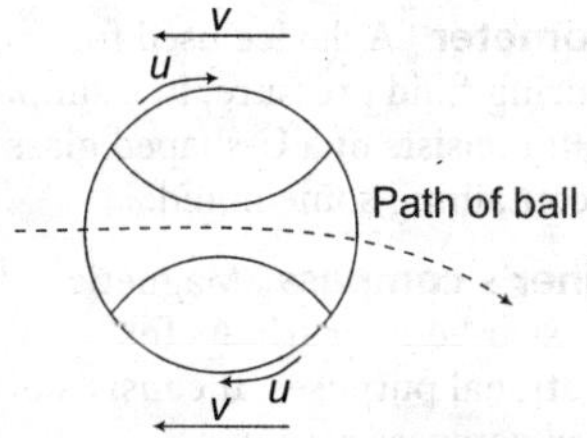

Representation of magnus effect

Figure shows the streamlines of air for a ball which is moving and spinning at the same time. The ball is moving forward and relative to it, the air is moving backwards. Therefore, the velocity of air above the ball relative to it, is larger and below, it is smaller. This difference in the velocities of air results in the pressure difference between the lower and upper faces and there is a net upward force on the ball. This dynamic lift due to spinning,is magnus effect.

majority carriers Charge carriers present in majority in any substance. Such as in p-type semiconductor, holes and in n-type semiconductor, electrons are majority charge carriers.

malleability The property of a substance that allows it to be beaten or rolled into thin sheets.

Malus law The intensity of light transmitted through an analyser, is proportional to $\cos^2\theta$, where θ = angle between the transmission planes of the polariser and the analyser.

manganese A transition metal occuring naturally as oxides. Nodules found on the ocean floor are about 25% manganese. Its symbol is Mn.

manganin Alloy of copper with manganese and nickel that exhibits high electrical resistance and which is used in resistors. It contains 13% to 18% of manganese, 1% to 4% of nickel and remaining part of copper.

manometer A device used for measuring fluid pressure. In a simple form, it consists of a U-shaped glass tube containing some liquid.

Mariner's compass Magnetic compass used by mariners for navigational purposes. It consists of a pivoted compass card in a gimbalmounted, non-ferrous metal bowl.

Mars The next planet in terms of distance from the Sun, is Mars or Mangal. It appears reddish and therefore, it is also called the red planet. It is visible from the Earth for most part of the year. It has two natural satellites named Phobos and Deimos.

MASER An abbreviation of Microwave Amplification by Stimulated Emission of Radiation. It is a device for producing an intense source of coherent microwave radiation. Masers, like lasers, operate by population inversion and stimulated emission.

m

mass Quantity of matter in an object. The SI unit of mass is kilogram.

mass absorption coefficient A measure of how well an object absorbs a given radiation. It is similar as linear absorption constant divided by density.

mass-energy relation Deduction from Einstein's special theory of relativity that all energy has mass;

$$E = mc^2,$$

where, E = energy,
m = amount of mass and
c = speed of light.

mass moment The product of the mass of an object and the distance to some point, line or plane. It depends on the situation, there are various mass moments for different situation.

mass spectrograph Vacuum system in which positive rays of charged atoms (ions) are passed through electric and magnetic fields, so as to separate them in order of their charge to mass ratio on a photographic plate. It measures relative atomic masses of isotopes with precision.

mass spectrometer Device used to measure the mass of atoms or molecules.

mass spectrum Indication of the distribution in mass, or in mass-to-charge ratio, of ionised atoms or molecules produced by a mass-spectrograph.

matter Substance that occupies space and has the property of inertia.

matter waves The waves associated with moving particles such as; electrons, protons, neutrons and other fundamental particles, and even atoms and molecules. These waves are also called de-Broglie waves.

Maxwell A unit of magnetic flux in CGS system. It is equal to 10^{-8} Wb.

Maxwell-Boltzmann distribution Law that describes the distribution of speed among molecules of a gas in thermal equilibrium. In a system consisting of N molecules that are independent of each other, except that they exchange energy on collision, it is clearly impossible to say, what velocity any particular molecule will have.

Maxwell's cork screw rule If a right handed cork screw is imagined to be rotated in such a direction that the tip shows the direction of the current, then the direction of rotation of thumb gives the direction of magnetic field lines.

Maxwell's distribution This distribution describes particle speed of idealised gases, where the particle moves freely inside a stationary container without interacting with one another or very brief collision.

Maxwell's equations A set of partial differential equations that form the foundation of classical electrodynamics, classical optics and electric circuits. The equations describe how electric and magnetic fields are generated and altered by each other and by charges and current. These are named after physicist and mathematician James Clerk Maxwell.

Point form	Integral form
$\nabla \times H = J_c + \frac{\partial D}{\partial t}$	$\oint H.\,dl - \int_S \left(J_c + \frac{\partial D}{\partial t}\right).\,dS$ (Ampere's law)
$\nabla \times E = -\frac{\partial B}{\partial t}$	$\oint E.\,dl - \int_S \left(-\frac{\partial B}{\partial t}\right).\,dS$ (Faraday's law, S fixed)
$\nabla . D = \rho$	$\oint_S D.\,dS = \int_r \rho\, dv$ (Gauss's law)
$\nabla . B = 0$	$\oint_S B.\,dS = 0$ (non-existence of monopole)

Mayer's relationship

$$C_p - C_V = R$$

where, C_p = molar specific heat of gas at constant pressure ($JK^{-1}mol^{-1}$),
C_V = molar specific heat of gas at constant volume and
R = gas constant (8.314 $JK^{-1}mol^{-1}$).

mean absolute error The arithmetic mean of all the absolute errors is taken as mean absolute error of the measured physical quantity. It is represented by Δa_{mean}.

mean deviation A measure of dispersion. It is computed by taking the arithmetic mean of the absolute values of the deviations.

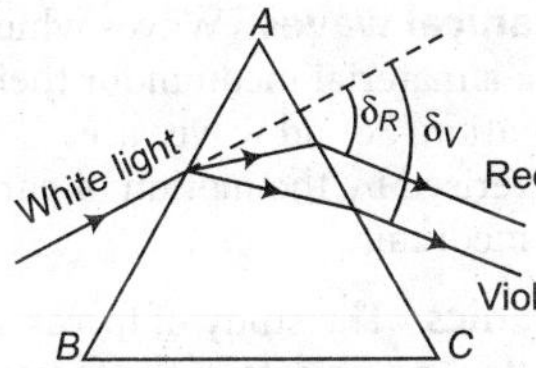

Dispersion of white light through a prism

$$\delta_m = \frac{\delta_R + \delta_V}{2}$$

mean free path The average distance of a molecule which can travel without colliding. The mean free path, in gases, is of the order of thousands of angstroms.

mean free time The average time that elapses between the collisions of the molecules in a gas.

mean life The average time for which a radioactive nucleus exists before it disintegrates. It is the reciprocal of the decay constant.

mean solar day Average value over a year of the solar day, the constant time between two transits of the Sun across the meridian. It equals to 24 hours.

mean velocity of fluid through the pipe

$$V_m = \frac{R^2}{8\eta}, \frac{\Delta p}{l}$$

mechanical advantage The ratio of output force to the input force applied to any mechanism.

mechanical energy The total sum of potential and kinetic energies.

mechanical equivalent of heat A constant which relates heat and work. If W work is done by heat Q, then

$$W = JQ$$

where, J is called mechanical equivalent of heat.Its value is 4.18 J/cal.

mechanical waves Waves which require a material medium for their propagation. Sound waves are characterised by the motion of particles in the medium.

mechanics The study of forces and their effect on objects. If the forces on an object or in a system ,cause no change of momentum, the object or system is in equilibrium. Its three divisions are kinematics, dynamics and statics.

mechanism A device designed to transform input forces and movement into a desired set of output forces and movement.

medium The nature of the space through which some sound or something is transmitted or propagated. It can be in the form of solid, liquid, gas or a vacuum. Sound moves through a medium from the point of generation to the listener.

medium frequency A radio frequency in the range between 3 MHz and 0.3 MHz (wavelength 100 – 1000m).

mega Metrix prefix meaning million times,
e.g. 1 Megahertz (MHz) $= 10^6$ hertz (Hz).

mega hertz Unit of frequency of one million hertz. Its symbol is MHz
i.e. $1\text{ MHz} = 10^6\text{ Hz}$.

megaton A unit used to express the explosive power of nuclear weapons. One megaton is an explosive power equivalent to that of one million tons of TNT.

megawatt hour One million watt hour.Its symbol is MWh.

Meissner effect The falling off the magnetic flux within a superconductor metal when it is cooled to a temperature below the critical temperature in a magnetic field.

melody Musical sound that gives a pleasing effect to the ear.

membrane A two-dimensional structure at the boundary between two distinct materials which resists the movement of molecules between the two phases.

meniscus The curved surface of a liquid or a column of a liquid in a tube or vessel. The shape of the meniscus depends on the angle of contact between the surface and the liquid. If the angle > 90°, the meniscus is concave. If it is < 90°, it is convex.

mercury A transition metal that is liquid at room temperature (bromine is the only other element with this property). The vapour is very poisonous. Mercury is used in thermometers, special amalgams for dentistry, scientific apparatus and in mercury cells.

mercury barometer A barometer in which the weight of a column of mercury in a glass tube having a sealed top, is balanced against that of atmosphere pressing on an open vessel of mercury at the base of the column. The height of mercury column changes with change in atmospheric pressure.

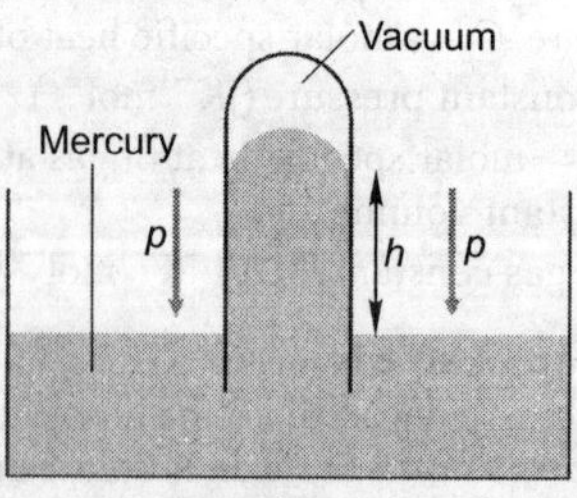

Mercury barometer

mercury cell A voltaic or electrolytic cell ,in which one or both of the electrodes consist of mercury or an amalgam. Amalgam electrodes are used in the Daniell cell and the weston cadmium cell.

mercury thermometer A liquid in glass thermometer that uses mercury as its working substance. It consists of a thin capillary tube graduated in degrees, at the base of which is a bulb containing mercury. When the temperature rises, the mercury expands along the tube. The position indicates the temperature.

meridian Refers to the great circle of Earth, that passes through the poles and any given point on the surface of earth.

mesa transistor A transistor designed in such a manner that its base region lies above the surface of the substrate.

MESFET Stands for metal-semiconductor field effect transistor. It is quite similar to a JEFT in construction and terminology. The difference is that instead of using a *p-n* junction for a gate, as Schottky junction is used.

mesh A network of lines joining nodes in particular in electric circuits.

mesons Elementary particles which are thought to be responsible for the exchange forces between nucleons in a nucleus. Their masses are more than that of an electron and less than those of nucleons.

mesosphere The region between the ionosphere and the exosphere, extending from about 250-650 miles above the surface of earth.

metacentre The point of intersection between two vertical lines, one through the centre of buoyancy of a hull in equilibrium and other through the centre of buoyancy when hull is slightly inclined to one side towards one end.

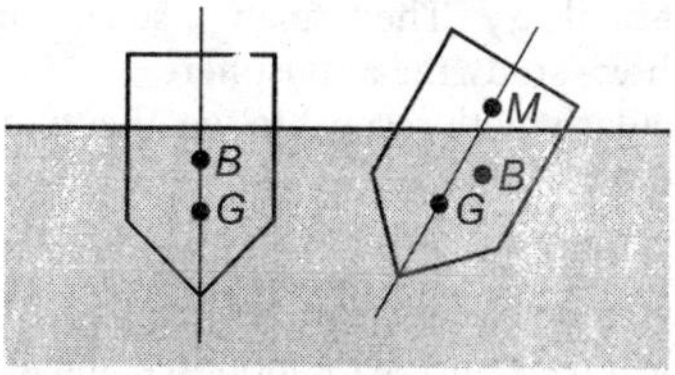

Metacentre

metal A material that is typically hard, opaque, shiny and has good electrical and thermal conductivity. These are generally malleable, ductile.

metamaterial A type of synthetic composite materials with a complex nanostructure, so as to have unusual properties that do not occur naturally.

metastable The state of equilibrium of a system where in the system though apparently state changes to new state on being disturbed slightly.

meteor Meteors are very small stone-like objects that are revolving around the sun. When some of them enter by chance into the earth's atmosphere, it gets heated due to friction of air.
The heat produced is so high that the meteor begins to glow and evaporates within a short time. The path of the meteor, therefore, appears as a streak of light in the night sky. The meteors are commonly known as shooting stars although they are not stars.

meteor shower When the earth crosses the tail of a comet, swarms of meteors are seen. These are known as meteor showers. Some meteor showers occur at regular intervals each year.

meteorite Some meteors are large so that they can reach the earth before they evaporate completely. The body that reaches the earth is called a meteorite. Meteorites help scientists in investigating the nature of the material, from which the solar system was formed.

meteorology The branch of science in which we study the atmosphere, particularly with respect to weather and climate.

meter bridge It is an application of Wheatstone bridge. A meter length of uniform resistance wire mounted above a scale marked in millimetre with suitable terminal points added to make the device adaptable either as a Wheatstone bridge.

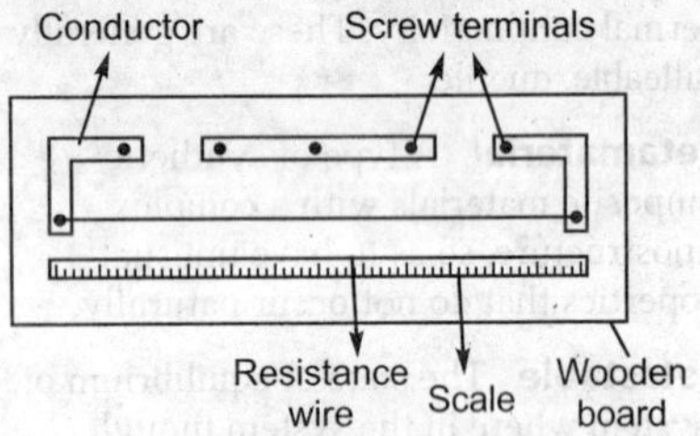

Meter bridge

The wire acts as two arms of the bridge resistors and as a potentiometer, the potential drop along the wire is proportional to the length of wire.

metre The SI unit of length, defined as the length of the path travelled by light in a vacuum in a time of 1/2, 77, 792, 458 second.

metric system A system of units based on the metre and the kilogram using multiples and submultiples of 10.

metric tonne A unit of mass equal to 1000 kg.

mho A unit of conductance

$$1 \text{ mho} = 1 \text{ ohm}^{-1} \text{ or amp/volt.}$$

Michelson-Morley experiment Experiment conducted by Michelson-Morley in 1881 to show that the velocity of light is not influenced by motion of medium, through which it passes.

microammeter The instrument used for measurement of very small electric currents calibrated in microamperes.

microbalance A balance for weighing masses of fraction of gram.

microgravity The condition in which people or objects appear to be weightless. This effect can be seen when astronauts and objects floats in space.

micron A unit of length

$$1\ \mu\text{m} = 10^{-6} \text{ m.}$$

microphone An instrument for converting sound waves into electric energy. The pressure variations of the sound wave are converted into variations in an electrical signal.

microscope A device used to obtain an enlarged image of very small objects that cannot be seen with unaided or naked eyes. A magnifying glass may be considered to be the simplest form of a microscope.
The most commonly used compound microscope has two convex lenses fixed at two ends of a small cylindrical tube. The lens fixed at one end of the microscope and towards the object is called objective and the second lens, through which we see the object is called eyepiece. The objective lens forms a real, inverted and enlarged image of the object. The distance between the two lenses of the microscope is so adjusted that the image formed by the objective falls between the eyepiece and its focus. The eyepiece, therefore forms a further enlarged but virtual image of the object.

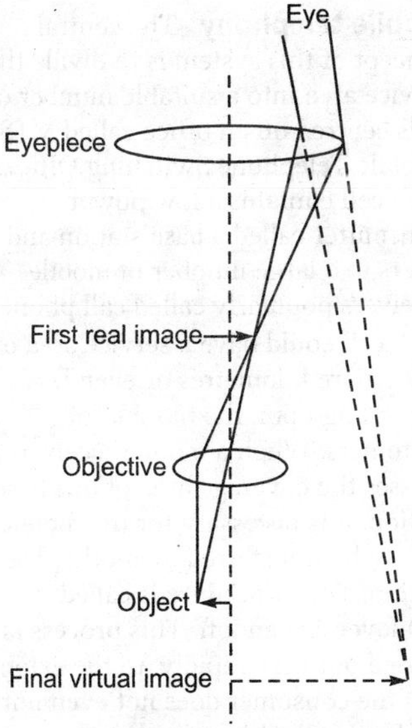

Compound microscope

microwaves A form of electromagnetic radiation, ranging in wavelength from about 1 mm. Microwaves are produced by various electronic devices including the klyston, they are often carried over short distances in tubes of rectangular section called waveguides.

migration The resultant movement of matter particles as a conclusion of their random motion under some force. This term is common in the case of the movement of ions during electrolysis and of dopant particles during semiconductor doping.

mil An abbreviation of either a milli metre (ml) or a thousand of an inch (0.001 inch, equal to 0.0254 mm).

mile A unit of length equal to 1760 yards.

miller indices A system of notation to represent uniquely the planes of atoms or molecules in a crystalline solid.

milli A prefix denoting 10^{-3}.
e.g. 1 millimetre (mm) = 10^{-3} metre.

milliammeter An instrument for measuring electric currents of a few milliamperes.

minimum deviation A convenient way to measure the refractive index of a prism is to direct a light ray through the prism, so it produces the minimum angle of deviation.

minority charge carriers In *p*-type semiconductors, the electrons and in *n*-type semiconductors, the holes are called minority charge carriers.

minute Unit of time equal to 60 seconds.

mirage An optical illusion caused by total internal reflection in the air. It is common when the ground is strongly heated by the sun so that the air in contact with the ground is much warmer than the air above.
Light from an object above the ground is refracted and totally internally reflected by the warm air to produce an image. Mirages are also sometimes observed next to very warm vertical surfaces.

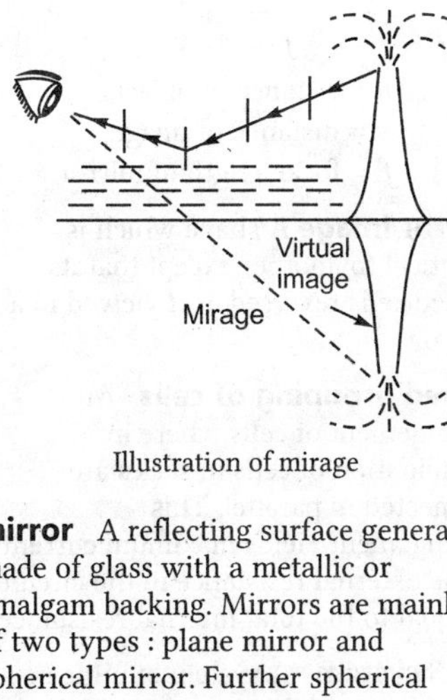

Illustration of mirage

mirror A reflecting surface generally made of glass with a metallic or amalgam backing. Mirrors are mainly of two types : plane mirror and spherical mirror. Further spherical mirrors are of two types : convex mirror and concave mirror.

Formation of image by spherical mirror are shown in the figure below

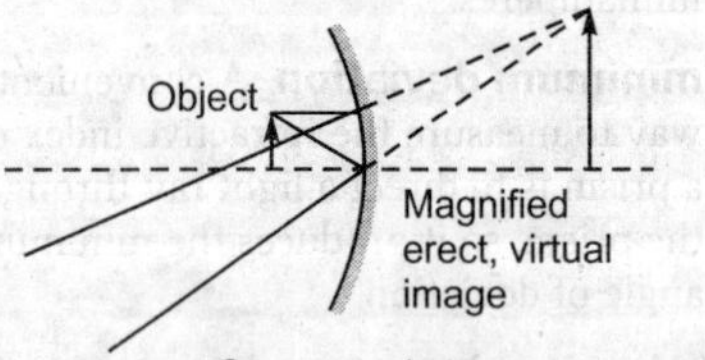

Concave mirror

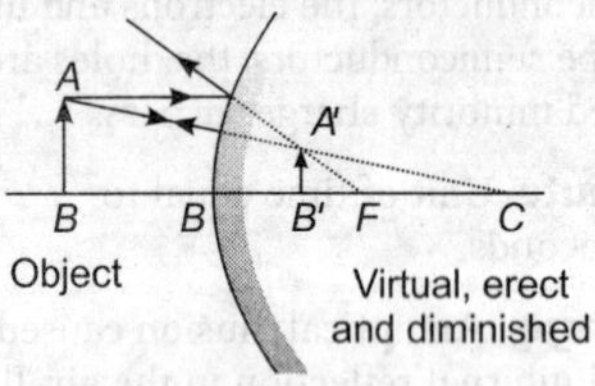

Convex mirror

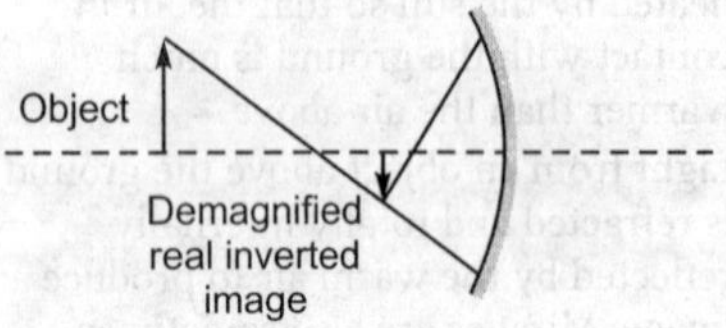

Concave mirror

mirror equation

$$\frac{1}{f} = \frac{1}{u} + \frac{1}{v}$$

where, u = distance of object,
v = distance of image,
f = focal length of mirror.

mirror image A shape which is identical to another except that its structure is reversed as if viewed in a mirror.

mixed grouping of cells An arrangement of cells where in combination of cells in series are connected in parallel. This arrangement yields maximum current, if the external resistance in the circuit is equal to the total internal resistance.

MKS system A system of units in which metre, kilogram and second are used as base units.

mobile telephony The central concept of this system is to divide the service area into a suitable number of cells centred on an office called MTSO (Mobile Telephone Switching Office). Each cell contains a low power transmitter called a base station and caters to a large number of mobile receivers popularly called call phones. Each cell could have a service area of a few square kilometres or even less depending upon the number of customers. When a mobile receiver crosses the coverage area of one base station, it is necessary for the mobile user to be transferred to another base station. This procedure is called handover or handoff. This process is carried out very rapidly, to the extent that the consumer does not even notice it. Mobile telephones operate typically in the UHF range of frequencies (about 800-950 MHz).

mobility The average drift velocity of a charge carrier per unit electric field is known as mobility. It is denoted by μ.

$$\mu = \frac{|\mathbf{v}_d|}{E}$$

The SI unit of mobility is m^2/Vs and its practical unit is (cm^2/Vs) and $m^2/Vs = 10^4\ cm^2/Vs$. Mobility is always positive.

mode

1. One of several wave frequencies which an oscillator can generate or to which a resonator can be turned.
2. Value of the abscissa corresponding to the maximum ordinate of a frequency distribution curve.

modem A device which converts the signals from one particular type of equipment into a form suitable for use in another.

moderator Material used to decrease speed of neutrons in nuclear reactor.

modulation The superimposition of a signal onto a carrier wave so that the information contained in the signal can be transmitted with the carrier wave.

modulation index The ratio of the frequency domination to the modulating frequency is known as the modulation index.

modulator A device that performs modulation, a process of varying one or more properties of a periodic waveform, called the carrier signal, with a modulating signal that typically contains the information to be transmitted.

modulus

1 Refers to the absolute value of a number. e.g. absolute value of −5 is 5.
2 Magnitude of a vector quantity.

modulus of elasticity The ratio of stress and strain, is found to be a characteristic of the material.

modulus of rigidity The ratio of shear stress to the displacement per unit sample length (strain).

moire fringes The pattern obtained when two regular sets of lines or points overlap. The effect can be seen through folds in netting drapes. Moire patterns can be used as models of interference patterns. Another application is in comparing two diffraction gratings by superimposing them and observing the more pattern produced.

molar Describing a physical quantity dividing by the amount of substance.

molar specific heat capacity The amount of heat required to increase the temperature of one mole of a substance through 1°C is called molar specific heat capacity. The SI unit of molar specific heat capacity is $J\ mol^{-1}K^{-1}$.

molar specific heat capacity at constant pressure If the gas is held under constant pressure, then amount of heat required to increase the temperature of one mole of gas through 1°C is called molar specific heat capacity at constant pressure. It is denoted by C_p.

molar specific heat capacity at constant volume If the gas is held under constant volume, then the amount of heat required to increase the temperature of one mole of gas through 1°C is called molar specific heat capacity at constant volume. It is denoted by C_V.

mole Amount of a substance which contains as many atoms molecules, ions, etc., as there are atoms in 0.012 kg of carbon-12. It is SI unit of amount of a substance.

molecular sieve A method used for seperating similar substances by absorbing the molecules of one substance within the structural cavities of another, such as a natural or synthetic zeolite.

molecular spectrum The absorption or emission spectrum that is the characteristic of a molecule. Molecular spectra are usually band spectra.

moment The turning effect of a force about a point. It is equal to the product of the force and the perpendicular distance from the point to the line of action of the force.
A body will be in rotational equilibrium if sum of the clockwise moment is equal to the sum of the anti-clockwise moments acting on it. This is called the law of moment.

moment of force The turning effect produced by a force is called its moment.

moment of inertia Moment of inertia of a particle about axis of rotation is equal to the product of its mass and the square of its distance from axis of rotation.

The moment of inertia of a body rotating about an axis is equal to

$$I = \Sigma m_i r_i^2$$

where, m_i and r_i are masses of the particles into which the body can be divided and their respective distance from the axis of rotation.

momentum The momentum, *p* of an object is defined as the product of its mass, *m* and velocity, *v* i.e. $p = mv$. Momentum has both direction and magnitude. Its direction is the same as that of velocity *v*. The SI unit of momentum is kilogram metre per second (kg ms^{-1}).

monoatomic Describing a molecule that consists of a single atom. The rare gases are monoatomic gases.

monochord An ancient musical and scientific laboratory instrument, also the class name for any musical stringed instrument having only one string. Most models of sonometer are monochords.

monochromatic light Light of a single wavelength.

monochromatic radiation Electromagnetic radiation of extremely narrow range of wavelengths. It is impossible to produce completely monochromatic radiation although the output of some lasers is not far off.

monochromator A device for providing monochromatic radiation from a polychromatic source. In the case of light, e.g. a prism or grating disperses the light and slits are used to select a small wavelength range.

monostable circuit An electronic circuit, usually a multivibrator, that has one stable state but can change to another state for a time after the application of a trigger pulse. Monostable circuits can be used for generating single pulses of a fixed duration, for shortening or lengthening pulses, or to delay pulses in computer logic circuits.

Moon The brightest celestial object except the sun. It is a natural satellite of the earth.

MOS Metal oxide semiconductor, a method of creating transistors. It consists of three layers, a metal conductor, insulating silicon layer, a semiconductor silicon layer.

Moseley's law Lines in the X-ray spectra of elements have frequencies that depend on the proton number of the element. For a set of elements, a graph of the square root of the frequency of X-ray emission against proton number is a straight line.

MOSFET A metal-oxide-semiconductor field effect transistor is used for switching electronic signals. It is a four terminal device with source (S), gate (G), drain (D) and body (B) terminals.

Mossbauer effect After an atomic nucleus has emitted a gamma-ray photon, the absorption of the momentum of the atom by the whole of its crystal lattice because it is so firmly bound that it cannot recoil. The same effect occurs with absorption of the gamma rays.

motion An object is said to be in motion if its position changes with respect to its surroundings with time.

motional electromotive force An emf induced,when a conducting rod moves perpendicular to a magnetic field then an emf is induced at its ends, which is called motional electromotive force. If conducting rod of length *l* moves normal to a magnetic field *B* with velocity *v*, then motion emf induced at its ends

$$e = Blv$$

motor A machine which can convert electrical energy into mechanical energy.

moving coil galvanometer It is a device used to detect the presence of current in a circuit or for measuring small currents. Its principle is based on the fact that when a current carrying coil is placed in a magnetic field a torque acts on it.

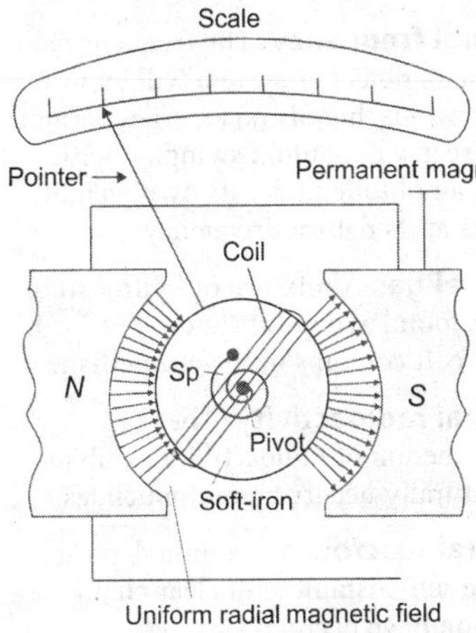

It consists of a coil having large number of turns wound over a soft iron core. The coil is placed in a radial magnetic field. One end of the coil is connected to hair spring and another end to phospher bronze strip.
When current is passed through the coil a torque $\tau = NBIA$ acts on it due to which the coil rotates and the phospher bronze strip gets twisted and a restoring torque acts on it.

moving iron instrument An electric meter in which the current passes through a fixed coil. There are two blocks of iron inside the coil, one is fixed and the other is free to move against a spring. The current in the coil magnetises the two pieces of iron which then repel.

multimeter An electrical measuring instrument designed to measure voltage and current over a number of ranges. It is a moving coil instrument with a switch enabling various resistors to be connected in series with the coil or various shunt resistances to be connected in parallel.

multiplier One of a set of resistor that is used in series with a voltmeter to allow it to measure a wide range of voltages.

mu-meson *See* muon.

muon A type of lepton with a mass 207 times that of the electron. There are two types, which have positive or negative charge.

mutarotation Change in optical activity of a solution containing photo-active substances, such as sugars.

mutual conductance The ratio of change of output current to the small change of input voltage causing it.

mutual induction The production of induced emf in one circuit by changing the magnetic flux linked with nearly circuit.

myopia Alternative name for short sightedness.

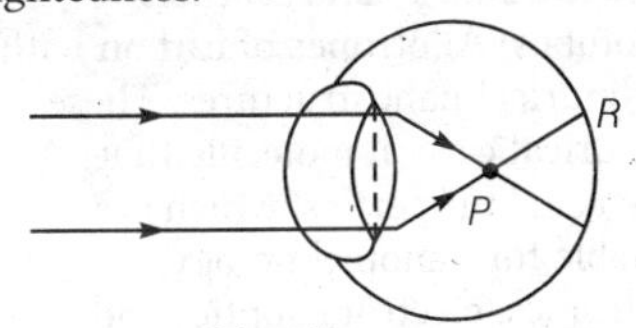

Myopia eye

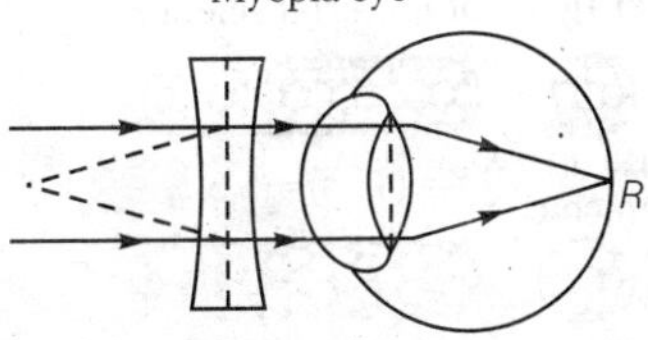

Correction of myopia

In this defect, a person can see near by objects clearly but cannot see far away objects clearly. It is normally caused if the distance between the lens and the back of the eyeball is too long or focal length of eye lens in spectacles.
This defect can be corrected by using concave lens of appropriate power is spactacles.

N

nano A prefix used in the metric system to denote 10^{-9}.

nanoparticles The particles between 1 and 100 nanometres in size. In nanotechnology, these particles act as a small object that behaves as a whole unit with respect to its transport and properties.

nanotechnology The branch of technology that is concerned with the production and behaviour of very small components, especially electronic devices that have a size of a few nanometres. Electronic devices of this type may use the movement of only a few electrons in their action.

nanotube (also CNT, carbon nanotubes) Allotropes of carbon with a cylindrical nanostructures. These cylindrical carbon molecule tubes have usual properties, which are valuable for nanotechnology electronics, electronic optics and other fields of material science.

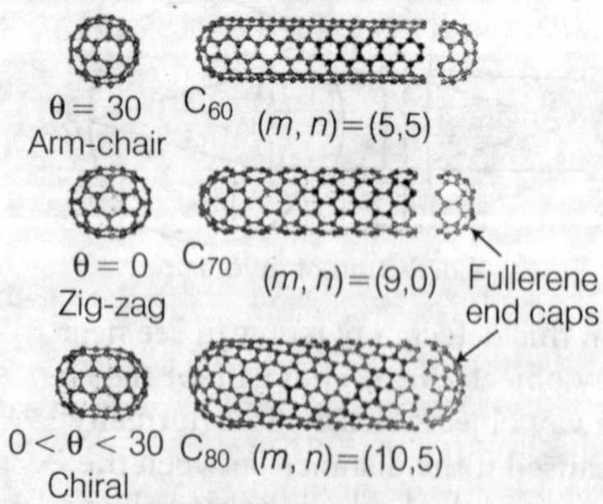

Carbon nanotube

natural convection *See* convection.

natural frequency The frequency at which an object or system will vibrate freely when there is no external periodic force. e.g. a pendulum swinging with small amplitude under its own weight, moves at its natural frequency.

natural gas A mixture of hydrocarbons and is found in deposits under the Earth's surface. It contains upto 90% methane.

natural radioactivity The phenomenon of radioactivity exhibited by naturally occurring radionuclides.

natural reactor A uranium deposit where self-sustaining nuclear chain reaction have occured.

nautical mile A unit of distance being equal to 6082.66 feet.

near infrared A part of infrared region of the spectrum close to the visible region.

near point The closest point to the eye at which an object can be clearly seen without excessive strain. The eye is then fully accommodated and has maximum power. The average near point distance for a normal adult is 25 cm.

nebula Originally, a fixed, extended and somewhat fuzzy white haze observed in the sky with a telescope. Many of these objects can now be resolved into clouds of individual stars and have been identified as nebula.

nebula hypothesis A theory which is based on the assumption that the solar system originated from the condensation of a nebula.

neel temperature Temperature above which an antiferromagnetic material becomes paramagnetic.

negative bias The potential that is applied to an electronic device. It is negative with respect to some fixed reference potential.

negative charge Means excess of electron on the object with respect to its natural state.

negative feedback Some part of output is again feed into input with phase difference of 180°.

negative lens A lens with a negative power.

negative mirror A mirror with a negative power.

negative pole A South pole of a magnet.

negative resistance The characteristic of certain electronic devices, in which current increases with decrease in voltage.

negative vector A vector having the same magnitude, as that of vector but has the opposite direction.

nematic Comes from a greek prefix nemato meaning thread like and is used here because the molecules in the liquid align themselves into thread like shape. Nematic liquid crystals are used in twisted nematic display.

neon lamp A gas discharge lamp which consists of small glass containing a mixture of neon and other gases at low pressure. When sufficient voltage and current is applied between the electrodes, the lamp produces orange glow discharge.

neptune The eighth planet in terms of its distance from the Sun. This is the second planet that was discovered with the help of telescope. Neptune has 8 satellites revolving around it.

neptunium A toxic radioactive silvery element of the actinoid series of metals that was the first transuranic element to be synthesised. Its symbol is Np and its melting point is 640°C.

Nernst calorimeter An apparatus for determining the specific thermal capacity of a metal.

Nernst effect When a magnetic field is applied at right angle to a conductor through which heat is flowing, an electric potential develops transversely across the conductor.

Nernst heat theorem Also called the third law of thermodynamics. It shows that for a chemical change occurring between pure crystalline solids at absolute zero, there is no change in entropy.

Nernst zero of potential An arbitrary zero of electrode potential, is defined as potential corresponding to the reversible equilibrium between hydrogen gas at 1 standard atmospheric pressure and hydrogen ions at unit activity.

net force Vector sum of all forces acting on an object.

network Refers to a system of interconnected points and their connections as a set of interconnected terminals online to one or more computers.

Neumann's law Whenever the flux of magnetic induction enclosed by a circuit is changing, there is an emf acting round the circuit, in addition, the emf is equal to the rate of diminution of the flux of induction enclosed by the circuit.

neutral An object that has no net electric charge, i.e. neither negative nor positive, e.g. a neutron is a neutral subatomic particle.

neutral equilibrium The equilibrium of a system, such that if it is disturbed a little, it shows no tendency to move further nor to return.

neutral point A point in a magnetic region, where the net magnetic field is zero.

neutral temperature The temperature of the hot junction of a thermocouple, at which there is maximum current in the circuit.

neutralisation The provision of negative feedback in an amplifier sufficient to neutralise any positive feedback, which thus, prevents oscillations.

neutrino An elementary, chargeless, massless, subatomic particle emitted with β-particles having only weak interactions.

neutron A nucleus contains a neutral particle. Its mass is almost the same as that of proton, i.e. 1.67492×10^{-27} kg. Neutrons are fermions with spin 1/2.

neutron bomb A nuclear bomb. It releases a shower of life destroying neutrons but has practically little blast and contamination.

neutron capture A capture by an atomic nucleus of a neutron which is often accompanied by the emission of gamma radiation.

neutron flux The quantity used in nuclear reactor physics corresponding to the total length travelled by all neutrons per unit time and volume or equivalently number of neutrons travelling through a unit area in unit time.

neutron multiplication ratio The ratio of the number of daughter neutrons inducting fission reaction to the number of parent neutrons in previous generation. Its symbol is k. If $k < 1$, then the fission reaction dies away. If $k = 1$, then the fission reaction continues indefinitely at a constant power level. If $k > 1$, then fission reaction grows exponentially till the system explodes.

neutron number The number of neutrons in the atom of an element.

neutron star A star in which nuclear sources are used and contracted upto the level of degeneracy under gravitational force.

new cartesian sign convention In the study of reflection of light by spherical mirrors, we shall use a set of sign conventions called the new cartesian sign convention. In this convention, the pole P of the mirror is taken as the origin. The principal axis of the mirror is taken as the X-axis XX' of the coordinate system.

The conventions are as follows

(i) The object is always placed to the left of the mirror and therefore, the light from the object falls on the mirror from the left hand side.

(ii) All distances parallel to the principal axis, are measured from the pole of the mirror.

(iii) All the distances measured to the right of the origin (along + X-axis) are taken as positive, while those measured to the left of the origin (along – X-axis) are taken as negative.

(iv) Distances measured perpendicular to and above the principal axis (along + Y-axis), are taken as positive.

(v) Distances measured perpendicular to and below the principal axis (along $-Y$-axis) are taken as negative.

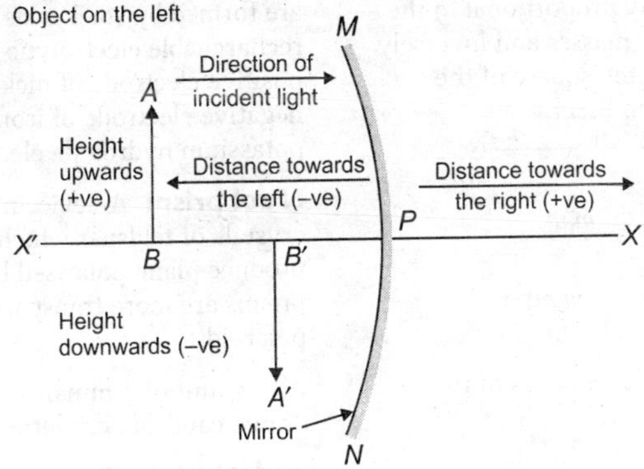

Representation of cartesian sign convention

newton The SI unit of force. It is equal to the force needed to accelerate one kilogram by one metre second^{-2}.

i.e. $1\text{ N} = 1\text{ kg ms}^{-2}$

Newtonian force The force between points that falls off as the inverse square of distance between them.

Newtonian physics The study of the motion of bodies in an ancient one, making classical mechanics one of the oldest subject in Science, engineering and technology.

Newtonian telescope A reflecting telescope in which a small plane mirror reflects the convergent beam from the objective to an eyepiece at one side of the telescope.

Newton's equation of sound This equation represents the velocity of sound in a gas. According to which, the speed of sound in a gas is given by

$$v = \sqrt{\frac{p}{\rho}}$$

where, p = pressure and
ρ = density of the gas.

For medium,

$$v = \sqrt{\frac{E}{\rho}}$$

where, v = velocity of sound,
E = elasticity of medium and
ρ = density of medium.

Newton's first law of motion An object at rest will continue to be in its state of rest or a uniform motion will remain in uniform motion in a straight line unless compelled by some external force. This law is also called law of inertia.

Newton's law of cooling When a hot body is cooling in air, the rate of transfer of heat is proportional to the temperature difference between the body and its surroundings. This is strictly true, only for forced convection.
This law holds good only for small difference of temperatures. Also, the loss of heat by radiation depends upon the nature of the surface of the body and the area of the exposed surface.

Newton's law of gravitation The gravitational force acting between two bodies is directly proportional to the product of their masses and inversely proportional to the square of the distance between them.

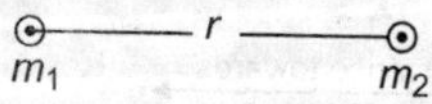

$$F \propto \frac{m_1 m_2}{r^2}$$

or $$F = G\frac{m_1 m_2}{r^2}$$

where, m_1 and m_2 = masses of two bodies,
r = distance between them.
G = constant called the universal gravitational constant whose value is
6.67×10^{-11} N-m^2/kg^2.

Newton's rings Interference pattern produced by placing a lens on a reflecting surface and illuminating it with monochromatic light from above.

Newton's second law of motion The rate of change of momentum of a body is directly proportional to the applied force and the change takes place in the direction in which the force acts,

i.e. $$F = \frac{dp}{dt} = ma$$

where, m = mass of the body and
a = acceleration produced in the body.

Newton's theory of light Newton introduced the corpuscular theory of light in 1678. A flight of material particles called corpuscular, was emitted by a light source, where the size of corpusculars were different. The impact of these particles on the retina produced the sensation of sight.

Newton's third law of motion To every action, there is always an equal and opposite reaction and both act on two different bodies.

nickel-iron accumulator A type of secondary cell, in which the electrodes are formed by steel grids. It is rechargeable electrolytic cell with a positive electrode of nickel oxide and a negative electrode of iron in a potassium hydroxide electrolyte.

Nicol prism A device made from crystals of feldspar which is used to produce plane polarised light. Nicol prisms are more transparent than polaroid.

nit A unit of luminance. It is defined as one candela per metre square.

nodal points Two points on the axis of a system of lenses, if the incident ray passes through one, the emergent ray will pass through the other.

node The positions of zero amplitude in a stationary wave. A distance of $\lambda/2$ or half a wavelength separates two consecutive nodes.

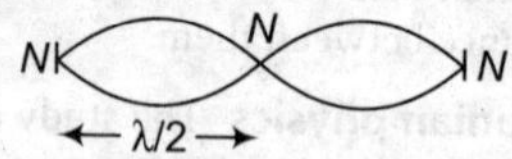

noise Sound composed of a random mixture of different frequencies.

noise factor A measure of noise. It is defined as the ratio of the signal-to-noise power ratio at the source to the corresponding ratio at the output.

non-inductive Describes a circuit component that has a low inductance.

non-inertial frame of reference The frame of reference accelerating with respect to each other.

non-linear optics A branch of optics that describes the behaviour of light in non-linear media in which the dielectric polarisation P responds non-linearly to the electric field E of the light.

non-magnetic substances Substances which on being placed in a magnetic field, are not attracted by magnet.

non-ohmic A circuit component, the current passing through which does not obey Ohm's law, i.e. the current is not proportional to the potential difference across the component. For these circuits, *V-I* graph is not a straight line.

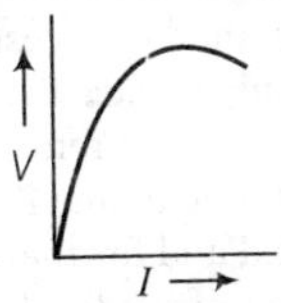

Non-ohmic *V-I* graph

non-polar dielectric A dielectric in the molecules of which the centre of positive charge coincides with the centre of negative charge. Each molecule has zero dipole moment in its normal state. These molecules are mostly symmetrical such as; nitrogen, oxygen, benzene, methane, etc.

non-polar molecules Molecules which get polarised within the external magnetic field.

non-radiating orbit The orbit in which electron does not radiate energy.

non-relativistic Related to any dynamic system in which relative velocity is much smaller than velocity of light, so that relativistic effects are negligible.

normal Perpendicular drawn on a reflecting surface at the point of incidence.

normal adjustment An image formed by an optical system, is in normal adjustment, if it is in a similar viewing position to the object. It refers to the adjustment of the system.

normal stress If the deforming forces are applied uniformly over entire surface of the body normally, so that change in volume of the body occurs without change in shape. Then, we call the stress produced as normal stress.

normal temperature and pressure (NTP) Now, known as standard temperature and pressure. *See* STP.

normalisation The process of heating steel above an appropriate critical temperature followed by cooling in still air.

North magnetic pole

1. The pole near the geographic North pole of the Earth is called the North magnetic pole.
2. The end pointing towards North is called North seeking or North pole.

note The sound having single fundamental frequency.

nova A star that over a period of only a few days becomes 10^3-10^4 times brighter than it was.

***n-p-n* transistor** See transistor.

***n*-type conductivity** The conductivity of an extrinsic semiconductor due to flow of additional electrons.

***n*-type semiconductor** A pure semiconductor doped with pentavalent impurity such as; antimony, bismuth, etc. and in which current is carried by electrons.

nuclear barrier A region which has a potential energy, so that a charged particle must pass through in order to enter or leave an atomic nucleus.

nuclear binding energy The energy required to separate all nucleons from the nucleus.

nuclear charge The product of atomic number having the charge of a proton.

Nuclear charge $= Z \times 1.6 \times 10^{-19}$ C.

nuclear cell A small electric cell which gains its power from the decay of a radioisotope, such cells are common in spacecraft and for polar systems.

nuclear density The ratio of mass of the nucleus to the volume of the nucleus. It is almost same for all atoms and is independent of mass number.

$$\rho = 2.97 \times 10^{17} \text{kgm}^{-3} = \frac{A}{\frac{4}{3}\pi R^3}$$

nuclear energy Energy derived from nuclear reactions either by the fission of heavy nuclei into lighter ones or by fusion of light nuclei into heavier ones. This energy is exploited both for weapons construction and for civil power supplies.

nuclear fission The process of splitting of a heavy atomic nucleus into two parts of nearly equal masses with the release of large amount of energy. Fission may be spontaneous or induced. In fission, nuclei usually disintegrate into two fragments of roughly comparable mass number along with few neutrons, e.g. ^{235}U splits into ^{90}Kr and ^{143}Ba along with 3 new neutrons.

$$^{235}_{92}\text{U} + {}^{1}_{0}n \longrightarrow {}^{92}_{36}\text{Kr} + {}^{143}_{56}\text{Ba} + 3\,{}^{1}_{0}n + \text{Energy}$$

nuclear force A strong attractive force which exists between the nucleons. It is a short range force with a range of few fermi (1 fermi $= 10^{-15}$ m) and is charge independent.

nuclear fuel The fuel required to start nuclear reactor.

nuclear fusion The process of fusing two light nuclei to form a heavier nucleus with the release of tremendous amount of energy. Also called the thermonuclear reaction.

nuclear isomers A pair of isotopes of the same proton and neutron numbers, but in different quantum states, which retain for long time period.

Nuclear Magnetic Resonance (NMR) A method of investigating the spins of atomic nuclei. This technique is used for the measurement of nuclear magnetic moments, precise magnetic field and for the determination of the location of nuclei in molecules and for chemical analysis.

nuclear magneton The unit of intrinsic magnetic moment of proton. Its value is

$$\mu_N = \frac{eh}{4\pi m_p}$$

where, e = charge and m_p = mass of proton, respectively.

nuclear mass The sum of masses of protons and neutrons minus the mass defect.

nuclear physics The branch of Physics which deals with nuclear structure, properties, reactions and their applications.

nuclear power The power produced by nuclear reaction. It is generally used for electric power generation.

nuclear reaction A reaction involving nuclei. An equation for a nuclear reaction shows the nuclides and particles involved by their symbols.

nuclear reactor A device in which nuclei reactions take place on a large scale. A reactor may be built for the purpose of providing useful energy producing new nuclides or research.

nuclear stability The average energy needed to liberate a nucleon from the nucleus.

nuclear transmutation Change of one nucleus into another as the result of a nuclear reaction.

nuclear waste The harmful radioactive by product of the nuclear industry particularly from the mining extraction and reprocessing of nuclear fuels and from decommissioned nuclear reactors.

nucleon A comparatively massive particle in an atomic nucleus, a proton or neutron.

nucleon number The number of nucleons (total number of protons and neutrons) in an atomic nucleus.

nucleus The most massive central part of the atom of an element which contain total positive charge of the atom. It consists of positively charged protons and natural neutrons. The number of protons in the nucleus is called atomic number *Z* and the total number of protons and neutrons in the nucleus is called mass number *A* of the nucleus.

nuclide Atomic nucleus defined by its atomic number and neutron number. e.g. $^{12}_{6}C$, $^{14}_{7}N$, etc., are different nuclide.

nullification A conclusion of combining normal and negative matter, there being no energy output when this happens.

numerical aperture A dimensionless number that characterise the range of angles, over which the system can accept or emit light.

null vector The vector whose magnitude is zero.

n

O

object A source of diverging light rays. It may be luminous or illuminated. It may be real or virtual.

objective A lens or a combination of lenses of an optical system such as microscope or telescope that is nearest to the object.

ocean thermal energy The energy exploited from the sea or ocean due to difference in temperature in the layers of water at the surface and in deeper section of the sea or ocean. Ocean thermal plants can operate if the temperature difference between the water at the surface and water at depths up to 2 km is 20°C or more. The warm surface water is used to boil a volatile liquid like ammonia. The vapours of the liquid is used to run the turbine of a generator, which produces electricity.

octave The interval between two musical notes whose frequencies are in the ratio 2 : 1.

octet Group of eight electrons in the outer shell of an inert gas (except helium). Every atom wants to complete its octet to become more stable.

odd-even nucleus Atomic nucleus with an odd number of protons and an even number of neutrons.

odd-odd nucleus Atomic nucleus with an odd number of both protons and neutrons.

oersted CGS unit of magnetic field strength. It was named after the Danish physicist Hans Oersted.

Its value is $\frac{10^3}{4\pi}$ Am^{-1}.

ohm SI unit of electrical resistance. It is named after the German physicist George Ohm.

$$1 \text{ ohm } (\Omega) = 1 \text{ volt/ampere}$$

One ohm is the electrical resistance of a conductor in which 1 ampere of current flows when a potential difference of 1 volt is applied across its ends.

Ohm meter An instrument for measuring electrical resistance in ohm.

Ohm's law If physical conditions of a conductor such as temperature remains unchanged, then the electric current (I) flowing through it is directly proportional to the potential difference (V) applied across its ends,

$$V \propto I$$

or

$$V = IR$$

where, R is the electrical resistance of the conductor.

ohmic A resistance or other re-electric device that obeys Ohm's law. It describes a substance in which the flow of current is proportional to the voltage difference between them.

ohmic substance A substance, the current flowing through which is in accordance with Ohm's law.

oil-drop experiment An experiment performed by Millikan in 1913 to determine the charge on an electron.

opacity The ratio of the radiant flux incident on an object to the flux transmitted. It is the reciprocal of transmittance. It is a measure of the ability of a solid, liquid or gaseous body to absorb radiation.

opalescence A type of dichroism seen in highly dispersed systems with little opacity. The materials appear yellowish red in transmitted light and blue in the scattered light perpendicular to the transmitted light. The phenomenon is named after the appearance of opals and is an example of Tyndall effect.

OP-amp It stands for operational amplifier which produces thousands times larger output voltage than the input voltage.

opaque A substance that does not transmit light. A substance that is opaque to one type of electromagnetic radiation may be transparent to other radiation, such as glass is transparent to visible radiation but is opaque to most infrared radiation.

open circuit An electric circuit through which no current passes.

open tube monometer It is a device that can be used to measure pressure.

operating point A specific point with in the operation characteristic of a technical device. This point will be engaged because of the properties of the system and the outside influences and parameters. In electronic engineering, an operating point is named as biasing.

ophthalmoscope An instrument for examining the interior structure of the eye, especially the retina, consisting essentially of a mirror that reflects light into the eye and a central hole through which eye is examined.

optical activity Phenomenon exhibited by some chemical compounds which, when placed in the path of a beam of plane polarised light, rotate the plane of polarisation to the left or right.

optical axis A line passing through the optical centre and the centre of curvature of a spherical lens or mirror. It is also called principal axis.

optical bench A track on which optical components can be mounted and moved. It is used widely in optic experiments.

optical centre The geometric centre of a spherical lens is called its optical centre.

optical instrument A device that incorporates optical components, which improves seeing.

optical fibre A type of transmission line through which a signal can propagate in the form of light. It consists of high quality glass or quartz. The refractive index of internal core is higher than the cladding surrounding the internal core.

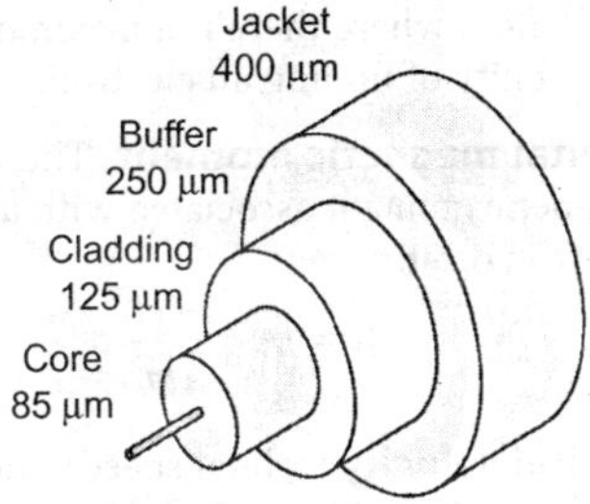

Optical fibre

When light enters at its one end, it undergoes repeated total internal reflection along the length of the fibre and finally comes out at the other end.

optical flint Any of various types of high dispersion optical glass.

optical glass Very pure glass free from streaks and bubbles, used for making lenses. Precautions are taken during its manufacturing to avoid mechanical and optical defects such as density, strain, heterogeneity, colour, refractive index, etc.

optical path The product of the distance travelled in a medium and the refractive index of the medium, i.e. $d = l \times n$.

optical rotation Rotation of plane polarised light by an active substance.

optics A branch of physics which deals with the study of light.

orbit

1. In astronomy and space science, the path of a heavenly body moving round another heavenly body such as the path of the earth round the sun, the path of the moon round the earth, etc.
2. In atomic physics, the path of motion of an electron round the nucleus of an atom.

Therefore, orbit is a closed path of an object moving in a central force field.

orbital The space around the nucleus in an atom where there is a maximum probability of finding an electron.

orbital magnetic moment The magnetic moment associated with an electron orbit.

$$\mu = IA = \frac{-eL}{2m_e}$$

orbital velocity (orbital speed) The speed of an object in an orbit average the earth or around some other celestial body.

order of magnitude A value expressed to the nearest power of ten.

organ A musical instrument which consists of one or more sets of pipes sounded by means of compressed air. It is played with the help of one or more key boards.

organ pipe A wooden or metal pipe used for producing musical sound is called an organ pipe. If both of its ends are open, then it is called an open organ pipe. If its one end is closed and other end is open, then it is called a closed organ pipe.

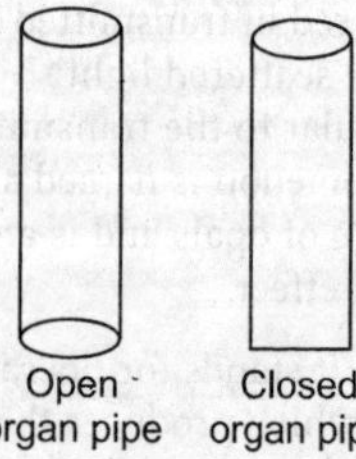

organic LED A light emitting diode in which the emissive electroluminescent layer is a film of organic compound which emits the light in response to an electric current.

origin starting point or a point corresponding to which the position of any object can be expressed.

Orion (*or Mriga*) Orion or Mriga is a most magnificent constellation in sky that can be seen during the winter. It has seven bright stars of which four appear to be arranged in the form of a quadrilateral.One of the largest stars, known as Betelgeuse, is situated on one corner of this quadrilateral while another bright star called Rigel is located on the opposite corner. Other three prominent stars of Orion constellation appear to be on a straight line in the middle of it.

oscillation A regularly repeated motion or change of small frequency. Simple harmonic motion is the simplest form of oscillatory motion.

oscillation magnetometer A device in which a freely suspended magnet is allowed to vibrate in a magnetic field (of earth). The time period of vibration is given by the formula

$$t = 2\pi \frac{K}{MH^2}$$

oscillator A circuit whose output is in the form of alternating current while input is direct current.

oscillatory circuit An AC circuit having a capacitor and an inductor in such a way that their capacitive reactance and inductive reactance are equal. The frequency of electrical oscillations produced by such a circuit is given by

$$f = \frac{1}{2\pi\sqrt{LC}}$$

where, L is the inductance and C is the capacitance in the circuit.

oscillograph An instrument for measuring alternating or varying electric current in terms of current and voltage.

oscilloscope A device that shows periodic changes in an electric quantity such as voltage, current., etc, on a screen using a cathode ray tube or any other instrument.

ossicles The three bones in either middle ear that are among the smallest bones in the human body. They serve to transmit sounds from air to the fluid filled labyrinth.

otto cycle The ideal reversible cycle of four operations occurring in a perfect from stroke gasoline engine.

ounce One sixteenth of a pound equal to 0.028349 kg.

out of phase If the two or more cyclic processes not peaking together, i.e. at the same time or in the same place and they arc fully 180° out of phase, then there is a destructive interference at that point.

output

1. Power, voltage or current delivered by any circuit, device, or plant.
2. Terminal or other place where the signal is delivered.

over-current A situation in an electric power system where a larger than intended electric current exists through a conductor, leading to excessive generation of heat and the risk of fire or damage of equipment.

overload When the current drawn from any device such as a machine transformer, generator, etc., is more than the permissible limit then this device is called overload.

overtone The note of higher frequency each being an integer multiple of the natural (lowest) frequency.

oxygen point The temperature of equilibrium between liquid and gaseous oxygen at a pressure of one standard atmosphere, taken as a fixed point in the international temperature scale at 90.188 Kelvin.

P

packing fraction The difference between the actual mass of a nuclide and the nearest whole number divided by the mass number.

pair production (pair creation) The simultaneous production of an electron and its antiparticle (positron) from a gamma ray photon. The process can occur in the field of an atomic nucleus. The minimum energy of such a photon must be 1.022 MeV, being equal to energy equivalent to the sum of the rest masses of the electron and positron.

panchromatic film A normal black and white film which is sensitive to light of all visible colours (electromagnet wavelengths approximately 400 nm to 700 nm). Objects of different colours are distinguishable in panchromatic film with grayscale tones closely approximating the brightness of the object.

parabolic mirror

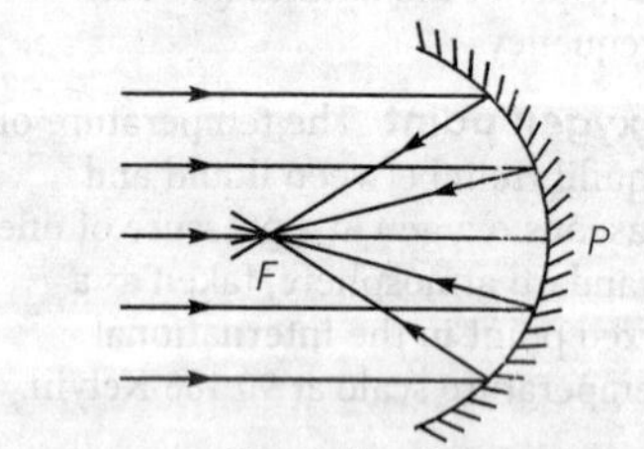

Parabolic mirror

It is a reflector with a parabolic section. Wide parallel beams can be converged accurately by the converging type into its focal point. This is used in reflection telescopes and solar power applications.

parallax Apparent change in the position of an object when it is observed from two different view points. If there is no parallax between two objects, they must be at effectively the same place.

parallel

1. Denoting lines and planes that are at the same distance from each other at all points.
2. Denoting a mode of connection of electric apparatus such that the current divides between them.

parallel axes theorem

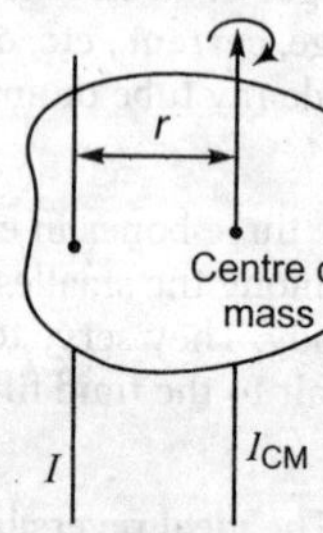

The moment of inertia (I) of any object about an axis is equal to the sum of its moment of inertia about its centre of mass (I_{CM}) and the product of its mass and the square of the perpendicular distance between the two axes,

i.e. $$I = I_{CM} + Mr^2$$

parallel circuits

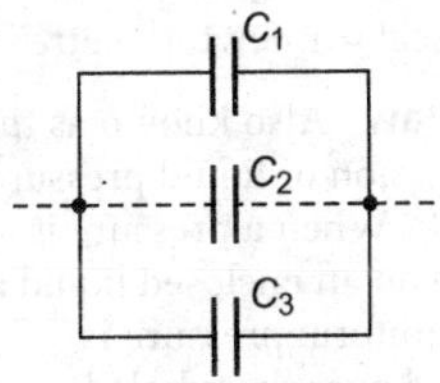

Capacitors in parallel

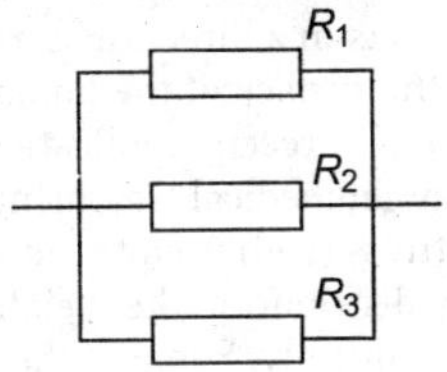

Resistors in parallel

Parallel circuits

Elements in an electrical circuit are in parallel if connected so that the current divides between them and rejoins at the other side. In parallel combination, the potential difference across the each element remains same. If capacitors of capacitances C_1, C_2, C_3 ..... are connected in parallel, then the resultant capacitance is given by

$$C = C_1 + C_2 + C_3 + ...$$

If resistors of resistances R_1, R_2, R_3 ... are connected in parallel then the resultant resistance of the combination is given by

$$\frac{1}{R} = \frac{1}{R_1} + \frac{1}{R_2} + \frac{1}{R_3} + ...$$

parallel forces The forces acting on a body having parallel line of action of force are called parallel forces.

parallel-piped (parallelopiped) It is a solid having six faces, all of which are parallelograms.

parallel plate capacitor A combination of two plane parallel conducting plates separated by a small distance.

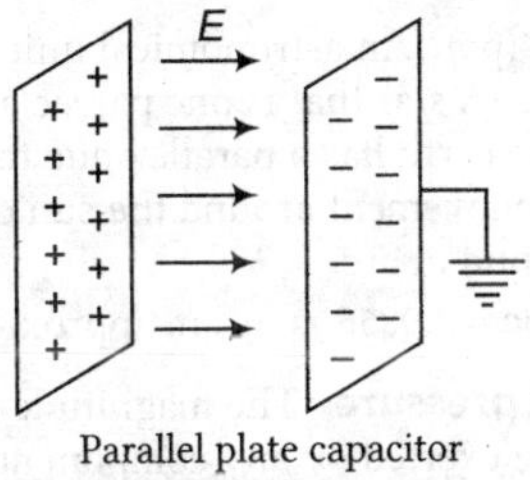

Parallel plate capacitor

The two plates have equal and opposite charges $+Q$ and $-Q$ and therefore surface charge densities $+\sigma$ and $-\sigma$. An electric field is established between the plates from positive charged plate towards negative charged plate.

parallelogram law of vectors The resultant of two vectors intersecting at a point is equal to the diagonal of the parallelogram formed with the vectors as the two sides and passing through the point of intersection of the vectors.

paramagnetism Properties of substances that possess a small permanent magnetic moment because of the presence of odd electrons, the substance becomes magnetised in a magnetic field as the magnetic moment aligns. Paramagnetic substances have tendency to move from a region of weak magnetic field to strong magnetic field.

paraxial rays Incident rays parallel and close to the axis of a lens. Only paraxial rays pass through the focal point of a spherical reflecting or refracting surface.

parent A nuclide that undergoes radioactive decay to another specified nuclide.

parent nucleus The nucleus which undergoes radioactive decay to another nucleus. The resulting nucleus is known as the daughter nucleus.

parity A property of the wave functions that describe physical system in quantum mechanics.

parsec (pc) An astronomical unit of distance–A star that is one parsec away from the earth has a parallex due to the Earth's movement around the sun of one second of arc.

$$1\ \text{pc} = 3.0856 \times 10^{16}\ \text{m approx.}$$

partial pressure The magnitude of pressure exerted by any component of a mixture of gases, if it was present alone in a container.

partials These are components of sound wave with frequencies above the fundamental frequency. The partials include the overtones together with non-harmonic components.

particle An abstract simplification of a real object the mass is concentrated at the object's centre of mass, its volume is zero.

particle accelerator A device that uses electromagnetic fields to propel charged particles to high speeds and to contain them in well defined beams.

1. *Electrostatic accelerators* like cathode ray tube, van de Graaf generator use static electric fields to accelerate charged particles.
2. *Oscillating field accelerators* like cyclotron, betatron use radio frequency electromagnetic fields to accelerate the particles.

particle physics The branch of physics that deals with elementary particles, their properties and interactions.

particle velocity The alternating component of the velocity of a medium transmitting sound, i.e. the total velocity of the medium less than the velocity due to sound propagation.

partition coefficient The ratio of the equilibrium concentrations of a solute dissolved in two specified immiscible solvents.

pascal SI unit of pressure;

$$1\ \text{pascal} = 1\ \text{newton metre}^{-2}$$

Pascal's law Also known as the law of transmission of liquid pressure. It states that "When a pressure is applied anywhere on an enclosed liquid at rest, an equal uniform pressure is transmitted over the whole liquid. It gets transmitted throughout the liquid and acts in a direction at right angles to the surface of the liquid everywhere." A recent application of Pascal's law in medical treatment is the water mattress (bed) used to cut down be-sore by distributing the weight of the body uniformly. Some of the important applications of Pascal's law are, (i) hydraulic press (or hydraulic lift), (ii) hydraulic brakes.

Paschen series A series of lines, in the infrared part of spectrum emitted by excited hydrogen atoms. The lines correspond to the atomic electrons falling into the third lowest energy level and emitting energy as radiation.

passive circuit Any circuit or network containing only passive component. Such a combination is capable of only attenuation. Such circuits are generally designed for use as passive filters.

path length The total length of the path traversed by an object.

Pauli paramagnetism Paramagnetism in which the susceptibility is very small but positive. It appears in alkali metals due to free electrons.

peak value The maximum value attained by an alternating quantity (like current, voltage, etc.).

peak value of alternating current The maximum value of current in either direction.

p

peak value of voltage The maximum value of voltage in either direction.

Peltier effect The absorption or evolution of heat at a junction when a current is sent through a thermo-couple is known as the Peltier effect. The energy absorbed or evolved at a junction, when a unit charge passes through it is called the Peltier coefficient and is denoted by π and expressed in joule/coulomb, i.e. volt. This coefficient depends on the temperature and material of the junction. The Peltier effect is reversible.

pendulum A simple pendulum consists of a weight at the end of a string, which swings with simple harmonic motion over small angles.

pentode A thermionic valve with five electrodes – cathode, anode and three grids between them.

penumbra

1. A fringe region of half shadow resulting from the partical obstruction of light by an opaque object.
2. The grayish outer part of a sun spot.

perfect gas A gas which obey the gas laws exactly. It consists of perfectly elastic molecules, their volume and the intermolecular forces between them being zero.

perfectly elastic The body which completely attains its original state on the removal of the deforming force is called perfectly elastic.

perfectly inelastic collision A collision in which conservation of momentum hold good but conservation of kinetic energy does not hold good. After such a collision the two colliding bodies stick together.

perfectly plastic If the body completely retains its modified form even on removing the deforming force, i.e. it shows no tendency to recover, it is said to be perfectly plastic. Plasticin may be considered perfectly plastic.

perigee The shortest distance between a satellite and the earth.

perihelion The point in a solar orbit which is nearest to the sun.

period Time taken to complete a regular cycle, such as a complete swing of a pendulum or one cycle of any type of simple harmonic motion.

periodic Which occurs at equal intervals.

periodic motion Any kind of motion that repeats itself at regular intervals of time is called periodic motion as the swinging of a pendulum, the vibration of a source of sound, the orbiting of a satellite or an electromagnetic wave. There are two classes of periodic motion: non-oscillatory motion and oscillatory motion.

periscope A device for seeing objects, that are above the eye level of the observer, or for which direct vision is obstructed. In its simplest form, it consists of two plane mirrors at 45° to the direction being viewed.

permanent magnet Substances which at room temperature retain their ferromagnetic properties for a long period of time are called permanent magnets. Permanent magnets can be made by holding an iron rod in the north-south direction and ring it repeatedly or by placing a ferromagnetic rod in a solenoid and passing a current.

permanent set When the applied stress is zero, but the strain is not zero, then the material is said to have a permanent set. The deformation is said to be plastic deformation.

permeability

1. Rate at which a substance diffuses through a porous material.
2. Magnetisation developed in a material placed in a magnetic field is equal to the flux density produced divided by the magnetic field strength, i.e. $\mu = \frac{B}{H}$.

   Its unit is henry per metre.

permittivity The degree to which the medium can resist the flow of electric charge through it. According to Coulomb's law, the electrostatic force acting between two charges q_1 and q_2 at the distance r from each other is given by $F = \frac{q_1 q_2}{4\pi\varepsilon_0 r^2}$, where, ε_0 is a constant, the permeability of the free space. The permittivity of free space ε_0 has a value 8.854×10^{-12} farad/metre.

perpetual motion Constant motion occurring without any external energy supply. These machines are impossible to construct because of frictional and other forces dissipating the original energy.

persistence It means continued existence or occurence. It is also used for the light which continue ever after electric spark is switched off in gas.

persistence of vision The impression of an image that persist on the retina of the eye for some time after its withdrawl. The impression on human eye lasts for 1/16 of a second. Successive images at the rate of 16 per second of the same scene give, therefore the impression of continuity.

persorption Physical chemical sorption in which molecules of a gas enter pores in a solid that are only a little larger than themselves.

perturbation theory An approximation method to solve the effect of other electrons on any electron in atom.

perversion Alternate name of lateral inversion. The effect produced by a mirror in reversing images apparently left to right. Thus, writing appears backwards when reflected, the image of a person raising the right hand appears to raise the left hand.

petrol engine An internal combustion heat engine in which a mixture of vapours of petrol and air is exploded in a cylinder by an electric spark. It is a four stroke engine.

Pfund series When an electron jumps from energy levels, $n_i = 6, 7, ...$ to energy level 5 (i.e. $n_f = 5$) the series of spectral lines obtained are called Pfund series. These lie in the far infrared region.

phase Any homogeneous and physically distinct part of a system that is separated from other parts of the system by definite boundaries, e.g. ice mixed with water.

phase angle An angle whose sine or cosine at a given instant indicates the position and direction of motion of the oscillator. It is expressed in radians.

phase contrast microscope Microscope that uses the principle that light passing through materials of different refractive indices undergoes a change in phase, transmitting these changes as different intensities of light given off by different materials.

phase diagram A graph combining two conditional parameter of a substance drawn so that a particular curve shows the boundary between two phases of the substance.

phase difference The difference in the phases of two coherent radiations travelling in the same direction in a superposition region.

phase discriminator A discriminator whose output signal is proportional to the phase difference between its input signals. It is utilised for reception of FM signals.

phase modulation A type of modulation in which a carrier wave is made to easy the information in a signal by fluctuations in the phase of the carrier.

phase rule (Gibbs phase rule) For any equilibrium system, the expression

$$P + F = C + 2$$

which relates the number of degrees of freedom F, to the number of phases P, and the number of components C.

phase shift The function is horizontally to the right of the usual position. It is typically measured in degrees where a complete cycle is 360 degrees.

phase space A multidimensional space that can be used to define the state of system.

phase velocity The velocity of propagation of phase in a travelling wave. Its value is given by $\frac{\lambda}{T}$, where λ is the wavelength and T is the time period.

phases of the moon The various shapes of the bright part of the moon as seen during a month.

phasor A quantity that varies sinusoidally with time and may be represented as the projection of a rotating vector . The projection of the vector on a fixed axis represents the amplitude variation with time.

phon A unit for measuring the loudness of sound.

phonetics The science of speech sound and their production transmission reception and their analysis.

phonograph A sound producing machine using records.

phonon It is quantum of elastic vibration in crystals. It is given by hn where, h is the Planck constant and n is the frequency of vibration.

phosphor bronze An alloy of copper, tin and phosphorus. Its conductivity and elasticity is high.

phosphorescene The absorption of energy by atoms followed by emission of electromagnetic radiation. The emission continue even after the light has been cut-off.

phot An unit of illumination of CGS system. It is defined as the illumination of one lumen per cm^2.

$$1 \text{ phot} = 10^4 \text{ lux}$$

photocathode A negatively charged in a light detection device such as a photomultiplier or phototube that is coated with a photosensitive compound. When this is struck by the quantum of light, the absorbed energy causes electron emission due to the photoelectric effect.

photocell Any device for producing an electric signal from electromagnetic radiation. Its working is based on photoelectric effect. It consists of a semi-cylindrical photosensitive metal plate C, called emitter, a wire loop A called collector supported in an evacuated glass or quartz bulb. When light of suitable frequency is incident on emitter, photo electrons are emitted.

These photoelectrons are attracted by the collector (*A*) and photo current of few microampere flows through the circuit.

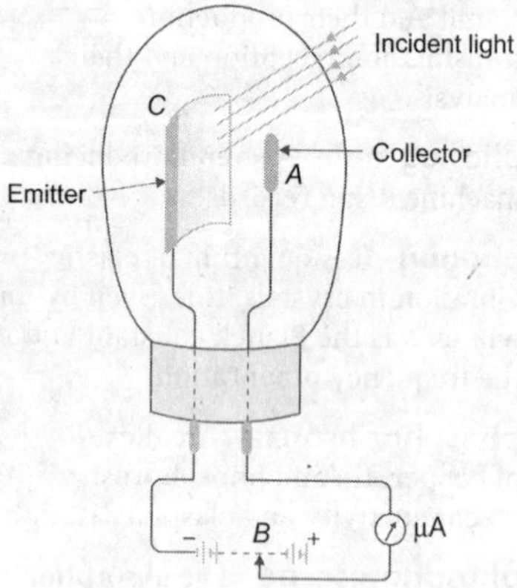

Photocell

photochemistry The branch of chemistry concerned with the chemical effects of light. Generally, this term is used to describe a chemical reaction caused by the absorption of ultraviolet, visible or infrared radiation.

photocurrent When the junction is reverse biased, the current flows due to minority carriers and produced current is called photocurrent.
This photocurrent is much larger than the reverse- saturation current which is much smaller in the ordinary *p-n* junction diode. A photo-diode can turn its current ON and OFF in nano (10^{-9}) seconds.

photoconductivity The increase of electrical conductivity in certain materials, produced by incident electromagnetic radiation.

photo disintegration The disintegration of an atomic nucleus by a gamma ray photon or an X-ray photon.

photodiode A special *p-n* junction diode fabricated with a transparent window to allow light to fall on the diode. It is used in reverse biasing. When light (photons of energy–$h\nu$ greater than the energy gap) is incident on photo diode, electron-hole pairs are generated due to the absorption of photons. Due to electric field of the junction, electrons and holes are separated before they recombine. Electrons are collected on *n*-side and holes are collected on *p*-side giving rise to an emf. If external circuit is completed using some load a photo current flows.

photoelectric absorption A phenomena in which the incident X-ray or γ-ray photon interacts with an atom of the absorbing material and the photon completely disappears; its energy is transferred to one of the orbital electrons of the atom.

photoelectric cell The device which converts light energy into electrical energy.

photoelectric effect The ejection of electrons from the surface of substances by ultraviolet radiation or from atoms within a substance by X-rays or gamma radiation is called photoelectric effect. The ejection of photo electrons takes place only when the frequency of incident radiation is greater than certain frequency, called threshold frequency (ν_0).

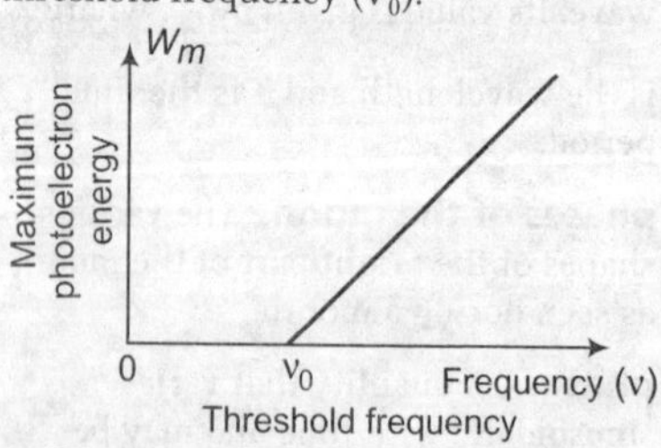

Representation of photoelectric effect

The number of electrons emitted is proportional to the intensity of radiation at a given frequency.

photoelectrons Some electrons produced by the photoelectric effect.

photoemission The emission of photoelectrons by the photoelectric effect or by photoionisation.

photofission A phenomena in which a nucleus after absorbing γ-ray, undergoes nuclear fission (splits into two or more fragments).

photographic camera A device that makes use of the properties of lenses. It consists of a light proof box fitted with a convex lens at its one face while a photographic film is kept at the opposite face. The lens makes an image of the object to be photographed, which is real, inverted and smaller in size. To focus images of the objects at different distances on the film, the distance between the lens of the camera and the film can be adjusted.

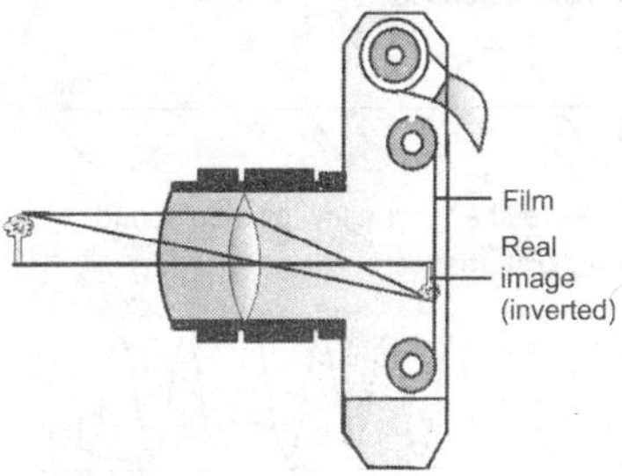

Photographic camera

photographic film The photographic film is made from thin, transparent sheets of special type of plastics. The plastic sheets are coated with a few layers of light sensitive chemicals.

photography The science, art and practice of creating durable images by recording light or other electromagnetic radiation, either electrically by means of an image senses or chemically by means of a light sensitive material such as photographic film.

photo lithography A technique used in manufacturing of semiconductor components, integrated circuit, etc.

photolysis A chemical reaction in which a chemical compound is broken down by photons. It is an interaction of one or more photons with one target molecule.

photometer An instrument for determining illumination or luminous intensity by comparisons made with the eye.

photometry The branch of Physics concerned with measuring intensity, illumination, etc., for visual radiation. The main physical quantities measured in photometry are luminous intensity, luminous flux, illuminance of the surface, etc.

photomultiplier A device in which electrons are originally emitted from a photocathode and initiate a cascade of electrons by secondary emission in an electron multiplier.

photon A quanta of light. The energy of a photon of light radiation of frequency f is given by $hf = hc/\lambda$, where, λ is its wavelength.

photon accelerator A device that is designed to raised the frequency of laser light pulses that may also one day come to be used to accelerate the charge particles.

photonuclear reaction A nuclear reaction resulting from the collision of photons with a nucleus.

photosensitive Any substance which when exposed to electromagnetic radiation produces photoelectric effect.

photosensor An electronic component that defects the presence of visible light, infrared transmission and ultraviolet energy.

photosphere The inner part of the sun whose temperature is about 5800 K. It contains highly ionised gases which continuously receives energy from interior of the sun and gives it out in the form of heat, light and other radiations.

Above the photosphere, temperature continues to fall for some distance (about 500 km) and reaches down to about 4300K. This layer is responsible for absorption lines in the solar spectrum. It is called the reversing layer or chromosphere.

phototransistor A transistor that is sensitive to electromagnetic radiation. It acts like a photodiode with an amplifier.

photovoltaic cell A device that converts electromagnetic radiation into electrical energy.

photovoltaic effect The basic physical process through which a solar cell converts sunlight into electricity. It is the creation of voltage or electric current in a material upon exposure of light and in a physical and chemical phenomenon.

physical change Any change in a substance which does not involve any alteration in its chemical composition.

physics The world physics comes from a Greek word meaning nature. Therefore, physics is that branch of science in which we study the basic laws of nature and their manifestation in different natural phenomena.

physisorption A process in which the electronic structure of the atom or molecule is barely perturbed upon adsorption.

pico Prefix denoting a factor of 10^{-12}.

Piezo-electric effect The generation of a small potential difference across certain materials when they are subjected to a stress.

pi-mesons Exchange particles responsible for strong nuclear forces. Their charge can be positive, negative or zero. The mass of meson is nearly 270 times the mass of an electron.

pin-hole camera A closed box in which light can enter only through a very small opening. It gives an inverted image of any object placed in front of the opening. The image is formed on the wall opposite to the opening.

pion A type of meson. There are three types of pion, having positive, negative or zero charge. Pions are strong interacting bosons with zero spin.

piston A disc or cylinder that moves within a tube exerting pressure on or receiving pressure from a fluid or gas within the tube.

pitch Pitch is the characteristic of musical notes that enables us to classify a note as 'high or low'. It depends on the frequency of sound.

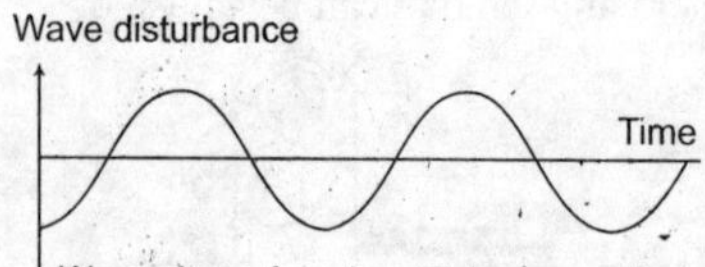

Wave shape for a low pitched sound

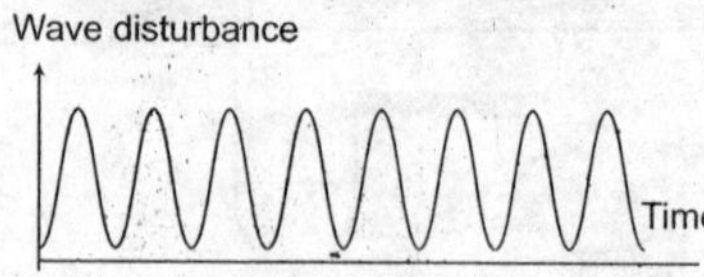

Wave shape for a high pitched sound

A shrill, sharp or acute sound is said to be of high pitch and a dull, grave and flat note is said to be of low pitch.

Planck's constant A fundamental constant and the ratio of the energy carried by a photon to its frequency. Its value is 6.626×10^{-34}. The energy of each photon is given by $E = h\nu$, where ν is the frequency of radiation.

Planck's formula or black body radiation The energy radiated per unit area time at a given wavelength λ, from a black body is given by the expression

$$E_\nu = \frac{2\pi hc^2}{\lambda^2} \frac{1}{\exp\left(\frac{hc}{kT}\right) - 1}$$

where, c is the velocity of light, h is the Planck's constant, and T is the absolute temperature of the black body, while k is the Boltzmann's constant.

Planck's law From Planck's quantum theory, Einstein postulated that the energy content E of an energy packet or photon is related to its frequency ν by

$$E = h\nu$$

This is often referred to as Planck's law.

plane of polarisation A plane perpendicular to the plane of vibration and containing the direction of propagation of light. It is also the plane containing the direction of propagation and the magnetic vector of the electromagnetic light wave.

plane of ecliptic The plane of Earth's orbit.

plane polarisation A type of polarisation of electromagnetic radiation, in which the magnetic oscillations are all parallel and occur in one plane containing the ray. The electric oscillations are all parallel and occur in a plane containing the ray and perpendicular to the plane containing the magnetic oscillations.

planet The heavenly bodies which revolve around the sun are called planets. In hindi, these are called grah. They do no emit their own light but appears bright due to the reflection of sunlight that falls on them. There are eight planets in our solar system—Mercury (budh), Venus (shukra), Earth (prithvi) Mars (mangal), Jupiter (brihaspati), Saturn (shani), Uranus, Neptune. The ninth planet pluto is now called a dwarf planet.

plano-concave (convex) **lens** A converging lens with one plane face and one convex or concave face.

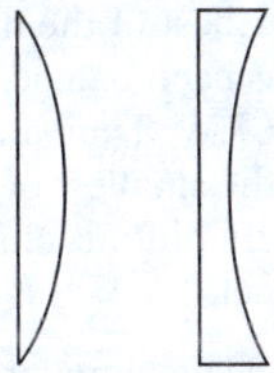

Plano convex and concave lens

plasma A mixture of free electrons and ions or atomic nuclei. It is a highly ionised gas in which the number of free electrons is approximately equal to the number of positive ions. Plasmas occur in thermonuclear reactions, as in the sun. Sometimes plasmas are referred to as a fourth state of matter.

plastic The substances such as a lump of putty or mud are deformed, they have no gross tendency to regain their previous shape, and they get permanently deformed. Such substances are called plastic and this property is called plasticity. Putty and mud are close to ideal plastics.

plasticity A property of a substance not to return to its original shape and size after a deforming force has been removed.

plate resistance The ratio of change in the plate voltage to the consequent change in plate current at constant grid voltage, i.e.

$$\frac{\Delta V_p}{\Delta I_c} = R_p$$

platinum A silvery-white malleable ductile transition metal used as a catalyst for ammonia oxidation and in making jewellery. Its symbol is 'Pt' and its melting point is 1772°C.

platinum resistance thermometer A type of thermometer used for measuring temperature in the range 170°C to 200°C.

plumline A cord having a metal bob attached to one end. It is used for determining the depth of water.

pluto The farthest of the nine planets and has been named as pluto, discovered by T.W. Tombaugh in 1930. Pluto is the smallest of all planets. Recently pluto is announced as a dwarf planet.

***p-n* junction** The boundary between *p* and *n*-type materials in semiconductor crystals.

***p-n-p* transistor** *See* transistor.

point charge A charge whose physical dimension is almost negligible.

poise A unit of dynamic viscosity. If the shearing stress in a liquid is expressed in dynes/cm^2 and the velocity gradient perpendicular to the direction of flow is in sec^{-1}, then the viscosity is defined in units of poise (or alternatively gram per cm per sec).

Poiseuille's formula An equation which gives rate of flow of a liquid. The amount of liquid flowing per second through a circular tube of radius *r* and length *l* when its ends are maintained at a pressure differences *p* is given by

$$V = \frac{\pi p r^4}{8 \eta l}$$

where, η being the viscosity of the liquid, *V* is volume per second.

poison A substance which reduces the efficiency of a process. It is most commonly used in nuclear reactor physics.

Poisson's ratio A measure of how a material changes shape when it is stretched. It is equal to minus the fractional change in cross-sectional area divided by the fractional change in length.

polar coordinates A system used in analytical geometry to locate a point *P*, with reference to two or three axes.

polar dielectric These type of dielectrics have a symmetric shape of the molecules such as water, CO_2, NH_3, HCl, etc. In such molecules, the centre of positive and negative charges does not coincide and they have some permanent dipole moment.

polarimeter An instrument used to determine the angle through which the plane of polarisation of plane polarised light is rotated.

polaris The stars appear to move from east to west because the earth rotates from west to east about an imaginary axis that passes through its centre. A star which is situated in the north direction and appears stationary to us is known as polaris or pole star or dhruv tara. The pole star had been one of the most familiar stars to travellers in earlier times to find directions at night.

polarisation Whether polar or non-polar, a dielectric develops a net dipole moment in the presence of an external field. The dipole moment per unit volume is called polarisation and is denoted by **p**. For linear isotropic dielectrics,

$$\mathbf{p} = \lambda_e \mathbf{E}$$

where, λ_e is a constant characteristic of the dielectric and is known as the electric susceptibility of the dielectric medium.

polarity An attribute with two possible values. An electric charge can have either positive or negative polarity. A voltage or potential difference between which two points of an electric circuit has a polarity, describing which of the two points has the higher electric potential.

polariserA device or arrangement producing plane polarised radiation from incident unpolarised radiation. e.g. nicol prism and polaroid are polariser.

polarising angle See Brewster law.

polarity of charge The property which differentiates the two kinds of charges.

polaroid A polaroid is a synthetic doubly refracting substance, that strongly absorbs polarised light in one plane, while easily passing polarised light in another plane at right angles. It consists of long chain of molecules aligned in a particular direction, if unpolarised light is incident on such a polaroid, then the light wave will get linearly polarised with the electric vector oscillating along a direction perpendicular to the aligned molecules. Polaroids can be used to control the intensity in sunglasses, windowpanes, etc. Polaroids are also used in photographic cameras and 3D movie cameras.

pole of mirror The geometric centre of a spherical mirror is called its pole. When a light ray is incident on pole, then angle of incidence (i) is equal to the angle of reflection (r).

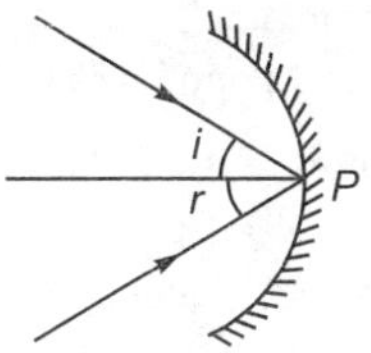

pole strength The force exerted by a given magnetic pole when it is one metre from a unit pole in vacuum.

polonium A rare radioactive metallic element of group 16.

polyatomic A molecule consisting of three or more atoms. e.g. methane (CH_4), ethane (C_2H_6), etc.

polychromatic Describes the radiation with a number of different frequency or energy components whether of similar intensity or not.

population inversion A situation when the number of atoms in excited state becomes greater than the number of atoms in ground state.

posistor A thermistor whose resistor increases with temperature.

positive charge Positive charge on a body means deficiency of electrons on it.

positive feedback The output in an oscillator is self-sustained. To attain this, an amplifier is taken. A portion of the output power is returned back (feedback) to the input in phase with the starting power. This process is termed as positive feedback.

positive rays A stream of positive ions.

positron The antiparticle of the electron, a particle with the same mass as the electron but with a positive charge. These are found in cosmic-ray showers, where they result from pair production.

post office box

A device containing resistances arranged in such a way that they can be used as a Wheatstone bridge. It was used earlier to find the resistance of long wires and thus to find any defects in the telephone or telegraph wires.

potential barrier The potential in a region where the force exerted on a carrier is such that it opposes the passage of the carrier through the region.

potential difference The difference in electric potential between two points in an electric field. It is equal to the work done per unit charge when a test charge is displaced between the points, by any path. Its SI unit is volt. The potential difference is measured by means of an instrument called the voltmeter. The voltmeter is always connected in parallel across the points between which the potential difference is to be measured.

potential depression A region of low potential energy.

potential energy The energy possessed by an object by virtue of its position or configuration. The potential energy of a body is equal to $E_p = mgh.$

potential energy of a charge Potential energy of a charge q at a point (in the presence of electric field) is the work done by an external force (equal and opposite to the electric force) in bringing the charge q from infinity to that point.

potential gradient The rate of charge of potential in the direction giving a maximum value.

potential well A region in a field of force surrounded by a higher potential region, the transition between the two being abrupt.

potentiometer A device which can be used to measure potential difference between two points in a circuit, the emf of a cell, the internal resistance of a cell or to compare the emf's of two cells. Its working is based on the principle that the potential difference in a current carrying wire of uniform cross-section area is directly proportional to its length. It consists of a wooden board on which a number of resistance wires of maganin or nichrome having uniform cross-sectional area are stretched parallel to each other. These wires are joined in series by thick copper strips. In this way these wires together act as a single wire of length equal to the sum of the length of all the wires. The end terminals of the wires are provided with connecting screws.
A meter scale is fixed on the wooden board parallel to wires. A jockey (a sliding contact marker) is provided with the arrangement. It makes a knife edge contact at any desired point on the wire.

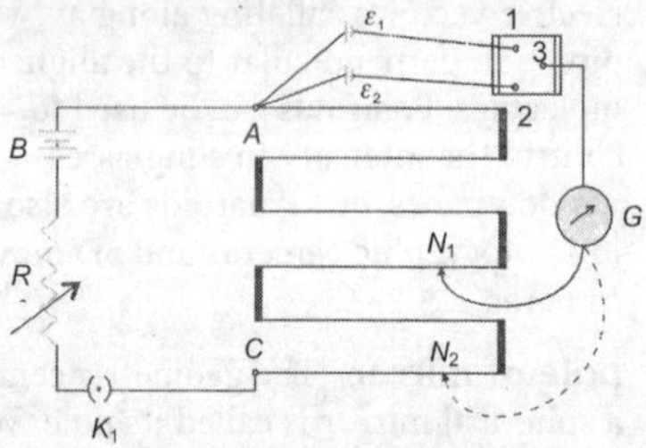

Potentiometer

pound An imperial unit of mass in FPS system.

$$1 \text{ pound} = 453.59 \text{ g}$$

poundal A unit of force in the FPS system equal to 0.138 newton.

power The rate of work done on energy consumption.

$$\text{Power} = \frac{\text{Work done}}{\text{Time taken}}$$

Its SI unit is 'watt' and

$$1 \text{ watt} = 1 \text{ joule/second.}$$

power amplification The ratio of the output power to the input power.

power factor In an electrical circuit, it is the ratio of the power dissipated P to the product of the electromotive force E and the current I. The power factor is given by cos ϕ, where ϕ is the phase angle between the EMF and the current.

power line transfer The transfer of signals through a power cable rather than through a special channel. This is quite common on a domestic scale as well as for communication through the national power grid of the country.

power of a lens The power of a lens is defined as the reciprocal of its focal length. When it is measured in metre, it is represented by the letter *P*. The power *P* of a lens of focal length *f* is given by

$$P = \frac{1}{f}$$

The SI unit of power of a lens is 'dioptre'. It is denoted by the letter D. The power of a convex lens is positive and that of a concave lens is negative.

power of accommodation The ability of the eye lens to adjust its focal length using ciliary muscles.

power reactor A nuclear reactor which is used to generate power. In this, nuclear fission takes place as a controlled chain reaction, producing heat energy that is used to drive turbines and provide electric power.

power supply An electronic device that supplies electrical energy to an electrical load. Its main function is to convert one form of electrical energy to another.

Poynting vector A vector that gives a measure of the flow of energy in an electromagnetic field.

practical units Ampere, volt and ohm are known as the practical units of current, potential difference and resistance respectively.

precession If a body is spinning on an axis, the axis of rotation can itself move around another axis at an angle to it. It can take place only when a couple is applied about an axis which is perpendicular to the axis of rotation. The gravitational fields of the moon and sun acting on the equatorial bulge of the earth causes the precession of the equinoxes, that is the axis of rotation of the earth sweeps out a cone with semi angle $23\frac{1}{2}^{\circ}$ in a period of 26000 years.

precision Precision tells us to what resolution or limit the quantity is measured.

presbyopia The power of accommodation of the eye usually decreases with ageing. For most people, the near point gradually recedes away. They find it difficult to see nearby objects comfortably and distinctly without corrective eye glasses. This defect is called presbyopia. It arises due to the gradual weakening of the ciliary muscles and diminishing flexibility of the eye lens.

pressure Force applied to or disturbed over, a surface, measured as force *F* per unit area *a*; $p = F/a$. The SI unit of pressure is pascal.

pressure gauge Device for measuring fluid pressure.
e.g. barometer, manometer, Bourdon gauge.

pressure head Height of liquid capable of exerting a given pressure.

primary cell An electrolytic cell in which the chemical reactions , that cause the current flow are not readily reversible and the cell cannot easily be recharged, e.g. a dry cell.

primary colours Red, green and violet, which give all other colours when light producing them is combined in various proportions. All three mix to give white.

primary winding The winding on the input side of transformer or induction coil.

p

principal axis of lens In the case of spherical lenses, the principal axis is the line joining the optical centre with its principal focus.

principal axis of mirror The line joining the pole and the centre of curvature of the spherical mirror.

principal focus It is also called second focus. Principal focus is a point on the principal axis through which parallel light rays passes after refraction through a lens.

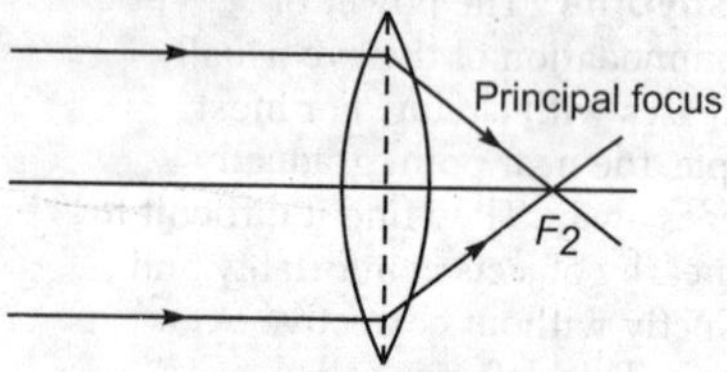

principle of calorimetry When bodies at different temperatures are mixed in the calorimeter, exchange of heat takes place between them. Bodies at higher temperature lose heat, while those at lower temperature gain heat. If no heat is lost to surroundings, the heat lost by hot body must be equal to the heat gained by cold body.

Heat lost = Heat gain

principle of conservation of energy It states that energy can neither be created nor be destroyed, but can be transformed from one form to another form.

principle of floatation A body floats on a liquid when the weight of the liquid displaced by it is equal to its weight.

Let w = weight of body.

w' = weight of the liquid displaced by the body.

if $w > w'$, body will sink.

$w = w'$, body will float being wholly immersed anywhere in the liquid.

$w < w'$, body will float being partially immersed in liquid.

principle of homogeneity of dimensions The physical quantities may be added or subtracted from one another only if they have the same dimensions. Thus, velocity cannot be added to force, or an electric current cannot be subtracted from the thermodynamic temperature. This simple principle called the principle of homogeneity of dimensions.

principle of moments For a system in rotational equilibrium, the sum of the clockwise moments is equal to the sum of the anti-clockwise moments.

principle of superposition When two or more waves of the same type passes through the same region, the amplitude of vibration at any point is the algebraic sum of the individual amplitudes. The waves emerge from the region of superposition unaffected.

principle of Wheatstone bridge If four resistances P, Q, R and S are connected along the arm of a parallelogram $ABCD$ as shown in figure, a battery and key K_1 along diagonal AC and a galvanometer and key K_2 along diagonal BD and there is no deflection in galvanometer, then it is called a balanced Wheatstone bridge

$$\frac{P}{Q} = \frac{R}{S}$$

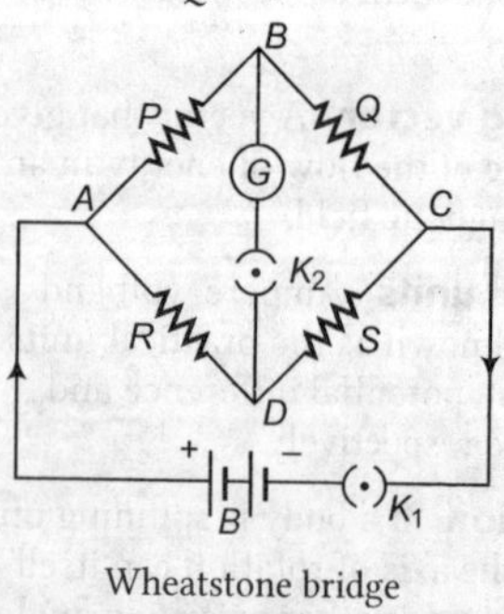

Wheatstone bridge

principal plane A plane perpendicular to the principal axis of a lens and passing through the optical centre. A thick lens has two principal planes.

printed circuit board A self-contained module of interconnected electronic components found in devices ranging from common beepers, pagers and radios to sophisticated radar and computer system.

prism A piece of a transparent material bounded by two plane surfaces inclined at an angle is called a prism. The angle between the two plane surfaces is called the angle of the prism. When a prism refracts sunlight, it splits into its seven colour components.

probe A device which is able to obtain a signal from some space while causing a little disturbance in space.

progressive wave (travelling wave) A wave motion in which the whole periodic displacement advances through the medium. At any instant, the disturbance changes with time and is represented by the equation

$$y = a\sin 2\pi\left(t\nu - \frac{x}{\lambda}\right)$$

where, a is the amplitude, ν is the frequency and λ is the wavelength of the wave.

projectile An object projected from horizontal at an angle and falling freely under gravity.

projectile motion Motion that has constant velocity in a certain direction and constant acceleration in the direction perpendicular to that of velocity.

projectors An optical instrument which can produce a large real image on a screen.

propagation constant A measure of change in amplitude of a wave when it propagates in a given direction.

proton Fundamental elementary particle with a positive charge equal in magnitude to the negative charge on an electron, i.e. $+1.6\times10^{-19}$ C, and with a mass about 1850 times that of an electron. Protons are constituents of the nucleus in every kind of atom. Its mass is 1.672614×10^{-27} kg.

proton decay A hypothetical form of radioactive decay in which the proton decays into lighter subatomic particles such as a neutral pion and a position.

proton number The number of protons in the nucleus of an atom. It is also called atomic number and is denoted by Z.

proton-proton cycle A chain of nuclear fusion reactions which are thought to be responsible for the production of energy in the sun. In this cycle hydrogen gets converted into helium.

$${}_1H^1 + {}_1H^1 \longrightarrow {}_1H^2 + n + e^+$$
$${}_1H^2 + {}_1H^1 \longrightarrow {}_2He^3 + n$$
$${}_2He^3 + {}_2He^3 \longrightarrow {}_2He^4 + 2\,{}_1H^1$$

p-type semiconductor Semiconductors in which conduction is the result of motion of holes.

pseudo force Forces which creates an effect of push or pull but are not physically visible.

pulley A simple machine used to transfer the direction of applied force. It has a wheel engrooved at its circumference and a string passes through the engrooved region.

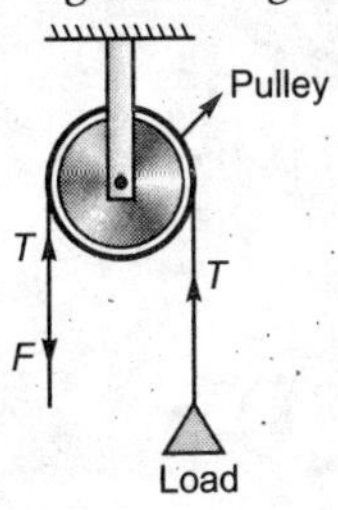

pulsating stars A type of variable star, the variation in the brightness resulting from expansion and subsequent contraction of star.

pulse In physics and telecommunications, brief disturbance propagated in similar way as a wave, but not having the continuous periodic nature of a wave.

pulse modulation The modulation in which information is transmitted by controlling the amplitude, duration, position or presence of a series of electric pulses.

pump A device that imparts energy to a fluid in order to move it from open place to another.

pupil The central circular region of the iris in human eye. It appears black because it does not reflect light and light enters the eye through it.

pure semiconductor Pure semiconductors are called 'intrinsic semiconductors'. The number of electrons (n_e) is equal to the number of holes (n_h) in intrinsic conductors. Holes are essentially semi-electron vacancies with an effective positive charge.

purely inductive or capacitive circuit If the circuit contains only an inductor or capacitor, then the circuit is known as purely inductive or purely capacitive circuit.

push pull amplifier These design operates with neither a phase splitter input or an impedance matching output transformer. Instead, it uses a complimentary pair of transistors, that is one *n-p-n* and one *p-n-p* transistor connected in common collector mode.

pyrometer Instrument for measuring light temperatures, above the range of liquid thermometers.

pyrometry Measurement of high temperatures.

Q

Q-factor It refers to the quality factor. It is the measure of the quality of performance of a resonant circuit. It represents the ability of the system to produce a large output at the resonant frequency. It is given by

$$Q = \frac{V_L \text{ or } V_C}{V}$$

$$= \frac{L\omega}{R} \text{ or } \frac{1}{C\omega R}$$

$$Q = \frac{1}{R}\sqrt{\frac{L}{C}}$$

quadrature A state of being out of phase by 90°.

quadripole An electrical network which has only four terminals, a pair of input terminals and a pair of output terminals. It is used for filters and alternators for which a number of impedances are arranged in series and in parallel in a ladder shaped network.

quadrupole A distribution of charge or magnetisation which is equivalent to two equal electric or magnetic dipoles arranged very close together in opposite directions. The potential at a distance r from a quadrupole is given by

$$V = \frac{1}{4\pi\varepsilon_0} \cdot \frac{q}{r^3}$$

where, q is the quadrupole moment.

quality or timber of sound A musical instrument vibrates with many frequencies at the same time. The quality of any musical sound is determined by the number of overtones and their relative intensities.

quanta of energy *See* quantum.

quantisation of charge Charge on any body can be an integer multiple of a smallest charge *e*. Therefore, charge on any body is given by

$$q = \pm ne$$

where, n is an integer and

$$e = 1.6 \times 10^{-19} \text{ C}.$$

quantitative

1. Relative to quantity.
2. Of, relating to, or susceptible of measurement.
3. Of or relating to number of measurement.

quantised Any physical quantity is said to be quantised if it has only certain discrete values and cannot change continuously.

quantum (Pl. quanta) The smallest amount of energy that a system can gain or loose. The quantum of electromagnetic radiation is the photon.

quantum dot A quantum mechanical system usually made from semiconductors in which electron can be confined into a small region of almost few nanometre size.

quantum electrodynamics The study of properties of electromagnetic radiation and the way in which it interacts with changed matter in terms of quantum mechanics.

quantum mechanics A mechanics that developed from quantum theory and is used to explain the behaviour of atoms, molecules, etc.

quantum number An integer or half integer that specifies the value of a quantised physical quantity such as energy, angular momentum, etc.

quantum state A state of a physical system, e.g. a crystal lattice or an atom, in which its constituent particles are defined by a unique set of quantum numbers.

quantum statistics A statistical description of a system of particles that obeys to the rules of quantum mechanics rather than classical mechanics. In quantum statistics, energy states are considered to be quantised.

quantum theory This theory was introduced by Max Planck (1900). According to this theory, the energy is emitted from any source in the form of packets or bundles of energy called photon. The energy of each photon is $E = h\nu$, where h is Planck's constant and ν is the frequency of the radiation.

quarks There are two types of quarks: up quark (u) and down quark (d). Up quark has a charge + 2/3 the proton charge and down quark has a charge – 1/3 the proton charge. Protons and neutrons are made up of quark as
Proton → *uud*, it means two up quarks and one down quark.
Neutron → *udd*, it means one up quark and two down quarks.

quarter-wave plate A crystal plate that changes the phase difference between the two components of polarised light by traversing it by one-fourth cycle-compare half-wave plate.

quartz The most abundant mineral, consisting of crystalline silicon dioxide (silica, SiO_2). It is a piezoelectric crystal and therefore used in piezoelectric oscillator. It produces double refraction, it can rotate the plane of polarisation to the left or right, it can transmit wavelengths from 180 nm (in ultraviolet) to 4000 nm (in infrared).

quartz clock The clock based on piezoelectric crystal of quartz. It is used to activate digital display.

quasi crystal A structure that is ordered by non-periodic. A quasi crystal line pattern can continuously fill all available space, but is lacks transactional symmetry.

Quasi static process The thermodynamic process that happens infinitely slow.

Q-value In a nuclear reaction, the quantity Q is called the energy balance or Q-value. In an endothermic reaction, the energy is released and Q is negative. In an exothermic reaction, the energy is absorbed and Q is called positive.

R

rad The unit of absorbed dose of ionising radiation. It is equivalent to 100 erg per gram or 0.01 J kg^{-1} of absorbing material. Its SI unit is the gray.

radar Abbreviation of Radio Detection And Ranging. It is used to locate, guide or identify objects; such as airplanes, ships, missiles, satellites, etc. A continuous or pulsed radio waves are sent towards the object and received back after its reflection from the objects.

radial acceleration The centripetal acceleration directed along the radius. It is denoted by a_r.

radial component The resolution of a vector in a circular motion, along the radius.

radial field A field in which lines are along the radii and radiate from the centre. A point charge have radial electric field and a point mass have radial gravitational field.

radial velocity Component of velocity which is along the radius of circle when an object is moving in circular path.

radian A unit of measurement of angles equal to about 57.3°, equivalent to the angle subtended at the centre of a circle by an arc equal in length to the radius.

radiance The radiant flux emitted, reflected, transmitted or received by a surface per unit solid angle per unit projected area.
This is the directional quantity and has a unit, watt per steradian per square metre (Wsr^{-1} m^{-2}).

radiant efficiency In optics, it is the energy conversion efficiency with which the system converts electrical power into optical power. It is the radio of radiant flux to the input electrical power.

radiant flux (radiant power) The total power emitted or received by a body as radiation. It is measured in watt.

radiant heat The rate of flow of radiant energy. Its SI unit is watt.

radiant heating The term refers to heating by radiation.

radiant intensity The radiant flux per unit solid angle emitted by a point source. It is measured in watt per steradian.

radiation

1 The energy emitted by a body in the form of electromagnetic waves due to its temperature.

2 The emission of alpha or beta particles and gamma rays by radioactive substance.

radiation pressure The pressure exerted by electromagnetic radiation on a surface.

radiation pyrometer A type of pyrometer that depends upon the thermal radiations from a hot body for its action.

radiative It is associated with the output of the radiation.

radiator

1. An object that emits radiation.
2. A heat exchanger.

radio The process of communication across the space by the transmission and reception of electromagnetic waves of radio frequency without using wires.

radio astronomy The study of astronomical bodies and events by the radio waves which they emit.

radio frequency A frequency between 30 kHz and 300 GHz (wavelength 1 cm-100 km).

radio telescope A concave reflector and is used to gather radio waves given out by celestial bodies. It helps to bring all such rays to a receiver placed at its focus.

radio transmission The transmission of radio waves from a transmitting aerial to a receiving aerial.

radio wave Radio waves are the result of charges accelerating through conducting wires. They are generated in such electronic devices, as *L-C* oscillators and are used extensively in radio and television communications. They are generally in the frequency range from 500 kHz to about 1000 MHz. The AM (Amplitude Modulated) band is from 530 kHz to 1710 kHz. Higher frequencies upto 54 MHz are used for short wave bands. TV waves range from 54 MHz to 890 MHz. The FM (Frequency Modulated) radio band extends from 88 MHz to 108 MHz. Cellular phones use radio waves to transmit voice communication in the Ultra High Frequency (UHF) band.

radioactive An element or nuclide that exhibits natural radioactivity.

radioactive dating A method of measuring the age of a specimen using the principles of radioactivity.
The method consists of determining the ratio of $_6C^{12}$ to the $_6C^{14}$ (radioactive isotope of carbon with a half-life of 5730 years).

[illegible]e decay The phenomenon [illegible] stable radioactive element to [illegible] α,β and γ particle[illegible]s to become stable.

radioactive element An element subjected to spontaneous degeneration of its nucleus accompanied by the elements with atomic number greater than 83 are radioactive.

radioactive series A series of radioactive nuclides, each of its member being formed by the decay of the previous one. All such series terminate in the product of a stable nuclide e.g. thorium series. It starts with ^{232}Th and terminates in ^{208}Pb after emitting six alpha particles and four beta particles.

radioactive waste The waste material containing radio-nuclides. It may come out from the mining of radioactive ores, nuclear power stations, manufacturing of nuclear weapons and from laboratories.

radioactivity The phenomenon of the spontaneous disintegration of certain unstable nuclides with emission of α-particles, β - particles or γ-rays.

radio altimeter An air borne electronic device capable of measuring the height of the aircraft above terrain immediately below the aircraft.

radiocarbon dating *See* radioactive dating.

radiograph Photographic image that results from absorption of penetrating radiation by an object e.g. an X-ray photograph.

radioisotope A radioactive isotope of an element. e.g. tritium is a radioisotope of hydrogen.
Radioisotopes are used in research as a source of radiation, as tracers in studies of chemical reactions, in medicine for diagnosis and treatment.

r

radiology The study of X-rays, γ-rays and radioactivity, especially as used in diagnosis and medical treatment.

radiolysis The dissociation of molecules by nuclear radiation. It is the cleavage of one or several chemical bonds resulting from exposure to high energy flux.

radiometer An instrument used for detecting and measuring radiation.

radiotherapy Therapy in which X-rays are used for the treatment of a disease.

radium A white radioactive luminescent metallic element, found in uranium ores; such as oxides, pitchblende and carnotite. It is used in radiotherapy and in luminous paints, its symbol is Ra and its melting point is 700°C.

radius of curvature The radius of the hollow glass sphere of which the spherical mirror is a part.

radius of gyration The distance from the axis of rotation at which the total mass of the object might be concentrated without changing its moment of inertia. It is denoted by K and expressed as

$$K = \sqrt{\frac{I}{m}}$$

where, I = moment of inertia of the object about axis of rotation and m = its mass.

radius vector A vector pointing from the origin towards a point in a plane with the polar coordinates $(r, 0)$.

rainbow A natural spectrum of sunlight appearing in the sky. It is formed due to the dispersion of white light by tiny water droplets present in the atmosphere. Rainbow can be seen when your back is towards the Sun. In primary rainbow, the violet colour is obtained at bottom and red colour at the top, while in secondary rainbow, the red is at the bottom and violet is at the top.

Raman effect When monochromatic light is allowed to pass through a transparent medium, it gets scattered and the scattered light contains original wavelengths as well as lines of larger wavelength than the original lines. These lines of larger wavelengths are known as Raman lines and effect is known as Raman effect.

Ramsden eyepiece An eyepiece consisting of two identical planoconvex lenses with their convex surfaces facing each other and separated by a distance equal to two-thirds of the focal length of either lens.

random errors The random errors are those errors, which occur irregularly and hence, are random with respect to sign and size. These can arise due to random and unpredictable fluctuations in experimental conditions (e.g. unpredictable fluctuations in temperature, voltage supply, mechanical vibrations of experimental setups, etc.), personal (unbiased) errors by the observer taking readings, etc.

random motion The motion of an object in all possible directions and with all possible speeds e.g. Brownian motion of gas molecules.

range The maximum distance between a source and a destination upto which the signal is received with sufficient strength.

range of molecular attraction The distance upto which forces of cohesion or adhesion are effective. It is of the order of 10^{-9} m, i.e. the order of the size of the molecules.

Rankine An absolute scale of temperature. In scale, the degree intervals are equal to those in the Fahrenheit scale. In this scale, Rankine is equal to $-459.7°$ F.

Rankine temperature scale A temperature scale that expresses absolute temperatures in °F having absolute zero = 0° R.

rarefaction When the vibrating object moves backwards, it creates a region of low pressure called rarefaction *R*. Rarefactions are the regions of low pressure, where particles are spread apart and are represented by the valley, i.e. the lower portion of the curve. A peak is called the crest and a valley is called the trough of a wave.

ray A very narrow beam of radiation such as; light, cathode rays, etc.

ray diagrams Accurate or approximate diagrams showing how selected rays pass through a lens; prism or a microscope. It also show details of the image formed.

ray of light A very narrow beam of light radiation.

Rayleigh criterion A generally accepted criterion for the minimum resoluable image processed and diffraction limit of a source point.

Rayleigh scattering The amount of scattering is inversely proportional to the fourth power of the wavelength.

***R-C* circuit** A resistor capacitor circuit used to filter a signal by blocking certain frequencies and passing the other.

reactance Measure of the resistance offered by an inductance and capacitance to an AC current of frequency ω. The reactance of an inductor of inductance L is given by $X_L = \omega L$, while for a capacitor of capacitance C, it is given by

$$X_C = 1 / \omega C$$

reactor Alternative name for a nuclear reactor. It is a device in which energy is produced.

real image If the ray actually pass through the mirror, it is called the real image, and generally will become invisible.

Reaumur scale A scale of temperature with 0° R at the freezing point at 80° R at the boiling point of water at normal pressure.

receiver The part of a communication system that extracts the desired message signal from the received signals.

recoil To move in backward direction.

recoil electron An electron that has been set into motion by a collision.

recombination In semiconductor, the elimination of mobile charge carriers (electrons and holes) cross over.

rectification The process of obtaining a direct current from an alternating electrical supply.

rectifier A device which converts alternating current into direct current and *vice-versa.* A diode valve or *p-n* junction can be used as a rectifier.

rectilinear motion Motion of an object in a straight line. It is also known as motion in one dimension.

rectilinear propagation Passage of radiation in straight line in a constant medium.

red A colour that is associated with low energy, low temperature visible radiation.

red giant A giant star which is the later stages of stellar evaluation. Its diameter is 10 to 100 times of the Sun and the temperature of its surface is 2000-3000 K.

red shift Astronomers call the increase in wavelength due to Doppler effect as red shift, since a wavelength in the middle of the visible region of the spectrum moves towards the red end of the spectrum.

reference circle The circle around which the point moves in circular motion.

reference level Location at which potential energy is chosen to be zero.

Reference tone Stable tone of known frequency continuously recorded on one track of multitrack signal recordings and intermittently recorded on signal track recordings by the collection equipment operators for the subsequent use by the data analysts as a frequency reference.

reflectance The ratio of the intensity of the reflected radiation to the intensity incident radiation.

reflected ray The ray that comes back from the surface after reflection.

reflecting telescope An astronomical telescope that uses mirror as objective. It has several advantages over refracting telescope. First, there is no chromatic aberration in a mirror. Second, by using a parabolic concave mirror, spherical aberration is removed. Third, a mechanical support can be easily given to a mirror.

reflection The phenomena of rebouncing back of light rays in to the same medium when it strikes on a smooth surface, such as a plane mirror.

reflectivity *See* reflectance.

refracted wave If a wave is incident obliquely on the boundary between two different media, the transmitted wave is called the refracted wave. The incident and refracted waves obey Snell's law of refraction, the usual laws of reflection.

refracting angle The dihedral angle (as of a prism) included between the planes of two sides through which the refracted beam passes.

refracting telescope A type of optical telescope that uses a lens as its objective to form an image. Its design was originally used in spy glasses and astronomical telescopes but is also used for long focus camera lenses.

refraction of light The phenomena of deviation of light rays from its path when it travels from one transparent medium to another transparent medium. The cause of refraction is the different speed of light in different media.

refractive index The absolute refractive index of any medium is equal to the ratio of speed of light in vacuum c to the speed of light in that medium v.

$$\mu = \frac{\text{speed of light in vacuum, } c}{\text{speed of light in medium, } v}$$

The refractive index of second medium with respect to first medium is equal to the ratio of speed of light in medium I to the speed of light in medium II.

$$\mu_2 = \frac{\text{speed of light in medium I } (v_1)}{\text{speed of light in medium II} (v_2)}$$

refractivity A measure of the ability of a medium to deviate radiation entering its surface.

refrigerator A refrigerator is the reverse of a heat engine. Here, the working substance extracts heat Q_2 from the cold reservoir at temperature T_2, some external work W is done on it and heat Q_1 is released to the hot reservoir at temperature T_1. In a refrigerator, the working substance (usually in gaseous form) goes through the following steps

(i) Sudden expansion of the gas from high to low pressure which cools it and converts it into a vapour-liquid mixture.

(ii) Absorption by the cold fluid of heat from the region to be cooled converting it into vapour.

(iii) Heating up of the vapour due to external work done on the system.
(iv) Release of heat by the vapour to the surroundings, bringing it to the initial state and completing the cycle.

regelation The phenomenon of refreezing.

regenerator A device that used especially with hot air engines or gas furnaces in which incoming air or gas is heated by contact with masses previously heated by outgoing hot air or gas.

regular reflection Reflection from a smooth surface like that of a mirror. Images are formed by regular reflection.

rejector A parallel resonant circuit containing an inductor and a capacitor in parallel. The impedance of such circuit is maximum at a particular frequency called resonant frequency.

relative density The ratio of density of the substance to the density of water at 4°C.

Relative density

$$= \frac{\text{density of the substance}}{\text{density of water at } 4^\circ\text{C}}$$

relative error The ratio of the mean absolute error $\Delta\bar{a}$ to the mean value (a_{mean}) of any quantity.

relative humidity Ratio of the amount of water vapour present in the air to the maximum amount of water vapour of the air can hold at that temperature.

relative permeability The ratio of permeability of medium and free space.

relative permittivity (ε_r) The ratio C_m / C_0 where, C_m is capacitance of parallel plate capacitor with the medium inserted between the plate and C_0, the capacitance with air (or vacuum) between them.

relative velocity The rate of change of relative position of an object with respect to the other object is called the relative velocity of first object with respect to the other object.

relativistic mass The mass of an object measured by an observer at rest in a frame of reference in which the object is moving with a velocity v, is given by

$$m = \frac{m_0}{\sqrt{\left(1 - \frac{v^2}{c^2}\right)}}$$

where, m_0 = rest mass of the object,
c = speed of light in vacuum
and m = relativistic mass of the object.

relativistic particle The particle which is travelling at a relativistic velocity.

relativity The theory of relativity was proposed by Einstein which over ruled the Newtonian mechanics, mostly there are two widely accepted theories of relativity. First is special theory of relativity which refers to non-accelerating frames of references proposed in 1905. Second is general theory of relativity which was extended to accelerated system which was proposed in 1915.

relaxation Any phenomenon in which a system takes a significant length of time to react to a change. There are many cases or situation in physics, where return to equilibrium does not at one follow a change.

relay A device by means of which one circuit is indirectly controlled by change in the same or in another circuit. In a different sense, it is the process by which a signal, especially an electronic signal is passed on.

reluctance The magnetic analog of electric resistance, i.e. magnetic resistance. It is equal to the ratio of magnetomotive force to total magnetic flux in a magnetic circuit. Its SI unit is henry per metre.

reluctivity The reciprocal of magnetic permeability.

remote control Control of operation or performance of an apparatus from a distance, as a control the guided missile by radio signals.

remote sensing The process of gathering and recording of information about the Earth from a distance (without actual contact).

renewable energy source The sources of energy that do not use up the Earth's finite mineral resources.

repeater A combination of a receiver and a transmitter. A repeater picks up the signal from the transmitter, amplifies and retransmits it to the receiver sometimes with a change in carrier frequency. Repeaters are used to extend the range of communication system. A communication satellite is essentially a repeater station in space.

resilience The power to return to the original form or position after being bent or compressed.

resistance The obstruction posed by the conductor to the flow of electric current through it.

resistance box Set of combination of resistance coils arranged in such a manner that any desired value of resistance may be obtained using one or a combination of these.

resistance thermometer The thermometer that measures temperature by the change in electrical resistance of a conductor.

resistive circuit The AC circuit containing only pure resistance R. In this case $\phi = 0$, which implies maximum power dissipation.

resistivity The resistivity of a material is equal to the electrical resistance of its wire of unit length and unit area of cross-section.

Resistivity, $\delta = \frac{RA}{l}$.

where, A = area of cross-section,
l = length of the wire and
R = resistance of wire.

Resistivity depends on the nature of the material and is independent of its dimensions. Its SI unit is ohm-metre.

resistor-resistor logic A mean to connect logic gates as inputs in a logic gate circuit using a resistor for each gate to give a specified logic output. The technique is simple but needs the resistors to be accurate.

resistors in parallel The equivalent resistance of a set of resistors connected in parallel is given by

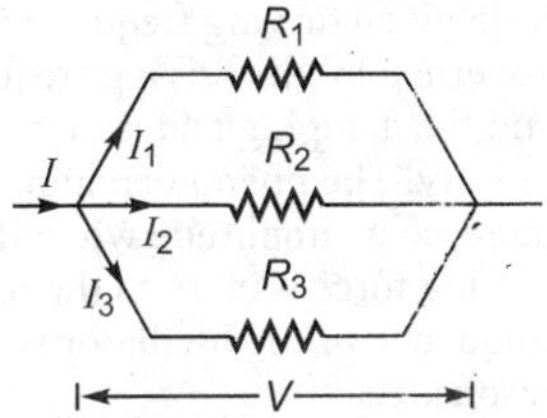

$$\frac{1}{R_P} = \frac{1}{R_1} + \frac{1}{R_2} + \frac{1}{R_3} + \dots$$

In a parallel combination, the potential difference remains same at the ends of each resistor.

resistors in series The equivalent resistance of a set of resistors connected in series is given by

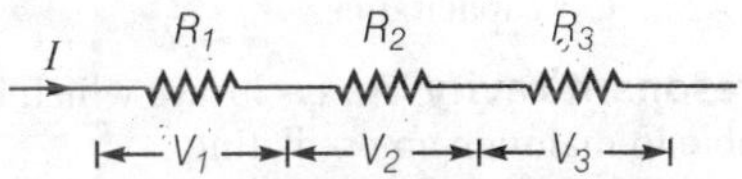

$$R_S = R_1 + R_2 + R_3 + \dots$$

In a series combination, the current flowing through each resistor remains the same.

resistor-transistor logic A class of digital circuits built using the resistors as the input network and bipolar junction transistors as switching devices.

resolution The ability to distinguish two close objects separately rather than as one single object.

resolution of vectors The division of a vector into its components which are at right angle to each other.

resolving power A measure of the ability of an optical system to form detectably separate images of close objects or to separate close wavelengths of radiation.

resonance

1. The particular case in which the natural frequency of the driver equals the natural frequency of the driven is known as resonance.
2. The maximum possible amplitude for a given driving frequency is governed by the driving frequency and the damping and is never infinity. The phenomenon of increase in amplitude when the driving force is close to the natural frequency of the oscillator is called resonance.

resonance circuit An electric circuit containing an inductance and a capacitance at a particular frequency at which inductive reactance and capacitive reactance are equal. This frequency is given by

$$f = \frac{1}{2\pi\sqrt{LC}}$$

where, L = inductance and C = capacitance.

resonant cavity An enclosure which is able to maintain an oscillating electromagnetic field when suitably excited. The geometry of cavity determines the resonant frequency.

resonator A device that is used for increasing sound by resonance or to detect the presence of particular frequency by resonance.

rest It refers to an object being stationary relative to particular frame of reference or another object. When the position of body with respect to its surroundings does not change with time, it is said to be at rest.

restitution coefficient The ratio of the relative velocity of two colliding bodies immediately after collision to their relative velocities before impact.

restoring force A force which changes on change in length, volume, size or shape of a body.

rest mass The mass of an object at rest as measured by an observer at rest in the same frame of reference.

resultant A vector quantity that has the same effect as two or more other vector quantities of the same kind.

retardation Negative acceleration.

retentivity The property measured by the residual magnetic induction corresponding to the saturation induction for the material.

retina Inner surface of the eye where image is formed by the eye lens. It contains lakhs of rod and cone cells which are sensitive to intensity and colours of light, respectively.

reverberation The repeated reflection that results in the persistence of sound. In an auditorium or big hall, excessive reverberation is highly undesirable. To reduce reverberation, the roof and walls of the auditorium are generally covered with sound-absorbent materials like compressed fibreboard, rough plaster or draperies. The seat materials are also selected on the basis of their sound absorbing properties.

reverse biasing When *p*-side of a *p-n* junction is connected to negative potential and *n*-side to positive potential, then this biasing is called reverse-biasing.

The applied voltage mostly drops across the depletion region. The direction of applied voltage is same as the direction of barrier potential. As a result, the barrier height increases and the depletion region widens due to the change in the electric field.

The effective barrier height under reverse bias is $(V_0 + V)$. This suppresses the flow of electrons from $n \rightarrow p$ and holes from $p \rightarrow n$. Thus, diffusion current, decreases enormously compared to the diode under forward bias.

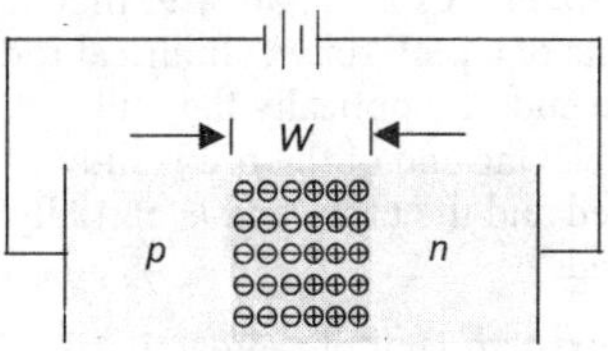

Reverse biasing

reversible process A process is reversible if it can be reversed such that both the system and the surroundings return to their original states, with no change anywhere else in the universe. The idealised reversible process is a quasi-static process with no dissipative factors such as; friction, viscosity, etc.

revolution Motion of a body about an axis or around an external point. In astronomy, revolution means the orbital motion of a body about its centre of mass.

Reynold's number A dimensionless number, whose value gives an approximate idea whether the flow of a liquid would be streamlined or turbulent.

$$R_e = \rho v d / \eta$$

where, ρ = density of the fluid flowing with a critical velocity v,

d = diameter of the pipe and

η = coefficient of viscosity of the fluid.

It is found that flow is streamline or laminar for R_e less than 1000. The flow is turbulent for $R_e > 2000$. The flow becomes unsteady for R_e between 1000 and 2000.

Rheology The study of flow of matter, primarily in the liquid state but also as soft solids or the solids under conditions in which they respond with plastic flow rather than deforming elastically in response to an applied force.

rheostat A variable resistor used to control voltage. It is a coil wound over a cylindrical block.

right hand rule

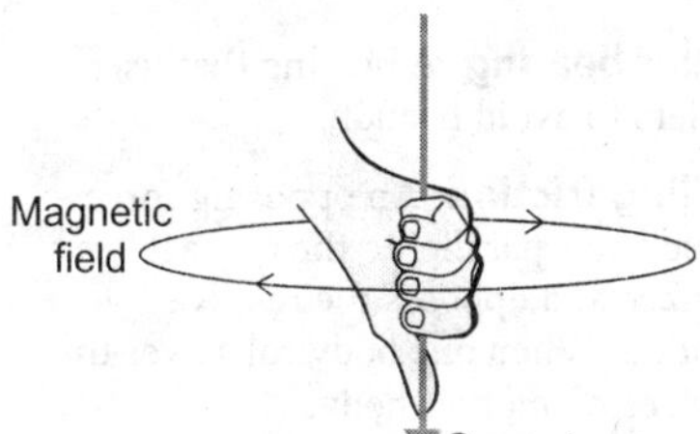

Grasp the wire in your right hand with your extended thumb pointing in the direction of the current. Your fingers will curl around in the direction of the magnetic field.

rigid body A body in which the relative position of its particles do not change on applying force on it.

ripple tank A device for producing waves (ripples) on the surface of water.

***R-L* circuit** An inductor-resistor circuit which is the analogous to infinite impulse response electronic filters.

robot A machine that is made to look like a human and capable of doing mechanical work, routine task on command.

Robotics The branch of technology that deals with the design, construction, operation and application of robots.

rods The light sensitive cells present on the retina of eye, which are sensitive for colours of light.

roentgen Its symbol is *R*, unit of radiation specially used for X-rays and γ-rays, defined in terms of the ionising effect on air. One roentgen induces 2.58×10^{-4} coulomb of charge in one kilogram of dry air.

roentgen rays Old name of X-rays.

roll Motion of an object about the long axis. It is common to use stabilisers to reduce this in the case of ships.

roller bearing A bearing that uses rollers to avoid friction.

rolling friction An opposing force which acts parallel to the contact surface and opposes the relative motion. When one body rolls over the surface of another body.

root mean square value (RMS value)

1. The square root of the mean or average of squares of speeds of a group of particles.
2. The root mean square value of alternating current is that value of steady current which will produce the same amount of heat in a circuit as by alternating current in the same circuit in the same time.

rotameter A device that measures the rate of flow of liquid or gas in a closed tube. It belongs to a class of metres called variable area metres, which measures the flow rate by allowing the cross-sectional area, the fluid travels through, to vary, causing a measurable effect.

rotor The non-stationary part of an electric motor operating with a stationary element.

rotation *See* rotational motion.

rotational frequency The magnitude of the vector quantity angular velocity. It is used as a synonym for the vector quantity angular frequency one revolution is equal to 2π radians.

rotational kinetic energy The kinetic energy of an object performing rotational motion.

rotational motion The motion of a rigid body in which all the particles of the body describe circular paths.

ruby laser A solid state laser that consists of a pink ruby cylindrical rod whose ends are optically flat and parallel. One end of the rod is fully silvered and the other end is partially silvered.

Rutherford Unit of radioactivity which has decay rate of 10 disintegrations per second. Its symbol is rd.

Rutherford scattering The scattering of an alpha particle through a large angle with respect to the original direction of motion of particle, caused by an atom with most of the mass and all of the positive electric charge concentrated at the centre of nucleus.

Rydberg constant A constant relating to the wave number of atomic spectrum lines. Its value for hydrogen is

$$1.09677 \times 10^{7}\ m^{-1}.$$

Rydberg formula A formula which describes all of the characteristics of hydrogen's spectrum, including the Balmer, Lyman, Paschen, Brackett and Pfund series.

S

Sabin formula In acoustics a formula giving the reverberation time of an enclosure

$$T = \frac{V}{20\sum_{r=1}^{n} a_r s_r}$$

where, T = reverberation time in seconds,
V = volume of enclosure in cu. ft.
$a_1, a_2, \ldots a_r$ = absorption coefficient across $s_1, s_2, \ldots$.

safety factor A term describing the structural capacity of a system beyond the expected loads or actual loads. Essentially, the safety factor is how much stronger the system is than it usually needs to be for an intended load.

safety valve A type of valve that automatically actuates when the pressure of inlet side of the valve increases to predetermined pressure.

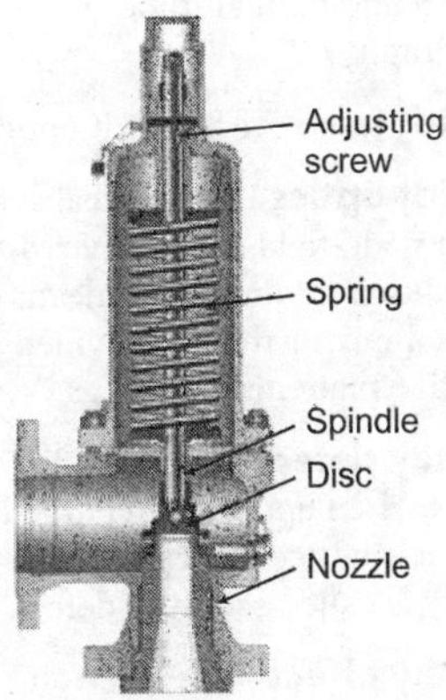

Safety valve

salt bridge An inverted U-tube containing a saturated solution of a salt such as potassium chloride. It is used to connect two half cells.

sampling A method of measuring only some portions of a signal, the resultant values are taken as representative of the whole. The rate of sampling of a periodic quantity must be at least double the frequency.

sand paper A strong paper coated on its surface with a layer of sand such a paper is used for smoothing or polishing.

satellites Heavenly bodies which revolve in orbits around other bodies of greater mass under the influence of their mutual gravitational field. Six of the major planets possess their own natural satellites. Moon is the natural satellite of the earth.

saturated It means to cause a substance to unite with the greatest possible amount of another substance.

saturated solution A solution that cannot take any more solute at a given temperature.

saturated vapour Vapour that can exist in equilibrium with its parent solid or liquid at a given temperature.

saturated vapour pressure Pressure exerted by a saturated vapour.

saturation Point at which no more of a material can be dissolved, absorbed or retained by another.

saturation current The maximum current, excluding breakdown current, that can be obtained from an electronic device.

Saturn Saturn is the most distant planet. Its distance from the sun is almost two times that of jupiter. It is cooler than jupiter. The most distinguishing feature of saturn is its beautiful rings that encircle the planet. Saturn is known to have 61 satellites or moons and is largest amongst all the planets.

sawtooth wave A waveform generated electronically (such as the variation of voltage with time), having a uniform increase that regularly and rapidly drops to the initial value. It is used as the time base for scanning circuits in a Cathode Ray Tube (CRT).

scalar Quantity that has magnitude but not direction are called scalars, e.g. length, area, volume, pressure, etc. It is specified completely by a single number, alongwith the proper unit. The rules for combining scalars are same as the rules of ordinary algebra. Scalars can be added, subtracted, multiplied and divided just as the ordinary numbers.

scalar potential A situation where the difference in potential energies of an object in two different position depends only on the initials and final position not the path taken.

scalar product The product of two vectors whose result is a scalar quantity. The scalar product of two vectors is equal to the product of magnitude of vectors and the cosine of the angle between them.

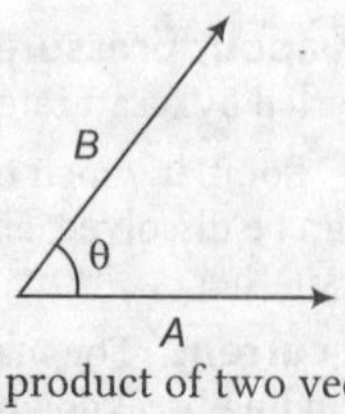

The scalar product of two vectors **A** and **B** are given by $\mathbf{A} \cdot \mathbf{B} = AB \cos \theta$, where, A and B are magnitude of vectors **A** and **B** and θ is the angle between them.

scalar quantity The physical quantities which do not require direction for their complete representation.

scanning The process of exploring area in a methodical manner, so as to produce an electrical output that varies with time and is proportional to the magnitude of the information scanned.

scanning electron microscope A type of microscope that produces images of a sample by scanning it with a focused beam of electrons.

scanning probe microscopy Branch of microscopy that forms images of surfaces using a physical probe that scans the specimen.

scattering The spreading out of a beam of radiation when it is incident on matter. According to Lord Rayleigh, the scattered light intensity varies as $1/\lambda^4$.

Schmidt camera A type of camera using a concave spherical mirror with a specially shaped lens in front of it to form the image. The lens is weakly converging near its centre and weakly diverging near the periphery, thus correcting the system for spherical aberration. It is used in astronomical research and high altitude photography.

Schmidt lens *See* Schmidt optics

Schmidt optics The optical system used in wide-field cameras. Errors are reduced to a minimum by means of a spherical mirror that is provided with a corrective plate near its focus.

Schottky defect In non-ionic crystals when oppositely charged ions leave their lattice site creating a vacancy is called schottky defect.

Schottky effect The electron emission that taken place in the field and temperature regime is called schottky effect.

Schrödinger equation An equation that treats the behaviour of an electron in an atom as a three dimensional stationary wave. Its solution is related to the probability that the electron is located in a particular place.

Schwarzschild radius A critical radius of a body of given mass that must be exceeded if light is to escape from that body. It is equal to $2GM/c^2$, where, G is the gravitational constant, c is the speed of light and M is the mass of the body. If the body collapses to such an extent that its radius is less than the Schwarzschild radius, the escape velocity becomes equal to the speed of light and the object becomes a black hole.

scintillation counter A device that counts the incident photons upon a material by the visible or near-visible light which is emitted.

sclera Separated from the cornea by corneal limbus.

scotopic vision The vision of the eye under low light conditions.

screen A surface on which image can be drawn.

screw A simple machine when given complete circular turn of radius. Due to friction, the efficiency of such machine is low. The force ratio, however can be quite high.

screw gauge A simple machine which on being given a complete circular turn moves forward linearly by a distance.

Searle's rod (Searle's apparatus) An apparatus used for measuring the thermal conductivity of a good conductor. It is a long metallic rod, which is heated at one end. The other end is cooled by a steady stream of water. The temperature of the rod is measured at two points along the length of the rod, separated by a distance I. If θ_1 and θ_2 are the temperature at these two points and A is the area of cross-section of the rod, the thermal conductivity of the rod is given by

$$\frac{KA(\theta_1 - \theta_2)}{I} = ms\,(\theta_4 - \theta_3),$$

where, m is the mass of water flowing per unit time, s is the specific heat of water and θ_3 and θ_4 are the temperatures at the inlet and outlet of water.

second It is the unit of time. The second is the duration of 9,192,631,770 periods of the radiation corresponding to the transition between the two hyperfine levels of the ground state of the cesium-133 atom.

second law of thermodynamics It states that the coefficient of performance can never be infinite. According to Kelvin-Planck statement–"Heat cannot be converted completely into work." According to Clausius–"Heat cannot be transferred from a colder object on towards a hotter object on its own."

second pendulum A simple pendulum whose period is two seconds.

secondary cell Electrolytic cell that must be supplied with electric charge before use of passing a direct current through it, but it can be recharged over and over again.

secondary colour Colour obtained by mixing primary colours.

secondary emission The emission of electrons when charged particles like electrons or ions in a vacuum tube strike a metal surface these are called secondary electrons.

secondary wavelets Every point of a wavefront can be regarded as a fresh source of light and called secondary source. It also emit waves, called secondary wavelets, which moves in the medium with a speed of the wave.

secondary winding The winding on the output side of a transformer irrespective of the transformer type.

sector A part of a circle bounded by two radii and the arc contained between them.

Seebeck effect The production of an emf in a circuit having two conductors, when the junction between the two conductors are at different temperatures. The emf developed in the circuit is called **thermo-electric emf** and is of the order of a few millivolt. This effect is called Seebeck effect.

seismic wave Vibrations propagated within the earth or along its surface as a result of an earthquake or explosion.

seismograph An instrument used for recording earthquake shocks.

seismology The scientific study of earthquakes and the propagation of elastic waves through the earth or through other planet like bodies.

self absorption The absorption of some part of its own radiation by a large radioactive source, it results in an overall decrease in external radiation.

self-inductance Resistance to a change in current in an electric circuit by the creation of a back electromotive force. This force is sometimes known as the back emf as its direction opposes the current change in accordance with Lenz's law. The unit of self-inductance is ohm-second. An ohm-second is called a henry (H).

semiconductor A material whose conductivity lies between a conductor and an insulator is called a semiconductor. e.g. germanium, silicon, etc. For a semiconductor conduction band is empty and valence band is fully filled and there is a small energy gap between them.

semiconductor diode
A semiconductor diode is basically a *p-n* junction with metallic contacts provided at the ends for the application of an external voltage. It is a two terminal device which can conduct current only in forward biasing.

semi-metal A material with a very small overlap between the bottom of the conduction band and top of valence band. According to electronic band theory, solids can be classified as insulators, semiconductors, semi-metals or metals.

sensitivity Generally, it is the response of a physical device to a unit change in the input. Its exact definition is different for different devices and circuits.

sensor Any device that is sensitive to light, temperature, radiation, etc. Which transmit a signal to a measuring or controlling device.

separation energy The energy needed to remove a nucleon or other particle from a nucleus.

series Element in an electrical circuit are said to be connected in series, if each of them carries the same current. Resulting resistance in series

$$R = R_1 + R_2 + R_3 + ...$$

Resulting emf for cells in series

$$E = E_1 + E_2 + ...$$

Resulting capacitance for capacitances in series

$$\frac{1}{C} = \frac{1}{C_1} + \frac{1}{C_2} + \frac{1}{C_3} + ...$$

sextant A navigational instrument used for the accurate measurement of the angle of a heavenly body above the horizon.

shadow The dark shade cast on a surface by an object through which light cannot pass as radiations travel in a straight line through a given medium.

shear modulus The ratio of shearing stress to the corresponding shearing strain is called the shear modulus of the material and is represented by G. It is also called the **modulus of rigidity**.

$$G = \frac{\text{shearing stress } (\sigma_s)}{\text{shearing strain}}$$

$$G = (F/A)/(\Delta x/L)$$
$$= (F \times L)(A \times \Delta x)$$

Similarly, $G = (F/A)/\theta = F/(A \times \theta)$

shearing force An unaligned force pushing one part of a body in one direction and other part in the opposite direction.

shearing strain When the deforming forces are tangential, then the shearing strain is given by the angle θ through which a perpendicular to the fixed plane is turned after deformation.

For small angle, $\theta = \dfrac{\Delta x}{y}$

shearing stress The restoring force per unit area developed due to the applied tangential force is known as shearing stress.

shell A set of electron orbitals having nearly the same energy and sharing the same first quantum number.

shielding The process of protecting certain region from external field.

shock wave Sound wave in air of exceptionally high intensity produced by an object travelling faster than the speed of sound on by the detonation of a high explosive.

short circuit It is an electrical circuit that allows a current to travel along an unintended path.

short sightedness Visual defect in which the eyeball is too long (front to back) so that rays of light entering the eye from distant objects are brought to a focus in front of the retina.

short wave An electromagnetic wave of wavelength 60 m or less.

shunt In physics, a low resistor connected in parallel with a circuit or device that reduces the amount of electric current flowing through it.

sideband Range of frequencies lying on either side of a modulated carrier wave.

siemens (mho) The SI unit of electrical conductance, defined as the conductance of an element that possesses a resistance of one ohm. The unit to be called the mho or reciprocal ohm.

signal The variable parameter, such as current or voltage, by means of which information is conveyed through an electronic circuit or system.

sign convention In cartesian sign convention, all distances are measured from the pole of the mirror or the optical centre of the lens.

The distances measured in the same direction as the incident light are taken as positive and those measured in the direction opposite to the direction of incident light are taken as negative. The height measured upwards with respect to x-axis and normal to the principal axis (x-axis) of the mirror/lens are taken as positive. The height measured downwards is taken as negative.

significant figures The reliable digits plus the first uncertain digit in measurement are known as significant figures. A choice of change of different units does not change the number of significant figures in a measurement. All the non-zero digits are significant. All the zeroes between two non-zero digits are significant no matter where the decimal point is, if at all. For a number with a decimal, the trailing zero's are significant. In multiplication or division, the final result should return as many significant figures as are there in the original number with the least significant figures.

In addition or subtraction, the final result should retain as many decimal places as are there in the number with the least decimal places.

silicon chip Integrated circuit made from a thin wafer of pure crystalline silicon. It is fabricated in such a way that it can perform large number of independent electronic functions.

simple harmonic motion Periodic motion of a particle whose acceleration is proportional to its distance (x) from a fixed point and is always directed towards that point, i.e. $a = -kx$, where k is a constant. The minus sign shows that as the particle moves to and fro its acceleration is oppositely directed to its displacement.

simple microscope A simple biconvex lens, usually referred as magnifying glass.

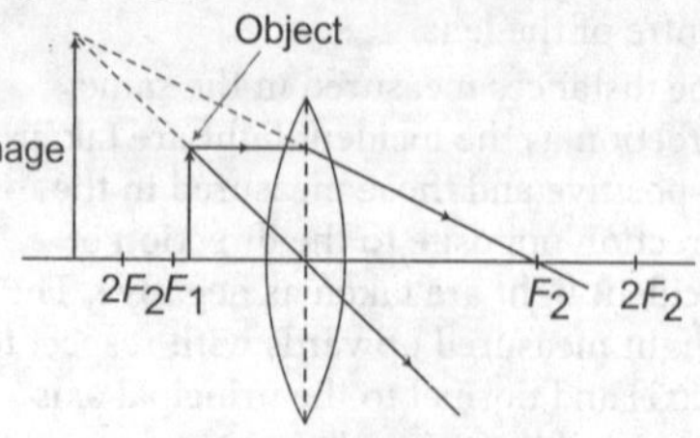

Simple microscope

It gives an enlarged image when object is place between principal focus and optical centre.

Its magnification $(m) = \left(1 + \frac{D}{f}\right)$

where, D is least distance of distinct vision.

simple pendulum It consists of a point mass suspended by an inextensible, massless string from a fixed point about which it can oscillate freely.

sine wave The waveform that represents the periodic oscillations of constant amplitude as given by the sine of a linear function.

single phase Single phase of electrical system or apparatus means, having only one alternating voltage.

sinusoidal wave A mathematical curve that describes a smooth repetive oscillation named after sine of which graph occurs.

SI units Abbreviation for System International *d'* Unites, an international system of scientific units. It has seven basic units—metre (m), kilogram (kg), second (*s*), kelvin (K), ampere (A), mole (mol), candela (cd) and two supplementary units radian (rad) and steradian (sr).

skin effect The phenomenon that causes very high frequency electric currents to travel through the thin outermost layer of metal in a conductor. The current density is greater at the surface of the conductor than at its centre. It is due to electromagnetic effects.

skip distance The minimum distance from the transmitter at which a sky wave can be received. This arises due to minimum angle of incidence at the ionosphere below which a sky wave is not reflected. This minimum angle is a function of the frequency.

sky wave The electromagnetic wave reflected downward towards Earth from the ionosphere. This mode of transmission is used for EM waves of wavelengths 200 m or less. The sky waves can reach the points on Earth where ground waves cannot reach due to curvature in Earth's surrounding.

sliding friction An opposing force acting between two objects which opposes the relative motion, when one body is sliding over the surface by another body.

slip The way in which plastic deformation of a metal occurs.

slip rings Conducting rings which are used in rotating electric machine. These are connected by brush due to which they are connected with moving parts. Moving wire slip on these rings.

slit A cut part, or small opening smelting from of entraction of base metal from its ore.

slow neutron A neutron with a kinetic energy less than 100 eV.

Snell's law The law of refraction

$$\frac{\sin i}{\sin r} = c$$

where, *i* is the angle of incidence, *r*′ is the angle of refraction, and *c* is a constant, now known to be the ratio, n / n', of the refractive indices of the initial medium and the refracting medium.

sodium vapour lamp A type of gas discharge lamp in which a discharge starts in an inert gas like neon at room temperature.

soft ferromagnetic material The class of ferromagnetic materials in which the magnetisation disappears on removal of the external field. Soft iron is one such material. There are a number of elements which are ferromagnetic like iron, cobalt, nickel, gadolinium, etc.

soft iron Iron that has a low content of carbon, unlike steel. It is unable to retain magnetism.

soft X-ray The X-rays of large wavelength having a low penetrating power are called soft X-rays.

solar cell Any device that uses solar radiation to drive an electric current. One type or solar cell is used in power equipment in spacecraft and artificial satellites and other types of solar cell is used in desert regions, water-heating systems, etc.

solar constant Energy received from the sun per minute per unit area placed at right angle to the incident radiation at the mean distance of the Earth from the sun. Its value is 2 cal/cm^2-min = 1400 J/s-m^2 nearly.

solar day The time interval between two successive appearance of the sun at the meridian.

solar eclipse *See* eclipse

solar energy Energy from the sun, mainly light and heat radiation. It can be harnessed to make electricity using photocells, or the sun's rays may be used directly to heat water in a radiator or, focused by mirror, in a solar furnace.

solar system The sun, the eight major planet (mercury, venus, earth, mars, jupiter, saturn, uranus, neptune) and their natural satellite, the asteroids, the comets and meteoroids all constitute solar system.

solar wind Continuous permanent stream of electrically charged particles that are emitted from the sun.

soldering iron An instrument used for melting and applying solder.

solenoid Cylindrical coil of insulated copper wire carrying an electric current, used to produce a magnetic field. It may have an iron core that moves, to work as a switch. It is used to obtain a uniform magnetic field.

solid angle (Ω) An angle subtended by a surface at a point.

solid state Physical state of matter that has a definite shape and the volume of a solid changes slightly with temperature and pressure.

solid state physics The branch of physics in which we study the physical properties of solids, with special emphasis on the electrical properties of semi-conducting materials in relation to their electronic structure.

solidification Alternative name for freezing. *See* freezing.

SONAR Abbreviation of Sound Navigation And Ranging. An apparatus for echo sounding that employs ultrasonic waves. It can detect echoes from under water objects and give their bearing and range.

sonic boom When a sound producing source moves with a speed higher than that of sound, it produces shock waves in air.
These shock waves carry a large amount of energy. The air pressure variation associated with this type of shock waves produces a very sharp and loud sound called the 'sonic boom'.

sonogram A diagnostic medical image created using ultrasound echo equipment.

sonography It is a diagnostic medical procedure that uses high frequency sound waves to produce dynamic visual images of organs, tissues, or blood flow inside the body.

sonometer Apparatus for investigating stretched wires or strings as sources of sound.

sound It is the sensation that is caused by stimulation of the organs of hearing by vibration transmitted through the air or another medium.

S

sound absorption The process by which a material, structure or object takes in sound energy when sound waves are encountered, as opposed to reflecting the energy.

sound wave A longitudinal wave in elastic medium.

south magnetic pole

1. The pole near the geographic south pole is called the south magnetic pole.
2. The points towards south is called south seeking or south pole.

space charge A region in a vacuum tube or semiconductor having some net electric charge because of excess or deficiency of electrons.

space wave A space wave travels in a straight line from transmitting antenna to the receiving antenna. Space waves are used for Line Of Sight (LOS) communication as well as satellite communication. At frequencies above 40 MHz, communication is essentially limited to line of sight paths. At these frequencies, the antennas are relatively smaller and can be placed at height of many wavelengths above the ground.

spark A visible disruptive discharge of electricity between two places at opposite high potential. It is preceded by ionisation of the path.

spark discharge A visible disruptive discharge of electricity between two points whose potential difference is high.

spark gap An arrangement of electrodes specially designed so that a disruptive discharge takes place between them when the applied voltage exceeds a pre-determined value.

speaker Transducers that convert electromagnetic waves into sound waves. The speakers receive audio input from a device such as a computer or an audio receiver.

specific charge The ratio of the electric charge to mass of an elementary particles is called its specific charge.

specific conductance The reciprocal of specific resistance.

It is denoted by σ. Therefore $\sigma = \frac{1}{\rho}$

It unit is $\text{ohm}^{-1}\ \text{metre}^{-1}$.

specific gravity Former name for relative density. The ratio of density of a substance to the density of water at 4°C.

specific heat The heat capacity of a body per unit mass of the body is called specific heat of the substance of which the body is made and is usually denoted by C or s.

$$\text{Specific heat, } C = \frac{Q}{m\Delta t}$$

It is also defined as the amount of heat required to raise the temperature of unit mass of a material for unit temperature change.
Its unit is kcal kg^{-1} K^{-1} or joule per kg per K.

specific heat capacity Measure of the capacity of heat needed to raise the temperature of 1 kg of material through 1 degree.

specific latent heat The energy released or absorbed by a body at a constant temperature process to change its state. e.g. ice melting.

specific resistance Resistance of a wire of unit length and unit cross-section area. The specific resistance of a material at a given temperature and does not depend on the size.

spectral line A line in spectrum corresponding to a particular wavelength of light emitted or absorbed by an atom, ion or molecule.

spectral series Sequence of lines in a line spectrum.

spectrograph An instrument for producing a photographic record of a spectrum.

spectrometer An instrument used for examining the different wavelengths present in electromagnetic radiation.

spectrophotometer Used for measurement of transmittance or reflectance of solutions, transparent or opaque solids, such as polished glass or gases.

spectroscopy The analysis of spectra. Spectroscopy is used for investigating energy levels in atoms, ions and molecules.

spectrum The band of coloured components of a light beam.

speed Rate at which an object moves, expressed as the distance travelled in a given time, measured in units such as ms^{-1}, km/h or mph. Unlike velocity it is independent of the direction of travel.

speed of sound Velocity of sound waves. In general, sound travels more rapidly through liquids than through gases and fastest of all through solids. As temperature increases, so does the speed of sound.

spherical aberration A defect of image formed by a lens. It arises due to the paraxial and marginal rays coming to focus at different points on the axis of the lens. It can be corrected by using parabolic surfaces as reflectors and refractors.

spherical mirror Spherical mirrors are the cut parts of a hollow glass sphere whose one surface is made reflecting by painting another surface. If reflection of light takes place from bulging out surface, then it is a convex mirror and if reflection takes place from bent in surface, then it is a concave mirror.

spherometer It is an instrument for determining the curvature of spherical objects.

sphygmomanometer A device used to measure blood pressure.

spirit level A device that is used for the determination of true horizontal or vertical direction by the centering of bubble in a slightly curved glass tube or tubes filled with alcohol and ether.

spontaneous fission Nuclear fission reaction that occurs on its own without the impact of a neutron or other energetic particle.

spring balance A device used for measuring the force acting on a body. It consists of a spring. When a body is attached to its lower end, spring gets stretched. Stretching of the spring is measured by a pointer on a graduated scale.

stable equilibrium A body is said to be in stable equilibrium if it tends to return to its original state when it is slightly disturbed from its state.

standard cell Electrolytic cell characterised by having a known constant electromotive force.

standard pressure An internationally agreed value of a barometric height of 760 mm Hg. It is equal to the 1.01×10^5 newton-metre^{-2}.

standard temperature An internationally agreed value for which many measurements are quoted. It is 0°C or 273 K.

standing waves Stationary wave caused by interference when two waves of the same wavelength move in opposite directions.

stars The celestial bodies which emits its own light are called stars. The sun is also a star. At night, we can see many stars twinkling in the sky. They appears as a point source due to very large distance from the earth.

stat coulomb (esu) Charge which when placed in air at a distance of 1 cm from an equal and similar charge repel it with a force of 1 dyne.

S

static friction If external forces are applied and object is still at rest in that case force of friction between object and surface is called static friction.

stationary wave Alternative name for standing wave. It is a superposition of two waves of the same wavelength, frequency and amplitude travelling in the opposite directions with the same speed.

stator The stationary part of a rotary system, found in electric generators, motors, siren etc.

Stator

steady flow The flow of fluid is said to be steady if at any given point, the velocity of each passing fluid particle remains constant with time.

steam A vapour into which water is converted when heated.

steam engine An engine which run through the mechanical energy by steam.

steam line The curve representing the change of the boiling point of water with pressure.

steam point It is the temperature at which water vapour condenses at a pressure of 1 atmosphere, i.e. 100°C.

Stefan's law It states that "The energy emitted per unit area of a perfectly black body per second is directly proportional to the fourth power of its absolute temperature (T), i.e. $E = \sigma T^4$, where, σ is Stefan's constant and its value is 5.67×10^{-8} J m^{-2}s^{-1}K^{-4}.

stellar The term related to research concerning the formation, evolution, interior and the atmosphere of stars.

step-down transformer A transformer which can change a low current of high voltage into high current of low voltage.

step-up transformer A transformer which is used to increase an available AC voltage.

steradian Supplementary SI unit of solid angle which is equal to the angle at the centre of a sphere subtended by part of surface whose area is equal to the square of the radius.

Stern-Gerlach experiment This is an important experiment in quantum mechanics on the deflection of particles.

stethoscope Optical instrument that gives a three dimensional illusion of depth, normally from a pair of flat photographs.

stimulated emission Process by which a photon causes an electron in an atom to drop to a lower energy level and emit another photon. It is the principle on which the working of lenses is based.

Stoke's law Sir George G. Stokes (1819-1903), an English scientist enunciated clearly the viscous drag force F, acting on a ball of radius r falling in a liquid of coefficient of viscosity η with terminal velocity v is given by

$$F = 6\pi\eta rv$$

stopping potential The retarding potential where the photocurrent becomes zero for a particular incident light frequency is called stopping potential V_0 for that frequency. The stopping potential increases with increasing frequency of the incident light, further more, the dependence is linear.

storage battery A voltaic battery made up of two or more storage cells.

STP Standard temperature and pressure. *See* standard temperature, standard pressure.

strain Deformation of an object due to stress. As a quantity it is equal to the amount of deformation divided by the original dimension. Strain has no units.

stratosphere The region of the atmosphere above troposphere. In this region, the temperature remains nearly constant and the atmosphere is calm and undisturbed.

streamer

(i) A column of light shooting across the sky in the aurora borealis.

(ii) An extension of rays from sun's corona.

streamline flow The path followed by an element of a moving liquid is called streamline, if energy element passing through a given point of the path follows the same line of flow as that of preceding elements.

stress Any force acting upon an object in such a way as to alter its size or shape. Mechanical stress is measured in units of force per unit area.

strong nuclear force The strongest force in nature, which is responsible for binding protons and neutrons inside a nucleus. These forces are very short range attractive forces which are neither electrostatic nor gravitational in nature. These forces are charge independent.

subsonic Speed less than that of the speed of sound in a medium.

sunspots The temporary dark spots on the sun's surface.

superconductor For some material below a certain temperature resistivity suddenly becomes zero. This temperature is called **critical temperature**. The material in this state is called superconductor and the phenomenon is called superconductivity. If an electric current is set up in a superconductor, it can persist for long time even for months and years after removing the applied potential difference. Superconductors are used to construct very strong magnets. Possible applications of superconductors are ultra fast computer switches and transmission of electric power through superconducting power lines.

supercooling Metastable state of a liquid in which its temperature has been brought below the normal freezing point without any solidification or crystallization occurring.

superheating Heating of liquid or gas above its boiling point in the liquid state by increasing the pressure above that of the atmosphere.

super high frequency *See* extremely high frequency.

super wave A steller explosion that briefly outshines an entire galaxy radiating much energy as sun or ordinary star.

superior planet The six planets from Mars onwards are known as the superior planets, since, their orbits are outside the orbit of the earth.

supplementary units The dimensionless units, the radian and the steradian.

surface charge density The charge per unit area of a surface is called surface charge density.

surface energy The sum of the energy of all the liquid molecules present in the surface.

surface tension Force per unit length acting along the surface of a liquid at right angles to any line drawn in the surface. It has the effect of making a liquid behave as if it has a surface skin and is responsible for capillarity and other phenomena.

surface wave A seismic wave that travels across the surface of the earth rather than through it. These waves usually travel more slowly and have larger amplitudes and longer wavelengths.

susceptance The opposite of reactance. It is measured in siemens.

$$B_C = \frac{1}{X_C}$$

or

$$B_L = \frac{1}{X_L}$$

where, B and X are susceptance and reactance respectively for L and C.

susceptibility The ratio M/H for a magnetic substance where, H is the applied magnetic intensity and M the magnetisation produced in the substance. $\chi < 0$ for diamagnetic substance and $\chi > 0$ for paramagnetic and ferromagnetic materials. Its value is very large for ferromagnetic materials.

switch Usually mechanical device for opening and closing of an electric circuit. A solid state switch has no moving parts.

system Collection of objects.

systematic error The systematic errors are those errors that tend to be in one direction, either positive or negative.

T

tachometer An instrument which is used to measure angular speed.

tachyon A hypothetical subatomic particle that can travel faster the speed of light.

tangent galvanometer A type of galvanometer which is based on the tangent law.

tangent law When a freely suspended magnet is acted upon by two uniform magnetic fields of strengths F and H at right angle to each other, the magnet comes to rest in a certain position, making an angle with H. In this position the moment of couple due to the field H is equal and opposite to the moment of couple due to field F.

$$F = H \tan\theta$$

tangential acceleration The tangential component of linear acceleration which is tangential to the path of particle moving in a circular path.

tape deck A unit that records audio or video signal on to a magnetic tape in cassettes and plays back signal from it.

target A substance, object or system subjected to bombardment by electrons or other particles.

technology

(i) Branch of knowledge that deals with creation and their interrelation with life, society and environment.

(ii) A scientific or industrial process, invention or method.

telecommunication The technology of communication by telephone, telegraph, etc.

telegraphy A type of telecommunication in which pulses of electricity are used as coded signals and carried along wires.

telemetry A method of sending information over long distances.

telephoto lens A photographic lens that can produce a large image of a distant object with normal camera extensions. It consists of a converging lens followed by a diverging lens with a separation, such that convergence to a real image occurs.

teleporting A regional telecommunication network that provides access to communication satellites and other long distance media.

telescope An optical instrument used to get an enlarged image of distant objects; such as the stars, the planets, etc. It consists of two convex lens fixed at two ends of a long cylindrical tube. One lens is of large aperture and large focal length is towards the object and called objective. The second lens is of small aperture and small focal length is towards the eye and called the eyepiece.

television A form of telecommunication in which radio waves are used to transmit video and audio signals over a large distance.

temperature The degree of hotness or coldness of a body. Heat always flow from a higher temperature body to a lower temperature body. Its SI unit is kelvin K. It is also measured in °C.

temperature coefficient A coefficient determining the rate of change of a physical quantity with change in temperature.

temperature gradient The rate of change in temperature with distance.

temperature of inversion The temperature of the hot junction of a thermocouple at which the current becomes zero and reversal of current is about to begin.

temperature scale A practical scale used in measuring temperature. It has two fixed points. The lower fixed point is ice point and the upper fixed point is steam point. Main temperature scales are Fahrenheit scale, Celsius scale and absolute scale of temperature.
In Fahrenheit scale, ice point is taken as 32° F and steam point is taken as 212° F and temperature difference between the two points is divided into 180 equal parts.
In Celsius scale, ice point is taken as 0° C and steam point is taken as 100° C and the temperature difference between the two fixed points is divided into 100 equal parts. In absolute scale of temperature, ice point is taken as 273 K and steam point is taken as 373 K and the temperature difference between the two fixed points is divided into 100 equal parts.

tempering The process of changing the physical properties of a metal or alloy by heating, if for a time and then cooling it gradually or quickly.

tensile stress The restoring force per unit area. If the body is compressed under the action of applied forces, the restoring force per unit area is known as compressive stress. Tensile or compressive stress can also be termed as longitudinal stress.

tension A stretching force.

Tera A unit prefix that equals to 10^{12}. e.g. 1 Tm = 10^{12} m.

terminal A point of an electrical circuit, where connecting lead can be connected.

terminal speed *See* terminal velocity.

terminal velocity The steady velocity with which a body falls through a viscous fluid (gas or liquid) under the influence of gravity.

terrestrial planets The four inner planets of the solar system, i.e. Mercury, Venus, Earth and Mars are relatively small, rocky bodies and thus, are also known as terrestrial planets.

tertiary colour A colour obtained by mixing two secondary colours.

tesla The SI unit of magnetic flux density. It is equal to 1 weber metre^{-2}.

test charge Charge used, in principle, to measure electric field.

theorem of parallel axes The moment of inertia of a body about any axis is equal to the sum of the moment of inertia of the body about a parallel axis passing through its centre of mass and the product of its mass and the square of the distance between the two parallel axes. Let z and z' be two parallel axes separated by a distance a. The z-axis passes through the centre of mass O of the rigid body. Then, according to the theorem of parallel axes

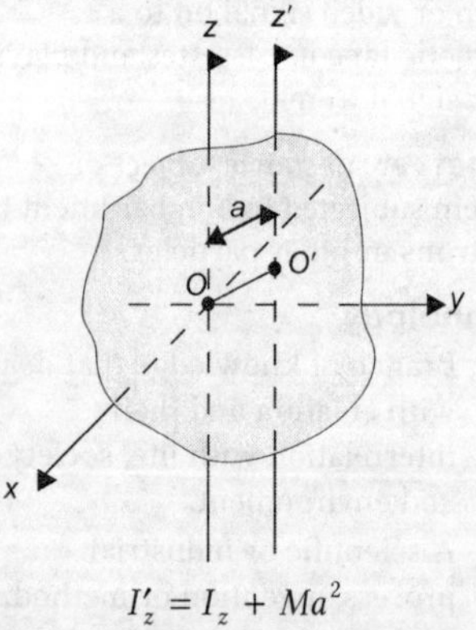

$$I'_z = I_z + Ma^2$$

where, I_z and I'_z are the moments of inertia of the body about the z and z' axes respectively, M is the total mass of the body.

theorem of perpendicular axes The moment of inertia of a planar body, such as a lamina about an axis perpendicular to its plane is equal to the sum of its moments of inertia about two perpendicular axes concurrent with perpendicular axis and lying in the plane of the body. An axis perpendicular to the body through a point O is taken as the z-axis. Two mutually perpendicular axes lying in the plane of the body and concurrent with z-axis, i.e. passing through O, are taken as the x and y-axes. The theorem states that

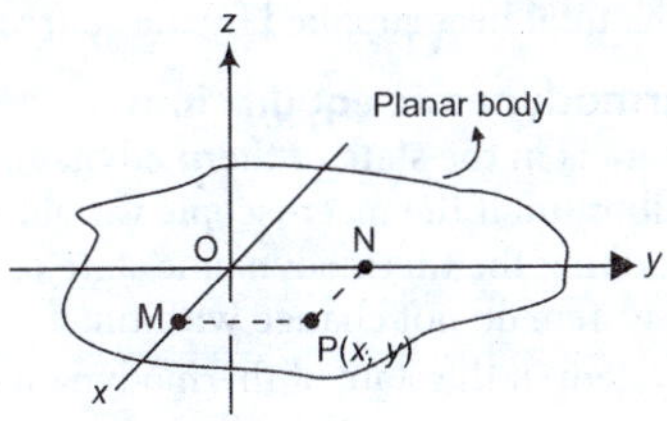

$$I_z = I_x + I_y$$

thermal agitation The random motion of molecules or other small components of particles of a substance that is associated with heat.

thermal capacity (heat capacity) The amount of heat energy required to increase the temperature of the body through 1 K. It is equal to the product of the mass of the body and its specific heat. Its unit is joule K^{-1}.

thermal conduction The process of transfer of heat from one place to another.

thermal conductivity The amount of heat passing normally per second through a plate of a material of unit cross-sectional area and unit length, when a steady difference of temperature between the two faces is one degree centigrade.

thermal diffusion A method of separating gas molecules of different masses by keeping one part of the gas at a lower temperature than the other.

thermal energy The potential and kinetic energy associated with the random motions of the particles of a material.

thermal equilibrium Two bodies are said to be in thermal equilibrium, if there is no exchange of heat between them when they are placed in contact.

thermal expansion The increase in the dimensions of a body due to the increase in its temperature. The expansion in length is called linear expansion. The expansion in area is called area expansion or superficial expansion. The expansion in volume is called volume expansion.

thermal generation of electron-hole pair Every liberated electron becomes conduction electron and leaves a hole in the valence band. A combination of such a free electron and a hole is known as electron-hole pair. This process is known as thermal generation of electron-hole pairs.

thermal neutron Neutrons of very low speed and energy of about 0.025 eV. These neutrons can be captured by an atomic nucleus to initiate nuclear fission.

thermal noise The electronic noise generated by thermal agitation of charge carriers inside an electrical conductor at equilibrium, which happens regardless the applied voltage.

thermal pollution A common cause of thermal pollution is the use of water as a coolant by power plants and industrial manufacturers. When water used as a coolant is returned to the natural environment at a higher temperature, the change in temperature decreases the oxygen supply and affects the ecosystem composition.

t

thermal radiation The electromagnetic radiation emitted by a body by virtue of its temperature. The radiation emitted by a red hot iron or light from a filament lamp are thermal radiation.

thermal reactor A nuclear reactor in which the nuclear fission reaction is carried out by thermal neutrons.

thermal stress When the thermal expansion of a rod is prevented by fixing its ends rigidly, then a compressive strain is produced in the rod due to the forces provided by the rigid support. The stress set up in the rod in this state is called thermal stress.

thermal transmittance The rate of transfer of heat through a structure divided by the difference in temperature across the structure. It is expressed in watts/metre^2-(kelvin) or W/m^2-K well insulated parts of building have a low thermal transmittance.

thermalisation The reduction of kinetic energy of neutrons in a thermal nuclear reactor with the help of moderator.

thermionic current The electric current produced due to flow of thermions.

thermionic emission The phenomena of ejection of electrons from a surface, when it is heated.

thermionics The branch of electronics which deals with the study of emission of electrons from metal surface as a result of high temperature.

thermistor An electrical component usually a semi-conductor, whose electrical resistance changes rapidly with temperature. It is used in sensitive temperature measuring device.

thermocouple A device used for measurement of temperatures. It consists of two metallic junctions of dissimilar metals, which are placed at different temperatures, an emf develops across these, whose magnitude depends on the temperature difference between the junctions. A measurement of the emf enables on to calculate the desired temperature.

thermodynamic cycle Cycle which consists of a linked sequence of thermodynamic process that involves transfer of heat and work into and out of the system while varying pressure, temperature and other state of variable.

thermodynamic efficiency The ratio of the work done by a heat engine to the total heat supplied by the source.

thermodynamic equilibrium A system is in the state of thermodynamic equilibrium if the macroscopic variables describing the thermodynamic state of the system do not change with time. A system in the state of thermodynamic equilibrium possess the following equilibria simultaneously.

(i) **Mechanical equilibrium** No unbalanced force in its interior or between the system and surroundings.

(ii) **Thermal equilibrium** All parts of system and surroundings are at same temperature.

(iii) **Chemical equilibrium** No change in internal structure due to chemical reaction, diffusion etc.

thermodynamic laws

First law The total heat energy given to a thermodynamic system is partially utilised by the system in doing work and the remaining part increases its internal energy, i.e.

$$\Delta Q = \Delta W + \Delta U$$

Second law Heat energy can not be converted into work completely or heat will not transfer from an object of low temperature towards an object of high temperature on its own.

Third law Entropy of a perfect crystal at absolute zero is equal to zero.

Zeroth law If two objects are in thermal equilibrium with a third object, then all three are in thermal equilibrium.

thermodynamic process A passage of a thermodynamic system from an initial state to a final state specified by a suitable set of thermodynamic state variables, that depends only on the current state of the system not the path taken to reach that state.

thermodynamics The branch of Physics which deals with the concepts of heat and temperature and the inter-conversion of heat and other forms of energy, particularly heat and mechanical energy.

thermodynamic state variables (or state function) A property of a system that depends only on the current state of the system, not on the way in which the system acquire that state.

thermoelectric effect The phenomenon of direct conversion of heat energy into electrical energy is known as thermo-electric effect. Thermo-electric effect is reversible effect. If a circuit contains conductors of different materials and the junctions between those conductors are maintained at different temperatures, then electric current is found to flow in the circuit. Three related effects of this kind are

(i) Seebeck effect (ii) Peltier effect, (iii) Thomson effect.

thermoelectric power The rate of change of the thermo emf of a thermocouple with the change of temperature of the hot junction.

thermoelectric series A list of metals; such as bismuth, nickel, cobalt, palladium, titanium, mercury, lead, tin, chromium, molybdenum, rhodium, iridium, gold, silver, zinc, tungsten, cadmium, iron and antimony.

thermo flask A special type of bottle devised by Sir James Dewar in year 1890. It is used for storing hot or cold liquid at the same temperature for long time. It has reflecting surface through which heat radiations can be stopped to avoid loss of heat. A vacuum is created outside the bottle to prevent heat conduction.

thermograph A chart recorder that records variations in temperature over a period in time on a graph.

thermometer A device used for measuring temperature.

thermometry The branch of Physics which deals with the study of methods of temperature measurement.

thermonuclear The process in which very high temperatures are used to bring about the fusion of light nuclei, such as those of the hydrogen isotopes deuterium and tritium, with the accompanying liberation of energy.

thermonuclear reaction A process in which energy is released by the fusion of atomic nuclei.

thermophone An electro acoustic transducer that forms sound waves by the expansion and contraction of the air adjacent to a conductor that varies in temperature according to the magnitude of the current passing through it.

thermopile An instrument used to detect radiant energy. It consists of a series of thermocouples connected in series. When heat radiation is allowed to fall on one set of junctions an easily measurable emf is produced.

thermosphere The region of the upper atmosphere, where the temperature increase with increase in height.

thermostat An instrument used for maintaining temperature within certain limits. In a thermostat, a device is used which cuts off the power when the required temperature is exceeded, and reconnects when the temperature falls.Commonly used in electric iron and geysers .

thick lens The lens whose faces are separated by large gap.

thick mirror A lens with one silvered face.

thin film A thin layer of substances deposited on the surface of another substance. Such thin solid films are used in many semiconductor devices.

Thomson effect When a temperature gradient exists along the conductor and a current is allowed to pass through the conductor, then the absorption or evolution of heat takes place in the conductor itself. This phenomenon is known as Thomson effect.

The rate at which Thomson heat (H) is transferred into a small region of a wire carrying current I and having temperature difference dT is proportional to IdT, i.e.

$$H = \sigma I dT$$

where, σ = Thomson coefficient.

Thomson scattering The scattering of electromagnetic radiation by free or loosely bounded electrons.

threshold The minimum value of a parameter that will produce a specified effect.

threshold audibility The threshold audibility at any frequency is the minimum intensity of sound at that frequency which can be detected.

threshold frequency For a given photosensitive material, there exists a certain minimum cut-off frequency of the incident radiation, called the threshold frequency below which no emission of photoelectrons takes place no matter how intense the incident light. It is denoted by ν_0. Above the threshold frequency, the stopping potential or equivalently the maximum kinetic energy of the emitted photoelectrons increases linearly with the frequency of incident radiation.

thrust The force acting on an object perpendicular to the surface.

thunder The sound caused by lightning. Depending on the distance and nature of lightning, thunder can range from a sharp, loud crock to a long low rumble. The sudden increase in pressure and temperature from lightning produces rapid expansion of the air surrounding and within a bolt of lightning.

thyristor A silicon controlled rectifier. Its anode-cathode current is controlled by a signal applied to a third electrode.

tidal energy Due to the gravitational pull of the Moon on the spinning Earth, the level of water in the sea rises and falls. This phenomenon is called high and low tides and the difference in sea-levels gives tidal energy. Tidal energy is harnessed by constructing a dam across a narrow opening to the sea. A turbine fixed at the opening of the dam converts tidal energy to electricity.

timbre The distinguishing quality, other than pitch or intensity of a note produced by a musical instrument. It depends on the number and intensity of the overtones present.

time A fundamental quantity usually indicating duration. The SI unit of time is second.

time lag Alternative name of time delay. The time that elapses between the closing of circuit in a circuit breaker, or similar apparatus and the response of the current in the main circuit.

time of flight The time of flight of a projectile is the time interval between the instant of its launch and the instant when it hits the ground.

time period The time taken to complete one vibration (oscillation). It is denoted by *T*.

tokamak An axially symmetric system in which the plasma suppresses the instability.

tolerance The degree of precision obtainable with a measuring instrument.

tone A vocal or musical sound with reference to its pitch, quality and strength.

tonne Unit of mass equal to 1000 kilogram. 1 tonne = 2,204.62 lb, slightly less than the imperial ton.

toroid An end less solenoid in the form of a ring. It is a hollow circular ring on which a large number of turns of a wire is closely wound.

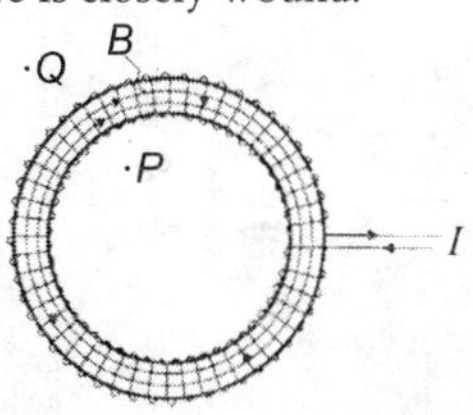

Toroid

If a toroid is carrying a current *I* and the magnetic field in the open space inside (point *P*) and exterior to the toroid (point *Q*) is zero, then the field inside the toroid is constant.

torque Turning moment product about an axis by force acting at right angle to a radius from the axis.

torr Unit of pressure equivalent to that produced by a 1 mm column of mercury. It is equal to 133.3 N m^{-2}.

Torricelli's theorem Gives the velocity of a fluid coming out of a vessel at a point distance *h* below its free surface. According to it,

$$v = \sqrt{2gh}$$

Torricelli's vacuum Refers to the space in which mercury vapours are present at the top of a column of mercury when a long tube which is sealed at one end is filled with mercury and inverted in a trough containing mercury.

torsion balance A device for measuring very small forces by the torsion they cause in a wire or fibre.

torsional pendulum In such a pendulum, moment of restoring torque

$$t = -\text{Kq}$$

and time period

$$T = 2\pi\sqrt{\frac{I}{K}}$$

where, *K*= constant torsion in the thread, *I* = moment of inertia of the rotating body about the thread.

total internal reflection Complete reflection of a light wave at a boundary between two media (glass, air). It occurs when the wave is incident at the critical angle.

total reflecting prism A right-angled crown glass isosceles prism. When light is normally incident on it, the light strikes the hypotenuse face at an angle of 45°; this is greater than the critical angle whose value for crown glass is 41°31′. This light is thus totally internally reflected.

tourmaline A complex blueish or brownish mineral important for its polarising effect on light. It is a dichroic material.

trajectory Path followed by a moving projectile acted upon by gravity or other forces.

transconductance The mutual conductance between the control grid of a thermionic value and its anode, it is expressed in mho.

transducer Any device that converts one form of energy into another. An electrical transducer may be defined as a device that converts some physical variables (pressure, displacement, force, temperature, etc.) into corresponding variations in the electrical signal at its output.

transformation Transmutation of one atomic nucleus into another by means of a nuclear reaction.

transformer Electrical device for changing the voltage of an alternating current without altering its frequency. The change in voltage is proportional to the ratio of the turns of wire on the primary and secondary coils of the transformer. The ratio of the voltages in the primary and secondary circuits V_1/V_2 is approximately equal to the ratio of the number of turns in the primary and secondary coils.

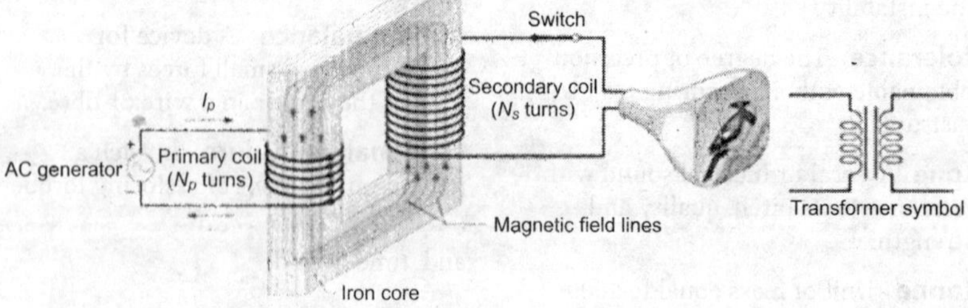

Transformer

transient A sudden brief disturbance of a system.

transistor A device commonly consisting of three layers, as either *p-n-p* or *n-p-n*, where *p* and *n* refer to *n* or *p*-type semiconductors. It allows amplification of an electric current. Both types of a transistor may be regarded as two diodes connected back to back, so that when a voltage is applied across the device one diode is forward biased and the other is reverse biased. Current flows across the forward biased junction. All the three segments of a transistor have different thickness and their doping levels are also different. A brief description of the three segments of a transistor is given below.

Emitter This is the segment on one side of the transistor. It is of moderate size and heavily doped. It supplies a large number of majority carriers for the current flow through the transistor.

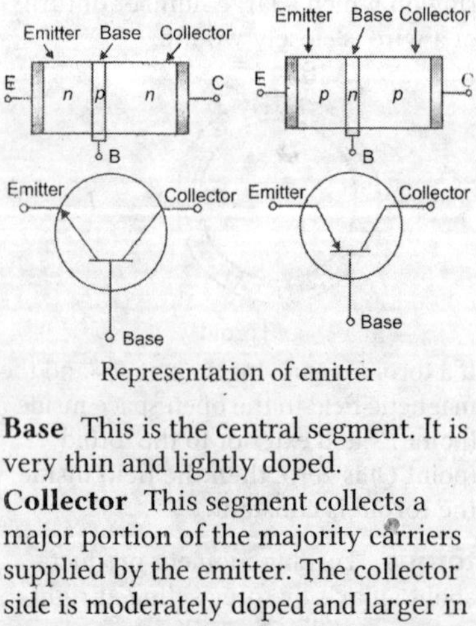

Representation of emitter

Base This is the central segment. It is very thin and lightly doped.

Collector This segment collects a major portion of the majority carriers supplied by the emitter. The collector side is moderately doped and larger in size as compared to the emitter.

transition temperature Temperature above and below which different allotropes of an element are stable.

translational motion If a rigid body moves in such a way that all its particles move along parallel paths, then its motion is called translational motion. Translational motion of the body may be represented by the motion of its centre of mass.

i.e. $$Ma = F_{ext}$$

translucent Permitting light to pass through but diffusion it.

transmission

(i) The mechanism by which power is transmitted from an engine to the axle in a motor vehicle.

(ii) The action of transmitting signals or data.

transmittance Ratio of transmitted energy to incident energy.

transmitter A device that converts electrical impulses into modulated radio waves.

transmutation

(i) **Dimensional transmutation** Physical mechanism providing a linkage between a dimensionless parameter and a dimensionful parameter.

(ii) **Nuclear transmutation** The conversion of an isotope into another. Atoms of one element can be changed into atoms of another element by a process which occurs through nuclear reactions.

transparent A surface that allows light (or other radiation) to pass through it with little or no diffusion in such a way that objects can be seen clearly through them.

transponder Refers to a radio or radar receiver, that automatically transmits a reply on reception of a certain signal.

transreceiver A device comprising both a transmitter and a receiver which are combined and share common circuitary or a single housing. When no circuitary is common between transmit and receive functions, the device is a transmitter receiver.

transverse wave A wave motion in which the motion or change is perpendicular to the direction of energy transfer. Velocity of transverse wave pulse is,

$$v = \sqrt{\frac{T}{m}}$$

e.g. electromagnetic waves .

travelling wave *See* progressive wave.

triangle law of vectors It states that, "If two vectors can be represented in magnitude and direction by two sides of triangle taken in order, then the resultant vector can be represented in magnitude and direction by the third side of the triangle taken in opposite order.

triode A thermionic tube with three electrodes, i.e. one grid called the control grid, in addition to the anode and cathode.

triplet In quantum mechanics, a quantum state of a system with a spin of 1, such that there are three allowed values of spin component – 1, 0 and 1.

triple point Temperature and pressure at which the three phases (solid, liquid and vapour) of a substance are in equilibrium. The triple point of water is 273.16 K.

tropopause The boundary in the Earth's atmosphere between the troposphere and stratosphere.

troposphere The lowest portion of Earth's atmosphere that contains 75% atmosphere mass and 99% of its water vapour.

trough A point of maximum negative displacement in a wave.

tuned circuit An electric circuit consisting of an inductor and a capacitor. The circuit can act as an electrical resonator, an electrical analogue of a tuning fork, storing energy oscillating at the circuit's resonant frequency.

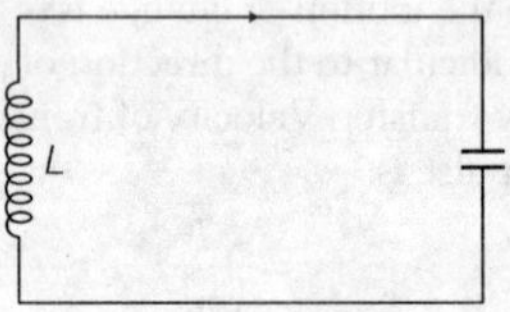

tuning fork Piece of metal shaped rod like an elongated letter U designed to produce a particular pure musical note when struck.

tunnel diode A type of semiconductor diode, i.e. capable of very fast operation well into the microwave frequency region, made possible by the use of the quantum mechanical effect called tunnelling.

turbine A mechanical device that extracts energy from a fluid flow and converts it into useful work. Early turbine example are windmills and water wheels.

turbulent flow If the velocity of flow exceeds the critical velocity v_c, the mixing of streamlines takes place and the flow path becomes *zig-zag*, the streamlines cutting each other and the motion is said to be turbulent.

turns ratio In a transformer; the ratio of turns of wire in primary winding to number of turns in secondary winding.

$$\text{Turns ratio} = \frac{N_P}{N_S}$$

twinkling (or scintillation) Variations in apparent brightness or position of a distance luminous object viewed through a medium. Twinkling of a star is caused by passing of light through different layers of a turbulent atmosphere.

tyndall effect A phenomenon first noticed by Faraday when a powerful beam of light is sent through a colloidal solution of high dispersity, the sol appears fluoroscent and the light is polarised, the amount of polarisation depend upon the size of the particle of the colloid, if the particles are much smaller than the wavelength of the radiation.

U

ultimate strength The limiting stress at which a material completely breaks down i.e. fractures or crushes. It is defined as force per original unit area of cross-section.

ultracentrifuge A centrifuge operating at a very high angular velocity suitable for use with colloidal solutions. It is used to separate colloidal particles and also can be used to estimate their size and measure the relative molecular, masses of very large molecules such as proteins.

ultra high frequency A radio frequency in the range of 0.3×10^9 Hz to 0.3×10^{10} Hz.

ultramicro balance A very sensitive balance for accurate weighing to 10^{-8} g.

ultramicroscope A modified compound microscope able to view the submicroscopic particles in a colloidal suspension when this is suitable illuminated, e.g. particles of smoke and fog.

ultrasonic Sound waves with frequencies above the audible range are termed ultrasonic. Ultrasound has many medical and industrial applications.

ultrasonic frequency A sound frequency above the range normally audible by humans, i.e. greater than about 20 kHz.

ultrasonic imaging (ultrasonography) By this, the image of soft tissues in human body produced by ultrasonic waves. These images are used in modern medicine.

ultrasound Vibrations of the ultrasonic frequency which can be generated using either the piesoelectric effect or magnetostriction, or by Galton whistle or Hartmann generator.

ultrasound scanning The process of passing an ultrasonic beam over an area of interest and studying the reflections.

ultraviolet radiation (UV radiation) A form of electromagnetic radiation, shorter in wavelength than visible light range between about 1 nm and 400 nm. Ordinary glasses are not transparent to these waves, quartz is a much more effective material for making lenses and prisms for use with ultraviolet. Ultraviolet photons carry more energy than those of light.
Sun is the important source of ultraviolet radiations.
Most of the ultraviolet light from Sun is absorbed by atoms in the upper atmosphere, i.e. stratosphere, which contains ozone gas. This ozone layer then radiates out the absorbed energy as heat radiations. Ultraviolet rays are used in killing the bacteria in drinking water, in sterilisation of operation theatres and also in checking the forgery of documents.

ultraviolet rays The electromagnetic radiation, shorter in wavelength than visible light. Ultraviolet wavelengths range between 1 nm to 400 nm. Ultraviolet radiation is produced by electronic transitions between the outer leads of atoms.

umbra

1. A region of complete shadow from which all light rays are excluded.
2. The central darker region of a sunspot.

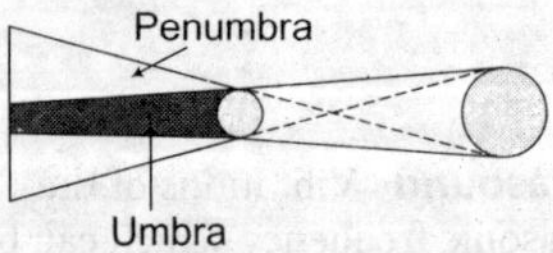

Representation of umbra

uncertainty principle According to uncertainty principle, it is not possible to find accurately and simultaneously both the position and velocity of a moving particle.
Mathematically,

$$\Delta x \cdot \Delta p = h/4\pi$$

where, Δx = uncertainty in position and Δp = uncertainty in momentum.

uncontrolled chain reaction If more than one neutron out of three neutrons obtained in the process of nuclear fission of one uranium nucleus further take part in the nuclear fission process, then chain reaction of fission takes place in uncontrolled manner and whole of the substance is fissioned in a few seconds with a great explosion. For an uncontrolled chain reaction, the size of the fissionable material should be greater than the critical size.

uniaxial crystal A type of birefringent crystal having only one axis along which the ordinary and extraordinary rays travel at the same speed.

u

unidirectional Moving in one direction.

uniform acceleration If the acceleration remains constant, i.e. it does not change with time, then it is called uniform acceleration.

uniform circular motion An object moving in a circular path with uniform speed, then its motion is known as uniform circular motion.

uniform motion If an object is moving with uniform velocity, then its motion is called uniform motion.

uniform speed When a body travels equal distances in equal intervals of time, then it is said to have uniform speed.

uniform velocity Constant velocity describing motion in a straight line with zero acceleration.

unijunction transistor A three-lead electronic semiconductor device with only one junction that acts exclusively as an electrically controlled switch. It is not used as a linear amplifier.

unipolar Having only one magnetic or electric pole.

unipolar transistor A transistor where in current flow is due to the movement of majority carriers only.

unit Measurement of any physical quantity involves comparison with a certain basic, arbitrarily chosen, internationally accepted reference standard. The units for the fundamental or base quantities are called fundamental or base units. The units of all other physical quantities can be expressed as combinations of the base units, are called derived units.

unit vector A unit vector is a vector of unit magnitude and points in a particular direction. It has no dimension and unit. It is used to specify a direction only, unit vector of a vector is given by

$$\hat{\mathbf{A}} = \frac{\mathbf{A}}{|\mathbf{A}|}$$

Unit vectors along the x, y and z-axes of a rectangular coordinate system are denoted by $\hat{\mathbf{i}}$, $\hat{\mathbf{j}}$ and $\hat{\mathbf{k}}$, respectively.
Since, these are unit vectors, we have

$$|\hat{\mathbf{i}}| = |\hat{\mathbf{j}}| = |\hat{\mathbf{k}}| = 1$$

These unit vectors are perpendicular to each other.

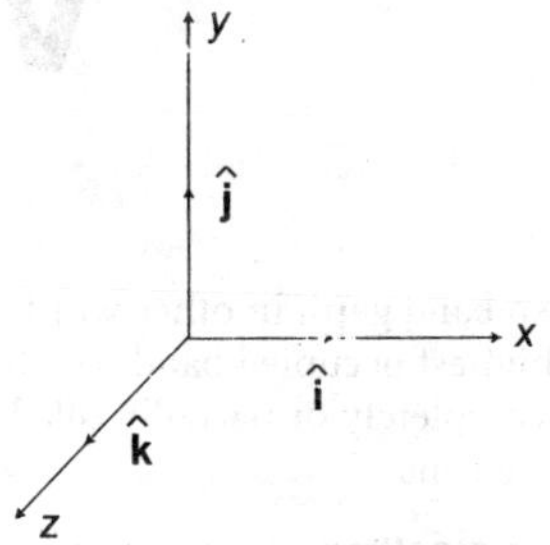

universe The whole of space and all the matter in it. The mass of matter is estimated at 10^{41} range 5×10^{9} year. The origin is a matter for speculations though the Big-Bang theory is now widely accepted.

universal gravitational constant The gravitational constant G is numerically equal to the force of attraction between two point masses 1 kg each placed at a distance of 1 m in air.

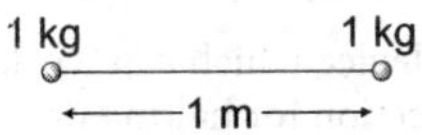

universal law of gravitation Everybody in the universe attracts every other body with a force called gravitation, which is directly proportional to the product of their masses and inversely proportional to the square of the distance between them.

unpolarised wave In an unpolarised wave, the displacement will be randomly changing with time though it will always be perpendicular to the direction of propagation.

unsaturated vapour A vapour at a certain temperature that does not contain the maximum amount of the substance in the gaseous phase.

unstable equilibrium A body is said to be in unstable equilibrium, if one being slightly disturbed from its equilibrium position tends to move away from its original position.

upper atmosphere The atmosphere above a height of about 30 kilometre. It includes part of the stratosphere.

upthrust An upward force acting on an object immersed in a fluid. The magnitude of the force is equal to the weight of the fluid displaced by it.

uranium lead dating A method of radioactive dating used for estimating the age of certain rocks. It is based on the decay of ^{238}U to ^{206}Pb (half-life 4.5×10^{9} years) or ^{235}U to ^{207}Pb (half-life 0.7×10^{9} years). The technique is useful for time periods from 10^{7} years ago back to the age of the earth (about 4.6×10^{9} years).

uranium series Radioactive series beginning with uranium-238, of half-life 4.5×10^{9} years, and ending with lead.

Uranus Uranus was the first heavily body to be discovered with the help of a telescope. William Herschely discovered the planet in 1761. When observed through a telescope, Uranus appears as a small disc although its diameter is almost four times that of the earth. Its distance from the Sun is almost two times that of Saturn. So far, 21 satellites or Moons of Uranus have been discovered.

V

vacancy In crystal, an unoccupied lattice position which is a result of an imperfection in lattice structure.

vacuum An enclosed space from which matter, especially air, has been partially removed so that the matter or gas remaining in the space exerts less pressure than the atmosphere. A good laboratory can maintain up to 10^{14} molecules of air per cubic metre compared with about 10^{24} molecules in a litre of air at ordinary pressure.

vacuum distillation Distillation under reduced pressure, which helps to lower the boiling point and hence reduce the risk of thermal dissociation.

vacuum flask A special container of double wall with a vacuum between them designed to keep hot liquid hot or cold liquids cold by minimizing heat transfer with the exterior.

vacuum gauge A device for measuring pressure below atmospheric pressure.

vacuum pump A device by which a partial vacuum can be produced.

vacuum tube (vacuum value) An electron tube from which almost all air or gas has been evacuated. It was earlier used in electronic devices which was farther replaced by semiconductor.

valence band The outermost shell of an atom in an insulator or semiconductor, in which the electrons are too tightly bound to the atom to carry electric current. [see also band gap]. In other words, this is the highest occupied band which is either completely or partially filled with electrons.

valence electron An electron in the outer shell of an atom is called valence electron, because by gaining, losing or sharing these outer-shell electrons, atom combine to form molecules. Therefore, the number of these outer shell electrons often determines the valency of an atom.

valence shell The outermost shell of an atom in which valence electrons are located.

value The amount or magnitude of a quantity or property.

valve A device which can work in single direction for halting or controlling the flow of liquid, gas or other material through passage, pipe, outlet, etc.

van de graaff generator It is a kind of generator having a positive-ion source fitted with an evacuated tube through which the particles can be accelerated with the help of high voltage produced by a large metal dome shaped terminal mounted on a hollow insulating support.
This generator consists of a silk belt running over two metallic pulley surrounded by a hollow metal sphere. Positive charges are sprayed on the belt which are collected from comb and transferred to the metallic sphere to produce required amount of potential for accelerating the particle.

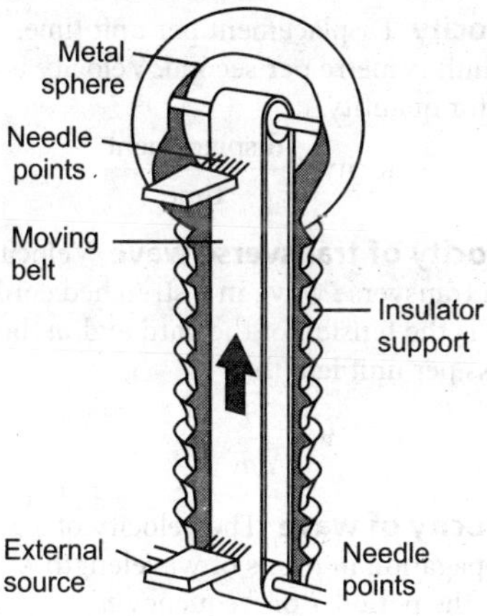

van de graaff generator

van der Waals' forces Interatomic or intermolecular forces of attraction due to the interaction between fluctuating dipole moments associated with molecules not passing permanent dipole moment. These forces are much weaker than chemical bonds and acts over short range and are inversely proportional to the seventh power of distance.

van der Waals' gas equation An equation of state for real gases. For one mole of gas, the equation is

$$\left(p + \frac{na}{V^2}\right)(V - nb) = nRT$$

where,

p = pressure of gas,
R = gas constant,
V = volume of gas,
T = absolute temperature,
n = number of moles of gas a and b are van der Waals' constant.

vapour A substance in gaseous state, but below the critical temperature. If a pure liquid partly filled in a close container is allowed to stand, the space in the container becomes filled with vapour which exerts vapour pressure with the help of atoms or molecules upto certain limit before coming to saturation. Such a body of vapour is not subjected to follow all gas laws. As, if the temperature is increased the pressure does not increase uniformly.

vapour density The relative gas or vapour compared to air, which has an arbitrary value of one. If a gas has vapour density of less than one it will generally rise in air. If the vapour density is greater than one the gas will generally sink in air.

vapour pressure The pressure exerted by a vapour consisting of atoms or molecules that have been evaporated from condensed form. The vapour pressure will reach an equilibrium value that depends only on the nature of substance and temperature but for pure substance it will only depend on temperature only.

vapour pressure thermometer A thermometer which depends on the fact that the saturated vapour pressure of a liquid is a function of temperature only. Such thermometers are most reliable at temperatures below 5 K, which is the boiling point of helium.

vaporisation The change of state from liquid to vapour (or gas) is called vaporisation. The temperature remains constant until the entire amount of the liquid is converted into vapour. During vaporisation both the liquid and vapour states of the substance coexist in thermal equilibrium.

variable The property or quantity that is altered to study the resulting change in another property or quantity. Usually all others of the system are kept constant.

variable capacitance diode, variable reactance diode or tuning diode It is a type of diode designed to exploit the voltage-dependent capacitance of reversed biased *p-n* junction.

V

variable forces When forces varies at it pushes or pulls an object with respect to the distance are called variables forces.
Work done by variable forces is given by

$$W = \int f \cdot dx$$

where, f = variable force.

variable resistor The resistor whose electrical resistance value can be adjusted as per requirement by adjustable component attached to it .

variance The number of degree of freedom of a system or the degree of freedom themselves.

vector A quantity with magnitude and direction. It can be represented by a line whose length is proportional to the magnitude and whose direction to that of the vector. A true vector or polar vector involves displacement, velocity, acceleration, force, electric and magnetic field strength.
A pseudo vector or axial vector, involves the orientation of an axis in space.

vector analysis The mathematical treatment of physical problems using vector notation.

vector product A multiplication of two vectors to give a vector. The vector product of A and B is written as $A \times B$. It is a vector of magnitude $AB \sin \theta$, where, A and B are the magnitudes of A and B and θ is the angle between A and B.
The direction of the vector product is at right angles to A and B. It points in the direction in which a right handed screw would move turning from A toward B.

vector quantity The quantities which require both magnitude and direction for their complete representation are called vector quantities.

V

velocity Displacement per unit time. Its unit is metre per second. Velocity is a vector quantity.

$$\text{Velocity} = \frac{\text{displacement}}{\text{time}}$$

velocity of transverse wave Velocity of a transverse wave in a stretched cord, if T is the tension of the cord and m the mass per unit length

$$v = \sqrt{\frac{T}{m}}$$

velocity of wave The velocity of propagation in terms of wavelength λ and the period T or frequency n

$$v = \frac{\lambda}{T} = n\lambda$$

velocity potential A scalar function of the position of a moving particle such that its gradient gives the particle velocity at any point. It has applications to fluid flow and to the movement of electric charge.

velocity ratio For a simple machine, it is the ratio of the distance moved by the load to the distance moved by the effort. Alternative name – distance ratio.

velocity selector (Wien filter) A device consisting of perpendicular electric and magnetic field, which can be used as a velocity filter for charged particle, such in microscope and spectrometer.

venturi A device to measure the flow speed of incompressible fluid. It consists of a tube with a broad diameter and a small construction at the middle.

venturi meter A device to measure the flow speed of incompressible fluid. It consists of a tube with a broad diameter and a small construction at the middle.

venturi tube The rate of flow of a fluid through the tube increases at the constriction and its pressure decreases. The difference in pressure between the ends of the tube and at the construction can be used to calculate the rate of flow.

Venus Venus or shukra is the second planet in terms of its distance from the Sun. It is a planet, which is often called an evening or a morning star. Venus occasionally appears as an evening star just above the western horizon and it also appears in the eastern sky as morning star. Venus appears the brightest of all celestial bodies, including all planets, the moon and stars. The mass of Venus is 4/5 times that of the Earth, while both are same in size. Venus has no moon or satellite of its own.

vernier Arrangement for measuring that permits more precise readings than a simple calibrated scale. It consists of a small movable scale graduated in intervals that are 9/10 of those on the main scale, allowing the latter to be read to a tenth of a division. A circular vernier is used on a micrometer gauge.

very high frequencies Radio frequencies lying between 3×10^7 to 3×10^8 cycles per second.

very low frequencies A radio frequency in the range between 30 kHz and 3 kHz.

vertex Point at which the optical axis intersects the surface of a lens.

vibration The to and fro or back and forth motion of an object is termed as vibration. This motion is also called oscillatory motion.

vibrational energy The sum of kinetic and potential energies of an oscillating body.
At maximum displacement, all the energy is potential; for zero displacement it is all kinetic.

vibrational energy level The value of the vibrational energy of an atom about its equilibrium position.

vibrator A device where in, by continued repeated impulses, a steady current is changed into an oscillating current.

virtual image Image brought to a focus by a lens, mirror or other optical system that can be seen by the eye but which cannot be focused on a screen.

virtual work The work done on a system when it is assumed to be displaced by an infinitesimally small amount. If the system is in equilibrium, virtual work is zero.

viscometer An instrument for measuring the viscosity of a fluid.

viscosity The property of a fluid by virtue of which a tangential frictional force acts between its layers. Viscous force acting between two layers of a fluid.

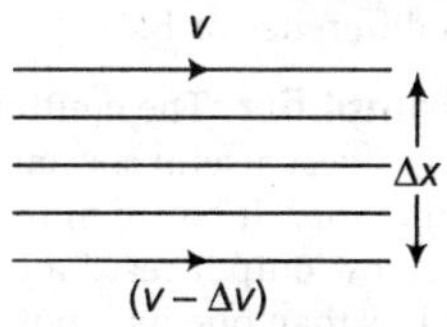

$$F = \eta A \frac{\Delta v}{\Delta x}$$

where, η is the coefficient of viscosity of the fluid.

viscous fluid Fluid that creates forces which opposes motion of objects through it.

visible light The EM waves that human eye can detect or to which the human retina is sensitive. These waves are produced by the rearrangement of electrons in atoms and molecules. When an electron jumps from outer orbit to inner orbit of lower energy, the balance of energy is radiated in the form of visible radiation. The wavelengths of visible lights ranges from violet ($\lambda = 4\times 10^{-7}$ m) to red ($\lambda = 7\times 10^{-7}$ m).

visible radiation The light having wavelength in the range between 4000-7000Å. It is visible to the human eye.

vision It refers to the sense of light, details sensitivity to visible light. The ability of an organism to distinguish objects of the light they reflect, emit or transmit.

vitreous humour A clear gel which occupied the posterior of compartment of the eye, located between the crystalline lens and retina and occupying about 80% volume of the eye ball.

volatile Liquid that gets easily evaporated at normal temperature, or in other words, having high vapour pressure.

volt It is a SI unit of electric potential, potential difference or EMF.

voltage amplifier The emitter follower is a very useful special form of voltage amplifier. It has high input resistance, low output resistance and a gain just less than one its input resistance is approximately equal to the load resistance at its output circuit multiplied by HFe.

voltage divider A number of resistors, inductors or capacitors connected in series with several terminals at intermediate points. The total voltage across the chain can split into known fractions by making connections at the various points.

voltage drop The electric potential difference across a resistor or other part of a circuit that consumes power.

voltage regulator It is a device which regulates voltage.

voltage sensitivity It describes the voltage per unit scale division of an electric instrument.

voltage stabiliser It is a device used for maintaining a constant output voltage in spite of variations in input voltage and load current.

voltaic cell An electric cell, inverted by voltage, consisting of two electrodes of different metals in a solution, so that the resulting chemical action produces an electromotive force.

voltmeter A meter used to measure electrical voltage. The commonest types are moving coil instruments with high series resistances to keep the current drawn to a low value. For alternating voltages, a rectifier must be used. Moving iron instruments with high series resistances can be used for both direct and alternating voltages. The cathode ray oscilloscope can also be used as a voltmeter.

volume Amount of space or capacity, measured in cubic units, that an object or substance occupies.

volume density of charge The electric charge per unit volume of a medium or body. It is measured in coulomb per cubic metre.

volume strain If by application of uniform pressure, the volume V of the body changes by ΔV without change of shape of the body, then volume strain

$$= \frac{\text{change in volume}}{\text{original volume}} = \frac{\Delta V}{V}$$

W

wafer A substrate on a thin slice of semiconductor material, such as a crystalline silicon, used in electronics for the fabrication of integrated circuit. Wafer mostly serves as the substrate for microelectronics.

water equivalent The mass of water that will absorb or lose the same amount of heat as the substance for same change in temperature.
Water equivalent,

$$(W) = mc$$

where, m = mass of the body and
c = specific heat of the body. Its SI unit is kg.

watt The SI unit of power. One watt is the power when one joule of work is done in one second.

watt hour A unit of work or energy, equal to one watt operating for one hour.

$$1 \text{ watt hour} = 3600 \text{ joule}$$

wattless current In a resistance less circuit the power consumed is zero, such a circuit is called wattless circuit and the current flowing is called the wattless current.

wattmeter An instrument used for measuring the power in watt in an alternating current electric circuit.

wave A wave is a periodic disturbance that moves through a medium or in space without any actual movement of the medium.
This disturbance may be continuous or transient travelling through a medium by virtue of the elastic and inertia factors of the medium or of the magnetic and electric properties of space.
In other words, energy is transferred from one place to another by vibration. The waves in which the disturbances are at right angles to the direction of propagation are called **transverse waves** and the waves in which disturbance is parallel to direction of propagation are called **longitudinal waves**.
The chief characteristics of a wave frequency, (ν) wavelength (λ), amplitude (a) and its speed ($v = \nu\lambda$).

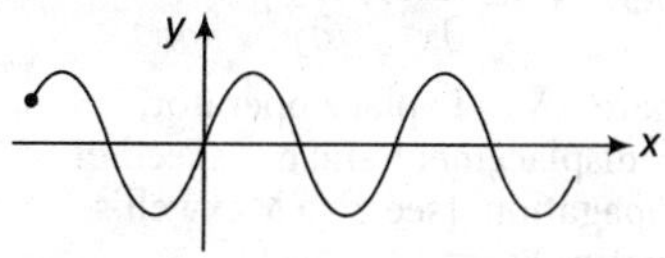

Wave

wave band A range of wavelengths in the electromagnetic spectrum, defined according to some property of the radiation, or some requirement of a detecting or transmitting system.

wave equation General classical equation at time t

$$y = a \sin(\omega t + \phi)$$

where, y = displacement,
ω = angular frequency,
t = time,
a = amplitude
and ϕ = phase.

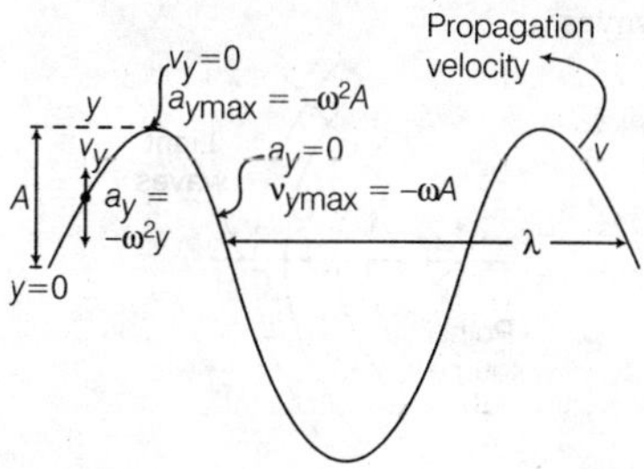

Here,

$$\frac{2\pi v}{\lambda} = 2\pi f = \omega, v = f\lambda$$

$$y(x, t) = A \sin \frac{2\pi}{\lambda}(x - vt)$$

$$v_y(x, t) = \frac{dy}{dt} = \omega A \cos \frac{2\pi}{\lambda}(x - vt)$$

$$a_y(x, t) = \frac{d^2 y}{dt^2} = -\omega^2 y$$

$$= -\omega^2 A \sin \frac{2\pi}{\lambda}(x - vt)$$

Maxwell's electromagnetic wave equation in partial differential equation form

$$\nabla^2 u = \frac{1}{c^2}\frac{\partial^2 u}{\partial t^2}$$

where, $\nabla^2 = \frac{\partial^2}{\partial x^2} + \frac{\partial^2}{\partial y^2} + \frac{\partial^2}{\partial z^2}$

where, ∇ = Laplace operator, u = displacement and c = speed of propagation. [see also Maxwell's equation)

de-Broglie matter equation,

$$\lambda = h / mv$$

where, λ = wavelength, h = Planck's constant, m = mass of the particle v = velocity of the particle.

waveform The shape of the graph obtained by plotting the instantaneous values of the quantity against time.

wavefront A locus of points, which oscillates in same phase. A point source has spherical wavefront, while a parallel beam has plane wavefronts. The wavefront is always perpendicular to the direction of propagation of light waves.

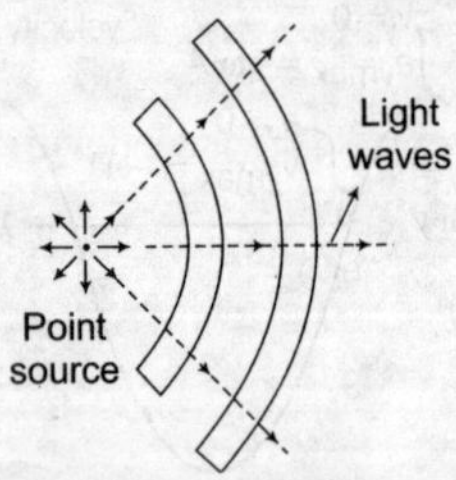

Spherical wavefront

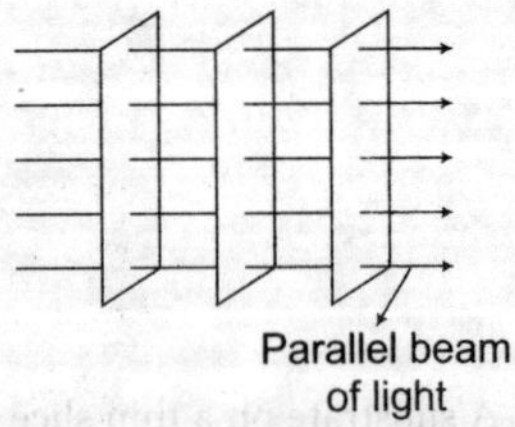

Plane wavefront

wave function Any simple wave can be described in terms of some quantities that varies in a wave-like function. The observed value of the wave depends on the location of that point and on the time at which observation is made. So, in general we can say sound waves and waves on strings are described by equation of Newtonian mechanics, light waves by Maxwell's equation and matter waves by Schrödinger's equation.

Therefore, we can summarise the wave equation as

(i) Classical wave, $y = a \sin(\omega t + \phi)$

(ii) Electromagnetic wave,

$$\nabla^2 u = \frac{1}{c^2}\frac{\partial^2 u}{\partial t^2}$$

(iii) Matter wave, $\lambda = h / p$

or $\Psi(x, y, z, t) = \Psi(x, y, z)\, e^{-i\omega t}$

[see also Schrödinger's wave function]

wave group The expanding of ring of wave within which one can discern individual wavelets of different wavelengths travelling at different speed.e.g. If a stone is thrown into the middle of a very still pond, a circular pattern of wave groups are originated from centre that appears in water.

wave guide The structure which guides the travelling waves, that is confining the propagation in one dimension. Commonly used guiding structures are typical coaxial cable, two wire, microstrip transmission line, hollow conducting wave guides and most commonly, now-a-days are optical fibre.

The choice of structure depends on factor (a) the desired operating frequency (b) the amount of power to be transferred (c) the amount of transmission loss can be tolerated.

wave intensity The energy carried by wave per second through per unit area is called wave intensity. It is proportional to the square of its amplitude.

Intensity of a wave $(I) = 2\pi^2 n^2 a^2 \rho v$

where, n = frequency,

a = amplitude,

v = velocity of wave

and ρ = density of the medium.

The intensity of wave at a distance, r from a point source is inversely proportional to the square of distance, r.

$$I \propto \frac{1}{r^2}$$

wavelength

1. The distance between the ends of one complete cycle of a wave.

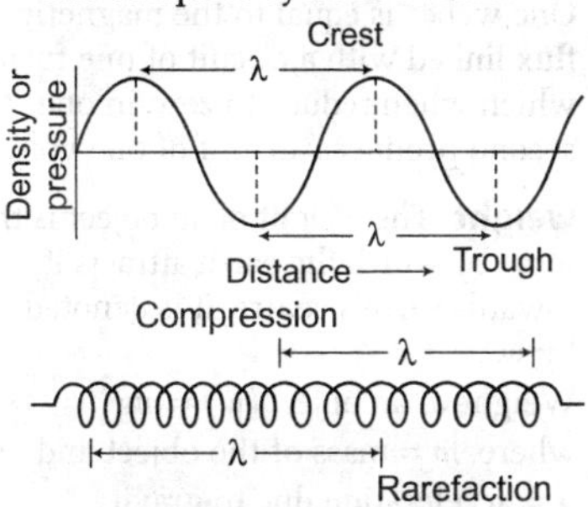

Representation of wavelength of wave

2. The distance between two consecutive troughs or two consecutive crests.
3. The distance between two consecutive compressions or two consecutive rarefactions. It is denoted by λ.

wavelet A small wave.

wave mechanics The branch of physics originated from the concept of de-Broglie hypothesis supporting the dual nature of matter. It is explained with the help of quantum mechanics and further advanced to more accurate explanation by the introduction of Schrödinger's wave function.

wave meter A device used for measuring the wavelength of electromagnetic radiation.

wave motion The energy transfer by propagation of a periodic disturbance which may be in the form of displacement of molecules of a gas, displacement of elements of a string, etc.

wave number The number of waves per metre. It is the reciprocal of the wavelength of the wave.

$$\text{Wave number } (\bar{\nu}) = \frac{1}{\lambda}$$

Its unit is metre^{-1}.

wave packet Wave packets are used to describe localised particle of both matter and photons. As, the motion of wave packet is in accordance with the motion of the corresponding classical particle, the localised wave action travels as a single unit.

Further, wave packet can be analysed into an infinite set of component of sinusoidal waves of different wave numbers, with phases and amplitudes such that they interfere constructively only over a small region of space and destructively elsewhere.

wave particle duality The concept of elementary particle or quantic entity exhibiting the properties of both matter and wave proposed by de-Broglie hypothesis. The wavelength of the particle associated with particle with momentum p is $\lambda = h / p$, where h is Planck's constant.

wave theory of light Newton was the first person to give the theory of light in which he proposed that light was made up tiny particles which was later over ruled by the Huygens' wave theory of light. Huygens' suggested light was made up of wave vibrating up and down perpendicular to the direction of propagation.

In 1803, Thomas Young studied the interference of light through a screen with two slits equally separated also supported the wave nature of light of Huygens' as two wavefronts overlap each other producing the light and dark area and the screen.

In 1900, Max Planck proposed the quantum theory of light in which he proposed light is a finite packets of energy which depends on the frequency and the velocity of the radiation.

In 1905, Albert Einstein coupled the idea of Maxwells and Planck's work on emission of light from hot bodies and suggested light is made up of tiny particles known as photons and each photon has energy hv while giving the theoretical explanation of photoelectric effect. Later de-Broglie proposed the idea of particles dual nature, of which suggested that right particles are of energy packet hv and having the wavelength, $\lambda = h / p$, which suggested greater the momentum of particle less will be the wavelength.

wave train A series of successive waves which are spaced at regular intervals.

wave vector This is the vector which helps in describing a wave, its magnitude is either the wave number of the wave and direction is ordinarily and the direction of wave propagation.

wave velocity Distance travelled by a wave in one second. It depends upon the nature of medium through which it passes.

waxing and waning of sound When two waves of slightly different frequencies travel along the same straight line and direction, they superimpose in such a way that the resultant intensity alternatively increases and decreases. This phenomenon of waxing and waning of sound is called beats. One waxing and one waning forms one beat.

weak nuclear force A weak nuclear force appears only in certain nuclear reactions such as the β -decay.

In β -decay, the nucleus emits a fast moving electron alongwith an uncharged particle called neutrino. The weak nuclear force acts over an extremely short range of about 2×10^{-18} m and are stronger than gravitational force but weaker than electromagnetic forces and nuclear forces.

weber The SI unit of magnetic flux.

$$1 \text{ Wb} = 1 \text{ volt sec.}$$

One weber is equal to the magnetic flux linked with a circuit of one turn which when reduce to zero in one second produces an emf of one volt.

weight The weight of an object is the force by which the earth attracts it towards earth's centre. It is denoted by w.

Weight of an object $(w) = mg$

where, m = mass of the object and

g = acceleration due to gravity.

The SI unit of weight is newton (N). It is a vector quantity.

weightlessness Practically weightlessness occurs when the gravitational attraction of the earth on a body in space is equal to centripetal force required by its orbital motion. Another example is freely falling condition where the body itself is moving with the acceleration equal to acceleration due to gravity.

weston cadmium cell Type of primary voltaic cell that produces a constant emf of 1.0186 volts at 20°C. It consists of an H-shaped glass vessel containing a negative cadmium mercury amalgam electrode in one leg and a positive mercury electrode in other leg. The electrolyte is saturated cadmium sulphate solution, which connects the two electrodes by means of the bar of the H.

Wheatstone bridge A special network designed to measure a resistance more accurately. This network was devised by Kristie and popularised by Wheatstone, therefore it is called Wheatstone bridge.

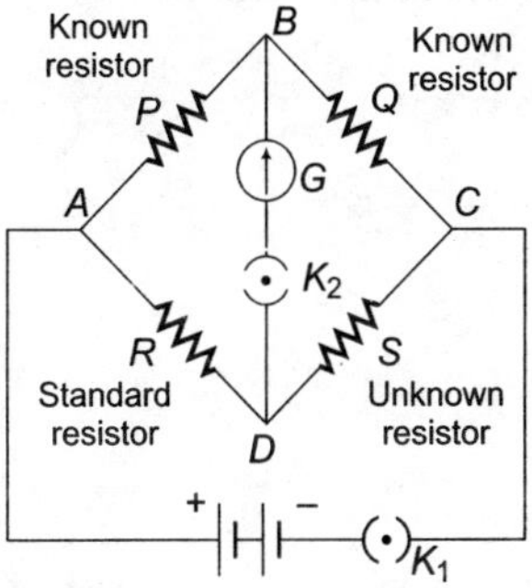

Symbolic diagram of Wheatstone bridge

It consists of four resistances *P*, *Q*, *R* and *S* connected along the arms of parallelogram. A galvanometer is connected along bridge arm *BD* and unknown resistance is connected along arm *CD*. First of all key K_1 is kept ON and then key K_2 is kept ON. If there is no deflection in galvanometer, then it is called a balanced Wheatstone bridge. In this state,

$$\frac{P}{Q} = \frac{R}{S}$$

white dwarf A very faint star in its last stage of steller evolution as its nuclear fuel is completely exhausted and later collapses under its own gravitation into a small but very dense body.

white light Visible radiation that gives a sensation of whiteness having spectrum similar to the spectrum of sunlight. Light from a lamp with filament temperature about 2000 K may be regarded as white. The sensation of whiteness can also be produced by suitable combination of parts of the spectrum, e.g. two complementary colours or three primary colours.

Wien's displacement law In the study of radiations emitted by a black body it was obtained by Wien that maximum energy emitted corresponding to wavelength λ_m, where, λ_m is inversely proportional to the absolute temperature of the black body, i.e.

$$\lambda_m \propto \frac{1}{T}$$

or $$\lambda_m \cdot T = \text{constant}$$

Thus, as the temperature rises the maximum of the spectral energy distribution curve is displaced towards short-wavelength end of the spectrum.

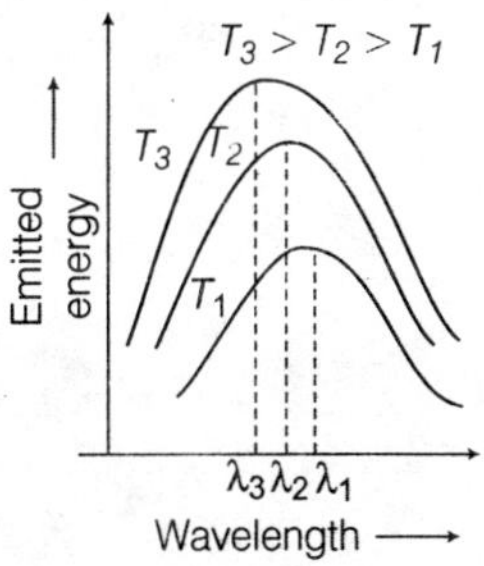

Graph between energy and wavelength

This is called Wien's displacement law.

windmill A machine which converts wind energy into mechanical energy.

wind power The utilisation of wind energy. Various types of windmills are being tried for converting wind energy to electric power. Wind power is a major source of renewable energy.

wire It is a sample of metal which is drawn into long uniform thread of varying radius.

work When a force is applied on a body and it undergoes a displacement, then work has been done by the force.

Work done $W = \mathbf{F} \cdot \mathbf{s}$

$= Fs \cos\theta$

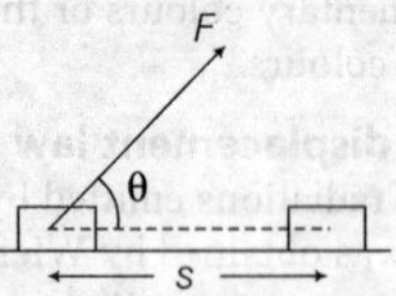

where, θ is the angle between the direction of applied force and displacement.

If a body undergoes an angular displacement θ when a torque τ acts on it, then work done

$$W = \tau \times \theta$$

Its SI unit is joule and CGS unit is erg.

$$1 \text{ joule} = 10^7 \text{ erg.}$$

work function The minimum energy required to eject an electron from a metal surface is called its work function. This energy can be given to metal either by heating it or by falling light of appropriate frequency on metal surface.

working substance A substance undergoing pressure and temperature changes in a heat engine.

X

X-axis The axis along which values of *x* are measured. It is perpendicular to both *Y*-axis, *Z*-axis, i.e., *yz*-plane.

X-component of a vector The resolution of vector along the *X*-axis is known as *X*-component of a vector.

xerography An electrostatic printing process for copying tent or graphics. In this process, on a sheet of paper corresponding to the image area of the original are sensitised with a charge of static electricity so that when powdered with a toner carrying an opposite charge, only charged areas retain the toner, which is fused to the paper to make it permanent.

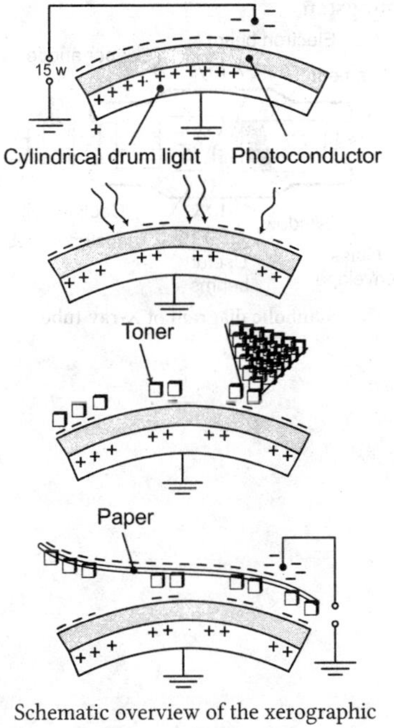

Schematic overview of the xerographic photocopying process

X-parameter A mathematical super set of S-parameter used for characterising the amplitudes and relative phase of harmonics generated by non-linear components under large input power level.

XOR-gate [or exclusive OR gate]

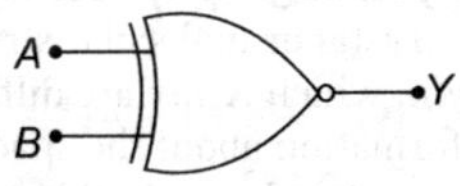

Traditional XOR gate symbol

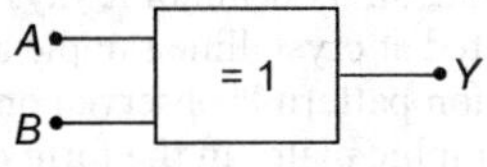

IEEE XOR symbol

A digital logic gate that implements an exclusive OR, i.e. if both the inputs are same, then the output is low, if both the inputs are different then output is high.

Boolean expression,

$$Y = A \,.\, \overline{B} + \overline{A} \,.\, B$$

Truth table

Input		Output
A	*B*	*A XOR B* = *Y*
0	0	0
0	1	1
1	0	1
1	1	0

X-ray A form of electromagnetic radiation of very short wavelength in the range of 10^{-10} m to 10^{-11} m. X-rays are produced when high energetic electrons are bombared on a metal target of high melting point, such as tungsten.

X-ray are used for detecting fractures in bones, presence of stones in body. It is also used in a treatment of certain forms of cancer and in the study of crystal structure.

X-ray analysis The study of the structure of crystalline substances by studying the X-ray diffraction patterns they produce.

X-ray astronomy An observational branch of astronomy which deals with the study of X-ray observation and detection from astronomical objects.

X-ray crystallography Use of X-rays to study crystal or molecular structure. The way in which X-ray are diffracted gives information about the spacing between crystal planes. In this technique, direct beam of X-rays is incidented at crystalline sample and the diffraction pattern is observed on photographic plates in the form of spots. From the position and intensity of the spots one can extract the information of electron density distribution in the ions, molecules or crystals.

X-ray diffraction Diffraction of X-rays by a crystal. The wavelength of X-rays are comparable with the spacing between the atoms of most crystals, and the repeated pattern of crystal lattice acts like a diffraction grating for X-rays.

X-ray fluorescence Softer (less energetic) secondary X-ray emitted by a substance bombarded by high energy electrons or primary X-rays.

X-ray microscope An instrument used to produce enlarged images of samples with X-rays as X-rays penetrate easier than visible light. It is used to achieve higher optical resolution due to shorter wavelength of X-ray.

X-ray spectrometer A spectrometer using X-rays to activate the inner electrons of an atom in order to separate and identify the chemical constituents of a substance and their concentration.

X-ıay tube The device for generating X-rays by accelerating electrons to a high energy by an electrostatic field and making them stripe a metal target. The target is made from a heavy metal usually tungsten.

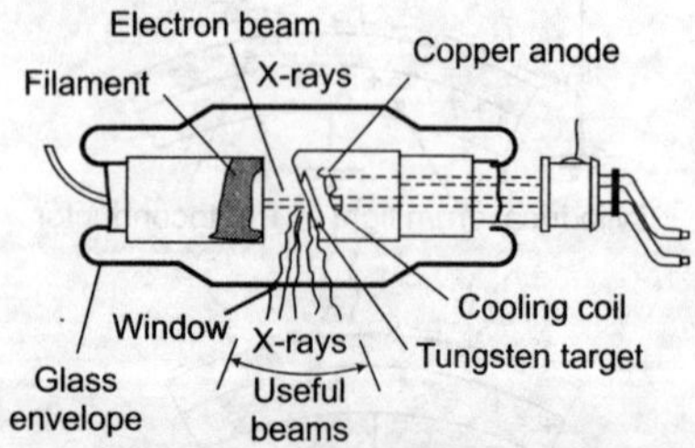

Symbolic diagram of X-ray tube

Y

Y-axis The line on a graph that runs vertically (up-down) through zero.

yard A fundamental unit of length in both the US customary system and the British Imperial System, equal to 3 feet, or 36 inches (0.9144 metre).

Y-component The resolution of vector along the *Y*-axis.

Y-current The current through one branch of star arrangement of three-phase circuit yards.

year The time taken by the Earth to complete one orbit around the Sun. The solar year is the time taken for the sun to make two successive appearances at the first point of Aries. It is equal to 365.242 mean solar days.

yellow spot The small area of few millimetre at the retina of human eye. It has a high concentration of rods cells giving high visual acuity and colour vision but low sensitivity to dim light.

yield To give way to force, pressure etc. so as to move or bend.

yield point On a stress-strain graph of an elastic material, the point beyond which the material ceases to behave elastically, i.e. stress is no longer proportional to strain linearly. In other words, the point on stress-strain graph beyond which material does not follow Hook's law is called yield point.

yield strength The maximum stress upto which a material can bear without coming its elastic nature or the maximum stress upto which material follows Hook's law.

yield stress The stress level at which material ceases to behave elastically.

yocto A prefix denoting 10^{-24}.
e.g. 1 yactometre (ym) = 10^{-24} m

yokes A piece of ferromagnetic metal that connects two or more magnetic cores.

yotta A prefix denoting 10^{24}.
e.g. 1 yottametre (Ym) = 10^{24} m

Young's double slit experiment In 1801, the phenomenon of interference of light was explained by Young's at which supported the wave nature of light. The apparatus known as Young's slit, light passes from a slit which is used to illuminate two adjacent slit on the second screen, light passing from second screen fall on third screen forming a series of parallel interference fringes having constructive fringes alternatively.

Young's modulus Within the limit of elasticity, the ratio of longitudinal stress to the longitudinal. It is denoted by *Y*.

$$\text{Young's modulus} = \frac{(F/A)}{(l/L)} = \frac{MgL}{\pi r^2 l}$$

Its SI unit is newton-metre^{-2}.

Y-parameter (admittance or Y-matrix) This is the property used in, electrical, electronic communication system engineering to describe the electrical behaviour of linear electric circuits.

Young thomas (13 June, 1773-10, May 1829) He was a British physicist and a physical who made his scientific contributions to the field of vision, light, solid mechanics, energy, Physiology, language, musical harmony and Egyptology. He is best known for the wave theory of light and his main article is Young's modulus.

Z

Z-axis The axis along which values of *Z* are measured. It is perpendicular to both *X*-axis and *Y*-axis. That is *xy*-plane.

Z-component of a vector The resolution of vector along the *Z*-axis.

Zeeman Dutch physicist who did study of light source in the pressure of external magnetic field leading to the discovery and explanation of Zeeman effect. For this work, he shared the Nobel prize in 1902 with Hendrick Lorentz.

Zeeman effect Further splitting of spectral lines of energy levels of an atom into a group of closely spaced lines when placed in an externaly strong static magnetic field. Splitting occurs because of the interaction of the magnetic moment of an atom with the external magnetic field.

Zener breakdown voltage
When a reverse biased heavily doped junction diode becomes conducting at a certain reverse voltage, that particular reverse voltage. This effect is due to electrons being excited directly from the valence band into the conduction band which further results in producing a large current just by changing very small reverse voltage or Zener voltage remains constant.

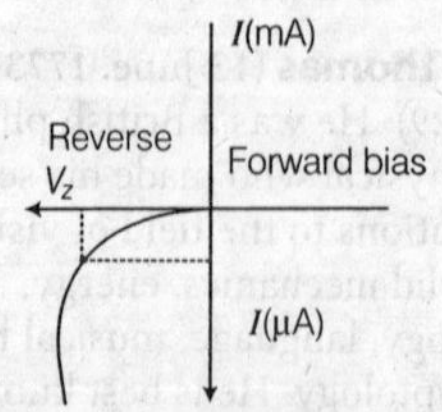

Graphical representation of zener breakdown voltage

This property of Zener diode is used for regulating voltage supply in I_c circuits.

Zener current When on a highly doped *p-n* diode, reverse bias is increased, the electric field also increases. At some stage, the electric field becomes so high, that it breaks the covalent bonds creating electron-hole pair, thus creating a large number of carriers which results in large current known as Zener current.

Zener diode A reverse biased heavily doped silicon *p-n* junction diode, which is operated in the breakdown region. The external resistance in the circuit and power dissipation of the diode limits the reverse current.

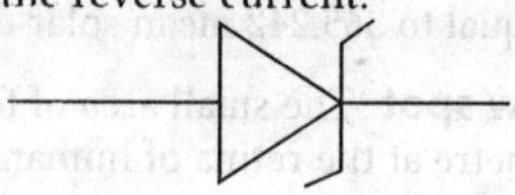

Zener diode

Zener effect If the *p* and *n* regions in a diode are heavily doped, the breakdown voltage can be reduced. Heavy doping reduces the width of the depletion region and the electric field at the barrier will be very high even for low voltage. The field is so strong that the electrons in the covalent bond can break away from the bonds. This effect is known as Zener effect.

zepto A prefix denoting 10^{-21}.

zero angular position The angular position is the measurement of an angle of position vector from the axis. If the position vector itself lies on the axis, then the angular position of a particle with respect to the axis is zero, therefore particle is supposed to have zero angular position.

zero gravity The condition where in the apparent effect of gravity becomes zero leading to the condition of weightlessness.

zero point A system consists of a point of reference known as origin or zero point and the line passing through the origin. One direction of the coordinate axis from the origin is chosen as positive and the other opposite direction as negative.

zero point energy The energy possessed by the atoms and molecules of any substance at absolute zero (0 K).

zero vector A vector whose magnitude is zero, is known as zero vector. The direction of zero vector is not defined.

zeroth law of thermodynamics If two systems A and B are separately in thermal equilibrium with a third system C, then systems A and B will also be in thermal equilibrium with each other.

zetta A prefix denoting 10^{21}.

zone melting A process of purifying any of various metals and other metals, such as germanium or silicon by passing it in bar form through an induction coil.

zone plate A plate or screen with alternating opaque and transparent concentric rings that focus light by diffraction.

zoom Focusing of zooming lens to examine more closely or in greater detail.

Appendices

Appendix-1

Basic Formulae of Physics

1. Density, $d = \frac{\text{Mass } (m)}{\text{Volume } (V)}$

2. Speed, $v = \frac{\text{Distance } (s)}{\text{Time } (t)}$

3. Velocity, $\vec{v} = \frac{\text{Displacement } (\vec{s})}{\text{Time } (t)}$

4. Force = Mass × Acceleration

5. Weight = Mass × Acceleration due to gravity

6. Pressure $= \frac{\text{Thrust}}{\text{Area}}$

7. Work = Force × Displacement × cos θ

8. Power $= \frac{\text{Work}}{\text{Time}}$

9. Potential energy = mgh

10. Kinetic energy $= \frac{1}{2} mv^2$

11. Equations of motion

    (i) $v = u + at$

    (ii) $s = ut + \frac{1}{2} at^2$

    (iii) $v^2 = u^2 + 2as$

    (iv) $s_n = u + \frac{a}{2}(2n - 1)$

12. Equation of projectile,

$$y = x \tan\theta - \frac{gx^2}{2u^2 \cos\theta}$$

(i) Time of flight, $T = \frac{2u \sin\theta}{g}$

(ii) Range $= \frac{u^2 \sin 2\theta}{g}$

13. Newton's Law of Universal Gravitation

    (i) $F = \frac{Gm_1m_2}{r^2}$

    (ii) $G = \frac{Fr^2}{m_1m_2}$

14. Relation between g and G,

$$g = \frac{GM}{R^2}$$

15. Equations of motion of an object under gravity

    (i) $v = u \pm gt$

    (ii) $h = ut \pm \frac{1}{2} gt^2$

    (iii) $v^2 = u^2 \pm 2gh$

16. Equations of motion for a freely falling body

    (i) $v = gt$ (initial velocity is zero)

    (ii) $h = \frac{1}{2} gt^2$

    (iii) $v^2 = 2gh$

17. Angular velocity,

$$\omega = \frac{\text{Angular displacement}}{\text{Time interval}}$$

18. Relation between angular velocity and linear velocity, $v = \omega r$

19. Angular momentum,

$$L = mvr = m\omega r^2$$

20. Centripetal acceleration, $a = \frac{v^2}{r}$

21. Moment of force = Force × Perpendicular distance

22. Cross product

$\Rightarrow \quad A \times B = AB \sin\theta\, \hat{n}$

23. Dot product

$\Rightarrow \quad A \cdot B = AB \cos\theta$

24. Resultant of vector

$\Rightarrow \quad R = \sqrt{A^2 + B^2 + 2AB\cos\theta}$

25. Torque $= R \times F$

26. Quantity of heat, $Q = ms\,\Delta t$

27. Specific gravity

$$= \frac{\text{Density of substance}}{\text{Density of water}}$$

28. Caloric value $= \dfrac{\text{Heat produced}}{\text{Unit mass}}$

29. Thermal efficiency

$$= \frac{\text{Heat utilised }(Q_1)}{\text{Total heat produced }(Q_2)}$$

30. Fundamental principle of calorimetry

Heat lost by the hot body
= Heat gained by the cold body

$\dfrac{V}{T} = \text{constant}$

31. Boyle's law $pV = \text{Constant}$

32. Charles' law $\dfrac{V}{T} = \text{Constant}$

33. Time period of a pendulum,

$$T = 2\pi\sqrt{l/g}$$

34. Velocity of sound, $v = n\lambda$

35. Distance between a crest and a trough $= \lambda / 2$

36. Distance between two consecutive crests or troughs $= \lambda$

37. Newton's formula,

Velocity of sound in a gas, $v = \sqrt{\dfrac{E}{\rho}}$

38. Newton-Laplace formula,
Velocity of sound in a gas,

$$v = \sqrt{\frac{\gamma p}{\rho}}$$

39. Velocity of sound in a solid,

$$v = \sqrt{\frac{Y}{\rho}}$$

40. Refractive index of the prism,

$$\mu = \frac{\sin\left(A + \dfrac{\delta m}{2}\right)}{\sin\left(\dfrac{A}{2}\right)}$$

41. Lens Makers formula

$$\frac{1}{f} = (\mu - 1)\left[\frac{1}{R_1} - \frac{1}{R_2}\right]$$

42. Number of images formed by two plane mirrors at an angle θ,

$$n = \frac{360^\circ}{\theta} - 1$$

43. Magnification, $m = \dfrac{\text{Size of image}}{\text{Size of object}}$

44. Snell's law ${}_1\mu_2 = \dfrac{\sin i}{\sin r}$

45. Relation between u, v and f

$$\frac{1}{f} = \frac{1}{u} + \frac{1}{v}$$

46. Power of lens, $P = \dfrac{1}{\text{Focal length}}$

47. Charge, $Q = CV$

48. Current, $i = \dfrac{Q}{t}$

49. Coulomb's Inverse Square Law,

$$F = \frac{1}{4\pi\varepsilon_0}\frac{q_1 q_2}{r^2}$$

50. Centripetal force, $F = \dfrac{mv^2}{r}$

51. Time period of simple pendulum,

$$T = 2\pi\sqrt{\frac{L}{g}}$$

52. Angle of banking $\theta = \tan^{-1}\sqrt{\dfrac{v^2}{rg}}$

53. Biot-Savart law $B = \dfrac{\mu_0}{4\pi}\dfrac{I\,dl\sin\theta}{r^2}$

54. Relation between absolute permeability (μ_0) and relative permeability (μ_r) of a medium,
$\mu_m = \mu_r \mu_0$

55. Magnetic moment, $\vec{M} = m(2\vec{l})$

56. Electrical potential,
$$V = \frac{\text{Work done } (W)}{\text{Charge } (Q)}$$

57. Ohm's law, $V = IR$

58. Resistance, $R = \rho \frac{l}{A}$

59. Combinations of resistances

(i) In series,
$$R = R_1 + R_2 + R_3 + \ldots + R_n$$

(ii) In parallel,
$$\frac{1}{R} = \frac{1}{R_1} + \frac{1}{R_2} + \frac{1}{R_3} + \ldots + \frac{1}{R_n}$$

60. Electric power, $P = VI = I^2R = \frac{V^2}{R}$

61. Einstein's mass-energy relation,
$$E = \Delta mc^2$$

62. Gauss law, $\int E \cdot ds = \frac{q}{\varepsilon_0}$

63. Ampere's law, $\oint B \cdot dl = \mu_0 I$

64. Equation of wave,
$$y = a \sin(\omega t + \phi)$$

65. Energy band gap $E_g = h\nu = \frac{hc}{\lambda}$

66. For common-emitter transistor,

(i) Input resistance,
$$R_i = \left(\frac{\Delta V_{BE}}{\Delta I_B}\right)_{V_{CE} = \text{constant}}$$

(ii) Output resistance,
$$R_o = \left(\frac{\Delta V_{CE}}{\Delta I_C}\right)_{I_B = \text{constant}}$$

(iii) Current amplification factor,
$$\beta_{AC} = \left(\frac{\Delta I_C}{\Delta I_B}\right)_{V_{CE} = \text{constant}}$$

(iv) DC current gain, $\beta_{DC} = \frac{\alpha}{1 - \alpha}$

(v) AC current gain,
$$\beta_{AC} = \left(\frac{\Delta I_C}{\Delta I_B}\right)_{V_{CE}}$$

(vi) Transconductance, $g_m = \frac{\beta_{AC}}{R_{in}}$

(vii) AC voltage gain,
$$A_V = \frac{\Delta I_C}{\Delta I_B} \times \frac{R_{out}}{R_{in}}$$
$$A_V = \beta_{AC} \times \text{Resistance gain}$$
$$[\because R_{out}/R_{in} = \text{Resistance gain}]$$

(viii) AC power gain = AC current gain × AC voltage gain

67. Truth table for NOT Gate

Input A	Output Y
0	1
1	0

68. Truth table for OR Gate

Input		Output
A	**B**	**Y = A + B**
0	0	0
0	1	1
1	0	1
1	1	1

69. Truth table for AND Gate

Input		Output
A	**B**	**Y = AB**
0	0	0
0	1	0
1	0	0
1	1	1

70. Truth table for NAND Gate

Input		Output
A	B	$Y = \overline{AB}$
0	0	1
0	1	1
1	0	1
1	1	0

71. Truth table for NOR Gate

Input		Output
A	B	$Y = \overline{A + B}$
0	0	1
0	1	0
1	0	0
1	1	0

Appendix-2

Conversion Factors

Length

1 km = 0.6215 mi

1 mi = 1.609 km

1 m = 1.0936 yd

= 3.281 ft = 39.37 in

1 in = 2.54 cm

1 ft = 12 in = 30.48 cm

1 yd = 3 ft = 91.44 cm = 36 inch

1 light year = 1 ly = 9.461×10^{15} m

1 Å = 0.1 nm

Area

1 m^2 = 10^4 cm^2

1 km = 0.3861 mi^2 = 247.1 acres

1 in^2 = 6.4516 cm^2

1 ft^2 = 9.29×10^{-2} m^2

1 m^2 = 10.76 ft^2

1 acre = 43560 ft^2

1 mi^2 = 460 acres = 2.590 km^2

Volume

1 m^3 = 10^6 cm^3

1 L = 1000 cm^3 = 10^{-3} m^3

1 gal = 3.786 L

1 gal = 4 qt = 8 pt = 128 oz = 231 in^3

1 in^3 = 16.39 cm^3

1 ft^3 = 1728 in^3

= 28.32 L

= 2.832×10^4 cm^3

Speed

1 kmh^{-1} = 0.2778 m s^{-1}

= 0.6215 mi h^{-1}

1 mi h^{-1} = 0.4470 m s^{-1}

= 1.609 km h^{-1}

1 mi h^{-1} = 1.467 ft s^{-1}

Magnetic Field

1 G = 10^{-4} T

1 T = 1 Wb m^{-2} = 10^4 G

Angle and Angular Speed

πrad = 180°

1 rad = 57.30°

1° = 1.745×10^{-2} rad

1 rev min^{-1} = 0.1047 rad s^{-1}

1 rad s^{-1} = 9.549 rev min^{-1}

Mass

1 kg = 1000 g

1 tonne = 1000 kg = 1 mg

1 u = 1.6606×10^{-27} kg

1 kg = 6.022×10^{26} u

1 slug = 14.59 kg

1 kg = 6.852×10^{-2} slug

1 u = 931.50 MeV/c^2

Density

1 gcm^{-3} = 1000 kg m^{-3} = 1 kg L^{-1}

Force

1 N = 0.2248 lbf = 10^5 dyne

1 lbf = 4.4482 N

1 kgf = 2.2046 lbf

Time

1 h = 60 min = 3.6 ks

1 d = 24 h = 1440 min = 86.4 ks

1 y = 365.24 d = 31.56 ms

Pressure

1 Pa = 1 Nm^{-2}

1 bar = 100 kPa

1 atm = 101.325 kPa = 1.01325 bar

1 atm = 14.7 lbf/in^2 = 760 mm Hg
= 29.9 in Hg = 33.8 ft H_2O

1 lbf in^{-2} = 6.895 kPa

Energy

1 kWh = 3.6 MJ

1 cal = 4.186 J

1 ft lbf = 1.356 J = 1.286×10^{-3} Btu

1 L atm = 101.325 J

1 L atm = 24.217 cal

1 Btu = 778 ft lb = 252 cal
= 1054.35 J

1 eV = 1.602×10^{-19} J

1 u c^2 = 931.50 MeV

1 erg = 10^{-7} J

1 torr = 1 mm Hg
= 133.32 Pa

Power

1 horse power, HP = 550 ft lbf/s
= 745.7 W

1 Btu min^{-1} = 17.58 W

1 W = 1.341×10^{-3} HP
= 0.7376 ft lbf/s

Thermal Conductivity

1 W $m^{-1}K^{-1}$ = 6.938 Btu in/hft^2°F

1 Btu in/hft^2°F = 0.1441 W/m-K

Appendix-3

The Greek Alphabet

Alpha	A	α	Nu	N	ν
Beta	B	β	Xi	Ξ	ξ
Gamma	Γ	γ	Omicron	O	ο
Delta	Δ	δ	Pi	Π	π
Epsilon	E	ε	Rho	P	ρ
Zeta	Z	ζ	Sigma	Σ	σ
Eta	H	η	Tau	T	τ
Theta	Θ	θ	Upsilon	Y	υ
Iota	I	ι	Phi	Φ	ϕ
Kappa	K	κ	Chi	X	χ
Lambda	Λ	λ	Psi	Ψ	ψ
Mu	M	μ	Omega	Ω	ω

Appendix-4

Common SI Prefixes and Symbols for Multiples and Sub-Multiples

Multiples

Factor	Prefix	Symbol
10^{18}	Exa	E
10^{15}	Peta	P
10^{12}	Tera	T
10^{9}	Giga	G
10^{6}	Mega	M
10^{3}	kilo	k
10^{2}	Hecto	h
10^{1}	Deca	da

Sub-multiples

Factor	Prefix	Symbol
10^{-18}	atto	a
10^{-15}	femto	f
10^{-12}	pico	p
10^{-9}	nano	n
10^{-6}	micro	μ
10^{-3}	milli	m
10^{-2}	centi	c
10^{-1}	deci	d

Appendix-5

Some Important Constants

Name	Symbol	Value
Speed of light in vacuum	c	2.9979×10^{8} ms^{-1}
Charge of electron	e	1.602×10^{-19} C
Gravitational constant	G	6.673×10^{-11} N m^{2} kg^{-2}
Planck constant	h	6.626×10^{-34} Js
Boltzmann constant	k	1.381×10^{-23} JK^{-1}
Avogadro number	N_A	6.022×10^{23} mol^{-1}
Universal gas constant	R	8.314 J mol^{-1} K^{-1}
Mass of electron	m_e	9.110×10^{-31} kg
Mass of neutron	m_n	1.675×10^{-27} kg
Mass of proton	m_p	1.673×10^{-27} kg
Electron-charge to mass ratio	e/m_e	1.759×10^{11} C / kg
Faraday constant	F	9.648×10^{-4} C/mol
Rydberg constant	R	1.097×10^{7} m^{-1}
Bohr radius	a_0	5.292×10^{-11} m

Name	Symbol	Value
Stefan-Boltzmann constant	σ	5.670×10^{-8} W m^{-2} K^{-4}
Wien's constant	b	2.898×10^{-3} mK
Permittivity of free space	ε_0 $1/4\pi\varepsilon_0$	8.854×10^{-12} C^2 N^{-1} m^{-2} 8.987×10^{9} N m^2 C^{-2}
Permeability of free space	μ_0	$4\pi \times 10^{-7}$ T m A^{-1} $\cong 1.257 \times 10^{-6}$ Wb A^{-1} m^{-1}
Mechanical equivalent of heat	J	4.186 J cal^{-1}
Standard atmospheric pressure	1 atm	1.013×10^{5} Pa
Absolute zero	0 K	– 273.15°C
Electron-volt	1 eV	1.602×10^{-19} J
Unified atomic mass unit	1 u	1.661×10^{-27} kg
Electron rest energy	mc^2	0.511 MeV
Energy equivalent of 1 u	uc^2	931.5 MeV
Volume of ideal gas (0°C and 1 atm)	V	22.4 L mol^{-1}
Acceleration due to gravity (sea, level, at equator)	g	9.78049 ms^{-2}
Bohr magneton	μ_B	9.27405 J/T

Appendix-6

Physical Quantities Expressed in SI Units

Physical Quantity	SI Unit
Area	m^2
Volume	m^3
Speed, Velocity	m/s or ms^{-1}
Angular velocity	rad/s or rad s^{-1}
Acceleration	m/s^2 or ms^{-2}
Angular acceleration	rad/s^2 or rad s^{-2}
Wave number	m^{-1}
Density, Mass density	kg/m^3 or kg m^{-3}
Current density	A/m^2 or A m^{-2}
Magnetic field strength, magnetic intensity, magnetic moment density	A/m or A m^{-1}
Concentration (an amount of substance)	mol/m^3 or mol m^{-3}
Specific volume	m^3/kg or m^{3}kg^{-1}

Physical Quantity	**SI Unit**
Luminance, intensity of illumination	cd/m^2 or $cd\ m^{-2}$
Kinematic viscosity	m^2/s or m^2s^{-1}
Momentum	$kg\ m\ s^{-1}$
Moment of inertia	$kg\ m^2$
Radius of gyration	m
Linear/superficial/volume expansivities	K^{-1}
Flow rate	m^3s^{-1}
Frequency	s^{-1}
Force	$kg\ m\ s^{-2}$
Pressure, stress	$kg\ m^{-1}s^{-2}$
Energy, work, quantity of heat	$kg\ m^2\ s^{-2}$ or $kg\ m^2/s^2$
Power, Radiant flux	$kg\ m^2\ s^{-3}$
Quantity of Electricity, electric charge	A-s
Electric potential, Potential difference, Electromotive force	$kg\ m^2\ s^{-3}A^{-1}$ or $kg\ m^2/s^3A$
Capacitance	$A^2s^4\ kg^{-1}\ m^{-2}$
Electric resistance	$kg\ m^2\ s^{-3}\ A^{-2}$
Conductance	$m^{-2}kg^{-1}\ s^3A^2$
Magnetic flux	$kg\ m^2\ s^{-2}A^{-1}$
Magnetic field, Magnetic flux density	$kg\ s^{-2}A^{-1}$
Inductance	$kg\ m^2\ s^{-2}A^{-2}$
Luminous flux, Luminous power	cd/sr
Illuminance	$m^{-2}\ cd\ sr^{-1}$
Activity (of a radio nuclide/radioactive source)	s^{-1}
Absorbed dose, Absorbed dose index	m^2/s^2 or m^2s^{-2}
Magnetic moment	$m^2\ A$
Dipole moment	m A s
Kinetic viscosity	$kg\ m^{-1}s^{-1}$
Couple, Moment of force	$kg\ m^2\ s^{-2}$
Surface tension	$kg\ s^{-2}$
Power density, Absolute value, Thermal flux density	$kg\ s^{-3}$
Heat capacity, Entropy	$kg\ m^2\ s^{-2}K^{-1}$
Specific heat, Specific entropy	$m^2\ s^{-2}\ K^{-1}$
Specific energy, Latent heat	$m^2\ s^2$
Radiation intensity	$kg\ m^2\ s^{-3}\ sr^{-1}$
Thermal conductivity	$kg\ m\ s^{-3}\ K^{-1}$

Physical Quantity	SI Unit
Energy density	$kg\ m^{-1}\ s^{-2}$
Electric field intensity	$kg\ m\ s^{-3}A^{-1}$
Electric charge density	$m^{-3}\ s\ A$
Dielectric constant	$kg^{-1}m^{-3}s^{4}A^{2}$
Magnetic intensity	$kg\ m\ s^{-2}A^{-2}$
Molar energy	$kg\ m^{2}s^{-2}mol^{-1}$
Angular momentum, Planck's constant	$kg\ m^{2}s^{-1}$
Molar entropy, Molar heat capacity	$kg\ m^{2}\ s^{-2}K^{-1}mol^{-1}$
Exposure time	$kg^{-1}\ s\ A$
X-rays and γ-rays	$m^{2}\ s^{-3}$
Compressibility	$kg^{-1}\ m\ s^{2}$
Coefficient of elasticity	$kg\ m^{-1}s^{-2}$
Pressure gradient	$kg\ m^{-2}s^{-2}$
Surface potential	$m^{2}\ s^{-2}$
Pressure energy	$kg\ m^{2}\ s^{-2}$
Impulse	$kg\ m\ s^{-1}$
Angular impulse	$kg\ m^{2}s^{-1}$
Specific resistance	$kg\ m^{3}s^{-3}A^{-2}$
Surface energy	$kg\ s^{-2}$

Appendix 7

Nobel Laureates in Physics

Laureate	Contribution
Isamu Akasaki, Hiroshi Amano and Shuji Nakamura (2014)	For the invention of efficient blue light-emitting diodes which has enabled bright and energy-saving white light sources
Francois Englert and Peter W. Higgs (2013)	For the theoretical discovery of a mechansim that contributes to our understanding of the origin of mass of subatomic particles, and which recently was confirmed through the discovery of the predicted fundamental particle, by the ATLAS and CMS experiments at CERN's Large Hadron Collider
Serge Haroche and David J. Wineland (2012)	For ground-breaking experimental methods that enable measuring and manipulation of individual quantum systems

Laureate	Contribution
Saul Perimutter, Brain P. Schmidt and Adam G. Riess (2011)	For the discovery of the accelerating expansion of the Universe through observations of distant supernovae
Andre Geim and Konstantin Novoselov (2010)	For groundbreaking experiments regarding the two-dimensional material graphene
Charles Kuen Kao (2009)	For groundbreaking achievements concerning the transmission of light in fibers for optical communication
Willard S. Boyle and George E. Smith (2009)	For the invention of an imaging semiconductor circuit -the CCD sensor
Yoichiro Nambu (2008)	For the discovery of the mechanism of spontaneous broken symmetry in subatomic physics
Makoto Kobavashi and Toshihide Maskawa (2008)	For the discovery of the origin of the broken symmetry which predicts the existence of at least three families of quarks in nature
Albert Fert and Peter Grunberg (2007)	For the discovery of Giant Magnetoresistance
John C. Mather and George F. Smoot (2006)	For their discovery of the blackbody form and anisotropy of the cosmic microwave background radiation
Rov J. Glauber (2005)	For his contribution to the quantum theory of optical coherence
John L. Hall and Theodor W. Hansch (2005)	For their contributions to the development of laser-based precision spetroscopy, including the optical frequency comb technique
Wilhelm Conrad Rontgen (First Noble Laureate) (1901)	In recognition of the extraordinary services he has rendered by the discovery of the remarkable rays subsequently named after him